From Humanism to the Humanities

From Humanism to the Humanities

Education and the Liberal Arts in Fifteenth-
and Sixteenth-Century Europe

Anthony Grafton & Lisa Jardine

Harvard University Press
Cambridge, Massachusetts
1986

Printed in Great Britain

10   9   8   7   6   5   4   3   2   1

Library of Congress Cataloging-in-Publication Data

Grafton, Anthony.
  From humanism to the humanities.

  Includes index.
  1. Education, Humanistic—Europe—History.
I. Jardine, Lisa.   II. Title.
LA106.G73   1986   370.11′2′094   86-22824
ISBN 0-674-32460-9

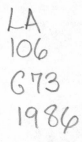

Contents

For the two Sams

Preface

The idea for this book was formed some ten years ago, when both authors were visiting scholars at Cornell University. Graduate students in Tony Grafton's seminar in the History Department and Lisa Jardine's seminar at the Society for the Humanities noted that both teachers adopted remarkably similar approaches to the history of humanist education. The seminars became collaborative, and the idea of a joint book followed. The authors' excitement at the discovery of such intellectual proximity, however, did not take account of the mundane problem of geographical distance. Close collaboration between Princeton, New Jersey and Cambridge, England proved to require ingenuity, patience and stamina. But the results, they feel, have been amply worth it. Each has learnt from the other. Each has profited from the extra charge produced when two people's combined efforts are brought to bear on apparently intractable problems.

Nor has this been the only fruitful coming together of minds. Both authors have had to combine their researches with demanding teaching programmes of their own. They are only too aware of the debt they owe to their own students at Princeton and at Jesus College, Cambridge, who, in the best tradition of classroom interaction, have contributed more than they know to the authors' understanding of their subject.

The passage of ten years has seen the passing of an era in Renaissance scholarship. The authors owe a great debt to D.P. Walker, R.R. Bolgar, E. Cochrane and C.B. Schmitt, none of whom has lived to see the completed volume in which their ideas and encouragement have played so considerable a part. This book is offered as a tribute to these great figures, without whom Renaissance studies and the histories of science and education would not have thrived as they have over the last thirty years.

We owe warm thanks for financial help to Princeton University and to Jesus College, Cambridge – especially to Princeton's Committee on Hellenic Studies, for a grant which made possible the research for Chapter Five. Audiences at Princeton University; the University of Pennsylvania; Brown University; the Warburg Institute; the American School of Classical Studies, Athens; the Institute for Historical Research; the 1982 Newberry Library Renaissance Conference; the University of Chicago; and seminars at the CNRS in Paris and the Universities of Cambridge and Oxford offered helpful comments on drafts of individual sections. The editors of *Past and Present*,

History of the Universities, *History of Education*, and the *Historical Journal* accepted, and constructively criticised, statements of our early findings. And many friends offered advice, information, and (most valued of all) criticism. In thanking Michael Baxandall, Paul Grendler, John Najemy, Renato Pasta, Keith Percival, David Robey, Quentin Skinner and Lawrence Stone with special warmth, we single out those to whose comments and to whose scepticism concerning our more far-fetched ideas, we owe the most. They are not, of course, responsible for our errors, nor will they necessarily agree with our views in their final form.

June 1986

A.G.

L.J.

Abbreviations

CTC　　*Catalogus translationum et commentariorum*, ed. P.O. Kristeller et al. (Washington, D.C. 1960-　)

BMC　　*Catalogue of Books Printed in the XVth Century now in the British Museum* (London, 1908-49)

Introduction

As educational systems contract, so the historiography of education expands. Until quite recently in early modern and modern Europe it was a genre composed by antiquaries, purchased by retired historians and read by almost nobody. The history of education was rarely taught or studied systematically outside faculties of education, and even within them it was pursued at too primitive a level to capture the interest of professional historians.

But the rise of social history in the 1960s and 1970s has had radical consequences in this as in so many other areas. Social historians have taken the history of education seriously, asked new questions about it and deployed new materials to answer them. They have quarried mountains of new evidence about student numbers, social origins and systems of patronage from university archives and college matriculation records. They have crystallised in precise graphs and tables the expansion and contraction of student bodies and endowments. They have called back to life the dead subcultures of past student generations; they have rehearsed the views of critics and reformers of a wide range of past curricula. For early modern Europe in particular the results of their labours have been striking. They have shown that between 1450 and 1650 there was a vast growth in the numbers of those involved in education at every level from the barely literate to the professional scholar. And they have firmly embedded this Educational Revolution in the general social and political history of early modern Europe.[1]

But this exciting body of work displays the weaknesses as well as the strengths of the new social history. Indifferent to those shades of local variation and individual experience that give history life, hostile to the systematic study of texts and ideas, the social historians have had little new to say about what went on inside the institutions they have reconstructed. The very iconoclasts whose archival research has shattered hallowed clichés about the clientèle and character of schools and universities have uncritically

---

[1] For samples of this body of work see e.g. J.H. Hexter, 'The education of the aristocracy in the Renaissance', *Journal of Modern History* 22 (1950), 1-20; P. Ariès, *L'enfant et la vie familiale sous l'ancien régime* (Paris, 1960); L. Stone, 'The educational revolution in England, 1560-1640', *Past and Present* 28 (1964), 41-80; G. Huppert, *Public Schools in Renaissance France* (Urbana, 1984); L. Stone (ed.), *The University in Society* (Princeton, 1975); R. Chartier, D. Julia and M.-M. Compère, *L'éducation en France du XVIè au XVIIIè siècle* (Paris, 1976).

repeated every received platitude about what teachers thought and students learned. And they have failed to confront the complementary evidence – as rich as that of the matriculation records – preserved in textbooks, student notes and theses.

Moreover, and more seriously, traditional intellectual historians have largely failed to tell the social historians what they could not learn by the application of their own methods. The few intellectual historians who have worked on early modern education have been more intent on grinding old axes than on testing new hypotheses. Themselves believing in the preeminent value of a literary education, committed to preserving a canon of classics and a tradition of humanism, they have treated the rise of the classical curriculum and the downfall of scholasticism as the natural triumph of virtue over vice. Like the humanists they study, whose words they often echo faithfully, they assume the barbarity and obsolescence of medieval education and the freshness and liberality of humanism. The new system, they hold, offered such vistas of intellectual and spiritual freedom as to make it irresistible.[2]

This book forms part of a wider, continuing effort to displace these present-minded pieties. It is informed by the social historians' findings, but does not seek to add to them, for its concern is not with context but with content. Our task is to reconstruct the key rituals, assumptions and methods of the humanists who revolutionised secondary schools and arts faculties in Renaissance Europe. Our method is one of case studies in a variety of different forms of evidence and levels of instruction. Each chapter differs from the rest in subject and structure, but each rests on primary sources and each seeks to shed light on innovative and influential scholars and teachers. Naturally this approach leads to many omissions. Questions will arise. What about Poland? Where is Spain? To these and similar objections we can reply only that we have chosen cases where the evidence was rich enough to yield a coherent story, and that we have tried so far as possible to concentrate on typical problems and solutions. We make no claim that our studies form a survey of Renaissance education, or even of humanist education.

We do, however, claim that they are linked together in a single argument: that the triumph of humanist education cannot simply be explained by reference to its intrinsic worth or practical utility. On the contrary, the literary education of the humanists displaced a system far better adapted to many of the traditional intellectual and practical needs of European society. Scholasticism was very much a going concern in the fourteenth and fifteenth centuries. At the level of the school, it offered literacy in Latin of a sort to thousands of boys. At the higher level of the university arts course, it provided

---

[2] For examples of this approach – some of which offer it with more qualifications than others – see e.g. E. Garin, *L'educazione in Europe, 1400-1600: problemi e programmi* (Bari, 1957); K. Charlton, *Education in Renaissance England* (London and Toronto, 1965); G. Muller, *Bildung und Erziehung im Humanismus der italienischen Quattrocento* (Wiesbaden, 1969).

a lively and rigorous training in logic and semantics. At the higher level still of the professional faculties of law, medicine and theology, it trained men for employment in powerful and lucrative occupations. And on its fringes, in the severely practical courses on the arts of the notary, it even taught the future estate manager, government clerk or solicitor how to keep books, draw up contracts and write business letters. This curriculum, in short, equipped students with complex skills and fitted them to perform specialised tasks. Its immense success is clearly visible from the enviable placement record enjoyed by the medieval alumni of Oxford and Cambridge, and more generally from the rapid expansion it was undergoing for at least a century before the humanists had any substantial impact. Above all, we know now that it was no sterile indoctrination in the authoritative messages of a few selected texts. Recent research in the history of fields as divergent as natural philosophy and political theory has brought to light vast, unsuspected veins of insight and speculation, long buried in forgotten summas and commentaries. The liquidation of this intellectual system was clearly the murder of an intact organism, not the clearing away of a disintegrated fossil.[3]

We do not seek to tarnish the reputations of individual humanist teachers. The secondary works on which we have relied most heavily – chiefly monographs by classicists and literary historians – confirm the brilliance of the humanists' work in their favourite fields. Their rigorous empirical investigation and codification of the grammar and syntax of the classical languages laid the foundation for modern philology. Their equally rigorous schooling in prose and verse composition, in the artful allusion and the striking metaphor, was a necessary precondition for the flowering of the modern European vernacular literatures. The prose of Rabelais, the lyrics of Ronsard and the plays of Shakespeare are only the most succulent of the fruits that grew from deep roots in the training the humanists offered. To have been the progenitors of modern scholarship and modern literature is no small achievement, and we would be among the first to claim it for the subjects of this book.[4]

What we would not accept is the traditional claim that these solid merits enabled humanism to win its battle against scholasticism. The older system had fitted perfectly the needs of the Europe of the high middle ages, with its communes, its church offices open to the low-born of high talents and its vigorous debates on power and authority in state and church. The new system, we would argue, fitted the needs of the new Europe that was taking

[3] Perhaps the best introduction is the *Cambridge History of Later Medieval Philosophy: From the Rediscovery of Aristotle to the Disintegration of Scholasticism*, eds. N. Kretzmann, A. Kenny and J. Pinborg (Cambridge, 1982).

[4] Our greatest debt – beyond what we owe to the general works of Professors Bolgar, Garin and Kristeller – is to the older studies of H.-I. Marrou, R. Sabbadini and T.W. Baldwin, cited profusely below. It is to be noted that all three of the latter knew the humanistic tradition intimately – and mistrusted it profoundly.

shape, with its closed governing élites, hereditary offices and strenuous efforts to close off debate on vital political and social questions. It stamped the more prominent members of the new élite with an indelible cultural seal of superiority, it equipped lesser members with fluency and the learned habit of attention to textual detail and it offered everyone a model of true culture as something given, absolute, to be mastered, not questioned – and thus fostered in all its initiates a properly docile attitude towards authority. The education of the humanists was made to order for the Europe of the Counter-Reformation and of late Protestant orthodoxy. And this consonance between the practical activities of the humanists and the practical needs of their patrons, we argue, was the decisive reason for the victory of humanism. Scholasticism bred too independent an attitude to survive. In the Renaissance as in other periods, in sum, the price of collaboration in the renewal of art and literature was collaboration in the constriction of society and polity.

The suggestion that it suited the ruling élites of fifteenth- and sixteenth-century Europe to support the new humanism as an educational movement is, we believe, an important one for modern professors of the humanities. This book concerns itself, in its detailed argument, with education during the fifteenth and sixteenth centuries, and the involvement of that education with the ideals and attitudes of government and those in power. But we also regard it as a book about arts education in general, and its institutionalised position in western Europe. It is, we feel, a timely subject to concern ourselves with, as professional teachers of the arts. For, both in North America and in Europe, the decline in prosperity of the industrial nations has brought with it a crisis of confidence in arts education as a 'profitable' undertaking. Where, it is asked, is the marketable end-product in the non-vocational liberal arts faculties that justifies the investment of public money? Where indeed? This book is offered in part as a contribution to our understanding of the long history of evasiveness on the part of teachers of the humanities – an evasiveness which has left them vulnerable to the charge of non-productiveness, irrelevance to modern industrial society, without those teachers themselves having deviated from their commitment to the liberal arts as a 'training for life'.

We do not pretend to offer a final judgment on the plausibility or otherwise of the view that western European culture – the underpinning of shared opinions and values in which our society is grounded – is rooted in the classics. We do consider it a matter of some urgency to confront the fact that for five hundred years or more it has been seen as such by the confraternity of teachers engaged in the crucial introductory stages of education; that that faith in the heritage of Greece and Rome was communicated as an act of faith to generations of students; and that the practical classroom activity which went to support the ideology of humanism was frankly inadequate to match the fervour of the ideal. As a result, we believe, western Europe as a whole (and we include along with it the continent of North America, which learned its academic lessons so early and so well from its European forebears) became involved in the mystification of arts education – a connivance in overlooking the evident mismatch between ideals and practice – which has clouded our intellectual judgment of the progress and importance of the liberal arts from the days of Guarino down to T.S. Eliot, Leavis and the twentieth-century guardians of European 'civilisation'.

To take a single, but central, example. In his essay 'What is a Classic?' (1944), T.S. Eliot affirms the centrality of Virgil's Latin to western European culture in a way that bears all the hallmarks of humanist ideology and mystification:

> When a work of literature has, beyond [its] comprehensiveness in relation to its own language, an equal significance in relation to a number of foreign literatures, we may say that it has also *universality* ... [To find such a work] it is necessary to go to the two dead languages: it is important that they are dead, because through their death we have come into our inheritance – the fact that they are dead would in itself give them no value, apart from the fact that all the peoples of Europe are their beneficiaries. And of all the great poets of Greece and Rome, I think that it is to Virgil that we owe the most for our standard of the classic: which, I will repeat, is not the same thing as pretending that he is the greatest, or the one to whom we are in every way indebted – it is of a particular debt that I speak. His comprehensiveness, his peculiar kind of comprehensiveness, is due to the unique position in our history of the Roman Empire and the Latin language: a position which may be said to conform to its *destiny* ... Virgil acquires the centrality of the unique classic; he is at the centre of European civilisation, in a position which no other poet can share or usurp. The Roman Empire and the Latin language were not any empire and any language, but an empire and a language with a unique destiny in relation to ourselves; and the poet in whom that Empire and that language came to consciousness and expression is a poet of unique destiny.[5]

Elsewhere in this essay Eliot specifies the salient qualities of a 'classic' as 'maturity of mind, maturity of manners, maturity of language and perfection of the common style'. The point is that Virgil's poetry is here inextricably bound up with the values of the society which recognises it as classic, just as (according to Eliot) such values were responsible for the quality of the original writing. Eloquence is synonymous with maturity; *recognition* of that eloquence on the part of modern Europe is equivalent to confirmation of contemporary values.

In so far as the humanities, as taught in schools and universities, are regarded as a significant, even a peculiarly apposite training for those destined to occupy key positions in society, that belief still rests, historically, on the assumption that 'the Roman Empire and the Latin language were not any empire and any language, but an empire and a language with a unique

[5] T.S. Eliot, 'What is a Classic?' (1944), repr. *On Poetry and Poets* (London, 1957), 53-71; 67-8.

destiny in relation to ourselves'. Yet *within* most humanities departments such an assumption would be strenuously rejected (or at least replaced by some notion that the unique position of the 'universal classic' derives from some intrinsic textual quality of a 'surplus of signifier').[6] It is our contention that teachers and students of the humanities today need to be fully aware of the discrepancy between these two positions, and of the fact that the security of the humanities within institutions of higher education in particular rests on the continuing assumption that they are intrinsically supportive of 'civilisation' – that is, of the Establishment. In our view, the most striking way of highlighting this is to turn our attention to the moment at which western Europe committed itself to humanistic education as the training for the ideal, cultivated citizen. But throughout this book we shall be drawing the reader's attention repeatedly, and in a variety of ways, to the gap between strongly held ideal views and the reality which is educational practice. Finally, we shall suggest that that gap becomes, for modern society, the gap between *humanism* – the zealous faith in an ideal – and the *humanities* – a curriculum training a social élite to fulfil its predetermined social role.

---

[6] F. Kermode, *The Classic* (London, 1975), 140.

CHAPTER ONE

The School of Guarino:
Ideals and Practice

Guarino Guarini of Verona (1374-1460) was the greatest teacher in a century of great teachers. He was also a preeminent example of a humanist whose level of cultivation and scholarship was unmatched since antiquity. Like Cicero he went to Greece to be educated – to Constantinople, the capital of the dying Byzantine empire. There he studied for some years with the most learned Greek scholar of the day, Manuel Chrysoloras. On his return to Italy in 1408 he taught first at Florence, then at Venice and Verona, and finally at Ferrara, where he established a school in 1429 at the request of the local ruling family, the Este. At Ferrara he taught the young Prince Leonello, and an ever-growing number of others, drawn at first from Ferrara, but eventually (as the reputation of his school grew) from a catchment area that ran from England to Hungary. His expanding school became the arts faculty of the new university of Ferrara. And it became the model for dozens of others that sprang up across Italy, whose masters looked back to Guarino as their inspiration – the modern equal of Theophrastus and Isocrates.[1]

Guarino believed in education in its fullest sense – the classical *educatio*.[2] A lengthy and arduous process, it involved the formation of character as well as the training of the mind. He saw as its ideal product not the professional scholar but the active man of affairs, who retains a solid and lasting interest

[1] For a general introduction to Guarino's life and work and to the secondary literature on him, see E. Garin, 'Guarino veronese e la cultura a Ferrara', *Ritratti di umanisti* (Florence, 1967), 69-106, which also provides a forceful statement of his general views on humanist education. On the culture of the Este court see in general E.G. Gardner, *Dukes and Poets in Ferrara* (London, 1904), 26-66; W.L. Gundersheimer, *Ferrara: The Style of a Renaissance Despotism* (Princeton, 1973). And on Guarino's position in the Ferrara *studio* – an astonishingly exalted one for a teacher of the humanities – see esp. F. Borsetti, *Historia almi Ferarriae Gymnasii*, 2 vols (Ferrara, 1735). It is revealing that Guarino gave the inaugural lecture after the university was reformed (really refounded) in 1442, and that when he died he received a monument deliberately designed to rival the splendid one given by Florence to the humanist chancellor Leonardo Bruni (ibid., i, 49, 59).

[2] On ancient education see H.-I. Marrou, *Saint Augustin et la fin de la culture antique* 4th edn. (Paris, 1958); H.-I Marrou, *Histoire de l'éducation dans l'antiquité* (Paris, 1965 edn.); S.F. Bonner, *Education in Ancient Rome* (London, 1977).

1

in the literary studies of his youth. And he was at pains to remind any friend
or alumnus who had passed through his hands that his literary, political and
military triumphs were owed directly to the lessons he had learned in his
Ferrara classroom. As early as 1419 we find him writing to his friend Gian
Nicola Salerno, then the *podestà* of Bologna:

> I understand that when civil disorder recently aroused the people of Bologna to
> armed conflict you showed the bravery and eloquence of a soldier as well as you
> had previously meted out the just sentence of a judge ... You therefore owe no
> small thanks to the Muses with whom you have been on intimate terms since
> your boyhood, and by whom you were brought up. They taught you how to
> carry out your tasks in society. Hence you are living proof that the Muses rule
> not only musical instruments but also public affairs.[3]

Once settled in Ferrara he hardly made a speech or wrote a letter without
returning to this point. In the dedicatory letters to Leonello which
accompanied his translations from the Greek of Plutarch and Isocrates,
Guarino liked to allude to the resemblance between their relations and those
that had obtained between the great Greek and Roman leaders and their
tutors, notably Aristotle's with Alexander the Great. More than once
Guarino pointed out that a heavy responsibility had fallen on him, since in
shaping the character of the prince he was also shaping the future of his
subjects.

These themes from the private flattery of Guarino's letters are also to be
heard in his public discourses. In the introductory lecture of his 1422 course
at Verona on Cicero's *De officiis*, for example, he explicitly argued that his
pupils' studies would equip them for an active life and in the end directly
benefit the society they served:

> What better goal can there be for our thoughts and efforts than the arts precepts
> and studies by which we may come to guide, order and govern ourselves, our
> households and our political offices. [Moral philosophy] arms us against being
> cast down by bad fortune or swelling with pride at good fortune. It provides us
> with weighty counsel for our action and enables us to avoid rashness, the enemy
> of reason. It teaches us faith, constancy, fairness and liberality towards friends
> and foreigners, and respect for all sorts of men. It sets in order the impulses of
> our souls, and reins in our desires, so that we do nothing effeminate, soft or
> unworthy. I shall venture to say something bold, but which you gentlemen will
> acknowledge to be true: the very art and method of public speaking which the
> Greeks call rhetoric must become mute and silent unless it derives subject
> matter from this philosophy ... I should argue that it was this very philosophy
> which once upon a time brought men out of their wild life into this gentle and
> domesticated condition and which gave them the laws that enabled those
> assembled together to become a civil society ... Therefore continue as you have

[3] Guarino Guarini, *Epistolario di Guarino Veronese*, ed. R. Sabbadini, 3 vols (Venice, 1915-19), i,
263; Italian translation in *Il pensiero pedagogico dello umanesimo*, ed. E. Garin (Florence, 1958),
326-8.

begun, excellent youths and gentlemen, and work at these Ciceronian studies which fill our city with well-founded hope in you, and which bring honour and pleasure to you, prosperity and happiness to your friends.[4]

Guarino weaves every cliché he can steal from Cicero into this elegant if platitudinous sampler, and he probably did not expect to be taken entirely seriously. Teachers notoriously court their students in their introductory lectures in the hope of high enrolments. Translators also notoriously flatter the achievements of their patrons in their prefatory epistles. In both cases, however, the generalities about the relationship between an arts education and individual integrity and maturity are produced with a confidence which suggests that they are an acceptable justification for devoting oneself to the close study of ancient literature. We all know, Guarino is saying, that this is the very reason why you sought out my school in the first place.

It does not follow, however, that we can simply assume that Guarino's classroom did provide the wherewithal for producing fine statesmen. Intellectual historians have long had an emotional vested interest in taking Guarino at his word on this matter. But it is curious nevertheless how readily generations of historians have seized on these prefatory boasts as proof of the success in the worldly arena of humanist teaching in the arts. What is in fact happening is that the *ideology* of Renaissance humanism is being taken over as part of a historical account of humanist achievement. But however persistently such ideal claims are made for a programme of study, its final achievement requires to be assessed independently of them.

One glance at the mass of surviving classroom material from the humanist schools of the fifteenth century must make it obvious that, whatever the principles on which it was based, the literary training it provided was a far cry from this sort of generalised grooming for life. Even a charismatic teacher presenting the information which survives in student notes and teachers' lecture notes would have been hard put to convert the dense accumulation of technical material into quintessential 'humanity'. Yet if we are to evaluate the impact of the humanist teaching curriculum on fifteenth-century 'life and thought', it is to this body of taught humanism that we must turn.

The task before the student of humanism confronting the schoolbooks of the Ferrara classroom is a complex one. He has in front of him two *different* kinds of assessment which must be combined to produce any final judgment of the impact of humanistic studies. On the one hand there is the general claim that the goal of *educatio* is the inspiring and transforming initiation into mysteries which really does make a student a born-again 'new man'. On the

---

[4] Text in R. Sabbadini, *La scuola di Guarino Guarini Veronese* (Catania, 1896), repr. in *Guariniana*, ed. M. Sancipriano (Turin, 1964), 182-4. For a similar oration from Guarino's Ferrarese period, see for example the introduction to his course on Pier Paolo Vergerio, *De ingenuis moribus*, in A. Gnesotto, 'Vergeriana', *Atti e memorie della R. Accademia di scienze lettere ed arti in Padova*, new ser., 37 (1920-1), 52.

other there is the immense task of the competent transmission of necessary literary skills. For the humanist teacher himself, what creates the bond between the two (practice and ideology) is the example of ancient Rome. There, according to the humanist, 'culture' in the broad sense of a preparedness to deal wisely with civilised communal existence went hand in hand with a programme for passing on the skills of eloquence which had come down almost intact to the modern world. Revive the latter, the humanist argument went, and 'new men' on the Roman model would inevitably follow.

It will help us to understand some of the largely unstated reasoning behind the fifteenth-century revival of a training in eloquence as the foundation for civic life if we turn briefly to its Roman prototype. Roman *educatio* in its turn had been a conscious emulation of a foreign ideal. The Greek programme of education had evolved in the course of the gradual conversion of Greek culture from oral to written form.[5] Inevitably the core of this education was the Greek epic poetry and drama which had originally provided the focus for ritual community activity, and the formal oratory on which public debate and negotiation depended. When the Romans became interested in Greek culture in the middle of the third century BC,[6] it was a programme of this kind that they encountered. When they looked to Greece for a detailed course of instruction to produce the kind of intellectuals and statesmen they admired, the Greek teachers whose advice they sought (or whose services they bought) introduced them to a carefully graded programme in literature and rhetoric, which in the first instance the Romans accepted intact and absorbed as their own. However much later shifts in attitude and more careful consideration of local problems of bilingual education altered the balance of the curriculum, Homer (and later Virgil) and Greek tragedy (later of Ennius) remained vital elements in the general Roman education. By Quintilian's day this was clearly intended as a grooming for political spokesmen and professional lawyers, but it remains his view that the foundations of oratory are laid on 'the art of speaking correctly' (*scientia recte loquendi*) and 'the literary interpretation of the poets' (*poetarum enarratio*).[7] This training, according to

[5] Throughout this work we shall use the word 'culture' in the sense of 'high culture'. See M.I. Finley, *Knowledge for What?* (Edinburgh, 1972), reprinted as 'The heritage of Isocrates' in *The Use and Abuse of History* (London, 1975), 193-214: 'Throughout I shall use the word "culture" to mean "high culture", "humanistic culture", in the sense in which we speak of a "cultured person", and not in the descriptive, non-normative sense in which an archaeologist speaks of "material culture", an anthropologist of the "culture of the Chippewa Indians" ' (195).

[6] See A. Momigliano, *Alien Wisdom* (Cambridge, 1975), especially 16-17; Bonner, *Education in Ancient Rome*.

[7] Quintilian, *Institutio oratoria* 1.4.5. There are, of course, conflicting views as to the extent to which Rome's assimilation of Greek education was critical or imitative. It now appears to be accepted (and we are inclined to believe) that Roman education was closely and self-consciously modelled on Greek, to an extent which might occasion surprise to anyone not familiar with the ordinary practice and attitudes of schoolteachers. If a programme exists in precise detail, and if you are a teacher, at least try the same recipe. This is the view of Bonner in the most complete recent treatment of ancient education. It was also the classic view of Marrou, in his *Saint Augustin*

Quintilian, will produce 'the man who can really perform his function as a citizen, who is fitted to the demands both of private and public business, who can guide a state by his counsel, ground it in law and correct it by his judicial decisions'.[8]

Both Greek and Roman teachers insisted that this literary training provided the individual with a secure foundation for full and active life in the service of his community. In the case of Greece such a view was at least plausible, if difficult to pin down in detail. For Greek culture, with its early oral roots and the focal position of the orator/narrator within it, was squarely grounded in Greek literature. Homer and Hesiod were treated as repositories of ancient lore and moral wisdom far beyond the time when 'myth' ceased to be the basis for Greek self-consciousness and was replaced by 'history'.[9] By the time Rome looked to Greece for a prototype education, the reading and study of Homer was a matter of careful textual study, supported by a vast apparatus of commentary material providing a detailed body of instruction in myth, history, morals, language and literature. The 'grammarian' and 'rhetor' could argue that this provided a key to a deep understanding of Greece and Greek values, and was essential to anyone in civic office; and he could expect to be believed.

To the educated Greek it did not seem at all implausible to maintain that a broadly oratorical training was absolutely basic as a 'training for life'. The boy born a member of the ruling élite grew up with a literary canon stemming from Homer and Hesiod so firmly a part of his background that he could hardly conceive of a context for social, ethical or political discussion in which that literature did not play a part.[10] Since it was customary to clinch a point in debate with a tag from an ancient poet, and to sift the texts for apposite

---

et la fin de la culture antique. Those like Astin and Bowersock who are less inclined to believe in such enthusiastic philhellenism on the part of Rome are driven to argue for a much later interest in Greek instruction (beginning their discussion at the point at which Roman practice had significantly diverged and evolved away from its Greek prototype), to maintain that initially interest in things Greek was more a question of attitudes, not a serious question of models for pedagogic instruction. See A.E. Astin, *Scipio Aemilianus* (Oxford, 1967), appendix 6, 'The "Scipionic Circle" and the influence of Panaetius', 294-306; G.W. Bowersock, *Augustus and the Greek World* (Oxford, 1965), e.g. Ch. 6, 'Romans and the Hellenic life', 73-84. The point we are concerned with here is that *initially* emulation of things Greek prompted wholesale borrowing from Greek education. Later developments are then of interest in their own right; but the starting point is wholehearted and flattering lifting from a Greek into a Roman context.

[8] *Institutio oratoria* 1.pr.10.

[9] See M.I. Finley, 'Myth, memory and history', in his *The Use and Abuse of History*, 11-33; M.I. Finley, *The World of Odysseus* (London, 1954 edn.), ch. 1, 'Homer and the Greeks', 17-29.

[10] Compare, in the modern period, Matthew Arnold's remarks about the crucial role of Greek literature in the formation of western morals, in *Culture and Anarchy*. For example: 'The best art and poetry of the Greeks, in which religion and poetry are one, in which the idea of beauty and of a human nature perfect on all sides adds to itself a religious and devout energy, and works in the strength of that, is on this account of ... surpassing interest and instructiveness for us ... Greece did not err in having the idea of beauty, harmony, and complete human perfection, so present and paramount' (*Culture and Anarchy*, ed. Dover Wilson (Cambridge, 1932), 1963 edn., 54-5).

references, it was easy to suppose that *all* relevant knowledge of ethics, social practice, even guidance in practical affairs, could be arrived at by conscientious study of the key ancient works and works subsequently drawing upon them.[11] So study of the ancient texts *per se* (with accompanying commentaries and glosses highlighting their instructive content) could plausibly be considered to provide a rounded preparation for civic life.[12]

When Rome in her turn adopted this programme, the close relationship between literature and the society sponsoring the educational programme was inevitably less obvious. Rome, after all, did not have her roots in the mythology of Homeric legend, even if cultivated Romans had begun to show a keen interest in Greek art and literature. And of course Greek, the language of Homeric epic, was not the Roman student's first but his second language. Nevertheless the literature of an alien culture, in a foreign language, was held out to the Roman public as the proper foundation for an education appropriate to Rome's new urbanity and sophistication. Although Roman teachers amended, shifted and altered some of the emphases in the Greek curriculum, they never modified its general insistence on the vitality of Homer on essentially traditional Greek grounds.[13]

The problem of providing a basic education in a language which was foreign to the student probably provided the most compelling grounds for Roman modification of the Greek curriculum. Ideally, as Cicero and Quintilian still maintain, the Roman child would learn Greek from a Greek 'pedagogue' in his own home.[14] This had the added advantage that it

[11] There is a well-known passage in Plato's *Republic* in which Socrates alludes in passing to such a commonplace attitude towards Homer: 'When you find admirers of Homer saying that he educated Greece and that he deserves to be taken up and his lessons learnt in the management and culture of human affairs, and that a man ought to regulate the whole of his life on his principles, you must be kind and polite to them ... and concede that Homer is the foremost and most poetical of the tragic poets' (*Republic* 606E), cited in Finley, *The World of Odysseus*, 17.

[12] Much the same might be thought to be the case, for instance, among arts students in England in recent decades. A middle-class student raised on a traditional 'literary heritage' might be prepared to grant that Shakespeare ought to provide the pivotal axis for his arts education, because the art and literature which provided part of the context for his 'middle-classness' is in that tradition, and substantially shaped by Shakespearean influence (sometimes strongly felt; sometimes in choice of imagery or poetic language). A student who is not from that background will find it odd that such texts could *ever* have been considered central or valuable for his general education. Confidence in a cultural tradition or heritage has always gone hand in hand with the social confidence of an élite. Pierre Bourdieu has pointed out how the traditional curriculum in the French lycée inadvertently discriminates against lower-class students who do not have the same privileged access to the cultural tradition of their middle-class peers. See e.g. P. Bourdieu, 'Systems of education and systems of thought', in *Readings in the Theory of Educational Systems*, ed. E. Hopper (London, 1971).

[13] For a fine account of the transfer of Greek educational ideals and practice to Rome, see Bonner, *Education in Ancient Rome*. Bonner's work clarifies and solidifies the standard earlier works on ancient education, notably those of H.-I. Marrou. See also, for the later period of Roman education, E. Jullien, *Les professeurs de littérature dans l'ancienne Rome et leur enseignement depuis l'origine jusqu'à la mort d'Auguste* (Parish, 1885); A. Gwynn, *Roman Education from Cicero to Quintilian* (Oxford, 1926); P. Riché, *Education et culture dans l'Occident barbare* (Paris, 1962).

[14] Bonner, op. cit., ch. 4.

followed Greek practice (early introduction to national culture in the home from a specially appointed slave), though for a different purpose. But it appears that when primary schools began to provide less fortunate children with public instruction, that instruction was predominantly in Latin, with Greek as a later addition to the syllabus.[15] Inevitably this meant that indigenous Latin works were introduced alongside the major Greek texts which were still promoted as repositories of general wisdom. Just as inevitably, these indigenous Latin works tended to be consciously emulative works which echoed the Greek tradition – in the first instance simply by translating Greek works, and then by writing creatively and originally within contours determined by Greek literary forms.[16] By the time that Quintilian details a comprehensive training in the arts, the programme (and the kind of grounding it gives) differs in all but its broad categories from its Greek antecedent. And yet it retains something of its Greek flavour, and, above all, Greek-style pedagogic justification for the value of the literary course as a general education.

If Romans could none the less be persuaded that there was some intrinsic (and almost mysterious) relevance of the adopted literary education to the society in which they lived, it was because of the complicated process of inter- and cross-fertilisation which goes on between a base-education and the institutional activities it supports. A clear example of this complexity occurs in the case of 'declamation', the most sophisticated exercise in the rhetoric programme, and the one which provided the prelude to the student's professional activity in the lawcourts.[17]

Controversiae, or simulated disputations on a controversial theme, were the final stage in the graded system of oratorical exercises in which the 'rhetor' instructed his students as the constructive part of the programme of analysis of ancient literature. Following close study of the ancient texts, the student imitated the techniques used in these, in a carefully graded sequence of imaginative exercises emulating their content and practice.[18] For the

[15] Ibid., ch. 14.

[16] Bonner documents this change interestingly. Livius Andronicus' translation of the *Odyssey* was a standard Roman textbook down to Horace's time: Bonner, op cit., 20. Ennius provided both epic and tragic writings for teaching purposes, which were used until Virgil's *Aeneid* provided the Romans with an epic comparable in stature to the great Greek works: ibid., 21, 213. Even with the introduction of Latin works into the literary curriculum, much time was spent on comparing and contrasting them with their Greek prototypes. 'Already in the first century A.D., the assessment of the degree of Virgil's success in "borrowing", or echoing, lines and passages from Homer, the Greek tragedians, and earlier Latin poets, such as Ennius and Lucretius, was a favourite occupation of the *grammatici*' (ibid., 213-14).

[17] This account is based on the important studies of Bonner and Winterbottom: ibid., ch. 21, 'Declamation as a preparation for the lawcourts', 309-27; S.F. Bonner, *Roman Declamation in the Late Republic and Early Empire* (Liverpool, 1949); M. Winterbottom, 'Schoolroom and courtroom' (Paper delivered at the First International Conference of Rhetoric, Zürich, 1977). See also, J. Fairweather, *Seneca the Elder* (Cambridge, 1981).

[18] For a detailed account of this part of ancient education, see Marrou, *Saint Augustin et la fin de la culture antique*; Bonner, *Education in Ancient Rome*, part 3, 'The standard teaching programme', 163-327. Bonner interprets the surviving material on *progymnasmata* so as to give a rather more

controversia, the student was set a problem in law, an outline situation and a set of laws relating to it (say), and was expected to argue the case convincingly. In the Greek programme, the cases chosen, and the laws selected as apposite related closely to Greek legal practice and custom. When the Romans produced their own curriculum equivalent to the Greek exercise, they started with the Greek examples and tinkered with them to bring them in line with Roman legal and oratorical practice.

Given the artificial nature of the transposition – lifting Greek examples and incorporating them in a Latin syllabus – one might expect that the *controversiae* provided an overtly fantastic and fictitious occasion for schoolroom debating. Many of the cases for debate involve bizarre combinations of rape, adultery, disinheritance and family dispute, and the penalties meted out are implausibly severe. But in spite of the fantastic nature of the configurations of circumstances, the cases are carefully selected for their ability to bring into play the kinds of debating strategy which *were* most frequently invoked in the Roman courtroom. Just this feature of the cases was what recommended them to the teachers who sifted the Greek cases for those elements which could most usefully be adapted for Roman use.[19] The *form* of argument would be perceived by student and teacher to be essentially Roman and relevant to practice, even as the case itself and accompanying salacious or scandalous details were enjoyed as unlikely and absurd.

At the same time, in the actual lawcourts, practice *was* affected by the rhetorical exercises. All those who became Roman advocates had passed through the hands of the rhetor and had been exposed to his graded exercises complete with ancient and stylised *controversiae* examples. Among like-minded initiates the temptation was therefore strong to make a disputational point by direct or allusive reference to a familiar schoolroom example. These were the shared commonplaces of an educated public. And cases contrived to illustrate a difficult and effective rhetorical strategy provided an ideal opportunity for rhetorical flourish where needed in real prosecutions. They even had a reassuring ring of familiarity which was an essential feature of justification by accumulated example. 'We all know it to be the case' was an argument which could be used with gratifying certainty of the examples every educated person had encountered in the classroom.

If at this point the Roman teacher had been asked what and how intimate was the link between a literary training on a foreign model and the practical

---

convincing acount of actual teaching practice, although this still owes a good deal to Marrou's original formulation.

[19] It is, of course, well known that testimony of witnesses ranked last on the scale of 'convincing' arguments in Roman law. Adducing comparable examples persuasively played a prominent part in making a case. The contrived examples of the schoolroom contribute effectively to this persuasiveness, since they are readily recognisable and thoroughly familiar. On types of evidence and their judicial use, see Quintilian, *Institutio oratoria* 5; Pseudo-Cicero, *Ad Herennium* 2.

exigencies of life in his own cultural milieu, he would be bound to sense strong and definite affinities which he would be hard put to it to explain. And his general and largely conventional remarks about an education producing a mature individual ideally equipped for life would have an appealing ring of truth. In our own culture, literary critics have advanced the same kind of arguments for a 'felt affinity' between the Virgilian epic and English vernacular literary practice, induced by a similarly complicated process of cross-fertilisation between classroom and 'real-life' practice.[20]

Such examples should make it clear that extreme caution needs to be exercised when confronting Guarino's extravagant claims for a natural and self-evident relation between an education in the revived humanities and 'preparation for life' as a mature citizen of integrity. There is no question of making serious headway in assessing the real achievements of humanistic education without probing the actual possibilities for linking Guarino's classroom teaching with the general claims he made for it as a propaedeutic for civilised living.

The question of what actually went on in Guarino's schoolroom to complement the elaborate claims to be found in his letters and orations can be answered with some precision. Detailed statements of his methods appear both in his own letters and in a general treatise produced by his son. Many of the schoolbooks he compiled and used survive. Taken together, these materials allow us to make detailed comparison between classroom practice and humanist theory concerning the merit and efficacy of an arts education. They reveal his curriculum as comprehensive and exacting. Like the Roman educators whom he took as his model (especially Quintilian) he expected his students to devote many years to the course: Leonello d'Este spent six years under Guarino's tuition, although he had only embarked on his studies at the age of twenty-two. On the whole Guarino preferred to have his students entrusted to him at an earlier age and for an even longer period.

The boys began with an 'elementary' course in which they learned to read and pronounce Latin. Guarino had learned from Chrysoloras to take pronunciation seriously, and he insisted that it be studied and practised attentively as an essential aid to cultivated speech, close reading of texts (he instructed his students always to read aloud) and even good digestion.[21] We do not have much information about the exercises he used for this elementary instruction, but his pupils probably read in unison from a basic Latin text like

---

[20] See for example F. Kermode, *The Classic*, ch. 1, 15-45.

[21] In the absence of statutes or a detailed description by Guarino himself it is necessary to follow such descriptions of his curriculum as his son Battista's *De ordine docendi et discendi*, ed. with Italian translation in *Pensiero pedagogico dello umanesimo*, ed. Garin, 434-71. For the most part we follow the detailed reconstruction given in Sabbadini, *Scuola e gli studi di Guarino Guarini*. Guarino Guarini's insistence on pronunciation can be seen in, for instance, his letter to Leonello, Summer 1434: Guarino Guarini, *Epistolario*, ii 269-70 (ed. Garin, 380); Battista Guarini, *De ordine docendi et discendi*, ed. Garin, 440.

the thirteenth-century *Ianua* (Gateway) which lists and analyses the parts of speech as a series of questions and answers: 'What part of speech is "poet"?' 'It is a noun.'[22] We can assume that the exercises were systematic, intensive and highly repetitive.

The second part of his course he called 'grammatical',[23] and (following Quintilian) he divided this into two parts. One, 'methodical', covered the rules of grammar and syntax. The other, 'historical', dealt with history, geography, mythology – all the facts needed to read and write classical Latin in an informed way.

The central text for the 'methodical' part of grammar was Guarino's own manual, the *Regulae*. This defines the parts of speech, gives detailed instructions for the inflection of verbs and nouns and formulates the basic rules of Latin syntax. Like its medieval antecedents (on which it draws substantially)[24] it crystallises these pieces of instruction into hundreds of mnemonic verses:

> *Flagito posco peto doceo rogo calceo celo*
> *Vestio subcingo moneo,* also *instruo iungo* –
> Two accusatives with all these verbs go.[25]

These verses were decidedly not merely ornamental; the student was expected to spend years committing them to memory, reciting them, being tested on them:

> They must learn grammar perfectly in every respect. As in buildings, where unless strong foundations are laid, everything that is built upon them must collapse, so in studies, unless they know the principles perfectly, the more progress they make the more aware they will become of their weakness. Therefore let the boys learn first how to inflect nouns and verbs, without which they cannot possibly understand what comes later. And the teacher must not be satisfied with teaching them once, but must train the boys' memories by going over the material again and again, and must ... test what and how much they have learned. He must sometimes give a wrong inflection to test how well they know their terms: for the ability to detect mistakes in others will be strong evidence of progress.[26]

---

[22] Sabbadini, op. cit., 35, 43-4.

[23] Battista Guarino, op. cit., ed. Garin, 440-3.

[24] On the sources of the *Regulae*, see Sabbadini, op. cit., 38-44, with W. Keith Percival, 'The historical sources of Guarino's *Regulae Grammaticales*: a reconsideration of Sabbadini's evidence', in *Civiltà dell'umanesimo: atti del VI, VII, VIII convegno del Centro di studi umanistici "Angelo Poliziano"* (Florence, 1972), 263-84; W. Keith Percival, 'Renaissance grammar: rebellion or evolution?', in *Interrogativi dell'umanesimo* (Florence, 1976), 73-90.

[25] Quoted in Sabbadini, *Scuola e gli studi di Guarino Guarini*, 42.

[26] Battista Guarino, *De ordine docendi et discendi*, ed. Garin, 440-1; see Guarino Guarini, *Epistolario*, i, 498 (ed. Garin, 344-5). Given the amount of noise involved in such activities it is not surprising that schoolmasters sometimes ran into legal difficulties with irate neighbours; see R.G.G. Mercer, *The Teaching of Gasparino Barzizza* (London, 1979).

Memorisation, repetition, catechism – these are the activities on which
Guarino's humane learning is firmly grounded. Written tests ensured that
the student was not mechanically repeating sounds he did not understand,
while oral practice gave him a fluency that would not necessarily have come
from written drilling alone.

This rigorous grounding in the formal rules was only the first assault. As
the pupil advanced he had to learn to write a 'pure' Latin – that is, a Latin
resembling as closely as possible that of the age of Cicero and Virgil. For this
he needed a guide to proper usage, to using only such terms as the Romans
had used and only in the senses in which they had used them. Guarino and
his pupils compiled a series of such guides. At their most elementary (like the
one by Bartolomeo Facio entitled 'The Differences between Latin Words')[27]
they amounted to little more than a preventive against elementary solecisms:
'This is the difference between a *fabula* and a *historia*: we call an invented
narrative a *fabula* and a true one a *historia*.'[28] Equipped with such simple
distinctions the pupil could at least avoid making a fool of himself on the
public platform.

Guarino's aim, of course, was for his pupils to achieve more than this
elementary level of security. He intended them to be in a position to use Latin
discerningly, after the manner of the great ancient authors. Classical Latin
vocabulary, like that of any sophisticated literary language, is highly complex.
Any word has a broad range of more or less unexpected connotations; for,
once a major author has used it in a particularly attractive extended sense, or
made it part of an elegant metaphor, others will make a point of imitating him.
The great Roman writers – the authors who formed the backbone of the
curriculum – pitched their works at a small and highly literate audience,
trained to detect and enjoy such covert allusions.[29] After several hundred
years of Latin literature, the language was developed into a tissue of implicit
allusion, glancing reference to metaphors and quotation from elsewhere in
the canon, and similar plays on words.[30] Renaissance humanists recognised

---

[27] See in general M. Baxandall, *Giotto and the Orators* (Oxford, 1971), 8-20.

[28] Quoted in C. Marchiori, *Bartolomeo Facio tra letteratura e vita* (Milan, 1971), 40.

[29] For a modern example see F. Kermode, *The Genesis of Secrecy* (Cambridge, Mass., 1979), 8:
'[The concourse] is often enough, indeed ostentatiously, compared to a graveyard, though it is a
real station in the *unreal City* of London, full of commuters, brothers and sisters of that *crowd that
flows over London Bridge* at nine and back at five-thirty: *I had not thought death had undone so many.*'
The passages italicised by us are unacknowledged quotations from T.S. Eliot's *The Waste Land*,
which the reader is expected to recognise. The passages in *The Waste Land* are themselves a
rendering of Dante, *Inferno* 3. 55-7, as the notes to the text provided by Eliot himself point out. It
has been argued recently by sociologists concerned with literacy in general that such borrowings
at textual level are a significant feature of 'advanced literacy'. They become apparent once texts
are treated as potential objects of interpretation, rather than simply as transmitters of information
or instruments of recall.

[30] In the Renaissance, humanist writers similarly enjoyed 'quoting' word play already
familiar to the well-read reader. See for example R. Guerlac, *Juan Luis Vives against the
Pseudodialecticians* (Dordrecht, 1979), 52: '*At isti non dico non intelliguntur a doctissimis latine, cum se*

quite early that this was a game the Romans had played – a game fostered by the habit of comparing Latin works with their Greek prototypes. The problem was to find a way of teaching the rules to students who could not immerse themselves in the classics as Petrarch might have done; how, in other words, to codify a practice which really depended on deep acquaintance with the entire canon of classical writing. For the aspiring Latinist whose native language was Italian, and whose knowledge of Latin was restricted (and coloured by church usage – a flexible but entirely non-classical idiom), the structure of the web of classical allusive usage was frustratingly hard to master.

Guarino devised an ingenious combination of pedagogical exercises in an attempt to overcome this problem. He amassed an elaborate corpus of linguistic information essential for an elegant Latin style, and he compressed it into a variety of readily retainable forms – on the one hand mnemonic verses packed with careful discriminations, on the other meticulous lexica dense with apposite quotation and citation.

The *Carmina differentialia* set out long mnemonic lists of homonyms, synonyms and words with other peculiar characteristics:

> A hill is a *collis*; a *caulis*, I'm told,
> Is a plant, and a *caula* keeps sheep in the fold.
> A *collum* bows down with the weight of the head
> That it holds, while a *colum*'s for spinning a thread.
> A philosopher's *radius* spans half a wheel;
> For the weaver it serves as a spindle or reel.
> But *radii* make up the light of the sun.
> *Liber* (of *libri*) is a *codex* which one
> Must never confuse with the bark of a tree –
> That's *cortex* – nor yet with *liber liberi*,
> Who is Bacchus, who gave us the great gift of wine,
> Or else a man born from a non-servile line.[31]

To complement this, Guarino's massive lexicon is a compilation of a much more detailed and sophisticated kind, which not only gives the common sense of Latin words, but explains their varying connotations and illustrates their usage with numerous quotations. Here is a single representative entry:

> *Canere*, 'To write verse about'. Virgil, *Arma virumque cano*. 'To praise', as *regemque canebat*. 'To divine', as *ipsa canas oro*. For although the Sybil is said to give her answers in verse, the word is none the less to be construed as 'divining'. This

---

latine dicant loqui, sed interdum, ne ab hominibus quidem ejusdem farinae, seu ejusdem potius furfuris' (But these persons are not only unintelligible to men expert in Latin, though they say they speak Latin; they are sometimes not understood by men of their own grain – or rather bran). Guerlac comments: 'A colloquial play on words common in Erasmus and More' (ibid., 214).

[31] Garin, *Pensiero*, 489-9. Another version of the poem is attributed to Barzizza; see Mercer, *Teaching of Gasparino Barzizza*, 66.

interpretation is well supported by another verse, *divique hominesque canebant* – that is, 'the gods and men divined'.[32]

Neither of these forms of instruction was original to Guarino. The mnemonic verses had a good medieval precedent, while the large-scale lexicon was substantially a rearrangement of entries from the vast late-antique commentary on Virgil by Servius (fourth century AD). The entry just quoted, for example, is closely adapted from one of Servius' notes on the first line of the *Aeneid*.[33] The novelty, however, was the marriage of these two very different sorts of approach in Guarino's programme of instruction. For, to judge from the one surviving commentary on the *Carmina differentialia* (not in fact by Guarino himself, but by a later and lesser schoolmaster, Ludovico da Puppio),[34] the *Carmina* were meant to serve not as a self-sufficient collection of mnemonic tags, but as an armature, to which the teacher could affix as much material as possible from other sources, and especially from such a lexicon as Guarino's own.

Ludovico tells us that his commentary rests on his teaching practice. His method was to explain the distinctions laid down in Guarino's verses, and then to amplify them, qualify them and take off from them into accounts of other related words, or even unrelated words for related things. He also managed to include a good deal of elementary historical and mythological information in his glosses, and once or twice he even enriched his teaching with relatively fresh material from recent works of text scholarship, such as Lorenzo Valla's *Elegantiae*.[35] For the most part, however, his method is Guarino's, and his chief source is once again Servius. On the single line from the *Carmina* – *Hic Cancer cancri crescit aquis caelesteque signum* ('Here the Crab grows in the water and appears as a constellation in the heavens') – Ludovico goes on for more than a page. He lifts a complete list of signs of the Zodiac from Servius, with the months they were held to rule and the spheres of the planets that were assigned to their control. Only then does he pass on to

[32] From the recension of Guarino's lexicon in A. Decembrio, *De politia litteraria libri septem*, IX.xxxiiii (Basle, 1542 edn.), 311 (here and elsewhere we follow the text of Decembrio's presentation copy in the Biblioteca Apostolica Vaticana, Rome, MS. Vat. lat. 1794).

[33] Servius on Virgil, *Aeneid* 1.1 (ed. G. Thilo and H. Hagen, 3 vols, Leipzig, 1881-7, i, 6): '*Cano* is a word rich in meanings, for it can signify three things: sometimes "praise", as in *regemque canebant*; sometimes "divine", as in *ipsa canas oro*; sometimes "sing", as here. For it properly means "sing", because poems are meant to be sung.' The quoted examples are from *Aeneid* 7. 698 and 6. 76 respectively; Guarino's final, added example is from *Aeneid* 12. 28.

[34] Guarino Guarini, *Carmina differentialia* (Parma, 1492); the Preface is given in *Pensiero pedagogico dello umanesimo*, ed. Garin, 499-500. Ludovico says that 'after interpreting [this poem] in my school and, as it were, within my own walls to my schoolboys, I have tried to produce some more diligent commentaries on it which, I hope, will be quite helpful to beginning students' – in short, he admits that his commented edition is a revised version of the notes he had used in the classroom.

[35] Guarino Guarini, *Carmina differentialia*, sig. Aiiii[v]: 'Valla distinguishes between *vir* and *homo* ...'. Valla's *Elegantiae linguae latinae* was completed circa 1444.

Guarino's original level of simple lexical distinctions, and even so he finds it necessary to amplify and to explicate Guarino's already very simple Latin: '*Cancer cancri* and *cancer canceris* of the third declension and masculine, of a disease feared by all. *Crescit* means "grows". *Aquis* means "in the water".'[36] One can imagine the cumulative impact of such lessons. The pupils were deluged with words, phrases and facts as they floated out of the teacher's memory, or out of Guarino's word lists. At the same time, the *Carmina* structured the mass of information, making it easy to retain, recall and put readily to use. By reciting (out loud or to himself) a section of the *Carmina*, the student would be induced to recall also much of the illustrative and supplementary matter that his teacher had provided. Such a system achieved what medieval grammar teaching had stopped short of: it turned out students whose grammar and usage were convincingly classical, who could read and write classical Latin with something like the native speaker's facility and sensitivity. The only wonder is that students were prepared to pay the high price in boredom and fatigue that entitled them to access to these mysteries.

Alongside this linguistic drilling, the student was expected to build up a large stock of pertinent factual information. The 'historical' part of grammar comprised far more than history alone. It began with the study of the Roman historians, 'so that the boys may adorn their speeches with examples relevant to every kind of virtue, to outstanding actions and sayings'.[37] But it also included the reading of poets whose graphic descriptions of everyday life were to be admired, and from whom 'they will learn the names and locations of rivers, mountains, cities and countries'.[38] And it extended to the few Latins who had written on elementary scientific matters, such as astronomy and geography. In other words, this part of the course attempted to use classical literature as the basis for detailed anthropological and geographical knowledge of antiquity, as well as a modicum of science. All this would make it easier for the student to read and write classical Latin like a 'native'.

One example of 'historical' grammar teaching comes from Guarino's lectures on Virgil's *Georgics* (a traditional source of instruction on Roman husbandry), as recorded by that amiable and adventurous Englishman, John Free, who came from Bristol to Ferrara to learn the more humane letters.[39] *Georgics* 1.43-4 reads:

[36] Guarino Guarini, *Carmina differentialia*, sig. [Av^{r-v}].

[37] Battista Guarino, *De ordine docendi et discendi*, ed. Garin, 454-5.

[38] Ibid. For an interesting sample of the variety and level of factual information that Guarino wished his pupils to master, see the mnemonic verses that he wrote for Leonello listing the names of the Seven Sages 'so that when you encounter them in reading, you will find all your difficulties removed' (Guarino Guarini, *Epistolario*, ii, 265-6).

[39] On Free, see R. Weiss, *Humanism in England during the Fifteenth Century*, 2nd edn. (Oxford, 1957), especially 106-12; R.J. Mitchell, *John Free: From Bristol to Rome in the Fifteenth Century* (London, 1955); W.F. Schirmer, *Der englische Frühhumanismus*, 2nd edn. (Tübingen, 1963), 114-27.

Vere novo gelidus canis cum montibus umor
Liquitur et Zephyro putris se glaeba resolvit.

(In the new spring, when the snow melts from the white mountains,
And the earth becomes soft under the West Wind.)

Here is Guarino's general note on line 43:

Vere novo: the word *annus* comes from *ananein* (renew, recover), because when the sun returns to the same degree then a year has passed. Romulus began the year from March; hence he called the first [month of the year] by his name, since he is called the son of Mars. The second month he named after Aeneas, from whom the Roman nation is descended. He is said to have been the son of Venus; Venus is called Aphrodite. Hence *Aprilis*, with the aspiration removed. And because the Roman people were divided into two parts, that is into the elders or *seniores* ... and the younger, he named May from the elders (*maioribus*) and June from the younger (*junioribus*).[40]

Guarino continues about the names of the months at some length. Floundering in this flood of detailed factual information, poor John Free's notes are peppered with grammatical errors as he struggles to keep up. What Free's note-taking shows us is something of the quality of erudition Guarino felt it essential for his students to acquire. It was not a deep knowledge of any one subject or subjects, but as comprehensive a catalogue as possible of disconnected 'facts' necessary for informed reading and writing in the classical tradition: etymological, geographical and mythological points have equal value for this purpose, and demand equal attention.[41] To this end Guarino's note on *Georgics*, 1.43-4, continues:

Vere novo: Each month has three parts. The first is called new or beginning; the second is called middle ...; the third is called last or final.

humor gelidus: That is, ice. *canis*: snowy.

Zephyros: in Greek means *Favonius* (west wind) in Latin. The opposite wind is called *Euros* in Greek, *Subsolanus* in Latin. *Notos* in Greek is *Auster* in Latin.

...

Boreas in Greek is *Septentrio* in Latin. [It is so called] because *meta boês reei*, that is, it comes with force.

putris: That is, easily broken.[42]

---

[40] Bodleian Lib., Oxford, MS. Bodley 587, fol. 137[r].
[41] The approach of the late-antique teachers from whom Guarino drew both information and inspiration had been quite similar; so, probably, was that of Chrysoloras and the other Byzantine teachers whom he heard as a young man.
[42] Bodleian Lib., MS. Bodley 587, fol. 137[r].

At the same time, Guarino encouraged his students to take up Greek. Here too, partly thanks to his teacher Chrysoloras, he made use of some ingenious pedagogical devices: short and pithy *sententiae*, some of which had been cited by Roman authors, made an attractive introduction; a short grammar in the form of a catechism provided the necessary details of noun- and verb-forms and syntax; and projects in translation, done under Guarino's no doubt vigilant eye, made the best students self-reliant and fluent in reading.[43]

In his general remarks on teaching methods Guarino's son Battista insists that this training must be supplemented by the student's independent reading. The student must study on his own the great encyclopaedic works of the empire: the *Attic Nights* of Aulus Gellius, the elder Pliny's *Natural History* and Augustine's *City of God*. Those with the stamina could also tackle Strabo's *Geography*, which Guarino translated and commented upon.[44] These works were meant to fill out the grammatical programme, particularly in subjects like the history of ancient science and philosophy. But Battista entrusted this supporting reading to the energy of the individual student, stopping short of providing aids for the study of these massive and largely disorganised texts.

On a more realistic level, the pupil had to collaborate with his teachers in assembling and collating lexical and factual material as part of the constructive element in his training. Guarino knew that no one could become a real master of classical Latin on the basis of memorised, predigested rules. He instructed even his most exalted students to extend their working knowledge by compiling their own lexica and compendia in the course of their reading. Every pupil was expected to compile his own collection of specimens of interesting usage and edifying anecdotes, and to set them out systematically in indexed notebooks:

> Whenever you read [he wrote to Leonello], have ready a notebook ... in which you can write down whatever you choose and list the materials you have assembled. Then when you decide to revise the passages that struck you, you will not have to leaf through a large number of pages. For the notebook will be at hand like a diligent and attentive servant to provide what you need. The ancient teachers and students considered this practice so valuable that many of them, including Pliny, reportedly never read a book without taking notes on its more interesting contents. Now you may find it too boring or too much of an interruption to copy everything down in such a notebook. If so, some suitable and well-educated lad – many such can be found – should be assigned this task.[45]

[43] See in general Battista Guarino, *De ordine docendi et discendi*, ed. Garin, 448-53. On Guarino's method of elementary Greek teaching, see R. Sabbadini, *Il metodo degli umanisti* (Florence, 1922), 20-2; on his and Chrysoloras' Greek grammars, see A. Pertusi, 'Per la storia e le fonti delle prime grammatiche greche a stampa', *Italia medioevale e umanistica*, V (1962), 321-51; on Guarino Guarini's use of translation as a teaching device, see J.R. Berrigan, 'The Latin Aesop of Ermolao Barbaro', *Manuscripta* 22 (1978), 141-8.

[44] Battista Guarino, *De ordine docendi et discendi*, ed. Garin, 456-9, 460-1.

[45] Guarino Guarini, *Epistolario*, ii, 270 (ed. Garin, 382-3). The practices that Guarino popularised long remained standard; Francis Bacon, for example, used secretaries to compile his notebooks, among them Thomas Hobbes.

This letter to his noble charge Leonello reveals the extent of Guarino's ambitions for the best of his pupils: they should master the classics just as the ancients did, from the inside. At the same time it reveals one of his principal merits as a teacher. He had a gift for order, and the system of keeping notebooks was a brilliant device for enabling his students to impose a form on their hard-won knowledge. It also reveals some of the openly élitist assumptions Guarino makes: his ideal student is the aristocrat like Leonello with the leisure and the means to read extensively in the classics to supplement the basic course of instruction. The technical work and the drudgery which form a part of the programme are to be left to the poor scholarship boy – whose careful notes often grew into textbooks, just as the same boys often grew up to become teachers in Guarino's school and elsewhere. Finally, the letter to Leonello also suggests the aim of all the years of grammatical study: the pupil needs to have his material 'ready', 'at his fingertips'. Guarino does not say what he must be ready for, but that is because the answer is obvious to him. The pupil must be ready to compose, spontaneously, or to command, *extempore* and aloud, or as a written composition.

The school exercise in which Guarino tested the pupil's 'readiness' in the Latin language was the formal Latin essay on a set theme. Here was the opportunity for practical application of everything the student had learnt from his reading and recorded systematically in his notebooks. Like all the other parts of the course the theme was carefully regulated: Guarino provided his students with detailed instructions on both choice of subject matter and treatment. Here, for example, are his instructions to a former pupil on how to write in praise of the countryside, first in prose and then in verse:

> Remember when you praise the countryside or denounce the city to take the reasons for the praise or blame from four 'places'. That is, show that utility, pleasure, virtue and excellence belong to the country. Contrariwise, damage, wretchedness, defects and flaws belong to the city. I recall that I set those rules out in a couplet. You should note it down and memorise it so that you will always have it to hand:
>
> > Four things to praise all topics amply go:
> > Virtue and use, pleasure and goodness show.[46]

The nature of the exercise is apparent from this example. The pupil is not expected to develop original or independent ideas; he is not to express his own emotions, or to treat the topic in a fresh or striking manner. Rather, he is to execute a stylised set-piece in a stylish way. Like the Roman student of formal declamation he must commit to memory a set of rhetorical *loci* (literally 'places') where subject-matter may be classified according to the key kinds of topic needed to make a case ('virtue', 'usefulness', 'pleasure', 'goodness' in the case above). These he must draw upon in his theme, not because he has thought the matter through and decided they are appropriate, but because

[46] Guarini, op. cit., i, 594-5; see Sabbadini, *Metodo degli umanisti*, 44-5.

they are the proper *loci* for this sort of theme. He is to be a virtuoso at writing by numbers. He should know what *loci* are required for any category of theme, and then fill each of these out with the metaphors and anecdotes and fragments of ancient lore collected in his notebooks.

Guarino himself practised this form of exercise seriously throughout his life, much as the master musician will spend hours each day on routine practice. For example, he wrote a praise of his country villa, in which he follows his own precepts as literally as he expected his students to do. He shows that his house is useful because it is healthful; pleasant and good because of the lovely views it affords; virtuous because of the opportunities it will provide for untroubled study. And when Guarino's students had completed their studies he would write to them and ask for a formal description of their new surroundings.[47]

The student's arduous training in grammar was followed by training in formal rhetoric. In theory this was a rounded education in philosophy as well as in expression: one that embraced Cicero's philosophical dialogues as well as his rhetorical works, and which went on to cover the Greek sources on which Cicero had drawn (the writings of Aristotle and Plato). At this stage the student was to make that life-giving contact with the ancient world, understood in all its historical vitality, that would enable him to be an active citizen in his own time. In short, Guarino's claims for his rhetorical training followed those made by Quintilian: it was to complete a full liberal education in the manner of the training assigned by antiquity to the rhetor.

In practice, as by now we might expect, Guarino's rhetoric course was considerably less ambitious than this. It seems to have centred on the *Rhetorica ad Herennium*, an anonymous work widely believed in the fifteenth century (though not ultimately by Guarino himself) to have been written by Cicero. Here are surviving notes on his opening lecture, on the first sentence of the text:

> *Etsi negotiis familiaribus impediti vix satis otium studio suppeditare possumus, et id ipsum quod datur otii libentius in philosophia consumere consuevimus, tamen tua nos, Gai Herenni, voluntas commovit ut de ratione dicendi conscriberemus ...*

> (Being kept busy by my private affairs, I can hardly find enough leisure to devote to study, and the little that is granted to me I have usually preferred to spend on Philosophy. Yet your desire, Gaius Herennius, has spurred me to compose a work on the theory of Public Speaking ...)

> *Etsi* (although) a conjunction which is properly connected with a verb in the subjunctive mood and differs from *quanquam* (also meaning 'although') because *quanquam* is usually connected with the indicative, as in Virgil: *quanquam animus meminisse horret* (although the mind shudders to recall).

> *Negotiis familiaribus* (private affairs) that is, 'those of my intimates and friends', not, as many think, 'those of my household'. For Cicero was extremely wealthy. For he had many under his patronage, like King Deiotarus, Marcus Marcellus

---

[47] Guarini, op. cit., i, 238-41, adapted from Pliny the Younger, *Epistulae* 5.6; cf. ibid., i, 487.

and many others whom he defended with speeches (in court).

Impediti (being kept busy, plural form, literally meaning 'we are kept busy') this is more elegant than if he had said 'impeditus' (I am kept busy), and was an attempt to avoid seeming arrogant, for the ancients considered it more humble to speak of oneself in the plural than in the singular.

...

Suppeditare (devote), *subiungere* (add), *subicere* (subjoin), from *sub* (under) and *pes pedis* (foot)

...

In philosophia that is moral philosophy, as he did in his book *De officiis*, in the *Tusculan Disputations*, the book *On Friendship*, and so on. For philosophy is threefold: one kind is natural, which is called 'physics' in Greek; the second is moral, which is called 'ethics' in Greek; the third is that of speech, which is divided into dialectic and rhetoric; dialectic is the method of arguing correctly, rhetoric is the art of speaking well, and Zeno compares dialectic to a closed fist [and rhetoric to an open hand] ...

...

C. Herennium Herennius is said to have been the brother or relative of Cicero's wife Terentia.

Commovit voluntas (your desire has spurred me) Herennius incited Cicero to write ... as he himself says in the book *On Friendship*, 'It is the property of friends to want the same things and to refuse the same things'.

Ut de ratione dicendi Cicero here makes his reader tractable by briefly explaining what he will say. Then, since an introduction should have a threefold effect – namely that the listener be made tractable, favourable and attentive – in what follows he makes him favourably disposed and attentive.[48]

The labour that must have been involved in the dictation and recording of these notes is considerable. Evidently, even in his advanced teaching,

---

[48] Text in Sabbadini, *Metodo degli umanisti* 43-4. Some students, to be sure, found what Guarino did with a text very exciting. Free wrote to him that 'nothing ever made me so eager to write as your lecture on Cicero yesterday' (Guarini, op. cit., ii, 652-3). But this enthusiasm may have stemmed from Free's lack of previous exposure to Italian culture. In fact, it had been common since the early fourteenth century for Italian teachers to make a detailed commentary on the *Ad Herennium* the centre of their rhetoric courses. See J. Monfasani, *George of Trebizond: A Biography and a Study of his Rhetoric and Logic* (Leiden, 1976), 262-5; J.O. Ward, 'From Antiquity to the Renaissance: glosses and commentaries on Cicero's *Rhetorica*', in *Medieval Eloquence*, ed. J.J. Murphy (Berkeley, 1978), 25-67. Moreover Guarino's commentary is fairly traditional in its method and contents. It seems to have owed a good deal to such earlier prototypes as the twelfth-century commentary of 'Alanus' (at least to judge from a comparison of the passage quoted in the text with the recension of Alanus' commentary in British Library, London, MS. Harley 6324, fol.3).

Guarino worked through his text slowly and meticulously, trying to discuss every phrase, almost every word, that presented a problem of interpretation or revealed a novel shade of meaning. Equally evidently, his students tried to take down verbatim what he said. They failed: when the note-taker in this case writes, 'Zeno compares dialectic to a closed fist', he is giving half of a popular ancient anecdote. Clearly he had no time to complete it with the other half of the comparison, which Guarino certainly did not omit ('and rhetoric to an open hand').[49] And the notes that appear in such terse phrases here were no doubt complete sentences as delivered.

The notes convey an overwhelming preoccupation with a profusion of tiny details. They also make it clear that the rhetoric course cannot possibly have covered all the works that Guarino wished to include. To cover texts in the gruelling detail shown here, given an hour's lecturing per day per text, can hardly have taken less than an academic year for each book. Accordingly, even a student who spent several years attending Guarino's lectures on rhetoric would probably have studied only the equivalent of a few hundred modern pages of text *in all*.[50] When we try to imagine what it felt like to be trained in rhetoric by Guarino we are faced with this mass of disparate information hung on a frame of one or two key texts. Plato and Aristotle can have been little more than names to most of those who listened to Guarino's dissection of philosophy into three parts.

The truth appears to be that the rhetoric course was simply a more elaborate introduction to the same sorts of material that had occupied the student of grammar: explanation of interesting words and constructions, very brief and sketchy discussions of historical points, bits of general information of the sort that a cultivated person should know and formal analysis of the rhetorical *loci* used by Cicero himself. There is little attention to Cicero's train of thought or line of argument – this is entirely lost in the scramble for detail.

Cicero's text becomes at once a scaffold to be decorated with all manner of general information, and a worked example of the very principles that the *Rhetorica ad Herennium* set out to instill, with a model formal *exordium* (introduction) constructed according to the set theme, and so on. It is as if the teacher had on his desk a beautiful completed jigsaw puzzle – the text. Instead of calling up his students to look at the puzzle, he takes it apart, piece by piece. He holds each piece up, and explains its significance carefully and at length. The students for their part busy themselves writing down each explanation before the piece in question vanishes into the box. And the vital question we have to ask ourselves is whether the accumulation of fragments which the student made his own could ever take shape as the whole from which they originated.

---

[49] This aphorism appears several times in Cicero; for example, in his *Orator*, 32. 113: 'Zeno, the founder of the Stoic school, used to give an object lesson on the difference between the two arts [logic and eloquence]; clenching his fist he said logic was like that; relaxing and extending his hand, he said eloquence was like the open palm.'

[50] R.R. Bolgar has found that the Renaissance grammar schools managed likewise to cover

But before we turn to the examination of this question, there is one further feature of Guarino's system of education to which attention needs to be drawn. That is the direct use of Guarino's dictated lectures as a kind of 'teacher's training'. For it was inevitable that once his commentaries had been painstakingly taken down from dictation other teachers should borrow directly from them, rather than from the sources on which he himself had drawn. The immediate consequence of this was bound to be distortion and lack of clarity even greater than that displayed by the student notes themselves. As we have seen, student transcripts suffered further reductions in clarity and accuracy. A set of lecture notes once in general circulation tended to undergo a process of watering down and loss of precise content. By the time it had passed through three or more redactions the lectures that a humanist teacher based on the notes would be no more than a clumsy outline of the cumbrous but meticulous original.

Here too a brief example is instructive. In 1467 Ludovico Sforza wrote out a brief manuscript of eight leaves to give to his mother Bianca Maria as evidence of the progress he had made under the tutelage of Francesco Filelfo. The manuscript survives in the Royal Library in Turin. It is prettily illuminated as befits a presentation copy, which is probably why it attracted sufficient attention for a modern fascimile to be produced in 1967.[51] The editor of the facsimile, Luigi Firpo, rightly points out in his introduction that the manuscript contains a set of notes on the *Ad Herennium*, and suggests plausibly enough that Filelfo might have dictated them to his fifteen-year-old pupil. What Firpo did not realise is that these notes are nothing more than a much reduced version of Guarino's notes on the same text, from which we gave an extract above. Evidently Filelfo used some short form of Guarino's commentary as the basis for his lectures. He made the occasional addition – a few Greek roots, which Ludovico omitted, and the open hand of rhetoric – but he left out the bulk of what Guarino had had to say (the notes are barely one-tenth as long as the record we have of Guarino's), so that his treatment is at best sketchy and, at its frequent worst, incoherent. Guarino would no doubt have said that Ludovico lost Milan because he understood his Cicero so poorly!

Now that we are familiar with the practical teaching in Guarino's classroom, we can return to our original question about the relation between the day-to-day achievement of his classroom instruction and any idealised achievement associated by propagandists (Guarino himself being foremost among these) with humanist instruction in general.

The pupil learnt to read and write a classical Latin. He learnt it with a thoroughness that would be the envy of the modern classics teacher (and probably of the modern teacher of any of the European vernaculars). When he

---

only a fragment of the projected curriculum. See R.R. Bolgar, 'Classical reading in Renaissance schools', *Durham Research Review* 6 (1955), 2-10.

[51] See *Francesco Filelfo educatore e il 'Codice Sforza' della Biblioteca Reale di Torino*, ed. L. Firpo (Turin, 1967). It was the normal fate of pedagogical works to be reworked, abridged and padded at will by their users; for another case, see W. Keith Percival, 'Textual problems in the Latin Grammar of Guarino Veronese', *Res publica litterarum* 1 (1978), 241-54.

graduated, even the slowest of Guarino's pupils probably possessed the ability to pronounce and write in Latin, on issues ancient and modern, 'like a native'. That was the real achievement of the relentless, saturating instruction in the finer points of classical Latin grammar, usage, history, culture, geography and rhetoric. The modern teacher is likely to observe wistfully that he would dearly like his own classroom to be frequented by students who were *prepared to endure* such a training in the interests of true Latinity.

The price Guarino paid for his success in training Latinists of this calibre, however, was high in terms of his humanist ideals. The very nature of the meticulous, readily retainable, ready-to-recall instruction he devised precluded any kind of rich overview. To embark on generalised discussion of the intrinsic value of a classical education for character formation, or as a grooming for the public servant, would have been to distract the pupil from the task in hand. It would have required a different kind of attention from the pupil: something more intellectual and less disciplined than the regimented note-taking, rote-learning, repetition and imitation in which he was engaged.

Naturally Guarino did include some moral comment in the course of his lectures; it would have been hard to avoid doing so when his subject text was the *De senectute* or Persius' *Satires*. But these observations inevitably became absorbed into the pedagogical routine – something to be recorded between etymologies and paraphrases, rather than a coherent contribution to a fully articulated moral philosophy. Here, for example, are Guarino's comments on some familiar lines from Cicero's *De amicitia*:

> *Ego autem a patre ita eram deductus ad Scaevolam sumpta virili toga, ut, quoad possem et liceret, a senis latere numquam discederem. Itaque multa ab eo prudenter disputata, multa etiam breviter et commode dicta memoriae mandabam, fierique studebam eius prudentia doctior.*

(My father brought me to Scaevola when I had put on the *toga virilis* on the understanding that so far as possible I would never leave the old man's side. Therefore I committed to memory many of his prudent arguments and pithy sayings and tried to make myself more learned through his prudence.)

a senis latere (the old man's side): this refers to a way of walking and sets out for youths the important principle that they should seek the company of old men from whom they can derive learning.

disputare [i.e. *disputata*] (arguments) means things said with art and reason; [the word] is derived from the pruning of trees and vines.[52]

---

[52] '*A senis latere: Denotat modum eundi et notabile tradit adolescentibus ut senum consuetudinem consequantur: a quibus disciplinas capere possunt. Disputare est cum arte et racione dicta: tractum est ab amputatione arborum et vitium.*' Brit. Lib. MS. Harley 2549, fols. 81ᵛ-82ʳ: Guarino's commentaries on the *De senectute, Paradoxa* and *De amicitia*, in a recension whose compiler has added some small amount of material of his own (see, for example, ibid., fol. 90ᵛ). In general the method Guarino uses in these commentaries is strikingly similar to that of the *Ad Herennium* commentary. He does briefly discuss Cicero's views on philosophical questions (and those of other philosophers), but he

Presumably Guarino hoped that eventually his students would become fluent enough – mature enough as readers – for Cicero's moral outlook as conveyed by his structured moral argument to become accessible to them. Meanwhile he gave them intensive drilling in the grammatical and rhetorical ground-plot for such study.

At the same time 'prospective employers', as we might term them, the patrons of Guarino's school, and the parents who sent their offspring in droves to sit at Guarino's feet, did apparently feel that he was providing a worthwhile and relevant training for future leaders and civic dignitaries. So, having pinpointed the discrepancy between the claims of humanists as educators to uphold the *dignitas hominis*, and the narrow cumbersomeness of classroom instruction, let us turn our attention to the *incidental* advantages of humanist pedagogy as actually practised.

In the first place, of course, humanist education was modish; it was in vogue with the élite. One ought not to underestimate the self-reinforcing quality of such preconceptions in the field of education. As recently as ten years ago there were still employers in England, for instance, who would always employ an arts graduate from Oxford or Cambridge in preference to a specialist from elsewhere on the grounds of his 'flexibility', 'cultivation' and general suitability to western cultivated styles of living and attitudes of mind. In other words, if an ability to quote Cicero is currently believed to be a mark of a much wider competence, then the ability to quote Cicero will go a long way towards satisfying an employer, even if this is the only skill the person has been taught.

But, beyond this, the actual classroom drill to which Guarino's pupils were subjected left its mark on them in ways that had a distinct and recognised value in Renaissance society. In the first place, the skills Guarino inculcated had an established practical value in fifteenth-century Italy. The ability to speak *extempore* on any subject in classical Latin, the ability to compose formal

---

also spends much of his time showing that a good *prohemium* makes its readers docile and attentive (ibid., fol.81ʳ), giving etymologies, and the like. And as the example in the text suggests, his discussions of moral philosophy are hardly at the level of sophistication and rigour that one would expect from secondary accounts. Indeed one is tempted to suggest that what Guarino regards as *moral* about his instruction is not in fact the content at all. The *activity* of learning to read perceptively trains the moral faculties, rather in the way that gymnastics and wrestling had also traditionally been considered part of the *educatio* of youth. Textual analysis teaches the student to identify those aesthetic qualities which are assumed to be the mark of superior moral sense on the part of the author, and hence passes on that sense to the student. One might compare Arnold or Leavis on the function of literary criticism. On these critics' persistent elision of aesthetic and moral judgment in literary criticism, see J. Casey, *The Language of Criticism* (London, 1966), especially ch. 9, 'Art and morality', 179-97. Casey concludes (as we would conclude for Guarino): 'Both Arnold and Leavis insist that the criticism of literature is inescapably moral, but they both see moral judgment as essentially the diagnosis of emotions, motives, character – the area where it is most like aesthetic judgment. The conclusion is, surely, unavoidable that their notion of the moral, in its extreme formalism, is fundamentally aesthetic' (ibid., 196).

letters to order in the classical idiom, the ability to teach exactly as they had been taught, were all valuable assets. Equipped with them the student could serve as an ambassador, or secretary to a government department, or could become an advocate, a priest, or a professor of the *studia humanitatis* in his turn. In other words, although the programme was strictly literary and non-vocational, it nevertheless opened the way to a number of careers (exactly as its Roman prototype had done in ancient Rome).

Secondly, Guarino's schooling fostered the sort of personality traits that any Renaissance ruler found attractive: above all, obedience and docility. Much of the time in Guarino's classroom was spent (as we have seen) passively absorbing information, accumulating and classifying predigested and processed material. Active participation, like the formal disputation (or obligation debate)[53] which had figured prominently in medieval training, played a comparatively small part in the programme; hence the insignificant place of dialectic or 'active thinking' in the course.[54] The consequences of this were much as they had been in late antiquity, or as they would be in the seventeenth and eighteenth centuries: students became accustomed to taking their orders and direction from an authority whose guiding principles were never revealed, much less questioned.[55] Passivity had been a feature of monastic education, but then it had been future clerics who had been prepared for a life of obedience;[56] in Guarino's school the pupils were laymen, often of high birth and destined for high office. Fluent and docile young noblemen were a commodity of which the oligarchs and tyrants of late fifteenth-century Italy could not fail to approve.

Guarino himself recognised that uncritical willingness to obey orders was the current road to preferment when he wrote to his son in 1443:

> Whatever the ruler may decree must be accepted with a calm mind and the appearance of pleasure. For men who can do this are dear to rulers, make themselves and their relatives prosperous, and win high promotion.[57]

Perhaps that vein of pragmatism contributed to his own belief in the appropriateness of his schooling for the future man of affairs. And some idea of the safe conformity of the Guarino school product can be gleaned by reading

[53] On such active debating exercises in the Aristotelian programme, see C.L. Hamblin, *Fallacies* (London, 1970), especially 125-33. For an entertaining 'worked example' for the schoolroom, see Agostino Nifo, *Dialectica ludicra* (Florence, 1520).

[54] This is in marked contrast to the central position occupied by logic in the scholastic programme. See *The Cambridge History of Later Medieval Philosophy*, eds. N. Kretzmann, A. Kenny and J. Pinborg (Cambridge, 1982).

[55] On late antique education, see Riché, *Education et Culture*; on seventeenth- and eighteenth-century education, see G. Snyders, *La pédagogie en France aux dix-septième et dix-huitième siècles* (Paris, 1965).

[56] On medieval education, see Garin, *Educazione in Europa*, ch. 1.

[57] Guarini, op. cit., ii, 439; see also ibid., 438, 441. This letter, incidentally, found enough readers that some twenty-seven copies of it survive.

between the lines of Carbone's funeral oration in praise of the great humanist. Students came to him, Carbone claimed, from Veneto, from Emilia, from Umbria, from Tuscany, from Calabria, from Sicily, from Germany, from Dalmatia, even from Britain: 'So many men, barbarian by nature, Guarino freed from barbarity of speech. He sent them back to their fatherlands as Latins in language and in culture.'[58] Such uncritical acceptance of homogeneity guaranteed the oligarchic supremacy of the Italian aristocracy, as it had once guaranteed the extent of the Roman empire.[59]

Seen from this point of view, the general approval expressed for Guarino's kind of humanist instruction by the Italian establishment has more to do with its appropriateness as a commodity than with its intrinsic intellectual merits. As long as humanist schools turned out such suitable potential servants of the state, they were prepared to endorse the enthusiastic claims of humanist idealists for their literary studies as 'a storehouse of recorded values', from which the individual acquired 'a general fitness for a humane existence'.[60]

No doubt there will be some readers whose response to all this will be to exclaim: 'Well, but what did you expect? It is inevitable that the elevated claims of all promoters of new educational programmes become more pedestrian when translated into classroom practice.' And we would be bound to agree. But the reader must remember that this is *not* what the student of humanism is led to believe if he relies upon the most influential accounts of the impact of humanist pedagogy. There he finds passages like the following, manifestly conflating professional ideals with actual results:

> Such was humanistic education: not as one has sometimes been led to believe, grammatical and rhetorical study as an end in itself, so much as the formation of a truly human consciousness, open in every direction, through historico-critical understanding of the cultural tradition. *Litterae* (literature) are effectively the means of expanding our personality beyond the confines of the present instance, relating it to the paradigmatic experience of man's history ... What matters is a moral preparation based not on precepts, but on the effective mastery of a critical understanding of the human condition itself. What matters is to engage in dialogue with those who express archetypal humanity – that is, with the true masters. Because in order to understand them, and in understanding them, that which is most elevated in us emerges.[61]

---

[58] L. Carbone, '*Oratio habita in funere ... Guarini Veronensis*', in *Prosatori latini del quattrocento*, ed. E. Garin (Milan and Naples, 1952), 398-9. See also Free's remark that Guarino's fame had induced him 'to come to Italy from, so to speak, another world' (Guarini, op. cit., ii, 653).

[59] On the homogenising aspirations of Roman education, see Marrou, *Saint Augustin et la fin de la culture antique*.

[60] L.C. Knights and D. Culver, 'A manifesto', *Scrutiny* 1 (1932), 5; F.R. Leavis, 'The literary mind', *Scrutiny* 1 (1932), 27.

[61] Garin, *Educazione umanistica in Italia*, 7. Here Garin grafts on to a description of humanist education ('Such was humanistic education ...') an ideological pronouncement concerning the

What we must now recognise is the inevitable *gap* between the beliefs which such passages articulate about the saving, civilising qualities of an arts education and the practical consequences for generations of students of pursuing the detailed curriculum to which the general pronouncements were affixed.

There is, in fact, one final piece of evidence concerning Guarino's school which suggests that contemporary humanists were aware of the problem of grafting a detailed curriculum on to a set of ambitious cultural ideals. In 1462 Angelo Decembrio, a pupil of Guarino's, published his *De politia litteraria*.[62] This consists of a series of dialogues between Guarino, Leonello and their circle, and purports to document the elevated intellectual activities of the Ferrara school and its progeny. We are presented with Guarino, Leonello and friends, seated under the great laurel at Belfiore, discussing the authenticity of the correspondence between Seneca and St Paul and the *Rhetorica ad Herennium*. Leonello neatly shows that the *Ad Herennium* cannot possibly be by Cicero, because it does not match his style, lacks the clear preface on the origin and issue of the work which marks any work as his, and receives no mention elsewhere in his opus. We even see the participants showing real literary perceptiveness in examining the habits of Roman writers: in particular, their habit of borrowing creatively from the works of earlier authors. And in other dialogues subjects are discussed as varied as the spoken Latin of the Romans and the nature of classical painting and gems.[63] Here is a côterie which fits readily into the framework of conventional accounts of the erudite achievement of the humanist schools of the quattrocento.

There is, however, another side to the work. In addition to the space devoted to elegant intellectual debate, large portions of the work are devoted to Guarino's instruction on such topics as homonyms, the rhetorical figures and Greek words with Latin derivatives. These consist of meticulously reproduced excerpts from Guarino's textbooks and lexica, alphabetically indexed and uncluttered with any kind of running narrative. What Decembrio appears to be trying to do is to provide an intellectual setting for

---

ultimate merits of an arts education which is exactly equivalent (we would maintain) to the fundamental axiom of the Leavisite 'Manifesto' in the first issue of *Scrutiny*: 'We take it as axiomatic that concern for standards of living implies concern for standards in the arts' (Knights and Culver, 'Manifesto', 2). The curiously impersonal construction Garin uses for his assessment of humanist achievement in the field of education in this introduction suggests that he is himself not entirely happy about bridging the gulf between theoretical boasts and classroom practice.

[62] On Decembrio, see R. Sabbadini, *Classici e umanisti da codici Ambrosiani* (Florence, 1933), 94-103.

[63] On the authenticity of the *Ad Herennium*, see Decembrio, *De politia litteraria*, I. x.63-4; for the study of borrowings and allusions, see ibid., VI. lxvi.477-86; for discussion of *objets d'art*, see ibid., VI. lxviii.500-13, which is presented and translated in M. Baxandall, 'A dialogue on art from the court of Leonello d'Este', *Journal of the Warburg and Courtauld Institutes* 26 (1963), 304-26. See also S. Rizzo, *Il lessico filologico degli umanisti* (Rome, 1973), 200-2; L.A. Panizza, 'Gasparino Barzizza's commentaries on Seneca's letters', *Traditio* 33 (1977), 297-358; 334-6.

such laborious and unwieldy material that will justify the claim that it has general cultural merit that goes beyond the skills it purveys. He makes no secret of the fact that the models for this type of justificatory fiction are Quintilian and the *Attic Nights* of Aulus Gellius.[64] These two ancient works present fragments of arts instruction in a narrative setting which underscores the full benefit which, it is argued, is to be derived from these. The narrative setting is designed to make explicit the implied connection between ideals and practice in the field of liberal arts education; Decembrio's dialogues make the same case for Guarino's humanistic training.

But the dialogues show only too clearly that the links between ideals and actual classroom achievement are by no means obvious. Indeed, on occasion the 'cultivation' (the goal) becomes disastrously separated from the rote-drilling (the practice): after Leonello's elegant analysis of the textual reasons why the *Ad Herennium* cannot be attributed to Cicero, the lexica which interrupt the poised dialogue nevertheless attribute it to him, and comment accordingly.

If Decembrio means to show how Guarino's school initiates the student into the whole of ancient culture, and the concomitant elevated attitudes and beliefs, then he fails. He fails because the process of initiation is not in the end conducted according to any set of rules. Nor is the transition from 'standards in the arts' to 'standards of living' made without intermediaries. Initiation of the kind Guarino believes in takes place, if it is to take place at all, as a lived emulation of a teacher who projects the cultural ideal above and beyond the drilling he provides in curriculum subjects – a charismatic teacher like Guarino. What shows up in the *De politia litteraria* is the discontinuity between the eloquent gestures of outstanding individual humanists and the body of classroom teaching embedded in the narrative text. On the one hand, we see the proliferation of discrete items of literary information, almost entirely without cohesive moral or intellectual comment. On the other, we see the effortless familiarity with antiquity of its literary products, the easy comparisons between authors and works, the critical acumen and moral poise of the ablest scholars and courtiers. In the end, Decembrio's work seems to indicate, the two can only be juxtaposed; the transition from one to the other will remain permanently mysterious.

We believe that the fact that individual gifted humanists succeeded in making that mysterious transition from classroom aptitude to rich familiarity with antique culture should serve to remind us of the magnitude of their intellectual achievement. We have shown that while the ruthless drilling of Guarino's classroom provided the foundation for their prowess, it was by no means a *sufficient* condition for their success. Guarino's pupils did include critical philologists like Fazio and Decembrio, and practising poets like Janus

---

[64] Decembrio, *De politia litteraria*, I. i.4; I. iii.9.

Pannonius, whose achievements were naturally adduced by propagandists to support their contention that a humanistic arts education was the ideal grooming for Renaissance civic life. In our view these scattered achievements, diverse in kind and quality, are in fact evidence of the *problematic* nature of any attempt to show a regular and causal link between routine competence and creative achievement, let alone civic qualities of leadership and integrity.

In private letters to his alumni Guarino appears to endorse this view. He urges his pupils to persevere with the studies to which he has introduced them, to carry on reading and writing in expectation of the enlightenment which he hopes will one day come to them. 'Don't be afraid, if at first you don't understand,' he exhorts them. 'Knock again, and it will open for you.' Even he could not claim to be sure quite how or when in this process his students would be metamorphosed into his erudite equals, and he was certainly aware that his instruction alone was not sufficient to produce 'new men' – even if he could only afford to admit as much to those initiates who had progressed far enough in their studies to deserve his confidence.

CHAPTER TWO

Women Humanists: Education for What?

In the last chapter we examined the way in which the ideals envisaged and propaganda claims made by a charismatic humanist teacher for his educational programme have to be scrutinised carefully before they can serve as evidence of the actual social and political impact of the *studia humanitatis* in fifteenth-century Italy. In the present chapter we turn from the teacher to the pupil, and specifically to a pupil who *fails* to meet implicit standards of 'suitability' as a candidate for such a training. From such a case, we shall argue, one gains valuable additional information about the limitations of the humanist liberal arts education as a general education, suitable for any cultivated person.

Somewhere between 1443 and 1448 the distinguished teacher Lauro Quirini,[1] a former pupil of Guarino's, addressed a letter of advice to the humanist Isotta Nogarola of Verona.[2] He was responding to a request from her brother for guidance on appropriate reading for an advanced student of the *studia humanitatis* in the technical disciplines of dialectic and philosophy:

> Your brother, Leonardo ... asked me some time ago if I would write something to you, seeing that at this time you are devoting extremely zealous study (as he terms it) to dialectic and philosophy. He was anxious for me to impress upon

---

[1] On Quirini see *Lauro Quirini umanista*, ed. V. Branca (Florence, 1977); *Isotae Nogarolae Veronensis opera quae supersunt omnia*, ed. E. Abel, 2 vols (Budapest, 1886), I, xliv, xccii; R. Sabbadini, 'Briciole umanistiche', *Giornale storico della letteratura italiana* 43 (1904), 247-50; L. Martines, *The Social World of the Florentine Humanists* (Princeton, 1963), 97-8.

[2] Isotta Nogarola (1418-1466): see most recently M.L. King, 'The religious retreat of Isotta Nogarola (1418-1466); sexism and its consequences in the fifteenth century', *Signs* 3 (1978), 807-22, which contains a full bibliography in an appendix. See also Abel's introductory essay in the *Opera*; M.L. King, 'Book-lined cells: women and humanism in the early Italian Renaissance', in *Beyond their Sex; Learned Women of the European Past*, ed. P.H. Labalme (New York and London, 1980), 66-90; P.O. Kristeller, 'Learned women of early modern Italy: humanists and university scholars', ibid., 91-116; D.M. Robathan, 'A fifteenth-century bluestocking', *Medievalia et humanistica*, fasc. 2 (1944), 106-11.

you, in most solid and friendly fashion, which masters above all you ought to
follow in these higher disciplines.[3]

Quirini prefaces his detailed suggestions for study with an elaborately
dismissive paragraph in which he is at pains to point out that to the learned
humanist with a real command of classical Latin (among whom he numbers
Isotta, some of whose writing he has been shown), all study of dialectic and
philosophy must appear uncouth and clumsy:

> For you, who have been thoroughly instructed in the most polished and
> excellent art of discourse, and who find that elegance in orating and suavity of
> speech come naturally, you are able of your own accord to expect the greatest
> perfection in eloquent speech. But we semi-orators and petty philosophers have
> most of the time to be content with mean speech – generally inelegant.[4]

He insists, however, that Isotta Nogarola should not therefore be misled by
difficulty for its own sake, even though 'now especially we pursue that
philosophy which in no way concerns itself with felicity of expression' (*eam
enim hoc potissimum tempore philosophiam sequimur, quae nullum sequitur florem
orationis*).[5] Technical scholastic dialectic is to be vigorously avoided:

> I absolutely insist, and I place the weight of my authority behind this, that you
> avoid and shun the new philosophers and new dialecticians as men minimally
> schooled in true philosophy and true dialectic, and that furthermore you harden
> your heart against all their writings. For they do not teach the approach to the
> old tried and tested discipline of dialectic, but they obscure the clear and lucid
> path of this study with goodness knows what childish quibbles, inextricable
> circuities and pedantic ambiguities. And while seeming to know a great deal,
> they distort the most readily intelligible matters with a kind of futile subtlety.
> So that, as the comedian would say, 'they find a knot in a bullrush' ['make
> difficulties where there are none' (Plautus, Terence)]. On which account,
> having been diverted by these obstacles, they are unable to aspire to the true
> philosophy, in which indeed, although they wish to seem sagacious debaters,
> they let slip the truth, as the old saying goes, with excessive cross-examination.[6]

---

[3] All passages are quoted from Abel's edition of Nogarola's works (hereafter 'Abel'). '*Leonardus
germanus tuus ... iam pridem me rogarat, ut nonnihil ad te scriberem, nam quoniam hoc tempore dialecticae et
philosophiae acrem, ut is aiebat, operam das, voluit, ut ipse fidelissime ac amicissime te commonerem, quos
praecipue magistros in his altioribus disciplinis sequi deberes*' (Abel, II, 10).

[4] '*Tu enim, quae politissima et exquisitissima arte dicendi edocta es assueta in eleganti oratione, suavitateque
dicendi, tuo iure perornatissimum exposcere potes eloquium, at nos semioratores minutique philosophi parvo et
illo ineleganti persaepe contenti sumus*' (Abel, II, 11).

[5] Ibid.

[6] '*Cupio, inquam, idque meo iure iubeo, ut novos hos philosophos novosque dialecticos tamquam homines
minime verae philosophiae veraeque dialecticae instructos non modo evites et fugias, verum etiam omnia eorum
scripta stomacheris, nam dialecticae quidem non viam disciplinae veteris iam probatae docent, sed nescio quibus
puerilibus captionibus, inextricabilibus circuitibus et scrupulosis ambagibus huiusce disciplinae claram et
dilucidam semitam obfuscarunt. Nam ut multa scire videantur, omnia etiam planissima futili quadam subtilitate
corrumpunt et, ut inquit comicus, "nodum in scirpo quaerunt". Quapropter his impedimentis detenti nequeunt ad*

According to Quirini the source of genuine understanding of dialectic and philosophy remains Aristotle (whose texts *veram et elegantem philosophiam continent* 'contain true and elegant philosophy'). And for a clear grasp of the sense of Aristotle's philosophical works he directs Isotta away from the newfangled, towards less pretentious expositors:

> Let me instruct you which authors you *should* follow. Read studiously the celebrated works of learned Boethius, easily the most acute of men, and fully the most knowledgeable. Read, that is, all those treatises which he composed with erudition on the art of dialectic, and the dual commentaries he published on Aristotle's *Categories* and *De interpretatione*, the first for understanding the texts, the second as an examination of the higher art. In these you will be able to find the pronouncements of almost all the most relevant and reliable of the Greek commentators.[7]

Having mastered dialectic with Boethius, Isotta should proceed to Aristotle's moral philosophy, and thence to mathematics, natural philosophy and metaphysics. Since she has no Greek, Quirini suggests the Arab commentators (in their Latin versions), as providing the best access to the nuances of Aristotle's texts. In spite of their 'barbarity', Averroes and Avicenna are preferable in this respect to any of the 'new' philosophers – a sign, incidentally, that Quirini takes Isotta's intellectual aspirations entirely seriously.[8] To these he adds Thomas Aquinas. However, Quirini concludes, in the end the Roman historians and moralists, and supremely Cicero himself, will add the final gloss and lustre to Isotta's grasp of higher learning, and the lessons in life it provides.

This leads him to round off his letter with a eulogy of philosophy as the supreme guide to virtuous conduct – *bonae artes* and right living go hand in hand:

> For nothing is more seemly than philosophy, nothing more lovely, nothing more beautiful, as our Cicero was wont to say; and I may perhaps add, more properly, nothing more divine in matters human. For this is the single, most sacred discipline, which teaches true wisdom and instructs in the right manner of

---

veram et solidam aspirare philosophiam, in qua etiam dum acuti disputatores videri cupiunt, veritatem nimium altercando, ut vetus sententia dicit, amiserunt' (Abel, II, 13-14).

[7] *'[His ergo explosis] quos sequi debeas, breviter edocebo. Lege igitur studiose Boetii Severini, viri facile acutissimi abundeque doctissimi praeclara monumenta, id est tractatus omnes, quos in arte dialectica erudite confecit, et eius commentarios, quos in Aristotelis Cathegoriis et Periermenias duplices edidit, primos ad litterae intelligentiam, secundos ad altioris artis indaginem. In quibus cunctorum fere probatissimorum Graecorum commentatorum sententias videre poteris'* (Abel, II, 15-16).

[8] For an account of the serious use of Averroes' commentaries on Aristotle's texts in the Renaissance which is entirely consistent with Quirini's advice to Isotta Nogarola, see C.B. Schmitt, 'Renaissance Averroism studied through Venetian editions of Aristotle-Averroes (with particular reference to the Giunta Edition of 1550-2)', *Convegno internazionale: l'Averroismo in Italia, Atti dei convegni Lincei* 40 (Rome, 1979), 121-42. Schmitt is, of course, concentrating largely on a later period.

living. Whence it comes about that to be ignorant of philosophy is not simply to go through life basely, but also ruinously. Accordingly, throw yourself wholeheartedly, as they say, into this one matter. For I wish you to be not semi-learned, but skilled in all the liberal arts (*bonae disciplinae*), that is, to be schooled in the art of discourse, and in the study of right debating, and in the science of things divine and human.[9]

Quirini's letter articulates a mature humanistic position on the type of rigorous study of language and *scientia* appropriate to *eloquentia*. But although the advice is standard, even commonplace, the circumstances in which it is given are unusual. It was not customary for a woman to pursue advanced humanistic studies. Indeed Leonardo Bruni's well-known letter to Battista Malatesta of some forty years earlier explicitly states that while the *bonae artes* are an appropriate occupation for a noblewoman (the favourite analogy is that it keeps their fingers out of mischief, like spinning or needlework),[10] public proficiency in advanced studies is indecorous:

There are certain disciplines which while it is not altogether seemly to be entirely ignorant of, nevertheless to ascend to the utmost heights of them is not at all admirable. Such are geometry and arithmetic, on which if too much time and energy is expended, and every subtlety and obscurity pursued to the utmost, I shall restrain you by force. And I shall do the same in the case of Astronomy, and perhaps in the case of Rhetoric. I have said this more reluctantly in the case of this last, since if ever there was anyone who has bestowed labour on that study I profess myself to be of their number. But I am obliged to consider many aspects of the matter, and above all I have to bear in mind who it is I am addressing here. For why exhaust a woman with the concerns of *status* and *epichiremata*, and with what they call *crinomena* and a thousand difficulties of rhetorical art, when she will never see the forum? And indeed that artificial performance which the Greeks call *hypocrisis*, and we call *pronuntiatio* (which Demosthenes maintained to rank first, second and third, such was its importance), as it is essential to performers, so it ought not to be pursued by women at all. For if a woman throws her arms around while speaking, or if she increases the volume of her speech with greater forcefulness,

[9] '*Nihil enim philosophia formosius, nihil pulchrius, nihil amabilius, ut Cicero noster dicebat, ego vero forsan rectius, nihil philosophia in rebus humanis divinius. Haec enim unica, sanctissima disciplina est, quae veram sapientiam edocet et rectum vivendi modum instruit, ex quo fit, ut ignari huius non modo turpiter sed etiam perniciose per vitam obirent. Proinde huic uni rei, toto, ut aiunt, pectore incumbe, volo enim te non semidoctam esse, sed cunctarum bonarum disciplinarum peritiam habere, id est et bene dicendi artem et recte disputandi disciplinam et humanarum atque divinarum rerum scientiam noscere*' (Abel II, 21-2).

[10] See, for example, Erasmus: 'The distaff and spindle are in truth the tools of all women and suitable for avoiding idleness ... Even people of wealth and birth train their daughters to weave tapestries or silken cloths ... It would be better if they taught them to study, for study busies the whole soul ... It is not only a weapon against idleness but also a means of impressing the best precepts upon a girl's mind and of leading her to virtue.' *Christiani matrimonii institutio* (Basle, 1526), ch. 17, unpaginated, cit. *Not in God's Image: Women in History*, ed. J. O'Faolain and L. Martines (London, 1979), 194. Politian, writing in praise of another woman humanist, Cassandra Fedele, commends her for having exchanged 'her spinning wool for her books, her rouge for a reed pen, her needle for a quill pen'. See *Clarissimae feminae Cassandrae Fidelis Venetae epistolae et orationes ...* ed. I.P. Tomasinus (Padua, 1636), 156.

she will appear threateningly insane and requiring restraint. These matters belong to men; as war, or battles, and also contests and public controversies. A woman will not, therefore, study any further what to speak either for or against witnesses, either for or against torture, either for or against hearsay evidence, nor will she busy herself with *loci communes*, or devote her attention to dilemmatic questions or to cunning answers; she will leave, finally, all public severity to men.[11]

'Cultivation' is in order for a noblewoman; formal competence is positively unbecoming. Presumably it is because encouraging her higher studies might be considered improper that Quirini insists at the beginning of his letter of advice to Isotta that it is specifically at the request of her brother (her father being dead) that he offers such advice.

So in the case of Quirini's letter to Isotta Nogarola we have familiar sentiments about the moral desirability of humanistic education, addressed to an unusual student – one of whom it can be said with certainty that full competence as a humanist would probably be construed as unbecoming, if not *immoral*. It is because this particular conjunction must concentrate our minds so remarkably well on the question of what 'moral' might possibly mean in the context of humanistic education that we choose it as the focus for this second chapter. It gives us striking additional information to bring to the general question (in relation to students of either sex): What was humanist education envisaged as an education *for*?

As we saw in the last chapter, propaganda documents issued by humanists on behalf of their emerging educational programme (epistles of advice, introductions and prefaces to texts and translations, epideictic orations for deceased humanist pedagogues) consistently (like Quirini's exhortation above) make the identity of humanist eloquence and moral integrity – right living – automatic and self-evident. Ludovico Carbone's funeral oration for Guarino is a masterly example of the form, and is particularly pertinent to the

---

[11] '*Sunt enim disciplinarum quaedam, in quibus ut rudem omnino esse non satis decorum, sic etiam ad cacumina illarum evadere nequaquam gloriosum; ut geometria et arithmetica, in quibus, si multum temporis consumere pergat et subtilitates omnes obscuritatesque rimari, retraham manu atque divellam. Quod idem faciam in astrologia, idem fortasse et in arte rhetorica. Invitior de hac postrema dixi, quoniam, si quisquam viventium illi affectus fuit, me unum ex eo numero esse profiteor. Sed multarum rerum habenda mihi ratio est et in primis, cui scribam, videndum. Quid enim statuum subtilitates et epicherematum curae et illa, quae appellantur crinomena, et mille in ea arte difficultates mulierem conterant, quae forum numquam sit aspectura? Iam vero actio illa artificiosa, quam Graeci* hypocrisim, *nostri* pronuntiationem *dixere, cui Demosthenes primas et secundas et tertias tribuit, ut actori necessaria, ita mulieri nequaquam laboranda, quae, si brachium iactabit loquens aut si clamorem vehementius attollet, vesena coercendaque videatur. Ista quidem virorum sunt; ut bella, ut pugnae, sic etiam fori contentiones atque certamina. Non igitur pro testibus neque contra testes dicere addiscet mulier, neque pro tormentis aut contra tormenta, neque pro rumoribus aut contra rumores, nec se communibus locis exercebit, neque interrogationes bicipites neque responsiones veteratorias meditabitur; totam denique fori asperitatem viris relinquet.*' *Leonardo Bruni Aretino Humanistisch-Philosophische Schriften mit einer Chronologie seiner Werke und Briefe*, ed. H. Baron (Leipzig, 1928), 11-12. In spite of Bruni's warning, Battista Malatesta delivered a public oration in Latin to the Emperor Sigismund. See Kristeller, 'Learned women of early modern Italy', 93-4.

present consideration of the humanism of Isotta Nogarola, which moves very much in the shadow of the great teacher's influence:[12]

> It was shameful how little the men of Ferrara knew of letters before the arrival of Guarino. There was no one who even understood the basic principles of grammar, who understood the propriety and impact of words, who was able to interpret the poets, let alone who was learned in the art of oratory, who professed rhetoric, who was competent to speak gravely and elegantly and dared to do so in public. Priscian was lost in oblivion, Servius was unheard of, the works of Cicero were unknown, and it was considered miraculous if someone mentioned Sallust, or Caesar, or Livy, or if anyone aspired to understand the ancient authors. At forty our citizens were still occupied with childish studies, still struggling and embroiled with the rudiments, until the liberal arts had been reduced entirely to ruins. But after a propitious star had brought this divine individual to Ferrara, there followed an extraordinary transformation in competence ... From all quarters they came to listen to that most felicitous voice, so that one might call him another Theophrastus (of whom it is said that his teaching attracted at least two thousand scholars). No one was considered noble, no one as leading a blameless life, unless he had followed Guarino's courses. So that in a short space of time our citizens were led out of the deepest shadows into a true and brilliant light, and all suddenly became eloquent, learned, elegant and felicitous of speech.[13]

The equation is unashamedly explicit: Guarino brought literary studies to Ferrara; literary studies transformed men overnight into paragons of virtue. All the detail is about grammar and oratory, all the evaluations concern 'leading a blameless life'. Good grammarians lead blameless lives.

Quirini's letter of advice to Isotta Nogarola is heavily ornamented with this assumed equivalence of proficiency in humane letters and personal virtue. What makes his insistence on this conventional humanist equation interesting is that, as applied to advanced studies in relation to a *woman*'s life,

---

[12] The Nogarola sisters were tutored in humanistic studies by Martino Rizzoni, one of Guarino's old pupils. This allows Sabbadini to claim them as members of Guarino's 'school'. In addition to corresponding with Guarino himself, Isotta Nogarola exchanged letters with a number of humanists of his circle, and received scholarly advice from Quirini, another graduate of Guarino's school.

[13] *Ludovici Carbonis Ferrariensis, artium doctoris et comitis palatini apostolici, oratio habita in funere praestantissimi oratoris et poetae Guarini Veronensis*, in *Prosatori latini del quattrocento*, ed. E. Garin (Milan and Naples, 1952), 381-417. '*Pudendum erat quam parumper litterarum sciebant nostri [Ferrarienses] homines ante Guarini adventum. Nemo erat, non dicam qui oratoriam facultatem nosceret, qui rhetoricam profiteretur, qui graviter et ornate diceret et in publico aliquo conventu verba facere auderet, sed qui veram grammaticae rationem cognosceret, qui vocabulorum proprietatem vimque intelligeret, qui poetas interpretari posset. Iacebat Priscianus, ignorabatur Servius, incognita erant opera Ciceronis, miraculi loco habebatur, si quis Crispum Sallustium, si quis C. Caesarem, si quis T. Livium nominaret, si quis ad veterum scriptorum intelligentiam aspiraret. Quadragesimus fere annus cives nostros in ludo puerili occupatos inveniebat in iisdem elementis semper laborantes, semper convolutos. Usque adeo bonarum litterarum ruina facta erat. Postea vero quam divinus hic vir dextro sidere Ferrariam ingressus est, secuta est mirabilis quaedam ingeniorum commutatio ... Currebatur undique ad vocem iucundissimam, ut alterum Theophrastum diceres, ad quem audiendum legimus perrexisse discipulos ad duo milia. Nemo putabatur ingenuus, nemo in lauta vitae parte, nisi Guarini esset auditor. Unde brevi de obscurissimis tenebris educti sunt nostri homines in veram et clarissimam lucem, omnes repente diserti, omnes eruditi, omnes limati, omnes in dicendo suaves extiterunt*' (390-2).

it lacks the comfortably self-evident quality of equivalent set-pieces addressed to men. Leonardo Bruni's view, in the passage we cited, that the virtuous woman should not pursue indecorously advanced studies, is typical not just of the humanist educators, but of generations of scholars and historians of humanism. Garin's footnote to this passage in his Italian abridgement of the text states firmly that 'the exaltation of ethico-political studies (which are concerned with the *vita civile*) evidenced in Bruni's treatise is the keynote in all early humanist pedagogy'; he then adds that Bruni would obviously not advocate pursuit of rhetorical studies to a noble *woman*, since she clearly ought not to be concerned with its 'excessive use, above all in a practical sphere'.[14]

The Latin letters which make up the two volumes of Isotta Nogarola's *Opera* testify eloquently to the intriguing social and practical difficulties which arise when it comes to extolling the virtue inseparable from eloquence of a female humanist. In 1436 Guarino was sent some of the Nogarola sisters' compositions (Isotta's and her sister Ginevra's) by Jacopo Foscari. Guarino replied with a letter of studied and effusive praise for their scholarly achievement and their manifest virtuousness. Their learning and their virtue brought glory to their native city, Verona (which happened also to be Guarino's):

> On this above all I bestow my admiration: such is the likeness of each sister's expression, such the similarity of style, such the sisterhood of writing and indeed the splendour of both their parts, that if you were to remove the names Ginevra and Isotta you would not easily to be able to judge which name you should place before which; so that anyone who is acquainted with either knows both together. Thus they are not simply sisters in birth and nobility of stock, but also in style and readiness of speech.
>
> Oh the glory indeed of our State and our Age! Oh how rare a bird on earth, like nothing so much as a black swan! If earlier ages had borne these proven virgins, with how many verses would their praises have been sung, how many deserved praises from truly unstinting authors would have consigned them to immortality! We see Penelope consecrated in the verses of the poets because she wove so well, Arachne because she spun a most fine thread, Camilla and Penthesilea because they were female warriors. Would they not have honoured these modest, noble, erudite, eloquent women, would they not sing their praises to the skies, would they not rescue them from the clutches of oblivion, by whatever means they please, and preserve them for posterity?[15]

[14] E. Garin, *L'educazione umanistica in Italia* (Bari, 1953), 32.

[15] Abel, II, 58-9. There is in fact a better text of this exchange of letters in *Epistolario di Guarino Veronese*, ed. R. Sabbadini, 3 vols (Venice, 1915-19), II, 292-309, and we have taken the Latin text from there. Sabbadini wrote a magisterial review of Abel's edition of Isotta Nogarola's works, in which he helpfully points out a large number of discrepancies between his versions of the letters and Abel's: 'Isotta Nogarola', *Archivio storico italiano*, 18 (1886), 435-43. He also redates some of the letters. '*Quodque praecipua admiratione prosequor, tanta est in utriusque dictione paritas, tanta stili similitudo, tanta scribendi germanitas et quidem utrobique magnifica, ut si Zinebrae nomen*

Here the virtue of the Nogarola sisters is characterised in two ways, neither of them 'civic': first, the sisters are indubitably virgins (Ginevra in fact fades from the scene when she marries);[16] secondly, they are represented as sisters in spirit to various magnificent women of classical antiquity. Humanists – male humanists – praising the Nogarola sisters liken them routinely to Sappho, Cornelia, Aspasia, Portia:[17] figures also invoked in defence of the education of women by Bruni in his epistle to Battista Malatesta.[18] Guarino's figurative selection of 'active' virtuous women is a particularly elegant literary ploy: Penelope and Arachne, spinners of exquisitely fine yarns, Camilla and Penthesilea, seductive Amazons and conquerors of entire male armies, deflect his compliments from any awkwardness over the public visibility of (real) women! The strategy of all such compliments is the same: they shift the focus of praise away from the engaged and civic (women speaking publicly), making figurative purity and iconic Amazon valour the object of attention. These are what brings glory to humanism, and to Verona for nurturing such distinction.

This method of celebrating the Nogarolas' virtue is essentially an evasion of the conventional humanist tactic of identifying the virtue of humanism with morality in the market place. And – as in the case of Bruni – this evasion in the sources is compounded in the scholarly secondary literature. In his *Vita di Guarino Veronese*, Sabbadini describes how Guarino chose to send Leonello d'Este copies of the pieces he had been sent by Foscari, during an absence from Ferrara, as follows:[19]

---

auferas et Isotae, non facile utri utram anteponas iudicare queas, adeo ut "qui utramvis norit, ambas noverit" [Terence]: *ita sunt non modo creatione et sanguinis nobilitate sorores, sed etiam stilo atque facundia. O civitatis, immo et aetatis nostrae decus! O "rara avis in terris nigroque simillima cygno!"* [Juvenal]. *Si superiora saecula hasce probandas creassent virgines, quantis versibus decantatae, quantas, modo non malignis scriptoribus, laudes assecutae immortalitati traditae fuissent. Penelopen quia optime texuit, Aragnen quia tenuissima fila deduxit, Camillam et Penthesileam quia bellatrices erant, poetarum carminibus consecratas cernimus; has tam pudicas, tam generosas, tam eruditas, tam eloquentes non colerent, in astra laudibus non eveherent, non ab oblivionis morsibus quavis ratione vendicarent et sempiterno donarent aevo?*

[16] There is a striking letter from Damiano Borgo to Isotta Nogarola describing how much changed Ginevra is for the worse since her marriage. The letter is preoccupied with virginity and defloration, and one can only take as the sense of the letter that Isotta's purity preserves for her a transcendent beauty which could not survive loss of virginity. Abel takes this quite naturally as an indication that Ginevra had lost her 'flair' for humanistic letters. See Abel, I, 261-7 for the letter, dated the last day of November 1440; Abel, I, xxxi-iii for Abel's verdict on Ginevra's 'Fall'.

[17] See Robathan, 'A fifteenth-century bluestocking', for some references to such compliments: Abel, I, 114, 125, 160, 180. Isotta also uses them of herself, for example, Abel, I, 256; I, 76.

[18] *Leonardo Bruni ... Schriften*, ed. Baron, 5-6. See below for a comparable letter from Politian to Cassandra Fedele, written in 1494, which opens with Virgil's *O decus Italiae virgo* (*Cassandrae Fidelis epistolae*, ed. Tomasinus, 155).

[19] Guarino's noble pupil replied exactly as he knew he was expected to. He praised the two sisters' work in the same figurative terms as his master: '*Hos igitur ingenii et studiorum fructus quos e duabus tuae civitatis virginibus collegisti collectosque ad me misisti non admirari non possum et summis prosequi laudibus eoque magis quod abs te, qui huiusce rei non negligendus testis es, mirum in modum*

How should he spend his time away? In correspondence. But Guarino did not want to send an empty vessel, so he included some fruits of the Verona school – not those which nourish the body, but rather those which provide fruit for the soul. And those fruits issued from the intellects of two Veronese virgins, the Nogarola sisters, Isotta and Ginevra ... These two women are among the most characteristic products of the Renaissance. In them for the first time, humanism was married with feminine gentility, especially in the case of Isotta, who remained in this respect unsurpassed. With the Nogarola sisters the Guarinian strain of humanist pedagogy reached its culmination.[20]

Sabbadini takes it for granted that the glory bestowed by Isotta and Ginevra on the school of Guarino derives from their *figurative* presence (as emblems of virtue rather than as real female performers on the public and professional stage). This is touchingly revealed in a later comment. Discussing abusive attacks on Isotta (to which we shall come shortly), he says that these were probably the work of jealous women, rather than of men, since 'envy is a peculiarly feminine passion'.[21] Real women are not the shining examples into which Guarino transforms the Nogarola sisters.

It proved almost impossible in practice, as it turns out, to sustain the equivalence of Isotta Nogarola's humanistic competence and her supreme virtuousness as a woman. Two exchanges of letters make this clear. The first is the exchange between Isotta and Guarino, preluded by the letter of praise from which we have just quoted (the exchange for which Isotta is remembered in histories of humanist education). Guarino's enthusiasm for Isotta's and Ginevra's compositions, expressed in a number of letters to male humanist colleagues and pupils, encouraged Isotta to write to him directly. Guarino failed to answer the letter.[22] At this point the social precariousness of Isotta's position as a humanist scholar becomes evident. Isotta was driven to write a second letter to Guarino, in which she positively begged for a response from the master. And the reason she gives is that her unanswered letter (publicly sent, publicly unanswered) compromises her as a woman. A woman of marriageable age has written an articulate (even pushy) letter, unsolicited, to a man of distinction. He has ignored her, and by so doing has exposed as illusory the notional 'equality' and 'free scholarly exchange' between them. In her first letter Isotta had expressed in entirely conventional terms her anxiety that, coming from a woman, her writing might be considered presumptuous – garrulous, a woman speaking out of turn:

Do not hold it against me, if I have transgressed those rules of silence especially

---

probantur extollunturque ... Illud equidem non parvi facio quod id mulierum genus etsi antea perrarum fuit, hoc tamen tempore perrarissimum esse consuevit' (*Epistolario*, ed. Sabbadini, II 298).

[20] R. Sabbadini, *Vita di Guarino Veronese* (Catania, 1896), 122.

[21] Ibid., 126.

[22] For Sabbadini's observations on the dating of this series of letters, as Abel presents it, see Sabbadini, 'Isotta Nogarola', 440.

imposed on women, and seem scarcely to have read that precept of Vergerio's, which warns against encouraging articulateness in the young, since in plentiful speech there is always that which may be censured. And Sophocles too called silence a woman's greatest ornament.[23]

In the absence of a reply from Guarino, convention has become a reality. Guarino's silence confirms Isotta's forwardness:

'You have treated me wretchedly, and have shown as little consideration for me as if I had never been born. For I am ridiculed throughout the city, those of my own condition deride me. I am attacked on all sides: the asses inflict their bites on me, the oxen attack me with their horns' [Plautus]. Even if I am most deserving of this outrage, it is unworthy of you to inflict it. What have I done to be thus despised by you, revered Guarino?[24]

'*S[a]epissime ... venit in mentem queri fortunam meam, quoniam femina nata sum*' (How often ... does it occur to me to lament my fortune, because I was born a woman), exclaims Isotta.[25]

The second epistolary exchange of interest to us here involved Isotta and Damiano Borgo.[26] Borgo had apparently challenged Isotta with the familiar claim that women outdo men above all in talkativeness. Isotta responded by claiming that to make such an accusation was to condemn all women on the strength of a few, and she challenged Borgo to maintain this view once he had considered the many examples of women who outdo both other women and all men 'in every kind of virtue and distinction':

Consider Cornelia, mother of the Gracchi, for eloquence; Amesia, who publicly pleaded to packed assemblies with most prudent speech; Afrania, wife of the senator Lucinius Buco, who argued the same kind of cases in public. Did not Hortensia do the same? Did not Sappho overflow with the perfection of her verses? Portia, Fannia and the rest are celebrated in the verses of countless most learned men. Take note of Camilla, whom Turnus, so the poet tells, supported with such honour. Did not Tamyris, Queen of the Scythians, massacre Cyrus, King of the Persians, and his entire army, so that indeed no witness survived to tell of so great a defeat? Did not the Amazons build a state without men? Did not Marpesia, Lampedo and Orithia conquer most of Europe and some states in Asia too, without men? For they were so strongly endowed

[23] '*Neque hoc mihi vitio dare, si tacendi leges mulieribus praesertim impositas praegressa sum illudque Vergerii praeceptum haud legisse videar, qui adolescentibus monet parum loqui prodesse, cum in multo sermone semper sit quod reprehendi possit. Et Sophocles quoque taciturnitatem in feminis singularem ornatum appellavit*' (Abel, I, 77: not in Sabbadini).

[24] ' "*Usa sum te nequiore meque magis haud respectus es quam si nunquam gnata essem. Per urbem enim irrideor, meus me ordo derided, neutrobi habeo stabile stabulum, asini me mordicus scindunt, boves me incursant cornibus*" [Plautus]. *Nam si ego hac contumelia digna eram maxime, tu tamen indignus qui faceres. Quodnam ob factum ita abs te contemnor, Guarine pater?*' (Abel, I, 80).

[25] Abel, I, 79. Eventually Guarino replied at length, and rebuked Isotta for panicking. A strikingly similar incident occurs in the correspondence between Politian and Cassandra Fedele, see below.

[26] On Borgo see Sabbadini, 'Briciole umanistiche', 250-1.

with *virtus* [valour/virtue] and with remarkable military skill, that to Hercules and Theseus it seemed impossible to bring the forces of the Amazons under their rule. Penthesilea fought manfully in the Trojan wars in amongst the strongest Greeks, as the poet testifies:

Penthesilea in fury in the midst of her thousands, rages.

Since this is so, I ask you whether you will grant that rather than women exceeding men in talkativeness, in fact they exceed them in eloquence and virtue?[27]

Here improper talkativeness is replaced by proper 'eloquence and virtue', and Isotta maintains that it is in these latter that women outdo men. But the rhetorical means to this end is an appeal once again to ancient female figurative *virtus* to displace social improprieties. Once again, also, the actual precariousness of Isotta's own position is the most obvious feature of such an argument. 'Virile' argumentative ability and 'Amazon-like' independence from men may make nice points in arguing for the appropriateness of female humanistic education. But they can all too readily be seen in a 'real-life' context as a socially indecorous absence of modesty and due deference, if not as a real social threat – the proverbial husband-beating shrew.[28] Isotta's Amazon citations are taken almost verbatim from Justin, and it is striking that in incorporating the example of Tamyris she herself tacitly acknowledges the awkwardly threatening possibilities of such illustrations – she stops short where Justin embellishes the story of Cyrus' defeat (exacted by Tamyris to avenge the death of her only son at Cyrus' hands):

Having hacked off Cyrus' head, Queen Tamyris hurled it into a vat filled with human blood, at the same time exclaiming with cruel venom: 'Sate yourself with blood, you who were always thirsty and insatiable for it.'[29]

Triumphant warrior-women all too easily become voracious, man-eating monsters.

[27] '*Volumus in eloquentia aspice Corneliam Grachorum matrem; Amesiam, quae Romano coram populo frequenti concursu prudentissima oratione causam dixit; Affraniam Lucinii Buconis senatoris coniugem, quae easdem causas in foro agitavit. Hortensia nonne hoc idem factitavit? Nonne Sapho mira carminis suavitate manavit? Portiam, Fanniam et reliquas quantis doctissimorum virorum versibus decantatas legimus? Volumus in bello aspice Camillam, quam Turnus, ut ait poeta, tanto honore prosequebatur. Nonne Thomiris regina Scytarum Cirum Persarum regem cum universo exercitu trucidavit, ut ne nuntius quidem tantae cladis superfuerit? Amazones nonne sine viris auxere rem publicam? Marpesia, Lampedo, Orithia maiorem partem Europae subiecerunt, nonnullas quoque sine viris Asiae civitates occupaverunt? Tantum enim virtute et singulari belli scientia pollebant, ut Herculi et Theseo impossibile videretur Amazonum arma regi suo afferre. Pantasilea bello Troiano inter fortissimos Graecos viriliter dimicavit; testis est poeta: "Pantasilea furens mediisque in milibus ardet" [Virgil]. Quod cum ita sit, te rogo, ut me certiorem reddas, si mulieres loquacitate vel potius eloquentia et virtute viros superent?*' (Abel, I, 256-7).

[28] For a general discussion of the way in which Renaissance literature transformed the 'forward' woman into insatiate man-eater and indomitable shrew, see L. Jardine, *Still Harping on Daughters: Women and Drama in the Age of Shakespeare* (Brighton, 1983), ch. 4.

[29] Justinus, *Epitome of Trogus*, I.8.

As it happens, Isotta's own fortunes poignantly illustrate the awkward 'moral' predicament of the unusually able, educated woman. (And once again, that awkwardness is common to her personal history and to the secondary literature upon it.) In 1438, a year after Isotta's difficult exchange of letters with Guarino, an anonymous pamphleteer addressed an invective against the vices of Veronese women (a popular brand of formal *vituperatio*). In it, having lashed out in conventionally Juvenalian fashion at female immodesty, vanity and promiscuity, he singled out the women of the Nogarola family for special blame. In a passage now much-quoted by feminist historians, he imputes to Isotta a sexual deviancy to match (according to his account) the grotesqueness of her public intellectual self-aggrandisement:

> She who has acquired for herself such praise for her eloquence behaves in ways utterly inconsistent with so much erudition and such a high opinion of herself: although I have believed the saying of numerous very wise men, 'the woman of fluent speech [*eloquentem*] is never chaste', which can be supported by the example of the greatest number of learned women ... And lest you are inclined to condone even in the slightest degree this exceedingly loathsome and obscene misconduct, let me explain that before she made her body generally available for uninterrupted intercourse, she had first submitted to, and indeed earnestly desired, that the seal of her virginity should be broken by none other than her brother, to make yet tighter her relationship with him. By God! ... [What inversions will the world tolerate], when that woman, whose most filthy lust knows no bounds, dares to boast of her abilities in the finest literary studies.[30]

The charge of incest is, of course, pure libellous invention, although, unfortunately, male scholars since the contemporary Veronese humanist Barbo have seen fit to leap to Isotta's defence as if the accusations might possibly be in earnest. The charge that she is *unchaste* challenges the view that as a woman she can be a prominent humanist and remain a right-living person ('the woman of fluent tongue is never chaste'). It is a studied part of the pamphleteer's contention that in Verona women regularly step out of line (are domineering), and that this is evidence of Verona's general decadence and erosion of morals. When Sabbadini maintains, in his account of the Nogarola sisters' importance, that 'the fruits of the Verona school ... issued from the intellects of two Veronese virgins ... In them for the first time, humanism was married with feminine gentility, especially in the case of

---

[30] For the text of this invective see A. Segarizzi, 'Niccolo Barbo patrizio veneziano del sec. XV e le accuse contro Isotta Nogarola', *Giornale storico della letteratura italiana* 43 (1904), 39-54; 50-4. '[Ea] que sibi tantam ex dicendi facultate laudem acquisierit, ea agat, que minime cum tanta eruditione et tanta sui existimatione conveniant, quamvis hoc a multis longe sapientissimis viris acceperim: nullam eloquentem esse castam, idque etiam multarum doctissimarum mulierum exemplo comprobari posse ... Nisi vero hoc nimium sane tetrum atque obscenum scelus sit aliquantulum a te comprobatum quod ante quam corpus suum assiduis connubiis divulgaret primo fuerit passa atque etiam omnino voluerit virginitatis sue specimen non ab alio nisi a fratre eripi hocque modo vinclo propiore ligari. Proh deum atque hominum fidem, "quis celum terris non misceat et mare celo" [Juvenal], cum illa, que in tam spurcissima libidine modum sibi non inveniat, audeat se tantum in optimis literrarum studiis iactare' (53). See also Jardine, op. cit., 57.

Isotta, who remained in this respect unsurpassed', we cannot help thinking that he too bonds Isotta's *chastity* with her acceptability as a humanist. Isotta is 'unsurpassed', her hymen intact until death; the bastions of Ginevra's humanist competence were penetrated at her marriage.

When a woman becomes socially visible – visible within the power structure – Renaissance literary convention makes her a sexual predator. We need only compare, for example, Boccaccio's influential Renaissance rendering of the story of Semiramis, the ancient Queen of the Assyrians. Boccaccio celebrates Semiramis among 'illustrious' women for successfully ruling in her son's place during his minority, thus preserving his patrimony:

> It was almost as if she wanted to show that in order to govern it is not necessary to be a man, but to have courage. This fact heightened that woman's glorious majesty as much as it gave rise to admiration in those who looked upon her.[31]

Then he deftly topples her manly valour into predatory sexuality:

> But with one wicked sin this woman stained all these accomplishments worthy of perpetual memory, which are not only praiseworthy for a woman but would be marvellous even for a vigorous man. It is believed that this unhappy woman, constantly burning with carnal desire, gave herself to many men.[32]

As in the case of Isotta, the heinousness of the sexual offence is intensified by its involving incest: Semiramis, it is claimed, had sexual intercourse with that very son whose power interests she had substituted for (one might remark that as Semiramis seized priority over her first-in-line son, so Isotta publicly obtrudes over her technically 'prior' brother).

So the charge against Isotta Nogarola is conventional. But that charge – and the public humiliation of Isotta it effected – does direct our attention to the *problem* of a mature woman who obtrudes herself, in her own right, beyond the bounds of social decorum. Her rank might have entitled her to be a modest patron of learning; it did not entitle her to participate actively within the public sphere.[33] When female patrons of this period write to female humanists it is striking how insistently they dwell on the celebratory and decorative nature of their scholarly aptitude – female patron and female

---

[31] *De claris mulieribus*, transl. G.A. Guarino (New Brunswick, 1963), cit. Jardine, op. cit., 182.

[32] *De claris mulieribus*, cit. Jardine, op. cit., 99.

[33] The issue of female patrons is an interesting one, and ripe for investigation. Where women were accidentally in control of *wealth* (through quirks in inheritance law), there appears to have been considerable social encouragement for their directing that wealth towards culture rather than towards power. On the unexpected prominence of noble women with charge of their own wealth in this period see Jardine, op. cit., ch. 3. On Mary Sidney, Countess of Pembroke, as exemplar of the wealthy woman directing that wealth to cultural manifestations of family power, see M. Brennan, *Aristocratic Patronage and Literature 1550-1650: The Herbert Family, Earls of Pembroke* (in press); M.E. Lamb, 'The Countess of Pembroke's patronage', *English Literary Renaissance* 12 (1982), 162-79.

scholar alike add lustre (they argue) to male achievement.[34]

Isotta and her family were away from Verona for three years from 1439 to 1441. After their return, Isotta no longer corresponds with other scholars as brilliant student of secular learning (*virilis animi*, learned 'beyond her sex'). Instead she is 'most learned and most religious'; *doctissima* becomes *sancta virgo, dignissima virgo, pia virgo*.[35] Her correspondents extol her for her Christian piety, her deep commitment to sacred letters. And they celebrate her celibacy, rather than her chaste purity. Not surprisingly, the 'illustrious women' with whom she is now compared are Mary and her mother Anna, the loved woman of the Song of Songs ('*Pulchra es amica mea et macula non est in te*').[36] Indeed Isotta's later male correspondents insist in a rather depressing and unhealthy way on the special importance in God's eyes (or perhaps their own) of her celibate state as confirmation of the admirable nature of her studiousness.[37] Isotta withdrew entirely from public view and became a virtual recluse in her family home (there are signs that her brothers were not entirely delighted with having to support a deliberately celibate sister as well as an aged mother).[38]

According to her nineteenth-century biographer Abel, Isotta totally renounced her secular studies, became a mystic and a saint, and devoted the remainder of her life to God. This is a version of events which feminist historians embrace, because it suggests 'thwarted ambitions', and the poignancy of a potentially brilliant career stifled by oppressive patriarchal intervention. But we need to be just as cautious at this point in Isotta's history as at earlier points at which critical prejudice obviously biased its telling. The letter of advice from Quirini on the advanced secular studies of logic and philosophy with which we opened this chapter dates from well after the return to Verona. The letters testifying to Isotta's asceticism, on the other hand, are all those of her 'mentor', Ludovico Foscarini (Isotta's letters to him do not survive).[39] Foscarini's correspondence with Isotta certainly depends for its propriety on the assumption that there could be no carnal involvement intended, so his insistence on Isotta's saintliness and spirituality is part of the strategy for 'coping' with a female scholar (even so, Abel claims a passionate love affair between the two).[40] The point is, whatever her continuing interest

[34] W.L. Gundersheimer is mistaken in thinking that a patron like Eleonora of Aragon did not correspond with female humanists ('her surviving correspondence with nonrelatives is with men', *Beyond their Sex*, ed. Labalme, 56). Cassandra Fedele made a point of corresponding with a number of female heads of state, including Eleonora, and the letters received are to be found in Tomasinus' edition of her letters. See below.

[35] Abel, II, 181; II, 96; II, 39; II, 105.

[36] Id., II, 25.

[37] Id., II, 23-7; 96-7; 98-100.

[38] Id., II, 73-87.

[39] Id., I, lvii.

[40] Id., I, lvii-lviii. Isotta Nogarola's one major published work was an epistolary dialogue between herself and Ludovico Foscarini entitled *De pari aut impari Evae atque Adae peccato* (a

in the *studia humanitatis*, there was no public outlet for Isotta's secular training once she became a mature woman, and there never had been, even before the libel of 1438.

So let us return to our general theme: Can we sustain historically the humanist propaganda claim that virtue and right living are the direct products of fifteenth-century humanist studies? The current view of the English-speaking scholarly community is that they were not, that a work like Vergerio's *De ingenuis moribus* 'does not lend itself readily to a civic interpretation as formulated by Saitta and Garin, and followed by many recent historians of humanism'.[41] But the critics of Saitta and Garin go on to say that if humanism provided an education in grammar and rhetoric which did *not* prepare its students morally for civic life, then it must have been a 'pure' intellectual training. When Vergerio writes that liberal studies are a preparation 'for every life' and 'for every kind of man', they argue, he means that studies are an end in themselves, a way of each individual's realising his full potential as a human being.

Isotta Nogarola's life shows us that this is not in fact the case. Certainly educators like Vergerio (and remember Isotta shows knowledge of Vergerio's treatise in one of the letters we used above) insist on the general civilising effect of the *bonae artes* without specifying either a moral or a civil context to which their training is attached. In other words, the educational programme of the humanist pedagogues is not job-specific. But the *value* attached to

---

set-piece debate on whether Adam or Eve was the more culpable in the Fall). This, however, does not mean that the case for Isotta's later spirituality and asceticism is proven, since the letters of Heloise and Abelard provide an impeccable model for an exchange of letters between a senior man and a secluded woman strenuously debating the relative culpability of mankind and womankind. It is therefore an eminently suitable form for the single public appearance of the work of a female scholar otherwise debarred on grounds of decorum from public display of her intellectual virtuosity. Although the Renaissance *fortuna* of the Abelard and Heloise letters is cloudy, we do know that Petrarch owned a copy of the medieval 'canon' of their exchange. Abel takes it for granted (a) that the dialogue between Isotta and Ludovico testifies to the repressed passion between them and (b) that it represents the core of Isotta's later preoccupation with spiritual as opposed to secular learning. But it is just as appropriate to regard the exchange as a virtuoso exercise by an exceptionally talented woman, in a suitably 'literary' context. For a discussion of some of these problems of 'reading' the exchange between Heloise and Abelard, see P. Dronke, *Abelard and Heloise in Medieval Testimonies* (Glasgow, 1976); P. Dronke, 'Heloise and Marianne: some reconsiderations', *Romanische Forschungen* 72 (1960), 223-56; P. Dronke, *Women Writers of the Middle Ages; A Critical Study of Texts from Perpetua (†203) to Margaret Porete (†1310)* (Cambridge, 1984), ch. 5, 'Heloise'; M.M. McLaughlin, 'Peter Abelard and the dignity of women: twelfth-century "feminism" in theory and practice', in *Peter Abelard – Pierre le Vénérable, Colloques Internationaux du CNRS no. 546* (Paris, 1975). On Isotta Nogarola's dialogue, see P. Gothein, 'L'amicizia fra Lodovico Foscarini e l'umanista Isotta Nogarola', *La Rinascita* 6 (1943), 394-413. As well as describing some of the central arguments of the Adam and Eve dialogue and the further exchanges of letters between Isotta and Ludovico to be found in Abel, Gothein also provides a perfect example of how ready a traditional critic can be to read spirituality and intense emotional involvement into every line of an exchange between a distinguished public man and a dependent secluded woman.

[41] D. Robey, 'Vittorino da Feltre e Vergerio', in *Vittorino da Feltre e la sua scuola: umanesimo, pedagogia, arti*, ed. N. Giannetto (Florence, 1981), 241-53; 252.

humanist studies does depend upon a particular ideology, and in this important sense it is firmly tied to its civic context. It is for precisely this reason that Isotta Nogarola failed to 'achieve', in spite of having access to humanist studies, as did others who failed to notice the tight inter-connectedness between the status of the *bonae artes* as a training and the political establishment and its institutions (other women, and those of inappropriate rank).[42] *Ad omne genus hominum*, 'for every type of person', has to be read out as 'for every appropriately well-placed male individual'. 'Opportunity', that is, is a good deal more than having ability, and access to a desirable programme of study. It is also being a good social and political fit for the society's assumptions about the purpose of 'cultivation' as a qualifying requirement for power.

If humanism has been of its nature tightly 'civic', then as a woman Isotta Nogarola would never have had the support of the community of distinguished humanist scholars and teachers in her pursuit of humanist studies. But equally, if humanism had really set as its highest goal the pursuit of learning for its own sake, she would not have disappeared so decisively from secular scholarly view in the mature years of her life – years in which she continued to excel in those studies. She could continue an excellent student of humanism in private, but she could not be publicly supported as 'virtuous' in doing so.

What we are stressing is that the independence of liberal arts education from establishment values is an illusion. The individual humanist is defined in terms of his relation to the power structure, and he is praised or blamed, promoted or ignored, to just the extent that he fulfils or fails to fulfil those terms. It is, that is, a condition of the prestige of humanism in the fifteenth century, as Lauro Martines stresses, that 'the humanists, whether professionals or noblemen born, were ready to serve [the ruling] class. The most apolitical of them could be drawn into the political fray'.[43] The fortunes of a gifted woman embarked on the humanist training show vividly how a programme with no explicit employment goals nevertheless presupposes those goals, and how the enterprise of pursuing secular humanist studies can be regarded as morally laudable (a 'virtuous' undertaking) only where achieving that goal is socially acceptable. A woman, as Bruni so eloquently insisted, was not available to be drawn into the public fray to marshal the morality of humanism in the service of the State in the fifteenth century. She could not argue politically in public without appearing indecorous; she could not even *pronounce* publicly without risking appearing 'threateningly insane

---

[42] Lauro Martines has been at particular pains to point out the close correlation between social rank and public prominence of the Florentine humanists. See Martines, *The Social World of the Florentine Humanists*, passim; L. Martines, *Power and Imagination: City-States in Renaissance Italy* (London, 1980), passim. See also Chapter One above.

[43] Martines, *Power and imagination*, 295.

and requiring restraint'.[44] Study, for her, consigned her to marginality, relegated her to the cloister. Because she could not enter the public arena, by virtue of her sex, Isotta Nogarola withdrew, figuratively and emotionally, from public intellectual intercourse to the nearest thing she could contrive to a secular cloister – her 'book-lined cell'.[45]

Isotta Nogarola, striking as her case is, is by no means unique among female pupils for whom the great fifteenth-century humanists served as teachers or mentors, and whose femaleness set them (and, in the eyes of historians of humanism, has continued to set them) awkwardly apart from their male counterparts. To consolidate our argument that the careers of such women are illuminating for our understanding of humanism as a movement in fifteenth-century Italy, let us turn to another surviving correspondence, this time between the learned Cassandra Fedele of Venice and the distinguished male humanist Politian.[46]

In about 1491[47] Angelo Poliziano began a correspondence with Cassandra Fedele, a learned young woman already noted in humanist circles for her ability as a Latinist.[48] Fedele initiated this exchange of letters by addressing

[44] Having looked at the careers of a number of other fifteenth-century educated women, including Cassandra Fedele and Laura Cereta (see below), it appears that all celebrated public performances by women humanists (orations before Emperors and prelates, disputations in the universities, invited lectures and so forth) are 'occasional' rather than professional. That is, an able woman might be afforded the unusual honour of a public appearance to 'show off' her talent, but it was on the strict understanding that this would not become a regular event. It is striking that we have not come across a single scholar, either of the fifteenth century or of the nineteenth or twentieth, who has suggested that any of these performances by exceptional women were other than outstanding (to us they seem competent but ordinary). *That* the woman performs is remarkable; *what* she performs is not to the point. For Fedele's orations, see *Cassandrae Fidelis epistolae*, ed. Tomasinus. For Laura Cereta's formal pieces see *Laurae Ceretae Brixiensis feminae clarissimae epistolae* ... ed. I.P. Tomasinus (Padua, 1640).

[45] See King, 'Book-lined cells', for references to both Matteo Bosso's and Ludovico Foscarini's representations of Isotta Nogarola's study as a 'cell' (74).

[46] See below, Chapter 4.

[47] G. Pesenti, 'Alessandra Scala: una figurina della rinascenza fiorentina', *Giornale storico della letteratura italiana* 85 (1925), 241-67; 248; see also W.P. Greswell, *Memoirs of Angelus Politianus, Joannes Picus of Mirandula*, etc. (London, 1805), 309.

[48] Cassandra Fedele (c.1465-1558). Although this is the date of birth which stands in the standard works, it is clearly incorrect. G. Pesenti, in a footnote to his seminal article on Alessandra Scala, cites Cesira Cavazzana as responsible for suggesting 1465 as Fedele's birth date, and indicates that this is a correction for the even less plausible 1456: 'Cesira Cavazzana, *Cassandra Fedele, erudita veneziana del Rinascimento*, Venezia, 1906 (estr. dall' *Ateneo Veneto*). C'é chi crede che la F. nascesse nel 1456; ma la data più plausibile è il 1465; certa è invece la data della morte [1558]: cfr. ibid., 13 sg.' (G. Pesenti, 'Alessandra Scala: una figurina della rinascenza fiorentina', *Giornale storico della letteratura italiana* 85 (1925), 241-67; 248). In a letter of 1488, Eleonora of Aragon calls Cassandra 'femina adolescens'; she was regarded as extraordinarily precocious when she performed publicly in an oration and disputation in 1487. 1470 is a more plausible birth date. It still leaves her five years older than Alessandra Scala, who certainly treats Fedele as senior to her in their correspondence (Politian also refers pointedly to Fedele's seniority over Scala). See Pesenti, 'Alessandra Scala', 243, for similar comments on the implausibility of the birthdate of 1450 proposed in the earlier literature for Alessandra Scala (see below). For Fedele's extant works, see I.P. Tomasinus, *Clarissimae feminae Cassandrae Fidelis venetae epistolae et orationes* ... (Padua, 1636); Pesenti, 'Alessandra Scala' (fn. 1), 266-7 (transcription of an

to Politian a letter of admiration – a suit for the great man's attention, and the established way of laying a claim to a place in the circle of erudite humanist scholars in the period. That letter is now lost, but an equivalent one addressed to Pico in 1489 survives, and gives us a good idea of the tone of Fedele's bid for intellectual recognition:[49]

> Although I had for a long time had the intention of writing to you, yet I was almost deterred by the renown of your divine gifts (described by many, and above all by Lactantius Thedaldus, most distinguished herald of your praises) and had rather determined to remain speechless than to appear deficient in brilliance and merely femininely pleasing when celebrating your achievements. But after your *Lucubrationes*, most rich in words and ideas, had been brought to me recently by that best of men, Salviatus, and I had often read them avidly, and had become acquainted with your intellectual skill and singular learning from them, I feared lest I might be reproved by many unless I celebrated your unheard-of gifts to the best of my feeble ability to all men, by whom you are held to be a miracle, you are praised and you are revered, especially as a result of the dissemination of your works. Because in those works are contained fine phrasing, most serious meaning, brilliance, divine sublimity of interpretation, and finally, all things cohere harmoniously by divine influence.[50]

Fedele here combines a display of Latinity with an indication of her serious and informed scholarship – she has already read Pico's latest theological work – and an extravagantly flattering exclamation of praise (which continues for a further half page), for the virtue, glory and honour of the age which Pico's intellect represents. We may take it she wrote similarly to Pico's friend and colleague Politian.

Politian, who claims already to be familiar with Fedele's work and reputation (he had probably seen the letter Pico had received, and heard of her widely acclaimed performance in a public oration in 1487),[51] replied with

---

unpublished letter from Fedele to Pico, 1489). On Fedele, see most recently King, 'Book-lined cells'; Kristeller, 'Learned women', passim; see also C. Cavazzana, 'Cassandra Fedele, erudita veneziana del Rinascimento', *Ateneo Veneto* 29 (1906), 2: 73-91, 249-75; Greswell *Memoirs*, 135-6; Pesenti, 'Alessandra Scala', 248-52.

[49] Pesenti, 'Alessandra Scala', 266-7. Politian mentions his close friend Pico in both his extant letters to Fedele.

[50] '*Etsi ad te iamdiu scribere proposueram, tuis tamen divinis virtutibus pene deterrita, perceptis a multis et maxime a Lactantio Thedaldo ornatissimo tuarumque acerrimo praecone laudum, potius obmutescere destinaveram, quam parum luculenter et femine(e) admodum tuas perlibare virtutes. Sed postquam his proximis diebus ab optimo viro Salviato tuae ad me lucubrationes ornatae verborum sententiarumque copiosissimae delatae essent, quas cum saepius lectitassem, ex his tui ingenii dexteritatem ac singularem doctrinam cognovissem, a multis reprehendi posse verebar nisi pro mei viribus ingenioli tuas inauditas dotes celebrarem, quibus ut miraculum teneris, laudaris ac veneraris, praesertim tuo opere edito; cui quoniam insunt dilucida verba, sensus gravissimi, splendor, sublimitas interpretandi divina, omnia denique divinitus quadrant. [Nec mirum; nam in omni disciplinarum genere fulges ac splendes, virtutes ornas, homines ad litteras capessendas incendis, quin immo inflammas]*' (267).

[51] See King, 'Book-lined cells', 69. For the text of this oration see *Cassandrae Fidelis epistolae*, ed. Tomasinus, 193-200.

an extended, set-piece panegyric on her peculiarly womanly achievement. This letter was followed by a visit to the Fedele household in June 1491,[52] during a trip to Venice with Pico. In public terms, the attention meant that Fedele's accomplishment was recognised in the Florentine humanist community, to which she was admitted, notionally, as a member.[53]

What was this group of which she had become a member? Well, essentially, it was a gentlemen's club of noble or nobly-connected scholar-courtiers, who depended upon the patronage of Lorenzo de' Medici.[54] When Politian reported back to Lorenzo, after the visit to Fedele's family home, he did so in terms of Fedele's gracious and courtier-like acceptance of an invitation to become part of his entourage (or at least to be associated with his court), an invitation extended by *Lorenzo* in the form of a greeting:

> *Item.* Yesterday evening I visited that learned Cassandra Fedele, and I greeted her, Excellency, on your part. She is a miraculous phenomenon, Lorenzo, whether in the vernacular or in Latin; most modest, and to my eyes also beautiful. I departed stupefied. She is a great admirer of yours, and speaks of you most knowledgeably, as if she knew you intimately. She will come to Florence one day, in any case, to see you; so prepare yourself to honour her.[55]

Most historians broadly agree that by the later decades of the fifteenth century the continuing support for humanism of the increasingly totalitarian Florentine ruling house tended to push scholarly energies to the margins of real political debate, and into 'contemplative' rather than 'active' studies – providing ornamental and propaganda proof of the civility and moral probity of the regime, rather than technical expertise in politics and government. Lauro Martines, who on the whole takes issue with those Italian historians of the school of Baron and Garin who characterise humanism as 'civic' and politically influential in the late trecento and early quattrocento, points out that on the late decades of the quattrocento he and they are in broad agreement. Pooling his own and Garin's views, he comments on Politian himself:

> 'He lives and works in a time when the new [humanistic] culture is no longer an

---

[52] The date is fixed by the account of the visit given by Politian to Lorenzo de' Medici in a letter written the following day. See below.

[53] Just as Isotta Nogarola's fame was established in the humanist circle around Leonello d'Este at Ferrara by the exchange of letters between herself and Guarino. See above.

[54] For the characterisation of the Florentine humanists of this period as scholar-courtiers, see Martines, *The Social World of the Florentine Humanists*, 5-6.

[55] '*Item*: visitai iersera quella Cassandra Fidele litterata, e salutai ec., per vostra parte. È cosa, Lorenzo, mirabile, nè meno in vulgare che in latino; discretissima, *et meis oculis etiam bella.* Partimi stupito. Molto è vostra partigiana, e di Voi parla con tanta pratica, *quasi te intus et in cute norit.* Verrà un di in ogni modo a Firenze a vedervi; sicche apparecchiatevi a farli onore' (I. Del Lungo, *Prose volgari inedite e poesie latine e greche edite e inedite di Angelo Ambrogini Poliziano* (Florence, 1867), 81). '*Quasi te intus et in cute norit*' is surely only decorous as a courtierly comment.

operative force in the city, in that very Florence of humanistic merchants and chancellors, now transformed into mere courtiers and professors, often courtier-professors'. The new type of chancellor, still a humanist, lost his political influence during the middle decades of the fifteenth century and became 'a solemnly haughty administrator like Bartolomeo Scala'.[56]

In this setting, the rhetoric of humanism represents the power of Latinity and eloquence as actual power – as meshed with civic activity in a close and influential relationship. But individual humanists are increasingly pursuing the recondite and arcane in scholarship as an end in itself. We might instance Politian's own dedication to Greek studies and textual problems in the last years of his life as evidence of this increasing tendency of humanists retained in official posts by those in power to busy themselves with erudition for its own sake.

The point of drawing attention to this unsignalled flight from political engagements to grateful courtiership at the time of the exchange of letters between Politian and Cassandra Fedele is that Fedele gained admission to a club which could not afford to recognise the implications of the fact that a woman *could* become a member. In a period which afforded no power to a woman in her own right, a woman's achievement in a sphere which supposedly stood in some active relation to power could not be allowed to stand *as* woman's achievement.[57] This, at least, is the explanation we offer for the fact that Politian assiduously *mythologises* Fedele into 'not-woman': into an emblem of humanistic achievement which avoids confronting her sex as a problem.

Politian's first letter to Fedele, his *laudatio* of female scholarly accomplishment, opens with a passage from Virgil's *Aeneid* (a passage which becomes, fascinatingly, a virtual synecdoche for the whole of Fedele's surviving reputation in later secondary literature on her):[58]

O decus Italiae virgo, quas dicere gratis
quasve referre parem

(O virgin, glory of Italy, what thanks shall I try
to utter or repay).[59]

In the Aeneid this exclamation of rapt admiration is addressed to Camilla,

---

[56] E. Garin, 'L'ambiente del Poliziano', *Il Poliziano e suo tempo, atti del IV convegno internazionale di studi sul rinascimento* (Florence, 1957), 24; Garin, 'I cancellieri umanisti della repubblica fiorentina da Coluccio Salutati a Bartolomeo Scala', *Rivista storica italiana* 71 (1959), 204; cit. Martines, *The Social World of the Florentine Humanists*, 5-6.

[57] Female heirs *substitute* for absent men; they do not hold power in their own right, and the male line is reinstated as soon as possible. See Jardine, *Still Harping on Daughters*, ch. 3.

[58] See, for instance, Del Lungo's footnote against her name in the letter to Lorenzo quoted above.

[59] *Aeneid* 11. 508-9.

supremely virtuous Amazon warrior-maiden, whose appearance at the end of the procession of protagonists rallied against Aeneas fills Turnus with rapture:[60]

> A warrior-maid, never having trained her woman's hands to Minerva's distaff or basket of wool, but hardy to bear the battle-brunt and in speed of foot to outstrip the winds. She might have flown o'er the topmost blades of unmown corn, nor in her course bruised the tender ears ...[61]

Politian's celebration of Cassandra proceeds self-consciously to sustain the same tone of wonder. This accomplished practitioner of the *studia humanitatis* is a latter-day paragon of 'manly' virtue (manly because active and productive; virtuous because employed in those studies associated with probity of character):

> What an astonishing impact it must make upon us, truly, that it was possible for such [letters] to be produced by a woman – what do I say, a woman? By a girl, rather, and a virgin. It shall therefore no longer be the exclusive privilege of antiquity to boast of their Sybils and their Muses, the Pythagoreans of their female philosophers, the Socratics of their Diotima, of Aspasia; and neither will the relics of Greece proclaim those female poets, Telesilla, Corinna, Sappho, Anyte, Erinna, Praxilla, Cleobulina and the others. Now we shall readily believe the Roman account of the daughters of Laelius and Hortensius, of Cornelia, mother of the Gracchi, as matrons of surpassing eloquence. Now we know, truly by this we know, that your sex has not after all been condemned to slowness and stupidity.[62]

And still in the vein of Camilla he exclaims:

> But truly in our age, in which few men indeed raise their head to any height in letters, you, however, stand forth as the sole girl who handles books in place of

---

[60] If *O decus Italiae virgo* became a catch-phrase for a female representation of learning or chaste wisdom, that might explain the fact that Botticelli's 'Pallas and the Centaur' was known as 'Camilla' in the fifteenth century.

[61] *Aeneid* 7. 803-17; 805-8. This passage is picked out by Auerbach as the acme of Virgilian 'sublime' – female valour sublimely idealised. E. Auerbach, *Literary Language and its Public in Late Latin Antiquity and in the Middle Ages*, transl. R. Manheim (London, 1965), 183-6.

[62] '*Mira profecto fides, tales proficisci a femina (quid autem a femina dico?) imo vero a puella, et Virgine potuisse. Non igitur iam Musas, non Sibyllas, non Pythias obijciant vetusta nobis secula, non suas Pythagorei Philosophantes feminas, non Diotimam Socratici, nec Aspaciam, sed nec poetrias illas Graeca iactent monimenta, Telesillam, Corinnam, Sappho, Anyte(m), Erinnem, Praxiham, Cleobulinam, et caeteras: credamusque facile Romanis iam Laelij, et Hortensij filias, et Corneliam Gracorum matrem fuisse matronas quantumlibet eloquentissimas. Scimus hoc profecto scimus, nec eum sexum fuisse a natura tarditatis, aut hebetudinis damnatum*' (*Cassandrae Fidelis epistolae*, ed. Tomasinus, 155-6). Guarino's celebratory letter in praise of Isotta and Ginevra Nogarola which gave rise to the correspondence between himself and Isotta is similarly extravagant in invoking ancient prototypes of outstanding female accomplishment; see above. For further comment on the routineness of such clusters of 'exemplary' women in compliments to living women see Robathan, 'A fifteenth-century bluestocking', 106-11.

wool, a reed pen instead of vegetable dye, a quill pen instead of a needle, and who instead of daubing her skin with white lead, covers paper with ink.[63]

Politian's enthusiasm culminates in an outburst of personal desire actually to confront this paragon of female virtue – a passion which, remember, precedes his ever having set eyes upon her. So vividly has he conjured up the warrior-maiden from her literary productions that her physical person, like her intact virginity, is vividly present to him in them:

> O how I should like to be transported where I might actually contemplate your most chaste visage, sweet virgin; if I might admire your appearance, your cultivation, your refinement, your bearing; if I might drink in your pronouncements, inspired into you by your Muses, as it were with thirsty ears; so that, finally, infused with your spirit and inspiration I might become most consummate Poet,
>
> > Not Thracian Orpheus, not Linus shall vanquish me in song though his mother be helpful to the one, and his father to the other, Calliope to Orpheus and fair Apollo to Linus.[64]

Here the personal homage – the cult of the virgin goddess – culminates in the final invocation of the Fates/the poet to the harbinger of the Golden Age (the return of the virgin Astraea, the age of the infant king):

> *aspice venturo laetentur ut omnia saeclo!*
> *o mihi tum longae maneat pars ultima vitae,*
> *spiritus et quantum sat erit tua dicere facta*

(Behold, how all things exult in the age that is at hand! O that then the last days of a long life may still linger for me, with inspiration enough to tell of thy deeds!)

From Camilla, warrior-maiden, Cassandra Fedele (practising Latinist) has become virgin Muse, object of poetic cult, herald of the Golden Age.[65]

Encouraged by the significant amount of attention accorded by Politian to

---

[63] '*At vero aetate nostra, qua pauci quoq(ue) virorum caput altius in literis extulerunt, vnicam te tamen existere puellam, quae pro lana librum, pro fuco calamum, stylum pro acu tractes, et quae non cutem cerussa, sed atramento papyrum linas*' (ibid.). See King, 'Book-lined cells', 76.

[64] '*O, quis me igitur statim sistat istic, vt faciem virgo tuam castissimam contempler, vt habitum, cultum, gestumq(ue) mirer, vt dictata, instillata tibi a Musis tuis verba quasi sitientibus auribus perbibam, deniq[ue] vt afflatu instin(c)tuq(ue) tuo consum(m)atissimus repente Poeta euadam,*

nec me carminibus vincat, aut Thracius Orpheus,
aut Linus: huic mater quamvis, atque huic pater adsit,
Orpheo Calliopea, Lino formosus Apollo. (Eclogues 4.55-7)'

(*Cassandrae Fidelis epistolae*, ed. Tomasinus, 157).

[65] For an interesting footnote on such 'becomings', see M.R. Lefkowitz, 'Patterns of women's lives in myth', in her *Heroines and Hysterics* (London, 1981), 41-7.

herself as a female scholar, and on the strength of some verbal commitment made by Politian during his visit to pursue the intellectual contact they had established, Fedele again wrote to Politian. This time he failed to reply. Perhaps the *actual* exchange of letters and views with the *real* girl ranked rather low on his list of intellectual priorities.[66] After a suitable wait she wrote again, this time a poignant letter of reproach; and in 1493 Politian replied, with a letter which keeps perfect decorum with the topos of 'lament' (woman abandoned) of her second letter.[67] Politian claims as his excuse that her intellectual performance on the occasion of his visit has left him absolutely tongue-tied – incapable of utterance. He makes this state allusively vivid with another quotation from the *Aeneid*, this time a passage from Book Three. Aeneas recounts to Dido the tale of his encounter with Andromache, whom he found passionately weeping and lamenting on her dead husband Hector's tomb. Aeneas' appearance further intensifies her grief, since it reminds her of the Troy that was, and she exclaims passionately to him. Confronted with this spectacle of majestic female fortitude in adversity, Aeneas is struck speechless:

'Hector ubi est?' dixit lacrimasque effudit et omnem
implevit clamore locum. vix pauca furenti
subicio et raris turbatus vocibus hisco.

('Where is Hector?' she spake, and shedding a flood of tears, filled all the place with her cries; to her frenzy scarce can I make a brief reply, and deeply moved gasp for broken words).[68]

Aeneas' reaction to Andromache's lament is particularly poignant, since it will soon be followed by Dido's own passionate lament when Aeneas himself abandons her. The passage encapsulates male admiration 'deeply moved with broken words', faced with the enormity of female grief 'manfully' endured.

In Politian's case it is, supposedly, awe and a sense of his own inadequacy at Fedele's superb Latinity and general cultivation which have left him thus rapt, but the implicit tone of contrition is elegantly appropriate as a response to female reproach.[69] Supposedly, because we must surely feel that the choice of

---

[66] Just as Guarino's correspondence with Isotta Nogarola rated sufficiently low on *his* list of priorities for him also to overlook replying to her in good time. See above.

[67] This is the same pattern as that followed in the exchange of letters between Guarino and Nogarola. Both women claim to have been publicly shamed by their male correspondent's prolonged silence, although undoubtedly such men habitually failed to reply to letters from less distinguished male colleagues. The shame is clearly *social* – the woman's overture if ignored is deemed forward. Later, in 1494, when she herself failed to answer a letter of Politian's promptly, Fedele wrote a humorous letter excusing her tardiness (*tibi debeo, ecce persoluo sero. tamen; sed melius sero quam nunquam*). *Cassandrae Fidelis epistolae*, ed. Tomasinus, 159-60.

[68] *Aeneid* 3. 312-14.

[69] It should be remarked that contrition was not a character trait in evidence anywhere else in Politian's public career aside from his studied dealings with female scholars; he was renowned

excuse is a choice of literary *topos*. As we saw, in an exactly similar situation (having made the same social gaffe of failing to reply to a letter), Guarino chose another plausible *topos* – the exhortation to the woman beset with adversity to remain *virilis animi*: it was Isotta Nogarola's 'manliness of mind' which persuaded him he could treat her *as* a man. And even if the vulgar crowd abuses her as a woman, her manly fortitude of spirit should allow her to rise above it:

> This evening I received your letters, full of complaints and accusations, in which you render me uncertain as to whether I should feel pain for you or congratulate myself. For when I saw fit to give my attention to that outstanding intellect of yours, with its attendant embellishments of learning, I was accustomed besides to express strongly my opinion that you were manly of spirit, that nothing could happen which you would not bear with a courageous and indomitable spirit. Now, however, you show yourself so cast down, humiliated and truly womanish that I am able to perceive nothing which accords with my previous magnificent opinion of you.[70]

This *topos* allowed Guarino to reprove Nogarola for allowing social convention (femaleness) any place in her scholarly life – how could a mere intermission in their correspondence threaten her womanly honour?[71]

Like Guarino's with Nogarola, Politian's relationship with Fedele is established entirely within the world of letters; confronted (physically) with her ability, he responds with the awe appropriate to a Muse or Goddess:

> For when some time ago I had come to your house for the purpose of seeing and greeting you (which was the chief reason for my visit to Venice), and you had presented yourself after a long wait, clothed beautifully, yourself most beautiful, like a nymph emerging from the woods before me, and when then you had addressed me compellingly with ornate and copious words, and, truth to tell, with a kind of echo of the divine about them, then my soul was of a sudden (as I think you remember) struck senseless at such a miracle and such a rarity, so that, as Aeneas reports of himself, 'I gasped with broken words', and could scarcely

for his ability to quarrel with other humanists, for example, with Alessandra Scala's father Bartolomeo and her future husband Marullus. On Politian's life, see F.O. Mencken, *Historia vitae et in literas meritorum Angeli Politiani* ... (Lipsiae, 1736). On his relations with Bartolomeo Scala see A. Brown, *Bartolomeo Scala, 1430-1497, Chancellor of Florence: the Humanist as Bureaucrat* (Princeton, 1979), 211-19.

[70] '*Hoc vesperi tuas accepi litteras querimoniae plenas et accusationis, quibus incertum me reddidisti tibine magis condoleam an mihi ipsi gratuler. Nam cum tuum istud perspexisse viderer ingenium adiunctis doctrinae ornamentis insigne, te adeo virili animo et opinari et praedicare solebam, ut nihil accidere posset quod non forti et invicto ferres pectore. Nunc autem sic demissam abiectam et vere mulierem tete ostentas, ut nihil magnifico de te sensui meo respondere te cernam*' (*Epistolario di Guarino Veronese*, ed. Sabbadini, vol. II (Venice, 1916), 306-7).

[71] There is, we think, a distinctly hollow ring to Guarino's protestations that Isotta's 'virility' of temperament precludes the possibility of attaching social blame to her actions. '*Cum enim intelligeres tuum in me pro litteraria inter nos necessitudine officium fecisse scriptis ad me tam suavibus tam ornatis tam laudatissimis litteris (nam sicut ex studiis arrogans esse non debes, ita bonorum tuorum aestimatrix non ingrata fias oportet) quid tibi obiectari potuit quod matronalem constantiam labefactaret?*' (ibid.)

even apologise for my inability to speak ... When therefore I returned to Florence, full of these impressions and totally overwhelmed by it all, I received from you your spectacular letters, to which I often tried to reply, but I know not how, my very writing fingers faltered, the very pen dropped from my hands. For I did not dare to submit to the unequal contest, whereby I was obliged to fear more the charge of insolence and baseness if I replied, than that of idleness or lack of courtesy if I remained silent. My failure to reply has not therefore come about out of negligence, but out of bashfulness, not from contempt, but reverence.[72]

At this point Politian intensifies the 'literary' quality of his celebration of the woman of letters. He introduces the figure of *another* young, beautiful and learned woman, the Florentine Alessandra Scala.[73] Too awestruck to answer Fedele's letters, Politian tells her, he took them instead to Alessandra Scala, and recreated the experience of Fedele's combination of learning and loveliness by having Scala read them aloud to the assembled company. Bartolomeo Scala, Marsilio Ficino and Pico della Mirandola praised their accomplishment.

This effects the metamorphosis of the individual talented woman into a *genus* of representatives of female worth, and it brings Politian to the substantial part of his letter, the offering, as it were, to Cassandra. On the occasion of a previous visit to the Scala household, he had joined the audience for a private performance, in Greek, of Sophocles' *Electra*, in which Alessandra Scala took the title role.[74] The central set-piece in Politian's letter is a description of the impression her performance made upon him:

But let me return to Alessandra. She busies herself day and night with the study of both Latin and Greek. And the other day, when the Greek tragedy of Sophocles was performed in her father's house, for which the greatest number of learned men had been assembled ... she took the part of Electra, one virgin playing another, and performed with such talent, art and grace, that all fastened their eyes and minds upon her. There was in her words that Attic charm,

---

[72] '*Nam cum te olim domi visurus salutaturusque venissem, qua maxime causa profectus Venetias fueram, tuque te diutus* [sic] *expectanti habitu quodam pulchro pulcherrima ipsa quasi nympha mihi de silvis obtulisses, mox ornatis copiosisque verbis atque ut verissime dicam divinum quiddam sonantibus compellasses, ita mihi animus repente (quod te arbitror meminisse) miraculo illo tanto et rei novitate obstupuit, ut quod de se ait Aeneas, "raris tubatus vocibus hiscerem", vixque illud saltem meam tibi excusare infantiam potueram ... Harum igitur imaginum plenus, atque hac undique rerum facie circumfusus, ut Florentiam sum reversus, litteras abs te mirificas accepi; quibus cum respondere saepius tentassem, nescio quo pacto digiti ipsi scribentes haesitabant, ipse de manibus calamus excidebat; nec enim subire impar certamen audebam, quasi magis mihi timendum crimen esset arrogantis et improbi, cum respondissem, quam desidis ac parum officiosi, cum tacuissem. Non igitur neglegentia factum est ut non rescripserim, sed verecundia, non contemptu, sed reverentia*' (G.B. Pesenti, 'Lettere inedite del Poliziano', *Athenaeum* 3 (1915), 284-304; 299-300).

[73] Alessandra Scala (1475-1506). See Pesenti 'Alessandra Scala'. Pesenti's article is a good starting point for work on Scala, in spite of its thoroughgoing sentimentalising of her relationships with all the men among her colleagues and tutors. Naturally all men become Scala's suitors in Pesenti's reconstruction of her life.

[74] An ostentatious display of learning on her father's part. He, according to Pesenti, knew no Greek. This performance also provided the occasion for Politian's first Greek epigram addressed to Alessandra Scala. See below.

utterly genuine and native, her gestures everywhere so prompt and effective, so appropriate to the argument, so covering the range of the various feelings, that they added greatly to the truth and believableness of the fiction. Nor was she so mindful of Electra that she forgot Alessandra. Altogether humbly and modestly, her eyes were not simply downcast to the ground, but firmly fixed there at all times. To see her you would have said she felt the difference between an actress and a virgin. For though she satisfied the requirements of the stage, yet she was in no way theatrical, as if she produced her gestures not for just anyone, but only for the learned and the upright.[75]

Once again, more than Alessandra's competence in Greek is at stake. What Politian celebrates is the *spectacle* of Alessandra performing as antique womanhood of supreme virtue (as his Greek epigram addressed to Alessandra herself on the occasion of this performance confirms).[76] It is the symbolic impact of the woman *verecunde omnia et pudenter, non modo ad terram demissis sed pene in terram semper defixis oculis* ('With shame and modesty in everything, her eyes not only constantly cast down to the ground, but fixed upon it'). The ideal nature of her performance does not derive from her impeccable Greek grammar and pronunciation (hardly at all, as Politian describes it), but almost entirely from her modesty, the probity of her person, her 'chastity' (that predictable invoking of virginity).[77] Alessandra/Electra is beauty/purity itself, a figure talismanic of the revival of Greek learning and culture which Politian and his colleagues are undertaking. And Politian closes his letter to Fedele by joining her and Scala in a single image of the exemplary learned woman:

> Alessandra Scala alone, therefore, is now talked of here, the Florentine Electra, a girl undoubtedly worthy for you, most learned Cassandra, to call sister, inasmuch as she alone of all our age, I shall not say, attains to your stature, but

[75] '*Sed revertor ad Alexandram. Dies ea noctesque in studiis utriusque linguae versatur. Ac superioribus diebus, cum graeca tragoedia Sophoclis in ipsius paternis aedibus maximo doctorum conventu virorum exhiberetur ... ipsa Electrae virginis virgo suscepit, in qua tantum vel ingenii vel artis vel gratiae adhibuit, ut omnium in se oculos atque animas una converteret. Erat in verbis lepos ille atticus prorsus genuinus et nativus, gestus ubique ita promptus et efficax ita argumento serviens, ita per affectus varios decurrens, ut multa inde veritas et fides fictae diu fabulae accederet. Nec tamen Electrae sic meminit ut Alexandrae sit oblita. Verecunde omnia et pudenter, non modo ad terram demissis sed pene in terram semper defixis oculis: sentire illam diceres quid ludiae alicui et mimae, quid ingenuae rursus ac virgini conveniret; nam cum scaenae satisfaceret nihil de scaena tamen sumebat, quasi non cuilibet, sed doctis tantummodo et probis ederet gestum*' (Pesenti, 'Lettere inedite', 300-1).*

[76] For the epigram see *Poliziano: Epigrammi greci*, ed. A. Ardizzoni (Florence, 1951; reprinted in A. Politianus, *Opera omnia*, Turin, 1970), 20 (Italian transl., 56): 'When the girl Alessandra took the part of Electra, she, virgin, the Sophoclean virgin girl, all were struck with utter amazement ...'

[77] Quentin Skinner has suggested to us that in their somewhat bizarre insistence on the virginity of the women humanists, the male humanists are 'doing the best that their moral vocabulary allowed them' by way of praising their *virtus* – for which chastity is the strict female equivalent. *Virtus*, the supposed product of the *studia humanitatis*, is a quality of a *vir*; in substituting the more appropriately female 'chastity' in the case of a woman we have gender creating a clear case of textual difficulty.

certainly follows in your footsteps.[78]

His letter here comes, as it were, full circle. From an encounter with a learned female Latinist, whose reproach allows him to applaud her typical pose of virtuous grief (whether or not expressed in impeccable Latin), he passes to the claim that Alessandra the Hellenist and Cassandra the Latinist are sisters in learning, and thereby sidesteps again the need to assess their *real* intellectual achievement, while for the time being celebrating 'female humanism' as a phenomenon worthy of the age.[79]

Now, like Alessandra Scala, Cassandra Fedele *was*, on the evidence of her published letters and orations, an accomplished humanist and scholar. And the problem which Politian's letters appear both to raise, and astutely to evade, is: What could such accomplishment be *for* in a woman?

The women humanists are accomplished; their accomplishment is celebrated by their male correspondents in terms of an abstract intellectual ideal (warrior-maiden, *virilis animi*; grieving spouse, majestic in suffering), or in terms of a social ideal (chastity, obedience, modesty, constancy, beauty). Guarino combines the two when he writes of the Nogarola sisters, Isotta and Ginevra (whom he has never met), on the strength of their display pieces of Latin prose:

> Why do the poets not honour these modest, noble, erudite, eloquent women? ...
> What are you doing, you noble young men of our city? ... Do you not fear that
> common outburst against you:
>
>> for indeed you young men display a womanish mind; while that virgin
>> displays a virile one [*De officiis* 1].[80]

---

[78] '*Sola igitur nunc in ore omnibus apud nos Alexandra Scala, hoc est florentina Electra, digna nimirum puella quam tu, doctissima Cassandra, sororem voces, utpote quae sola omnium nostra aetate, non dicam tecum contendat, sed tuis certe vestigiis insistat*' (Pesenti, 'Lettere inedite', 301).

[79] Guarino encouraged a correspondence between Isotta Nogarola and Costanza Varano, as Politian does one between Fedele and Scala, thus actually effecting a kind of merging of the female scholars into a composite figure of intellectual 'worth'. Similarly, women humanists exchanged complimentary letters with women in positions of civic prominence or power (confirming their mutual 'worth'). Fedele corresponded with Queen Isabella of Spain (*Cassandrae Fidelis epistolae*, ed. Tomasinus, letters 11 (Cassandra to Isabella, n.d.), 12 (Isabella to Cassandra, 1488), 13 (Cassandra to Isabella, 1487), 60 (Cassandra to Isabella, 1492), 66 (Cassandra to Isabella, 1495)); with Beatrice, Queen of Hungary (sister of Eleonora of Aragon and d'Este) (letters 21, 1488; 71, 1497; 78, n.d.); with Beatrice Sforza (letter 57 (Cassandra to Beatrice, n.d.), 58 (Beatrice to Cassandra, 1493)); and with Beatrice Sforza's mother, Eleonora of Aragon, Duchess of Ferrara, letter 105 (Eleonora to Cassandra, 1488). All these women were notable patrons of the arts, and Fedele presumably approached them with an eye to possible patronage (she was invited to Spain in 1488). Kristeller comments that on the whole patronage was sought for *vernacular* works from these female patrons. See Kristeller, 'Learned women', 93-4.

[80] *Epistolario di Guarino Veronese*, ed. Sabbadini, II, 293-4. Guarino used this same passage from the *De officiis* in his complimentary letter to Varano (see R. Sabbadini, *Vita di Guarino Veronese* (Catania, 1896; reprinted in *Guariniana*, ed. M. Sancipriano, Turin, 1964), 157-8).

On the other hand, humanistic accomplishment in the quattrocento is notionally the means of access to humanism as a *profession*, leaving aside for a moment whether what is envisaged is a political career, or a teaching career, or even a courtier's. When Isotta Nogarola writes to Guarino and receives a eulogy in reply, or when Fedele succeeds in eliciting a congratulatory response from Politian, they have apparently crossed the threshold from promising student to accomplished practitioner. The same might be said to be the implication of Politian's Greek epigram addressed to Alessandra Scala on the occasion of her performance as Electra: 'You have made it into the ranks of those honoured by society for their achievement as Latinists and Hellenists, those, that is, to whom our society looks as civic leaders and figureheads of the civilised community.' All three women certainly reacted to the great men's attention *as if* this had happened: Scala replied (as any male humanist would have done) with a competent Greek epigram praising Politian in his turn;[81] Nogarola and Fedele wrote letters in response to their mentors, which assume that an active and fully participating correspondence will now ensue. Fedele and Nogarola reacted to the subsequent *rebuff* with a personal and passionate intensity which suggests that they themselves had been well and truly deceived – that they had really expected to be treated from now on as equal intellectuals, not as forward women, or amorous encounters.[82]

It is this confusion on their part that we find deeply suggestive for our assessment of quattrocento Italian humanism as a whole. Within the humanist confraternity (sic) the accomplishment of the educated woman (the 'learned lady') is an end in itself, like fine needlepoint or the ability to perform ably on lute or virginals. It is not viewed as a training for anything, perhaps not even for virtue (except insofar as all these activities keep their idle hands and minds busy).[83] As signs of *cultivation* all such accomplishments

---

[81] See above.

[82] See above, and King, 'Religious retreat' and 'Book-lined cells'.

[83] A point regularly made in favour of education of girls by Erasmus and More. See, for example, More's letter to his daughter Margaret: '*Quaeso te, Margareta, fac de studiis vestris quid fit intelligam. Nam ego potius quam meos patiar inertia torpescere, profecto cum aliquo fortunarum mearum dispendio valedicens aliis curis ac negociis, intendam liberis meis et familiae*' ('I beg you, Margaret, tell me about the progress you are all making in your studies. For I assure you that, rather than allow my children to be idle and slothful, I would make a sacrifice of wealth, and bid adieu to other cares and business, to attend to my children and my family'. *The Correspondence of Sir Thomas More*, ed. E.F. Rogers (Princeton, 1947), letter 69 (134), transl. E.F. Rogers, *St. Thomas More: Selected Letters* (New Haven and London, 1961), 109. More makes the explicit point, in writing to Margaret after her marriage, that her learning is intended for *no other audience* than her father and her husband: '*Sed tu, Margareta dulcissima, longe magis eo nomine laudanda es, quod quum solidam laboris tui laudem sperare non potes, nihilo tamen minus pergis cum egregia ista virtute tua cultiores literas et bonarum artium studia coniungere; et conscientiae tuae fructu et voluptate contenta, a populo famam pro tua modestia nec aucuperis nec oblatam libenter velis amplecti, sed pro eximia pietate qua nos prosequeris satis amplum frequensque legenti tibi theatrum simus, maritus tuus et ego*' (But, my sweetest Margaret, you are all the more deserving of praise on this account. Although you cannot hope for an adequate reward for your labour, yet nevertheless you continue to unite to your singular love of virtue the pursuit of literature and art. Content with the profit and pleasure of your conscience, in your modesty you

satisfactorily connote a leisured life, a background which regards the decorative as adding lustre to rank and social standing, and the ability to purchase the services of the best available teachers for such comparatively useless skills. And there is supposed to be an evident discontinuity between such accomplishment and the world of the professional humanist, be he teacher, advisor or holder of public office. But that discontinuity is in practice, it appears, precariously established – sufficiently precariously for it to cause misunderstanding, puzzlement, uneasiness, textual difficulty in the letters exchanged between accomplished women and professional men, as the one strives for recognition, the other to evade it. Following receipt of Scala's Greek epigram, for instance, Politian addresses a succession of Greek epigrams to 'Alessandra poetess' which transform the exchange from one between Greek virtuosi into a series of formalised lover's addresses to an absent beloved, hoping for some substantial sign of favour ('To me who desire fruit you, however, send only flowers and leaves, signifying that I labour in vain').[84] Scala is thus effectively excluded from the exchange altogether, in spite of Politian's continuing protestations of admiration.[85] Only if mythologised can the woman humanist be celebrated without causing the male humanist professional embarrassment.

But if the gap between accomplishment (the ability of the noble, leisured pupil) and profession (the learned training of the active civic figure) is problematic in the case of women, might it not be so for men in a comparable position? That is to say, do the exchanges of letters between Guarino and Leonello d'Este or between Politian and Lorenzo de' Medici prove anything more about the noble pupil-patron than that he is accomplished, in currently validating social terms? It seems that for the nobleman also, who did not in practice earn a living or pursue a career, humanist learning provided the male equivalent of fine needlepoint or musical skill: it provided the fictional identity of rank and worth on which the precarious edifice of the fifteenth-century Italian city state's power structure depended. It read out as 'valour', 'manliness', 'fortitude', 'benevolence', the male equivalents of 'modesty' and 'chastity', but less readily discernible to our modern eye as culturally constructed 'moral' attributes – that, at least, is what we seem to begin to see when we 'look to the ladies' in the humanist case.

---

do not seek for the praise of the public, nor value it overmuch even if you receive it, but because of the great love you bear us, you regard us – your husband and myself – as a sufficiently large circle of readers for all that you write). Rogers, *Correspondence*, letter 128 (302), transl. Rogers, *St. Thomas More*, 155.

[84] Ardizzoni, *Epigrammi greci*, epigram XXXII (22) (Italian transl. 58).

[85] A number of humanists wrote Greek 'love' poems addressed to Alessandra. One of them, Marullus, eventually married her.

CHAPTER THREE

Humanism in the Universities I:
the Search for a Programme

In the autumn of 1465 Lorenzo Guidetti and Buonaccorso Massari embarked on a lively correspondence about the comparative merits of two competing schools of rhetorical teaching. Guidetti was a disciple and friend of Cristoforo Landino, the most famous (and most highly paid) teacher of rhetoric in the Florentine Studio. Massari was a pupil of a less illustrious rhetoric teacher from Lucca, Giovanni Pietro.

Massari had heard that Landino would lecture on Cicero's letters to Lentulus during the academic year 1465-66. 'I am an eager student,' he wrote to Guidetti on 14 September,

> and I would be grateful to know what Landino said when he explained the first letter. For in my view it is quite hard, thanks to the historical questions involved, and few have the ability to tackle so great an enterprise.[1]

Guidetti's answer was civil and clear. Landino, he explained, had just finished a course of lectures on 'the precepts of poetics and rhetoric'; he would use Cicero's letters to illustrate some of them:

> My teacher set out ... to give some instructions in letter-writing, and in order to make them easier and more accessible he decided to explain Cicero's first letter to Lentulus. (*Fam.* 1.1).

As to the historical difficulties posed by the letters, Guidetti regards them as unimportant:

> I don't see why someone who wishes to attain style and elegance in writing letters should work very hard at this. My primary interest, and in this Landino's instruction confirms me, is to learn what style, what constructions, what 'flowers' and what 'sobriety' we should employ in writing letters.

---

[1] B. Massari to L. Guidetti, 14 Sept. 1465; R. Cardini, *La critica del Landino* (Florence, 1973), 267: '*Ego, qui discendi cupidus sum, libenter ex te cognoscerem quid in ea prima epistola exponenda dixerit: est*

Such matters were far more useful than minor details of the history of Cicero's Rome, 'which hardly anyone knew about even when they happened'; these 'seem the province of a pedantic and trivial mind rather than of one which diligently seeks important forms of knowledge'.[2]

Massari thanked Guidetti for his frank answer, but pressed him on the issue of the study of history. He argued that Cicero's letters, permeated as they were with the events of the Roman revolution that Cicero lived through, were unintelligible to anyone who lacked a firm grounding in the history of the Republic and its institutions. He also claimed that the technical terms of rhetoric that Guidetti had employed to characterise his own interest in the letters were arbitrary and vague:

> How and out of what words and tropes one constructs 'flowers' and 'sobriety' I do not understand, nor have I ever read or heard a satisfactory account.

To highlight the difference in their two approaches, Massari asked Guidetti to deal with a specific text: to give Landino's exposition of a difficult passage in the letter:

> I would like you to tell me what the meaning is of the sentence which reads: *senatus religionis calumniam non religione, sed malevolentia et illius regiae largitionis invidia comprobat.*[3]

Guidetti replied with some asperity and at great length. He admitted that one needed a minimum of historical knowledge, 'enough to make the argument of the letter clear'. But one should not make the hunt for such details an end in itself:

> For when a good teacher undertakes to explicate any passage the object is to train his pupils to speak eloquently and to live virtuously. If an obscure phrase crops up which serves neither of these ends, but is readily explicable, then I am in favour of his explaining it. If its sense is not immediately obvious, I will not consider him negligent if he fails to explicate it. But if he insists on digging out trivia which require much time and effort to be expended in their explication, I shall call him merely pedantic.

---

enim – ut arbitror – propter historiam difficilis, et pauci sunt qui tantae rei magnos conatus assequi possint.'

[2] Guidetti to Massari, ibid., 267-8: '*Praeceptor meus, vir omnium iudicio humanissimus atque doctissimus, cum superiori anno poeticae rhetoricaeque artis praecepta egregie exposuisset ... praecepta quaedam de scribendis epistolis dare aggressus est, atque, ut facilius apertiusque ea ante oculos poneret, primam Ciceronis ad Lentulum epistolam exponere instituit ... Equidem non animadverto, mi Bonaccursi, cur stilum atque elegantiam in scribendis epistolis cupienti tantopere haec res inquirenda sit. Itaque illud in primis placet et sequor, quod de Landino meo saepissime audio: esse ante omnia elaborandum, ut quo dicendi genere, qua verborum compositione, quibus flosculis quaque sobrietate contexendae epistolae sint intelligamus ...*'

[3] Massari to Guidetti, 26 Sept. 1465; ibid., 270-1: '*Quo pacto autem et quibus verbis et schematibus flosculi conficiantur et sobrietas equidem non intelligo, neque unquam inveni aut a quoquam audivi ... quaero ex te*

As to the particular passage which Massari had proposed to him, Guidetti continued:

> In my view the teacher's duty is first of all to show from history that the ancients took no public decisions in the Senate without first consulting the Gods. If they found that the Gods opposed their action, they said that it was forbidden 'by religion' [Cf. the first two words in the passage under discussion, *senatus religionis*]. If it is appropriate to the seniority of the students and the occasion, he may add an account of the different ways in which the Gods' opinion was sought, and explain briefly that there were two general methods, one natural and one artificial ... But if someone is absolutely insistent in asking to what *kind* of religion the Senate made its vague appeals, I would tell him if I knew; if not I would admit that I didn't, and I still would not be afraid that I had failed in the duties of a teacher ... After that I would come back to the sense and meaning of the individual words: I would explain what the Senate is, what the word is derived from, who founded it at Rome, who enlarged its powers, how great its worth and authority were within the state, how many sorts of senator there were ... I would also deal with the definition of 'religion' and whether the word comes from *religare* or *relegare* or *relegere*; I would deal with 'calumny' in the same way ...[4]

Massari was still unsatisfied. 'I asked you for an explanation of the passage,' he wrote plaintively,

> not the duty of an exegete, and the office of a teacher. I too have read Macrobius, Valerius Maximus, Aulus Gellius and Cicero *On Divination*, but I still do not know what Cicero means in that letter. Please explain to me the phrase *religionis calumniam*; I do not really care whether *religio* comes from *religare* or *relegere*, and *calumnia* from *calvere* or not.[5]

---

quo pacto locus ille intelligatur, qui ait: "senatus religionis calumniam non religione, sed malevolentia et illius regiae largitionis invidia comprobat".'

[4] Guidetti to Massari, ibid., 273-5: '*Est enim probi praeceptoris, cum aliquid explicandum assumit, et ad ornate loquendum et recte vivendum discipulos instruere. Locus aliquis obscurior inciderit, et in quo neutrum istorum versetur: hunc si, quoniam praesto se illi offeret, exponet laudabo, si non illi praesto succurret, non iccirco negligentem putabo si non exprimet. Si vero istud nescio quid minutum multa cura, multo temporis dispendio investigare volet, prorsus curiosum appellabo. Quod ut quid velim expressius tibi demonstrem, capiam locum ex eadem epistola quem tu a me cognoscere cupis. Is est: "senatus religionis calumniam etc.". Puto ergo expositoris officium esse primo ut ex historia hoc edoceat, nihil publice in senatu apud priscos actum, quin prius dii an id iuberent consulerentur, quod, si ea in re adversam illorum mentem reperirent, religione impediri dicebant. Addet, si eruditorum ingenia et tempus ita postulaverit, quot modis haec scrutarentur, proferetque breviter duo in ea re genera, naturae unum, alterum artis ... At siquis odiosius instet et quaenam in senatu religio iactaretur interroget, proferam si scivero, sin minus ingenue me nescire fatebor neque propterea non adimplesse expositoris munus verebor: ... Deinde ad singulorum verborum vim et notionem revertar: exprimam quid sit senatus, unde dictus, a quo Romae inventus, a quo auctus. quanta illi dignitas, quanta auctoritas in re publica fuerit, quot genera senatorum .... Nec tacebo de religionis diffinitione et sitne an "a religando" an "a relegando" an "a relegendo" dicta; eodem pacto calumniam prosequar et quare 'a calvendo' sit dicta ...'*

[5] Massari to Guidetti, 31 Oct. 1465; ibid., 279: '*Ego ex te loci illius explanationem amice requirebam, non interpretis munus et praeceptoris officium; et nos Macrobium, Valerium, Agelium et Ciceronis De divinatione librum vidimus, sed non tamen ex hoc quid sentiat illic Cicero cognoscere possumus. Dicas, oro, si*

For Massari the teacher's task in taking his student through the text is to decipher phrase by phrase the meaning of the passage as a whole; for Guidetti it is to amass generally useful information around individual words in the text as they occur.[6]

These exchanges between Guidetti and Massari reveal two different notions of classical scholarship and education in conflict. On the one hand Guidetti (and presumably Landino) saw the purpose of a classical education in precisely the same terms as Guarino: namely, to produce well-behaved young men capable of writing classical Latin. The teacher should equip his pupils with the tools of rhetorical analysis and a stockpile of generally useful information. These would enable the student to extract from his text a central core of broadly moral and rhetorical instruction – to attain to a 'reading' which would enhance his developing intellectual outlook and improve his Latin *style*. These, at least, are the kinds of ideal for textual exegesis which we indicated in the first chapter as underpinning the meticulous programme of gruelling drilling in the Guarino school. Landino's own remarks in his preface to Cicero's *Tusculan Disputations* are entirely consistent with this view of the importance of textual study and rhetorical instruction.[7]

Massari, on the other hand, saw classical studies as a body of exact knowledge concerning every minute detail of the ancient world, and providing sophisticated techniques for resolving difficulties in the ancient sources. For him the highest achievement at which a teacher could aim was an entirely original explanation of a corrupt or difficult passage. The harder the textual problem, the more stimulating and the more satisfying its 'cracking' to the scholar who undertook it, as well as to the students following his arguments.

One of the immediate consequences of these two different approaches is a different choice of suitable texts for study. What interested Guidetti in classical texts was their most typical and regular elements, the ones most frequently encountered and most readily reproduced in original compositions. The most regular texts – in our terms the most 'classic' ones – *ipso facto* deserve more attention from the scholar and reward that attention more richly. What interested Massari, on the other hand, was the irregular and recherché: the short obscure phrase which, if explicated, might reveal something novel and specific about Roman life and culture. Such phrases tended to occur in texts which (for that very reason) had been neglected and which were especially vulnerable to corruption because of their internal difficulties.

---

placet, quae sit illa "religionis calumnia"; utrum autem religio "a religando" an "a relegendo" sit dicta et calumnia "a calvendo" non laboro.'

[6] For a more detailed analysis of the correspondence, see Cardini's discussion, ibid., 39-65.

[7] Ibid., 294-308.

These letters condense in the space of a few pages one of the central dilemmas of Italian humanism in the second half of the fifteenth century. By the 1450s humanist schools had spread through much of Italy. The municipal schools and university-supervised rhetoric and grammar teachers in many areas followed humanist principles in their choice of texts and methods of instruction. As we have seen, Latin eloquence and a familiarity with ancient Roman culture had become part of the necessary equipment for 'getting on' in public affairs within the élite of patricians who controlled most North and Central Italian states (Guidetti himself came from one of the richest and most prominent Florentine families).[8] And there was a growing feeling among humanist teachers – especially those who held ill-paid, peripheral chairs of grammar and rhetoric in university arts faculties – that their methods and interests deserved more space and recognition within the university curriculum. In their view teachers of grammar and rhetoric deserved the sort of esteem and salaries that normally accrued to teachers of dialectic and natural philosophy, the advanced elements in the arts syllabus – or even to teachers of medicine and law, the two higher, professional studies which were the speciality of the Italian universities.[9]

As a competitor with the logical, medical and legal curricula, however, the sort of urbane general education based on a few core texts which Guidetti endorsed lacked backbone. It offered no readily identifiable core of rigorous technical skills. Moreover, as German printers settled in Italy, humanist grammars and commentaries began to be printed, and the basic skills thus became available to anyone with the money to buy books. If the humanists were to hold their value as innovatory teachers, they had to change their ways: to concentrate on dealing rigorously with difficult texts and their internal (and academically stimulating) problems. By doing so they might create an intellectually respectable kind of training in historical and philological techniques. This, for critics like Massari, would enable humanism to compete in rigour with the stringency of late-scholastic logic and philosophy. Moreover, selective adoption of an approach like Massari's could enable individual humanists to shine among their fellows. By the end of the century Massari's kind of approach to the humanistic study of texts had become standard in many Italian arts faculties. As it spread it brought with it a fresh need to clarify the educational ends that a humanistic programme was intended to serve.

The University of Rome sponsored and stimulated humanistic studies throughout this period, and we turn to it now to explore some of the

---

[8] L. Martines, *The Social World of the Florentine Humanists* (Princeton, 1963), 60, 65.

[9] Lorenzo Valla made this set of claims explicit, by producing a series of highly polemical scholarly works in which he tried to demolish the authority of contemporary Roman lawyers, canonists, theologians and dialecticians. See S.I. Camporeale, *Lorenzo Valla: umanesimo e teologia* (Florence, 1972); F. Gaeta, *Lorenzo Valla: filologia e storia nell'umanesimo italiano* (Naples, 1955).

consequences of the specialist philological bias that teachers like Massari were prompting. Economic prosperity had returned to Rome with the return of the Papal Curia from Avignon. Within the university salaries were reasonably secure, and there were plenty of private pupils willing to subsidise the professors in return for individual tuition.[10] In practical terms Rome was ideally situated. Antiquarians and scholars could find a lifetime's worth of study among the ancient ruins and relics of the antique city. Those hoping to enter papal service – which afforded better prospects of advancement than the bureaucracy of any secular state – could move back and forth between the university and the Curia. Cardinals too employed many scholars in their households. The presence of the Vatican library, and the regular flow of messengers, diplomats and merchants in and out of the city from East and West ensured a rich and varied supply of ancient manuscripts and modern texts. Book production had become a commercial undertaking, and competition increased the accessibility and availability first of manuscripts and then of printed sources.[11] Finally, humanistic studies were supported in Rome by a succession of enlightened Popes, above all Nicholas V. The University of Rome became a centre for classical studies which attracted bright young men from all over Italy. Both Martino Filetico, from the isolated town of Filettino (the highest hamlet in Latium), and Pomponio Leto, the bastard son of the noble Sansevino family from South Italy, flourished as professors in Rome.

In this privileged setting, some of the unresolved and undiscussed consequences of the increased professionalisation of humanist teaching emerged with great clarity. At least three sets of circumstances tended to force humanists towards a position like Massari's. For one thing, the nature of Roman cultural politics encouraged gifted scholars to jockey for position and financial reward within the university. Support for scholars came almost entirely from the reigning Pope and his intimates; there was no tradition of civic aid for humanistic studies, and no local élite of public-spirited patrons. To win a secure and well-paid post, then, one had to win the attention of a Pope or of a papal advisor like Bessarion. And the obvious way to do this was by scoring off colleagues in public. The teaching conditions that resulted from this state of affairs were often lamentably contentious. Eminent humanists with reputations for particular ways of approaching their teaching texts found up-and-coming students only too eager to tell them that everything they did was wrong.

When the elderly and famous Francesco Filelfo gave his popular lectures on

[10] See in general E. Lee, *Sixtus IV and Men of Letters* (Rome, 1978); D.S. Chambers, '*Studium urbis* and *gabella studii*: the University of Rome in the fifteenth century', *Cultural Aspects of the Italian Renaissance; Essays in Honour of Paul Oskar Kristeller*, ed. C.H. Clough (Manchester, 1976), 68-110.

[11] See in general R. Weiss, *The Renaissance Discovery of Classical Antiquity* (Oxford, 1968), chs. 5-6; L.D. Reynolds and N.G. Wilson, *Scribes and Scholars: A Guide to the Transmission of Greek and Latin Literature*, 2nd edn. (Oxford, 1974), 133-6.

Cicero's *Tusculans* during the 1470s, he soon found that his reputation had marked him out as a target. One day he argued in a lecture that Cicero had held a sort of informal master-class in oratory. Afterwards, when he was discussing the point informally with some students (this was the custom, and contributed to the prevalence of polemical debate), 'a certain grammarian' began to attack him, 'criticising not only his general sayings and actions, but individual words and gestures, and denying absolutely that Cicero had opened a school or held classes'.[12] Much against his will, Filelfo was forced to argue with his opponent at length, before others intervened and ended the discussion. He was not the only distinguished teacher to be attacked in public; Filetico was harassed at one point by a claque of hostile critics.

In the second place, the audiences who turned out for a well-known lecturer's classes were often mature and knowledgeable, and this no doubt encouraged the ferment and speedy development of ideas. Teachers had to take up a position rather than contenting themselves with routine remarks. In the 1440s Gaspare Veronese described himself as 'babbling happily to a hundred men, almost all bearded' about Virgil, Terence and Aristotle's *Ethics*.[13] In the 1450s Georgius Trapezuntius felt that he could use an analogy from physics in a lecture because 'some of those present were well acquainted with natural philosophy' – which suggests that they must have been senior arts students at least.[14] Professors and clerics of high standing also came to some courses, or at least to the inaugural lectures. Sometimes, indeed, lecturers admitted what a strain it was to speak to audiences which included both beginners and more advanced scholars; so Paolo Marsi, lecturing on Ovid's *Fasti*, excused himself for being prolix in the discussion of well-known points on the grounds that his audience included 'both the ignorant and the learned, both boys and their elders', so that he had to explain everything 'with the utmost clarity'.[15]

In the third place, the contents of a popular set of lectures tended to circulate with extraordinary rapidity in the form of student notes. As Marsi put it:

---

[12] Alessandro d'Alessandro, *Genialium dierum libri sex*, bk. i, cap. 23 (ed. Leiden, 1673), i, 177-80.

[13] G. Zippel, 'Un umanista in villa', *Storia e cultura del rinascimento italiano* (Padua, 1979), 280-7. It should be noted, however, that the key word *barbatis* is twice given wrongly as *barbaris* in this edition (283, 287); cf. Zippel's own correction in his preface to *Le vite di Paolo II di Gaspare da Verona e Michele Canensi, Rerum italicarum scriptores*, new ser., iii, pt. 16 (Città di Castello, 1904), xxviii.

[14] George of Trebizond, 'Adversus Theodorum Gazam in Perversionem Problematum Aristotelis', in L. Mohler, *Kardinal Bessarion als Theologe, Humanist und Staatsmann* (Paderborn, 1923-42), iii, 279-80.

[15] Ovid, *Fasti*, ed P. Marsi (*BMC* v, 322-3) (Venice, 1482), 'Praefatio in II librum Fastorum', sig. [e vi^v]: '*Non enim haec in nostro cubiculo, aut in amoeno secessu nobis ipsis et nostro arbitrio commentamur, sed in media urbe Roma, terrarum et gentium domina, et in publico gymnasio, tam rudibus, quam eruditis, tam pueris, quam grandioribus natu profitemur: ubi quidem et apud quos nihil erit silentio praetereundum: sed ut utrisque mos geratur, omnia sunt summa perspicuitate demonstranda.*'

Every word one utters is taken down, and once taken down it is published with unconsidered haste.[16]

He took this so much for granted that he explained how it facilitated publishing:

If I am to publish anything, I shall borrow my efforts back from my students, and publish them in the same order in which I first put them forth.[17]

All that was necessary, as Domizio Calderini explained, was to 'polish what one's students took down' before letting it be printed.[18]

The circulation of notes could lead to trouble, however. Sometimes a corrupt version of a professor's lectures reached the public without his knowledge or even without any mention of his authorship. Antonius Parthenius had to publish his lectures on Catullus sooner than he had wished 'because certain jealous men have got hold of the explications that I dictated to my students four years ago, and that had been gathered into a commentary without my name attached'.[19] And Pomponio Leto simply refused to acknowledge the printed version of his lectures on Virgil, which was so corrupt as to be literally unintelligible.[20]

Worse still, the circulation of lectures made it all too easy for one professor to keep abreast of his competitors' work and either steal their good ideas or abuse the bad ones. Calderini, for example, bitterly attacked Angelo Sabino for stealing matter from his lectures on Silius and Juvenal:

Do you not remember, plagiarist, what an outcry you made when I gave this suggestion in my public lectures on Silius? But now you have taken it over, and you have mixed it up and explained it badly.[21]

---

[16] Ibid., 'Praefatio in Fastos', sig. [a^v]: '*In quo nobis eo magis elaborandum fuit, quo ne verbum quidem unum efferri potest, quod non ab his quibus id praestatur muneris excipiatur, exceptumque temerario quodam impetu vulgetur.*'

[17] Ibid., 'Praefatio in II librum Fastorum': '*Ab illis deinde, siquid edituri sumus, labores nostros mutuamur, et quo ordine a nobis omnia prolata sunt, eo quoque edenda esse ducimus.*'

[18] D. Calderini, ep. ded. to his commentary on Ovid's *Ibis*, in Ovid, *Heroides*, ed. A. Volsco (Venice, 1484), sig. k ii^r ('.*Nam nec opus adhuc emendaveram ab auditoribus exceptum superioribus annis, quum publice in Academia id profiteremur …*').

[19] Catullus, ed. Parthenius (*BMC* vii, pp. 968-9) (Brescia, 1485), sig. [i vii^v]: '*Est praeterea quaedam alia editionis festinatae causa non minor in nonnullis hominibus invidis, qui enarrationes meas superiore anno quarto discipulis meis dictatas, et in commentarium sine nomine meo redactas dum inique intercipiunt, meum operis maturandi consilium everterunt.*'

[20] V. Zabughin, *Giulio Pomponio Leto: saggio critico* (Rome and Grottaferrata, 1909-12), ii, pt. 1, 60-6. Cf. Martial, ed. D. Calderini (Hain * 10814) (Venice, 1480), ep. to Lorenzo de' Medici, sig. a ii^v.

[21] Juvenal, ed. D. Calderini (*Gesamtkatalog der Wiegendrucke* 5886) (Rome, 1476-7), note on I.154: '*Meministine Fidentine plagiarie quantis vocibus olim clamabas, cum hanc sententiam in Silii interpretatione, quem publice profitebar, recitassem? Et tamen eam nunc accipis, inversam quidem et male expositam.*'

Sabino's reply was crisp and to the point: it was Calderini who was plagiarising from a set of Sabino's lectures that had fallen into his hands.[22] In such an atmosphere, as one might expect, commentaries and editions tended to begin or conclude with short, bitter diatribes in which the opponent's intellect and morals came in for much abuse. And the fact that most of the Roman teachers had publication in view – and thus felt it necessary to defend their originality and protect their results not only in the classroom but before a wide reading public – only fanned the flames of *odium philologicum*.[23]

All this is a far cry from the propagandist claims that humanism instilled moral integrity and probity of character into its practitioner. Competition for prominence and patronage drove humanism in Rome towards self-consciousness and contentiousness. It is not at all surprising that views like Massari's took root and flourished in the Roman Sapienza, for it was precisely by doing something novel, rigorous and contentious that one could win powerful backing, beat down opposition and hold on to an impressive audience. From the 1440s on, successive humanists of greater or lesser intellectual stature tried to stake out their own original territory in the field of classical studies. At one end of the scale, as we shall see, such attempts produced fragmentation and pedantry within humanist teaching. At the other, however, they put pressure on perceptive teachers to clarify and crystallise their notion of the foundation core of humanistic studies. Among these latter, probably the most notable example is Lorenzo Valla.

In the spring of 1450 the Byzantine scholar Georgius Trapezuntius was lecturing in the *studia humanitatis* in Rome. His public lectures were attended by students from all over Europe. As a rhetorician Trapezuntius was regarded as something of an innovator. He explicitly taught that his own systematic 'five books on rhetoric' were superior to both the *Rhetorica ad Herennium* and the *Institutio oratoria* of Quintilian, and asserted the general merit of rhetorical instruction based on Greek sources; it was voguish to attend his course. But around March of that year another eminent humanist, Lorenzo Valla, began a series of lectures in direct competition with Trapezuntius'. For six months or so the two professors vied with each other for their audiences; then Trapezuntius cancelled his course. He never lectured publicly in Rome again.[24] Valla, on the other hand, became the most original Roman teacher of his generation.

Valla was stung into his assault on the chair of rhetoric by Trapezuntius' aggressively 'anti-Quintilianist' teaching. Valla was a known admirer of Quintilian and objected to Trapezuntius' repeated disparaging remarks on

[22] A. Sabino, *Paradoxa in Iuvenali* (*BMC* iv, 55) (Rome, 1474), 2nd ep. ded. to N. Perotti.

[23] Cf. esp. C. Dionisotti, 'Calderini, Poliziano, e altri', *Italia medioevale e umanistica*, 11 (1968).

[24] J. Monfasani, *George of Trebizond: A Biography and a Study of his Rhetoric and Logic* (Leiden, 1976), 80-2; L. Frati, 'Le polemiche umanistiche di Benedetto Morandi', *Giornale storico della letteratura italiana* 75 (1920), 32-9.

Quintilian's competence as a rhetorician and teacher. As he later justified his contest with 'the most learned professor of the day':

> I was not prepared to put up with abuse of Quintilian. And furthermore many colleagues well-versed in oratorical skills urged me to lecture, and they also arranged with certain Cardinals that I should be hired to lecture at the same salary as Trapezuntius. Hence it arose that, rather than opening a school as [Poggio] implies, as the one who had proved himself a great *rhetor* I was enabled to teach the art of oratory to [Poggio] and your fellows.[25]

In the face of hostility to Trapezuntius' way of presenting rhetoric (Theodore Gaza also attacked Trapezuntius' notion of rhetoric in the same period), Valla was 'backed' financially and intellectually to establish an alternative intellectual position.

As the circumstances of the contest suggest, the roots of the hostility between the two protagonists went far deeper than an affection or otherwise for the works of one Roman rhetorician rather than another. By 1450 Valla was identified with a new movement among teachers of the *studia humanitatis* to rationalise and consolidate the intellectual foundation for humanistic studies. More traditional scholars like Poggio Bracciolini deeply mistrusted this movement, but it was to play an increasingly prominent part in the development of a coherent humanist teaching programme. When a distinguished rhetorician like Trapezuntius conceded victory in the public arena to an intellectual and polemicist like Valla he acknowledged the vigour of a fresh component in humanist thinking.

What characterised both the developing and increasingly clearly opposed schools of textual 'reading' which we presented through the letters exchanged between Guidetti and Massari was the lack of structured teaching on any selected text. Of their nature both approaches used the text as a frame on which comment and instruction were hung, more or less un-systematically. Whether the focus of teaching was technical skill in decoding of textual difficulties, or the accumulating of a body of worthwhile knowledge about ancient beliefs and modern morality, each point was taken as it was precipitated by the text. Apart from difficulties this must have caused in holding the student's attention and interest through long hours of construing, such a teaching procedure raised further problems. It was, for instance, unlikely that at the end of the day (or the text) the student concentrating on the gloss would retain any sense of the import of the work as a whole (its argument, as opposed to its literal sense, line by line). And on the whole it never allowed the student to confront larger questions concerning the attitudes and beliefs which structured an entire dialogue, say, either to endorse them, or to challenge them himself.

[25] Lorenzo Valla, *Antidotum*, II (1453); *Opera* (Basel, 1540; repr., ed. E. Garin, Turin, 1962), I, 348; quoted by Camporeale, *Lorenzo Valla*, 133.

Valla maintained that his preference for Quintilian's way of teaching rhetoric (as opposed specifically to that of Cicero) derived from his favourite author's much more systematic and pragmatic approach to the teaching of rhetoric as a curriculum subject. At the root of his allegiance to Quintilian lay something more considered than a preference for one kind of style, one period of Latin eloquence over another:

> Concerning the two authors [Cicero and Quintilian], here is what I feel: ... No one can understand Quintilian who has not mastered Cicero completely, nor can anyone follow Cicero rightly unless he complies with Quintilian. Nor has anyone ever been eloquent since Quintilian (nor can he be) unless he has devoted himself entirely to the art regulated by him and to imitation. Whoever has not done this, however great he is, I shall set myself far ahead of him in the art of speaking. Now do you see how much I attribute to Quintilian?[26]

If Cicero provides the preeminent model, Quintilian is the means to understanding that model and how to derive from it precepts for the contemporary author's own use. Quintilian provides the systematic treatment of oratory and eloquence as a foundation for intellectual activity in all fields without which Ciceronian eloquence is mere sophistry. This is the recurrent argument which Valla uses in his vigorous defence of his oratorical hero.

This 'Quintilianism' offers a new opportunity for humanists debating true eloquence and the ultimate goals of an education founded on the ancient literary texts to inject intellectual vigour into their programme of study. When Massari challenged Guidetti's account of how Landino would teach the text of a Cicero letter, it was in terms of the choice of words for gloss, and the kind of running commentary which Landino would provide. As far as both correspondents are concerned, the purpose of the instruction will emerge from the accumulation of comments provided: the teacher's preoccupations will be made explicit in repeated recourse to particular kinds of question, and types of observation (predominantly moralising, say, or predominantly technical and historical). By contrast Valla suggests that literary exegesis must be taught within a rigorous and structured framework if it is to provide the basis for general instruction.

For a charismatic teacher like Guarino, a systematic programme was not as essential a part of overall instruction as it became once more pedestrian teachers took over. If humanistic studies were to become a standard feature in advanced education, something like Valla's insistence on structured teaching was essential. Valla's commitment to Quintilian ('whom I have virtually by heart') is at root a commitment to systematic instruction in humanist studies on a level which can compete with the scholastic curriculum they set out to supplant.[27]

[26] Valla, *Opera*, I, 266; quoted by Camporeale, *Lorenzo Valla*, 127.
[27] Valla, *Opera*, I, 477; quoted by Camporeale, 124.

Contemporaries of Valla report that Valla's lectures for the University of Rome were vigorously iconoclastic disquisitions on the standard literary works of the *studia humanitatis*. Poggio claims that he passed disparaging comment on Virgil, and disagreed with the *Ad Herennium* during his course on these works;[28] he also derides Valla's enthusiastic and insistent lecturing on Quintilian himself. We should not overlook the fact that Valla's reputation for disagreeing with the major authors he studied does not simply mark him out as a polemicist – after all, those who levelled the accusation of attacking those authors were themselves past-masters at vituperative debate. Valla defended himself against his detractors when the going had got particularly tough by pointing out that the ancients themselves had disagreed with one another's opinions, that this indeed was of the very nature of intellectual debate:

> Who ever wrote anything original about any science or art which did not find fault with those who had written on the subject previously? Otherwise for what reason would they have written at all ... Take the example of philosophy, with its several sects. What Stoic did not call in question almost everything the Epicurean had said? And he in his turn put up with it. What Peripatetic did not disagree altogether with both Stoic and Epicurean? What Academic Sceptic did not disagree with all the other sects?[29]

In other words, he maintained that the alert reader was bound to take a point of view when assessing ancient pronouncements on any subject. It was not enough to teach the student how to collate information amassed from detailed study of antiquity (whether close technical information or points of history); he must be taught how to discriminate among positions taken. Where two ancient authorities differed in their Latin usage, or in their opinions on some moral dictum or historical point of fact, no intelligent reader could avoid having to decide which was the more acceptable. And it was in making just these kinds of judgment in his own lectures that Valla earned a reputation for constantly calling into question 'authoritative' remarks by established authors from the classical canon.

Essentially, Valla was asking that textual studies should be treated as the means of exploring intellectual problems on a larger scale than those concerning the minutiae of the text itself. This was the burden of all his own original work, from the *Elegantiae*, which showed how nuances of meaning in classical Latin could be used to clarify long-standing questions whose complexity lay in their linguistic formulation, to the exposure of the Donation of Constantine as a forgery.[30] In doing so he asked humanistic studies to

---

[28] See n.60 below.

[29] In his so-called 'epistola apologetica' to Serra, *Opera*, ii, 391.

[30] See e.g. Gaeta, *Lorenzo Valla*, 129-66; W. Setz, *Lorenzo Vallas Schrift gegen die Konstantinische Schenkung* (Tübingen, 1975).

shift ground from largely literary and textual interests to more centrally ratiocinative concerns. The work in which Valla makes clearest his desire to move humanistic studies to the centre of the academic arena (displacing entirely the scholastic philosophical curriculum which had continued alongside the philological activities of a humanist like Guarino) was the *Dialecticae disputationes*.[31] By substituting this new view of ratiocination for the *Ad Herennium* as the core of the *studia humanitatis* Valla maintained that humanistic studies could break free altogether from the old curriculum, and stand unsupported as an independent programme of instruction in the arts.

The original title of the *Dialecticae disputationes* appears to have been *Repastinatio dialecticae et philosophiae*; elsewhere among the redactions of the work which Valla completed and which are preserved in manuscript the titles *Retractatio totius dialecticae cum fundamentis universae philosophiae* and *Reconcinnatio dialecticae et philosophiae* also appear.[32] In all these versions a philosophical approach to language is coupled with *dialectic*, the technical study of ratiocination, and an area of study on which Guarino and his generation had deliberately turned their backs.[33]

As we pointed out in the first chapter, 'active thinking' did not figure prominently in Guarino's programme of instruction. Both the ideals and above all the method of the early humanist schools minimised the attention paid to the argued line. Phrase by phrase commentary on semantic and syntactic problems displaced logical analysis, and was considered truer to ancient preoccupations. Such instruction in polemic as found space in a broadly imitative and model-following training in creative writing was appropriately 'rhetorical': as in the *Ad Herennium*, a telling 'dialectical' form of argument was given as a worked example to be imitated, rather than as part of coherent instruction in forms of ratiocination *per se*, and the rules for their valid use. A glance back at the correspondence between Guidetti and Massari may make this distinction clearer.

The exchange between Guidetti and Massari is, of course, polemical. At root there is a disagreement about the aims of a humanist study of texts (specifically, the text of Cicero's letters). The polemical strategy both writers adopt is to counter each other's points with a contrasting or competing example (the series of extracts with which we opened this chapter gives a fair

---

[31] On the *Dialecticae disputationes* see P.O. Kristeller, *Eight Philosophers of the Italian Renaissance* (Stanford, 1964), ch. 2; C. Vasoli, *La dialettica e la retorica dell'umanesimo* (Milan, 1968); C. Vasoli, 'La retorica e la dialettica umanistiche e le origini delle concezioni moderne del "metodo" ', *Il Verri*, 35/6 (1970), 250-306; L. Jardine, 'Lorenzo Valla: Academic Skepticism and the New Humanist Dialectic', in *The Skeptical Tradition* ed. M. Burnyeat (Berkeley and Los Angeles, California, 1983), 253-86.

[32] See Camporeale, ch. I.1.

[33] See H.H. Gray, 'Renaissance humanism: the pursuit of eloquence', *Journal of the History of Ideas* 24 (1963); reprinted in *Renaissance Essays* ed. P.O. Kristeller and P.P. Wiener (New York, 1968), 199-216; J.E. Seigel, *Rhetoric and Philosophy in Renaissance Humanism* (Princeton, 1968).

sample of this approach). At one point the example adduced by Guidetti is a 'dialectical' one, and clearly labelled as such. Massari had argued as follows:

> Since history is the basis of [Cicero's] letters, how can we understand them properly if we are ignorant of history? If we neglect it, it follows of necessity that all understanding and true intelligence of those letters perishes. Truth is above all else the foundation of history, and the quest for and investigation of truth is an essential part of man's definition, as no one would deny. So why then should someone be considered merely frivolous if he investigates the truth of the matter and examines even some of the most minute possible historical details?[34]

What he has done here is to lump together a series of aphoristic remarks about the relation between 'history' and 'truth', to counter Guidetti's contention that the textual exegete's job is to invoke only as much 'history' as is necessary to clarify textual difficulties. Guidetti rounds on him as follows:

> Did I advocate a total neglect of history, or that what historians perspicuously and elegantly wrote ought not to be read? 'But,' you reply, 'you said one should ignore the minute and worthless details in [Cicero's] letters.' I grant that much; but look what you infer from that: do not overlook here the rule of dialectic, from which we learn that if one member of a genus is denied, the entire genus does not thereupon fall. If one was to say 'This is not a fly' it would be false to conclude 'Therefore it is not an animal'; so, by the same token, if I say 'A certain very small part [of history] ought to be ignored', I do not on that account say 'Therefore history ought to be ignored in [Cicero's] letters'. You argue besides that truth is the foundation of history, which indeed I would not dream of denying you. I grant it, I grant it most freely: but then what? 'The investigation of truth is part of the essential definition of a man': I grant that also; but that we should not therefore call someone merely frivolous and of little intellect if he investigates minute historical details – I deny that, and I assert that it does not follow from the premises. For who does not know that just as we can not infer the genus from a member except by confirmation, as I showed above, so a member can only be derived from a genus legitimately by negation? 'It is not an animal, therefore it is indeed not a man.' Thus correctly. 'It is an animal, therefore it is a man.' Utter nonsense. But here I leave dialectic.[35]

In retaliation Massari takes up the dialectical cudgels himself:

> Read your letter carefully and you will find that you at first show a measure of contempt for history, although a little after you say, 'Scant damage will be inflicted to whoever does not pursue the minutiae of historical detail.' I am not completely ignorant of dialectic, and I marvel at your writing: 'This is not a fly, from which one concludes falsely if one concludes, therefore this is not an animal.' I on the contrary say, 'This is not a fly, from which one concludes properly if one concludes, therefore this is not an animal, because it is a piece of paper or something else of the kind.'[36]

[34] Cardini, *La critica del Landino*, 269-70.
[35] Ibid., 272-3.   [36] Ibid., 278.

In this exchange the 'dialectic' is used illustratively, just like the citations from the classics, the pursuit of etymologies and other standard devices of rhetorical debating. It does not further the discussion materially, or give a coherent basis for Massari's passionate commitment to the transcendent value of historical study; it merely provides the occasion for a (misleading) show of supposedly pertinent material. Massari accords it the disdain it deserves as 'hard argument' when he deliberately misunderstands Guidetti's syllogism, interprets it as a rhetorical syllogism ('*This* is not an animal' instead of 'It (general) is not an animal', and dismisses the whole thing as mere quibbling. Of course, this little exchange does show that Guidetti and Massari are familiar with some of the *terms* of traditional dialectic. Similarly, a modern student might use technicalities like 'implies' or 'sufficient condition' without altogether understanding them, and certainly without intending to give them their formal weight. Dialectic, for the humanist student in the school of Guarino or Landino, is, like history or ancient anecdote, or the sacred texts, a repository of possibly pertinent material to be appealed to to shore up a suggestive and unashamedly rhetorical debate.

In Quintilian's systematic course of instruction in oratory, one entire book is devoted to proof techniques in debate, and that treatment stands at the central point in his programme. For Quintilian sees it as entirely consistent with Cicero's contention that the orator should be the fully competent amateur, equipped with all technical skills and with access to the precepts of all arts and sciences, to give a prominent place to a broad study of ratiocination and law-court procedure (since the single most professionally important forum for oratory is the law-courts). 'Quintilianism' which embraces Quintilian's programme of study as a model training for the orator includes a commitment to explicit instruction in ratiocination for all kinds of discourse.[37]

It does not, however, confine itself as high scholastic logic had to ratiocination whose goal is syllogistic proof or certainty. Indeed, as Quintilian's treatment makes plain, such techniques are rarely relevant to debates in law, ethics or politics. And it is this which makes Quintilian's art of clear thinking an attractive option to a humanist like Valla whose face is set against the narrow formalism of logic and disputation in the scholastic schools. '*Consuetudo*' (customary forms) is the yardstick for Quintilianist discourse, and the forms of ratiocination which such discourse will customarily employ.

Valla's decision to review Aristotelian logic (he takes as his texts for examination Paul of Venice and Albertus Magnus, the standard school texts of the day)[38] represents a radical departure from the approach to teaching of

[37] Guarino and other early humanists had admired Quintilian; what they did not suggest was that they admired his programme as a whole, rather than his learning and Latinity.

[38] On the standard texts see W. and M. Kneale, *The Development of Logic* (Oxford, 1962), and E.J. Ashworth, *Language and Logic in the Post-Medieval Period* (Synthese Historical Library, 12) (Dordrecht, 1974); for further bibliography see E.J. Ashworth, *The Tradition of Medieval Logic and Speculative Gramar from Anselm to the End of the Seventeenth Century: A Bibliography from 1836 onwards* (Subsidia Mediaevalia, 9) (Pontifical Institute of Medieval Studies, 1978).

other early humanists, and earns him the 'new wave' title which is implicit (if not explicitly voiced) in the suspicious and downright hostile attitude of contemporary textual scholars towards his lectures and writings. For Valla the *studia humanitatis* are not just character-forming, nor do they simply provide a specialist training in the ancient languages and the texts associated with them. They can provide a self-contained alternative education which gives access to as many and as vital areas of knowledge as any programme which rivalled it.

In the *Dialecticae disputationes* Valla combines assault on traditional dialectic with constructive thinking on the effective means of adding ratiocinative strength to the *Elegantiae*. His aim is to show (as he states in the preface to the third book of the *Elegantiae*) that in existing learning and philosophy 'the major source of error stems from their lack of an adequate understanding of language'; the humanist who has systematically studied the 'most regularly used conventions of discourse' will have a clearer route to 'truth' than the specialist in logical formalism.[39] If logicians constructed their propositions '*grammatice*' – in conformity with correct ancient usage – the majority of the intellectual issues clouded by contorted expression would be clarified without recourse to logic-chopping. And having disposed of the time-consuming problems which had vexed scholastic philosophers, the humanist can then turn his attention to the ratiocinative means of negotiating for an acceptable point of view on the numerous more vital questions concerning behaviour, ethics and politics, which preoccupy the active participants in society.

In this way Valla provides a justification in terms of the growth of knowledge (always the final court of appeal for the educator) for the painstaking sifting of alternative locutions and details of Latin usage which formed the core of humanist textual study. It could provide historical justification for supporting one *sense* of a problematic proposition over others, and obviate the need for surrounding it with unnecessary logical speculation; it could prevent the student's ever falling prey to those pitfalls of language usage which might distract him from important human concerns into the realms of artificial reasoning; and it could provide him with the means of himself establishing clearly the merits of any course of action which his own clear thinking led him to wish to advocate to the public at large. In other words, Valla's justification for humanist studies was Cicero's and Quintilian's for the intellectual centrality of the *ars oratoria* and the 'perfect orator'.[40]

Valla's best-known work, the *Elegantiae*, provides us with a range of examples of this approach to language in action. Book II, for example, opens with a long and detailed discussion of the possessive pronouns.[41] Priscian,

---

[39] Valla, Praefatio to *Elegantiae* III, in *Prosatori latini del quattrocento*, ed. E. Garin (Milan and Naples, 1952), 610; *Dialecticae disputationes* I.3, *Opera* ed. Garin, I, 651: '*At philosophia ac dialectica non solent, ac ne debent quidem recedere ab usitatissima loquendi consuetudine, et quasi a uia vulgo trita et silicibus strata.*'

[40] See Cicero, *De oratore*; Quintilian, *Institutio oratoria*.

[41] Valla, *Elegantiae*, II.1, *Opera*, I, 42ff.

Valla says, maintained that there was no distinction grammatically between
meus, tuus, suus (mine, yours, his) and *mei, tui, sui* – both denote 'belonging to':

> [Priscian says] What distinction is there between *meus est filius* [he is my son]
> and *mei filius*? And elsewhere, what difference is there between *mei ager est* [it
> is my field] and *mei agri instrumentum* [my field's stock], and *mei agro dedit* [he
> gave (it) to my field], and *mei agrum colo* [I cultivate my field]; similarly we say
> *mei agri, mei agrorum, mei agros.*[42]

Valla does not accept Priscian's point of view. He discriminates between the
active and passive genitive, and makes this the basis for a distinction in usage
between *meus, tuus, suus* and the genitive form of the personal pronoun *ego, te, se*
– *mei, tui, sui*:

> Every use of the genitive (for I shall confine myself to the genitive) is either
> meant actively or passively: I add, possessively, which I take as effectively active.
> The active form, as in *providentia dei* [God's providence], *bonitas dei* [God's
> goodness]; the passive as in *timor dei* [fear of God], *cultus dei* [worship of God]: in
> the first kind of case, God provides, and blesses, not is provided with, or is
> blessed by; in the second kind of case he is feared and is worshipped, rather than
> fearing himself, or worshipping. The possessive form, as in *sedes dei* [God's seat],
> *regnum dei* [God's kingdom]. And as the meaning of utterances like these is clear
> and simple, so it is confused and ambiguous in the following cases: *amor dei* [love
> of God], *charitas patris* (sic) [father's esteem], *suspitio uxoris* [wife's mistrust].
> Here it is not clear what precisely we are referring to: whether it is the love
> which God gives us, or the love which we give him; the esteem of the father for
> his sons, or of the sons for their father; the husband's mistrust for the wife, or
> the wife's mistrust of her husband.[43]

Valla goes on to suggest, by analogy with this argument and such examples
as these, that the pronouns *meus, tuus, suus* should be used for 'active'
possession, and *mei, tui, sui* for 'passive' possession. That is to say, *meus* should
be used where the noun it qualifies expresses something I do, *mei* if it is
something done to me. So we would say *crimen meum* (my offence) if I
committed a felony, *crimen mei* if it was committed against me; *memoria mea*
(my recollection) if I remembered something, *memoria mei* if it was a
recollection about me.[44]

In arguing his case thus carefully (and we have given only the opening

---

[42] Ibid., 42: '*Multis in locis Priscianus testatur nihil interesse' an utamur primitiuo an derivatiuo in illis
pronominibus, mei, tui, et sui. Quid est, inquit, meus est filius, nisi mei filius? Et alibi, mei ager est, et mei agri
instrumentum: et mei agro dedit, et mei agrum colo; similiter mei agri et mei agrorum, et mei agros dicimus.*'

[43] Ibid., 43: '*Genitiuus omnis (ut taceam, si qui sint alii modi) aut actiue aut passiue accipitur: Adde etiam
possessiue, quod pene pro actiue accipio. Actiue, ut prouidentia dei, bonitas dei. Passiue, ut timor dei, cultus dei.
Ibi deus prouidet, et benigne agit, non ipsi prouidetur, et benigne fit; Hic timetur et colitur, non timet, nec colit.
Possessiue, ut sedes dei, regnum dei. Atque in huiusmodi oratione, ut intellectus apertus atque unus est, ita in illis
ambiguus et anceps. Amor dei, charitas patris, suspitio uxoris: dubium est de utro loquaris, an de amore, quem
deus in nos habet, an de eo, quem nos in eum: de charitate patris in filios, an filiorum in patrem: de suspitione
maritali, an de suspitione uxoria.*'

[44] Ibid., 44.

argument in a lengthy survey of the varied uses of the pronouns denoting possession), Valla is doing more than quibbling with his ancient and not so ancient authorities. He is making a valuable contribution to an area of analysis of discourse which greatly exercised scholastic linguists: how to discriminate between the various possibilities of possessives in ambiguous sentences (like the much-discussed, 'Every man's donkey is running').[45] As long as word-order and nuance of meaning attributable to distinct forms of words and other such 'grammarian's' concerns were ignored by logicians, the possibilities which had to be considered in establishing the *suppositio* of a selected ambiguous word or phrase were practically limitless.[46] Valla's preparatory investigation of the real differences in usage between alternative forms offered the possibility of rejecting out of hand some 'readings' in favour of others, and thus of reducing the problem to one which might yield to less daunting forms of analysis than those the scholastic logician proposed. So important did Valla consider the issue of the varieties of genitive form, and the ambiguities of meaning caused by imprecise usage, that he devoted an entire treatise to repairing the 'faulty habit of speech' (*lapsa loquendi consuetudo*) which in his view had created the problem.[47]

In Book VI of the *Elegantiae* (to take an example more widely celebrated in the secondary literature), Valla challenges Boethius' designation of *persona* as a substantive. Appealing once again to distinctions in customary usage (the usage of the best authors), Valla rejects this in favour of adjectival force. When the early Church fathers use *persona* of the three 'persons' of the Trinity (he goes on to argue), they cannot, therefore, possibly have intended to mean three distinct and separate *subjects*; and this grammarian's insight can simplify theological discussions of quite what the 'attributes' associated with the three clusters of qualities referred to by three *personae* of the Trinity might be. Verbal analysis cuts away some of the undergrowth which has prevented scholars from taking hold of the central questions in theology.[48]

Valla's contemporaries in the traditional camp (most vigorously represented in the contemporary attacks on him by Poggio) were outraged at the systematic querying of ancient and respected judgments on questions of usage in which Valla engaged in the course of sorting out such intellectual problems:

> It does not surprise me [wrote Poggio] that some deluded and demented idiot spews out his madness at me, since the innate imbecility of his mind, the ingrained insanity of his heart, the inborn perversity of his soul, lead him to condemn, reprehend, blame and spurn with wild arrogance all those ancient

---

[45] On the knotty problems raised for scholastic logicians by such propositions see E.J. Ashworth, 'Multiple quantification and the use of special quantifiers in early sixteenth century logic', *Notre Dame Journal of Formal Logic* 19 (1978), 599-613; for a reference to this as a commonplace logical 'quaestio' see R. Guerlac, *Juan Luis Vives against the Pseudodialecticians*, (Dordrecht, 1979), 58.

[46] On 'suppositio' see N. Kretzmann, 'History of Semantics', in *The Encyclopaedia of Philosophy* (New York and London. 1967), VII, 371-3.

[47] *De Reciprocatione sui et suus, libellus plurimum utilis, Opera*, I, 235-49.

[48] *Opera*, I, 215-16; see also *Dialecticae disputationes*, I.13, ibid., 673.

and most learned men, whose memory has been venerated throughout all generations with celebration in the highest terms of praise. As if he held the wheel of fortune in his hand, and turned it to and fro, and whirled everything around, and twisted it to fit his judgment. To take the grammarians for a start: he begins by censuring Priscian, Donatus, Servius, Pompeius Festus, Nonius Marcellus, finally Marcus Varro himself, on matters of grammar ... He condemns everyone with the exception of only Quintilian, whom this fanatic strenuously maintains to have been the most learned of all who have ever lived, and prefers to Cicero himself for eloquence and the art of discourse.[49]

Now, of course, if your primary commitment is to retrieval of texts free from scribal corruption, and to the patient exegesis of those texts as part of a return to an ancient wisdom partially lost because of incompetence in the original languages, then this is how Valla's *Elegantiae* is bound to strike you. It is perhaps unfortunate that the scholarly literature has been too readily inclined to accept Poggio's condemnation of Valla's grammatical iconoclasm. Valla's comments are strongly critical, but that criticism is in the interests of clarifying questions of correct usage. If a grammarian's main task is to provide a prescriptive grammar for language tuition (a Kennedy's *Latin Primer*), then simplification and ignoring of internal contradiction may be proper for the purpose. But if the task is to excavate the nuances of meaning captured by differentiated usage, which have served historically to distinguish between subtly differing concepts, then it is up to the grammarian to select and compare, to reject one authority in favour of another, to discriminate and sift all the available evidence.

Indeed it is ironical that Poggio should finally throw up his hands in horror at Valla's lack of respect for Varro ('Finally he censures Marcus Varro himself'). For Valla regards Varro as the creator of the approach to grammar which he himself favours: grammar as a tool for distinguishing what the senses and the raw data in the mind fail to distinguish. The careful discrimination between apparently indistinguishable words can often have a profound philosophical importance – as Valla's long discussion of the two verbs *careo* and *vaco* (both of which have to do with 'lacking' or 'emptiness') in the *Elegantiae* suggests. This discussion appears to be meant as a step towards clarifying the vexed question of the nature of the void (*vacuum*), a problem in which Valla explicitly showed an interest in the *Dialecticae disputationes*.[50] Valla acknowledges his debt to Varro in the preface to *Elegantiae* II:

> I cannot see why anyone who writes on grammar and the Latin language should consider this so unimportant as to be beneath his office, when in fact there is nothing more excellent than grammar and Latinity, as I shall show in the next book. This being so, am I saying that all those who have omitted such studies have done so out of ignorance or through negligence? Not at all. But Caesar's and Messalla's works perished through the ravages of time, and those of Varro are only half discovered, though these, perhaps, contain the kind of things which I am now teaching.[51]

[49] Poggio, *Invectiva* I, quoted in Camporeale, *Lorenzo Valla*, 111-12.
[50] Valla, *Elegantiae*, V.85, *Opera* I, 191-2.
[51] *Prosatori latini*, ed. Garin, 604.

Whole sections of the *Dialecticae disputationes* follow the same strategy as that used in the more openly grammatical *Elegantiae*: different forms of words are only accepted as 'meaning the same thing' (*congruens*) if no grounds can be provided for taking the different construction as a mark of a subtly important difference in sense; or the same fixed 'sign' (the terms used by the logician to identify propositions which will yield to standard treatment) is shown to produce a significant difference of meaning in different phrases which it introduces. In either case, the effect is to throw responsibility for discriminating meanings on to the Latinist and grammarian. The grammarian will take in hand the logicians whose ignorance of Latin usage leads them into unnecessary quibbling, as Valla indicates when he discusses negation ('no' and 'not' words) in the *Elegantiae*:

> The other standard questions about the nature of negation we have gathered together in our *Dialecticae disputationes*. We omit them in this place because although they are not unknown to orators, they are not known by any of the dialecticians.[52]

Of course, Valla's approach ignores the importance of formalism to the logician, and the technical advantages of considering problems in a kind of 'machine language' sub-section of ordinary language. But Valla's inspired choice of poetic and literary examples which will not be crammed within the restricted bonds of formalism is so attractive that the humanist reader of his *Dialecticae disputationes* is bound to be reluctant to accept the traditionally narrow focus of scholastic logic. If sentences of the form 'It is necessary that' are to be studied, why not also those introduced by 'It is preferable that', or 'It is desirable that'? The metaphysical assumptions that underpin scholastic logic are swept away by a powerful tide of grammarian's analogies and intriguing examples from ancient literature.

Valla's defence of his critical approach to the writers of antiquity is that he is no servile rehearser of ancient opinions as enshrined in respected texts, but is undertaking the same kind of active intellectual appraisal as those in which the great grammarians of antiquity were engaged. And his working model for this kind of approach is Quintilian. Quintilian in action, appraising and analysing the works of eloquence he most admires (and specifically Cicero's writings), provided the second strand of thinking in the *Dialecticae disputationes*. After reducing traditional logic in scale by using the grammarian's skills to eliminate needless complexity, Valla offers his own positive instructions for relating 'active thinking' more closely to the needs of the humanist orator. Quintilian's *Institutio oratoria* allows Valla to substitute for it a classified programme of debating techniques suitable for the task

---

[52] *Elegantiae*, III.27, *Opera*, I, 97: '*Caetera quae de natura negationum disputari solent, in libros Dialecticae nostrae contulimus, quae ideo praeterimus, quod fere non sunt ignota oratoribus, dialecticorum uero nemini cognita.*'

which Quintilian and Valla see as crucial to the orator – to teach, delight and move.

Quintilian says in the introduction to the *Institutio oratoria* that he does not consider it enough for the teacher of oratory to assume that his pupils have already been 'educated', and simply want to acquire an additional skill in public speaking:

> For almost all others who have written on the art of oratory have started with the assumption that their readers were perfect in all other branches of education and that their own task was merely to put the finishing touches to their rhetorical training ... I on the other hand hold that the art of oratory includes all that is essential to the training of an orator, and that it is impossible to reach the summit of any subject unless we have first passed through all the elementary stages. I ... propose to mould the studies of my orator from infancy, on the assumption that his whole education has been entrusted to my charge.[53]

It is in the context of such a 'whole education' that Quintilian includes copious instruction in ratiocination and 'invention' (as he labels the rhetorico-dialectical portion of his work) of all kinds.[54] And it is in the interests of such a compendious education of orator-humanists that Valla supplements his abbreviated Aristotelian logic with an array of techniques useful and effective in oratorical debate, but not traditionally accorded any place within the study of dialectic.

The result is a highly original compound of simplified logical terminology in the Aristotelian tradition (a tradition on which of course Cicero and Quintilian had themselves drawn), and a systematised treatment of argument strategies which logicians had tended to discard with barely a mention as 'sophistical' – effective in practice, but either of dubious general validity, or apparently not susceptible to satisfactory treatment within the framework of instruction in the syllogism. We shall see that the originality of Valla's hybrid dialectic earned it an enduring place in the history of humanist education.

Some of Valla's new topics in dialectic are taken over intact from the *Institutio oratoria*: Quintilian's treatment of *loci* (a retrieval system for debating material), of *exempla* (types of supporting evidence) and of *epicheireme* (curtailed argument form). These help to bulk out the *Dialecticae disputationes* from a grammarian's attack on scholastic quibbling (in Valla's sections on the modals, the transcendentals, the syllogism) into a handbook of sensible strategies for embarking upon a reasoned discourse. The leading note in all Quintilian's (and therefore Valla's) discussion of argument and proof is the practical effectiveness of such techniques faced with an actual debate. For instance, here is part of the section on *exempla* which Valla incorporates:

---

[53] *Institutio oratoria* 1.pr.4-5.
[54] Ibid.

But while examples may at times, as in the last instance, apply in their entirety, at times we shall argue from the greater to the less or from the less to the greater. 'Cities have been overthrown by the violation of the marriage bond. What punishment then will meet the case of adultery?' 'Flute-players have been recalled by the state to the city which they left. How much more then is it just that leading citizens who have rendered good service to their country should be recalled from that exile to which they have been driven by envy.' Arguments from unlikes are most useful in exhortation. Courage is more remarkable in a woman than in a man. Therefore, if we wish to kindle someone's ambition to the performance of heroic deeds, we shall find that parallels drawn from the cases of Horatius and Torquatus will carry less weight than that of the woman by whose hand Pyrrhus was slain, and that for dying Cato and Scipio carry less weight than Lucretia. This too is from the greater to the less. Let me give you some separate examples of these classes of argument from the pages of Cicero; for where should I find better? The following passage from the *Pro Murena* is an instance of argument from the like: 'For it happened that I myself when a candidate had two patricians as competitors, the one a man of unscrupulous and reckless character, the other a most excellent and respectable citizen. Yet I defeated Catiline by force of merit and Galba by my popularity.'[55]

Here we have a preoccupation with 'what will work in public debate', coupled with desirable reference to 'worked examples' surviving in Cicero's speeches. The contrast with the arid (as they seemed to humanists) formalisms, extended technical terminology and hair-splitting distinctions of Paul of Venice or Albertus Magnus (who was only called 'the Great', according to Valla, because that was his surname!) could hardly be more pronounced.[56] At the same time, the possibility of relating instruction on ratiocination directly to the texts of that most eloquent of orators, Cicero, makes the approach irresistible to the student of classic Latinity.

The final book of the *Dialecticae disputationes* offers the student an alternative set of ratiocinative techniques to substitute for the laborious (and in Valla's eyes, largely irrelevant) treatment of syllogistic which dominated fifteenth-century Aristotelian treatments of inference. The orator, according to Valla and Quintilian, argues *probabiliter,* or *verisimiliter* – for 'likelihood', or the closest approximation to truth that circumstances will allow. In this he is no different from the scientist or traditional philosopher, except in that he is aware that his reasoning is precarious, his truths mere approximations to truth. As Quintilian puts it:

Rhetoric is the art of speaking well [*ars bene dicendi*], and the orator knows how to speak well. 'But he does not know whether what he says is true.' Nor indeed do those who teach that all things are made up of fire, or water, or four elements, or indivisible particles, nor those who infer the distances between the stars and

---

[55] Ibid. 5.11.9-11.
[56] Camporeale, *Lorenzo Valla,* 123.

the sizes of the sun and the earth ... What if rhetoric does not infallibly consist in always speaking the truth, but always speaking true-seemingly [*verisimile*]? At least they are aware that what they say is true-seeming.[57]

Accordingly, Valla shifts the focus of ratiocination away from the pseudo-certainty of syllogistic (whose certainty is no stronger than the certainty of its premises, from Valla's point of view), and incorporates a varied armoury of more or less sophisticated strategies for arguing 'true-seemingly', including topics like 'sorites' and 'dilemma' whose argumentative force he insists on despite their dubious (or indeterminate) logical status.[58]

The overall effect of Valla's pioneer work is to reinstate a 'dialectic' (albeit one rather different from that promoted by conventional Aristotelian teachers) as a necessary rigorous component in humanist arts instruction. It is certainly no accident that when Erasmus was in search of rhetorical instruction in a formal mould Gaguin should have sent him, along with Trapezuntius' compendious *Rhetoricorum libri V*, Valla's *Dialecticae disputationes*.[59]

Valla had developed much of his programme in the course of an intellectual and personal odyssey that had taken him from his native Rome to Pavia, Naples, and then back to Rome. What the new context offered him was the opportunity to apply his views to teaching in a prominent place. That he did so is clear from contemporary reports of his lectures. 'Last year', Poggio wrote in 1454 to B. Ghiselardi,

> when I was in Rome, he was teaching Virgil and Cicero's *Ad Herennium*. He criticised both of them viciously all of the time, the former as a negligent and unpolished poet, the latter as going wrong in the art and method of speaking. The fanatic could not have brought forth any clearer proof of his madness. He claimed that he was superior to any ancient writer; his folly was so great that he openly said that he was more learned than Varro, whom, as you know, both Cicero and Augustine praise with the utmost lavishness. Therefore one needed not words but cudgels, and Hercules' club, to beat down this monster and his pupils.[60]

---

[57] *Institutio oratoria* 2.17.38-9.

[58] On 'sorites' and 'dilemma' in the *Dialecticae disputationes* see Jardine, 'Lorenzo Valla', 272-5; L. Jardine, 'Lorenzo Valla and the intellectual origins of humanist dialectic', *Journal of the History of Philosophy* 15 (1977), 143-64; 161-3.

[59] Monfasani, *George of Trebizond*, 318-19.

[60] Poggio to B. Ghiselardi, quoted by Camporeale, *Lorenzo Valla*, 137: '*Etiam anno praeterito dum Romae essem, cum Virgilium et Ciceronis Ad Herennium libros legeret, utrumque acriter quotidie reprehendebat: alterum ut parum consideratum poëtam ac politum; alterum ut in arte et dicendi praeceptis aberrantem, quo nullum majus, fanaticus ille, dementiae et insaniae vestigium edere potuisset; se autem ita jactabat, ut omnibus antiquis scriptoribus anteponeret: eo autem stultitiae progreditur, ut se palam dicat M. Varrone doctiorem, quem scis adeo a Cicerone non solum laudari, sed etiam a beato Augustino, ut in nullum majores laudes conferri possint. Itaque opus esset non verbis, sed fustibus, et clava Herculis, ad hoc monstrum perdomandum, et discipulos suos.*'

Poggio clearly saw Valla and his works through an obscuring veil of indignation; but even this hostile testimony shows that Valla's teaching was as self-consciously aggressive and avant-garde as his formal writings.

But some of the very features of the Roman environment that encouraged Valla also worked against the spread and further development of his doctrines. In the first place, his rivals among the humanists bitterly resented his attempts to reverse the methods and priorities on which they had been brought up – his enthusiastic setting of Quintilian above Cicero. Hence they accused him – unfairly, as we have seen, but not ineffectively – of being a wild man, an iconoclast without judgment or perspective. In the fifteenth century, as now, academics who wanted to get on could not afford to have their views labelled as 'unreliable' or 'unsound'. Valla's reputation, and his ability to produce a school of followers, clearly suffered from Poggio's relentless abuse, and his lack of adherents to defend him encouraged further attacks from scholars in the next generation, anxious in their turn to make their own names. Everyone used the *Elegantiae* as a fundamental reference book; few admitted that they were imitating its methods.[61]

Valla's intellectual independence and aggressive attacks on the lawyers and theologians also won him many enemies, especially among those trained in the theological faculties which were growing up in Italy during the fifteenth century. The Roman Dominicans did not enjoy the playfulness Valla showed when he came to preach their annual sermon in honour of Thomas Aquinas. He turned the occasion on its head by preaching in favour of patristic, rather than scholastic, models in theology: at least one member of his audience thought that he must have taken leave of his senses.[62]

In the third place, the exigencies of teaching limited Valla's ability to pass on his system as anything like a complete theory. His ideas were complex; the examples in which he gave them definite form were numerous and varied. Few of his pupils could master the full body of ideas and matter presented in the *Elegantiae* and the *Dialecticae disputationes*. They lacked direct access to the texts; they lacked the training in traditional scholastic dialectic that Valla took for granted on the part of any serious reader of his works. It is, of course, a persistent failing of educational reformers to assume that their pupils share their own understanding of the old curriculum which the reformers are setting out to supplant. Accordingly, students had to depend on Valla's

---

[61] Domizio Calderini, one of the dominant Roman scholars of the generation after Valla's, was particularly vehement in his attacks on Valla. See e.g. A. Grafton, 'On the scholarship of Politian and its context', *Journal of the Warburg and Courtauld Institutes* 40 (1977), 159. Niccolò Perotti, on the other hand, was an enthusiastic proponent of Valla's approach to linguistic studies (see e.g. Camporeale, *Lorenzo Valla*, 137). Yet his way of emulating Valla was to compile an enormous semi-lexical work, the *Cornucopiae*; he did not attempt to provide language study with a systematic foundation.

[62] H.H. Gray, 'Valla's encomium of St. Thomas Aquinas and the humanist conception of Christian antiquity,' *Essays in History and Literature ... Presented to Stanley Pargellis*, ed. H. Bluhm (Chicago, 1965), 37-52.

lectures. And there, however aggressively he presented his general views, he also had to accommodate himself to more elementary teaching requirements. He had to go through his texts word by word (even the text of Quintilian), giving the sort of paraphrase, rhetorical analysis, and basic information that beginning students needed. Sometimes, as Poggio's remarks indicate, he had to teach the traditional texts rather than his favourites, or those he considered doctrinally most important; in such cases his own ideas had to be presented in the awkward form of attacks on the authors whose texts he was meant to be explicating. In the end, then, Valla's example could not be followed by the majority of his Roman students, even though, as we shall see, his broad reform of dialectic was to prove far more influential.[63]

[63] See Chapter Six below.

CHAPTER FOUR

Humanism in the Universities II: Competition between Schools

The generation of Roman teachers after Valla – Calderini, Filetico, Leto – responded to the pressure of the Roman intellectual environment rather differently. Instead of adopting a provocatively novel system of teaching, they tried to renovate the traditional word-by-word method by applying it to an unfamiliar set of texts. The works of Cicero and Virgil which had been the traditional lynchpins of the curriculum offered few opportunities for the display of learning and brilliance. But another range of works, which had previously lain outside the central humanist curriculum, fitted their needs more closely. The vast historical epics of Lucan and Silius Italicus, the shorter poems of Statius and the epigrams of Martial, the satires of Juvenal and Persius, Ovid's *Fasti*: these texts required much wit and even more erudition to teach. They were the works of poets who had taken pride in exuberant displays of learning. They were studded with little-known place names and allusions to minor mythological characters, and (with the possible exception of Ovid) they were rich in tricky bits of syntax. Such texts necessarily called for a sort of decoding on the teacher's part. And decoding offered plenty of opportunity for proving linguistic virtuosity in public.

The very choice of such works as subject matter was an act of audacity, and might be enough to make a reputation. Domizio Calderini, for example, repeatedly emphasised his boldness in lecturing on Statius' *Sylvae*, 'which nobody dared to do before me', and Ovid's *Ibis*, 'a work full of anger and obscurity'.[1] He had his rewards: a chair in the university by 1470, while he was still in his early thirties, a papal secretaryship by 1471 and a salary that quickly doubled.[2] The lesson was not lost on contemporary observers. 'Calderini,' recalled his young acquaintance Raffaele Maffei,

---

[1] See e.g. A. Grafton, 'On the scholarship of Politian and its context', *Journal of the Warburg and Courtauld Institutes* 40 (1977), 158 and n. 24; J. Dunston, 'Studies in Domizio Calderini', *Italia medioevale e umanistica* 11 (1968).

[2] E. Lee, *Sixtus IV and Men of Letters* (Rome, 1978), 179-82.

was a man of sharp intellect. He was the first in our time who began to give thorough interpretations of the harder poets, and to publish commentaries on them while still quite a young man. Therefore he won the esteem of powerful men, and became a wealthy man and an Apostolic Secretary.[3]

No wonder that four Roman professors lectured on the *Punica* of Silius, or that several competed in teaching the satirists.[4] That way lay academic power and social prestige.

Some of Calderini's competitors surpassed Calderini himself in their search for novel texts and novel points to make about them. Paolo Marsi took on Ovid's *Fasti*, an extensive learned poem on the first six months of the Roman calendar which included detailed information on Roman topography, history and ritual. Even so, the issues he chose to discuss were sometimes even more refined than the text demanded. At 1.63 ff. Ovid describes the rites that take place on 1 January. Line 76 reads:

> *et sonet accensis spica Cilissa focis*

> (and (see how) the Cilician *spica* (top of a plant) crackles on the kindled hearths).

The line does not appear to pose any problem, but Marsi managed to find one: what sort of *spica* was burnt on the hearths? He recalled:

> When I lectured on this passage both father Sabino, who was then alive, and others attacked me because I took it as referring to a *spica* of nard, while they thought it should be taken as the very fine saffron that came from Cilicia.[5]

After all, Marsi's opponents pointed out, Pliny praised Cilician saffron and did not mention Cilician nard. But Marsi stuck to his guns. Pliny, he replied, did not deny that nard grew in Cilicia. Indeed he praised Syrian nard, and Syria was next to Cilicia, 'so what grows in Syria can grow in the part of

[3] R. Maffei, *Commentariorum urbanorum libri XXXVIII* (1506), Bk.21 (ed. n. p., 1603), col. 777 (cf. also A. Perosa, 'Calderini ... Domizio', *Dizionario biografico degli italiani* 16 (1973), 597-605): '*Domitius Calderinus patria Veronensis his omnibus statim successit. Acri vir ingenio, primus qui hoc tempore poetas duriusculos diligentius coeperit enarrare, et in eos commentarios aedere admodum iuvenis. Quare in principum virorum dignationem venerat, divesque propterea ac apostolicus Secretarius factus.*'

[4] On Silius see the article by E.L. Bassett, J. Delz and A.J. Dunston in *CTC* iii, 341-98; on Juvenal, the article by E.M. Sanford in *CTC* i, 175-238; cf. also the useful case study by Sanford, 'Bread and circuses', *The Classical Weekly* 45 no. 2 (26 November 1951), 17-21. That these poets were seen as 'difficult' and recondite is clear from many texts. See e.g. Pietro Marsi's preface to his commentary on Silius (1483), quoted by Bassett et al. in *CTC* iii, 387: '*Primus patrum nostrorum memoria huius poetae sacros fontes reserare arcanaque ingredi ac publice in hac florentissima urbis Romae academia profiteri ausus est Petrus Montopolita ...*' (our emphasis). Martial, ed. Calderini, sig. a ii[v]: '*Nusquam obscurior quam ubi peculiarem sibi assumit elocutionem. Latent verborum involucro plerunque aculei ...*'

[5] Ovid, *Fasti*, ed. Paolo Marsi, sig. [a viii[v]]: '*Cum legerem hunc locum et pater Sabinus, qui tunc vivebat et alii in me invehebantur, quoniam de spica nardi voluerim intelligi, cum ipsi de croco ex Cilycia laudatissimo provenienti intelligendum esse censerent. Nec advertebant quo in errore versarentur ...*'

Cilicia nearest to Syria'. He clinched his case with an appeal to personal experience:

> I myself picked a *spica* [of nard] on the shore of Cilicia with my own hand, and I showed it to my listeners when I lectured on this line.[6]

Later in the book Ovid refers to the health-giving spring of the nymph Iuturna in the Roman forum. Marsi not only set out at length the literary evidence for the spring's location, establishing it near the temple of Vesta, but testified that he had actually examined the place, where he found 'a half-ruined tower at the Church of St. George, under which is the very spring ...' To establish beyond question that he had discovered the nymph's beneficent waters he added:

> I took a student who had dermatitis there five times to bathe, and his entire infection cleared up at once.[7]

These long excursuses, with their careful citations of evidence, references to public controversy and appeals to *son et lumière* where the textual evidence gives out, are no doubt the kind of thing Massari was invoking in the letters cited in the last chapter.

This system of instruction had its merits. In particular, the persevering student at Rome really was likely to learn something new about the ancient world. For example, Silius mentions 'an enormous temple of Juno'. In his comment on the line Pomponio Leto observed:

> We have not been able to find out that mortals worshipped Juno in Carthage or in Africa ... But the Carthaginians worshipped in a temple dedicated to Hercules and built by Dido. For the Poeni, who sprang from the Phoenicians, followed the ancestral rite and worshipped Hercules, but not Juno.[8]

This was a novel and perceptive observation on the religious history of the

---

[6] Ibid.: '*Et si cilyssum nardum non legas apud Plynium, non refert; non enim inquit Ply. non nasci in Cilycia nardum, sed in primis laudat syriacum ... Adde quod Syria iuncta est Cilyciae, ut quod in Syria nascitur possit in ea parte Cilyciae nasci, quae Syriae iuncta est. Ego autem in ora Cilyciae spicam meis manibus legi, et auditoribus meis ostendi, cum haec legerem.*'

[7] Ibid., sig. [e vi^r]. (the end of a digression started on e v^v): '*Est enim apud templum divi Georgii turris semiruta sub qua est ipse fons, et aquae quidem salubres. Quod ego experiri volui, quo certior fierem an ea esset aqua Iuturnae, praesertim cum Varro diceret "nympha Iuturna: quae iuvaret. Itaque multi egroti, propter id nomen, hinc aquam petere solent". Duxi igitur illuc ad abluendum quinquies discipulum scabidum, protinusque ab omni scabie liberatus est.*'

[8] From a fair copy made from notes on Pomponio's lectures, now Biblioteca Laurenziana MS 52, 8¹, written *c.* 1473, and published by J. Dunston, 'A student's notes of lectures by Giulio Pomponio Leto', *Antichthon* 1 (1967), 88-9 (c.f. *CTC* iii, 373-83): '*Iunonem apud Carthaginem nec in Africa coluisse ipsos mortales comperimus ... sed templum Carthaginenses Herculi dicatum et constructum a Didone colebant. Nam et a Phoenicibus ipsi Poeni ortum habentes ritum secuti patrium Herculem colebant, non autem Iunonem.*'

ancient world – one so far from obvious that it was not repeated until the nineteenth century. A student who understood such remarks was not likely to follow the common Renaissance habit of treating all the ancients as devotees of a single, interchangeable set of gods.

On the whole, however, the disadvantages of the system more than outweighed its virtues. Continual recourse to showmanship tended to undermine the teachers' integrity. Some of them fabricated evidence to give their lectures more spice: Pomponio Leto pretended to have a full text of the long-lost *Annales* of Ennius, and Calderini invented an ancient biographer of Suetonius.[9] The full effects of the pressure upon individual teachers can be seen in the case of Filetico. He began as a faithful follower of Guarino, whose commentary on Cicero's *De senectute* provided much of the material for Filetico's own commentary (no doubt he had a full set of notes dating from his attendance at Guarino's course). Cicero attributes the substance of the work to the elder Cato, in order, as he himself said (I.3), to give it greater authority. According to a set of surviving notes on Guarino's lecture course, Guarino had remarked:

> *M. Catoni* [to M. Cato]: His words, as Pliny the historian says, were oracles, and he had three very great qualities. For he was a very great orator, a very great general, and a very great senator. Manuel Chrysoloras adds a fourth: that he was a very great *prae mamilias*.[10]

Prae mamilias would remain the mangled nonsense it no doubt seemed to the anonymous student who recorded these notes if we did not have Filetico's comment on the same passage, which makes Guarino's meaning clear:

> And the discourse clearly 'has more authority' because it is Cato who gives the arguments. His words, as Pliny says in the *Natural History*, were taken as oracles by the Romans. He also says that Cato had three outstanding qualities. He was a great orator, a great senator, a great general; and my teacher Guarino added a fourth, that he was a great and fine *paterfamilias*.[11]

Cato the *paterfamilias* makes a good deal more sense than Cato the *prae mamilias*. When Filetico prepared his commentary for public circulation he deleted the phrase 'and my teacher Guarino added', and replaced it with,

---

[9] Grafton, op. cit., 161.

[10] *Commentum Guarini de Senectute*, British Library MS Harl. 2549, fol. 4ʳ: '*M. Catoni cuius verba dicit Plinius historicus oracula fuisse atque in eo viro tria maxima extitisse. fuit enim maximus orator: maximus imperator: et maximus senator: Manuel Crisolora quartum addidit quod fuit maximus prae mamilias.*'

[11] M. Filetico, Commentary on the *De senectute*, British Library MS Add. 10384, fol. 26ᵛ: '*Et bene disputante Catone: maiorem habet auctoritatem oratio: cuius verba ut ait Plinius de naturali historia pro oraculis apud Romanos habita sunt. Quem etiam dicit tria in se habuisse praeclara. quod summus orator: summus senator: summus Imperator fuit: et quartum addebat praeceptor meus Guarinus* (a second hand has lined through the words "*addebat ... Guarinus*" and replaced them with "*etiam recte adiungere possumus*"): *quod summus et optimus pater familias fuit.*'

'and we can properly add'. This small act of intellectual dishonesty is, in a sense, all the more revealing because of the comparatively trivial nature of the point at issue.

From the standpoint of the ordinary student these lecture courses, however original and exciting, were inevitably too dense and complex to be easily followed. One's heart goes out to the student whose efforts to keep up with Pomponio Leto's lectures on Silius are recorded in a Florentine manuscript studied by John Dunston. He gave up in despair when his teacher listed in rapid succession the seven polysyllabic names of the seven mouths of the Nile:

> Sebanium, Gutterium, Pannicum, and the rest, Mendesium, Tarenticum [the names are all fantastically distorted]; I say there are others. My teacher spoke too quickly for me.[12]

The subscription at the end of the same student's notes on Book II captures his mood as he followed the course yet more vividly:

> I am glad to have collected all this from my teacher Giulio Pomponio. O immortal Gods, could you not grant me the knowledge of shorthand, so that I could follow Giulio's ideas that he discusses in lecture? At least you could grant that I be freed from my dermatitis.[13]

Students like this one, baffled by the speed with which their teachers poured forth their treasures of geography and myth, cannot have drawn the fullest benefit from the experience. And their profit was also lessened by the limitations of the Roman teachers' expertise and methods: above all by their emphasis on Latin texts at the expense of Greek.

One or two of the Roman teachers (particularly Pomponio Leto) did show some ingenuity in teaching their difficult material. Both as aesthete and a serious scholar, Pomponio not only loved the intellectual pursuit of the idealised dream-world that was his vision of Republican Rome, but tried to revive it as a way of life. He lived and dressed austerely, cultivated his own small farm in imitation of the elder Cato, and tried to follow the stiffest dictates of Roman Stoic ethics in his personal conduct. When the family from which he came, attracted by his fame as a teacher, tried to reestablish their connection with him, his answer was as brief and final as a Roman epitaph (a form of relic he collected): '*Pomponius Laetus cognatis et propinquis suis salutem.*

---

[12] Dunston, 'A student's note of lectures by Giulio Pomponio Leto', 87: 'On I.197 (where Pomponio read off Pliny's list of the seven mouths of the Nile: *proximo Alexandriae Canopico, dein Bolbitino, Sebennytico, Phatnitico, Mendesico, Tanitico, ultimoque Pelusiaco): Septem hostia ut hostium Sebanium Gutterium Pannicum et cetera Mendesium Tarenticum. Dico alia. Celeritas dicentis praeceptoris oppressit.*'

[13] Dunston, ibid., 90: 'On II fin.: *Iuvat haec collegisse Iulio Pomponio praeceptore. O dii immortales quid si mihi notarii manu adderetis ut Iulianas partes quas in lectione retractat assequi possem. Saltem et hoc praeberetis me scilicet scabie atrocissima liberar[i] ...*'

Quod petitis fieri non potest. Valete' (Pomponio Leto greets his relatives. What you ask cannot be granted. Farewell). And he instilled his love for what Rome had once been into a large group of friends, who assembled, taking mock-Roman names and titles, to study antiquarian questions and to celebrate the anniversary of the founding of the city (carefully established as 21 April).[14]

Pomponio set out to share both his antiquarian expertise and his love of antiquity with his students as well as with fellow humanists. He did use standard methods of teaching, as we have seen, but he also introduced some notable innovations. In particular, he presented the essential facts of ancient Roman government and religion in a series of concise textbooks on the magistrates, priests and laws of the city. Other humanists had written on these subjects: Flavio Biondo in Rome and Andrea Fiocchi of Florence had produced systematic works on a much larger scale. What Pomponio added was not so much new information as a gift for sticking to essentials. For example, the student who looked up 'Aedile' in Fiocchi found an account so wordy, so elaborate and so heavily documented as to be hard to follow:

> The job of holding the games, however expensive and spectacular, belonged to the Aediles. No small part of the Aedileship was also that each Aedile saw to holding the games at his own expense, in proportion to his patrimony and station. Cicero provides an ample account of this in his books entitled *De officiis*, when he recalls his own Aedileship and that of Pompey. But Asconius Pedianus says that when Pompey was made Aedile, he dedicated the theatre that he had built at vast expense with splendid games, in which he introduced chariots with elephants. This is also easy to see from the 'argumenta' of the comedies, in which the names of the Aediles who oversaw the games were entered.[15]

Leto is more straightforwardly explanatory, and still manages to compress most of this and rather more into his account.

> When the Plebs returned to the city from the Mons Sacer, it won from the Patres the concession that it might elect other magistrates to help the Tribunes; they were to oversee sacred and private buildings and see to the grain supply. They therefore created four Aediles. Two, who were called *curules* from their ivory chairs, used royal insignia and wore purple, and were in charge of the sacrifices and the games ...[16]

Leto's works were less technically meticulous than Fiocchi's, but their conciseness and remarkable comprehensiveness established them as standard teaching texts until the seventeenth century. Indeed they became the object

---

[14] J. Wardrop, *The Script of Humanism* (Oxford, 1963), 20-3.
[15] A. Fiocchi, *De potestatibus Romanorum* Bk. II, ch. 13, in *Respublica Romana*, ed. P. Scriverius (Leiden, 1626), 86.
[16] P. Leto, *De magistratibus Romanorum*, Bk. I, ch. 20, ibid., 136-7.

of printed commentaries and classroom lectures in their own right.[17]

It is a problem familiar to historians of education that the mere existence of books tells one nothing about their effect on readers. Pomponio's students *could* have learned a good deal about Rome from his work, but whether they actually did so is another matter. Fortunately other evidence enables us to be sure that some of his educational innovations had a considerable impact. As a way of giving his students more direct contact with the reality of Roman culture, and ultimately more command of its details, he revived the custom of performing Roman comedies and modern tragedies in public. His friend and biographer Sabellico described these productions:

> Pomponio was the one who restored to the city the ancient custom of watching plays, using the courts of the greatest cardinals as his theatre. There the plays of Plautus, Terence, and even some modern authors were put on. He both taught the noble youths these plays and served as director when they acted them.[18]

As we have pointed out, testimony of this kind from laudatory humanist biography cannot be trusted or evaluated without confirmation. In this case, however, independent confirmation is available. In the 1480s Pomponio found an ally in another Roman teacher, Giovanni Sulpizio, who combined an interest in ordinary literary texts with the study of ancient architectural methods, as preserved in the systematic handbook by Vitruvius. This work described Roman staging techniques in some detail. Leto and Sulpizio tried to apply the description to their own productions, thanks to the support of a generous patron, Cardinal Raffaele Riario. And Sulpizio's preface to his edition of Vitruvius – a dedication to Riario – both confirms and enriches Sabellico's testimony:

> For you were the first to adorn a stage, five feet high and in the middle of the Forum, for tragedy, which we were the first in this century to teach, in the hope of arousing the young to act and sing. Rome had not seen productions of plays for centuries. After the play had been acted in the Castel Sant' Angelo before Innocent, you brought it back to your house, as into the central auditorium of a circus, admitting both the public and your colleagues, and protecting the whole audience with awnings. You were the first to reveal the appearance of a decorated stage, when Pomponio's troupe played a comedy.[19]

---

[17] A copy of the Paris 1552 edition in Princeton University Library (Adams P 1841) has both a printed commentary by Richardus Gorraeus Parisiensis and marginal notes that apparently derive from lectures in a Paris college.

[18] M.A. Sabellico, '*Pomponii vita*', in P. Leto, *Romanae historiae compendium* (*BMC* v, 549) (Venice, 1499), sigs. P ii^v – [P iii^r].

[19] G. Sulpizio, preface to Vitruvius (1484), quoted by B. Pecci, *L'umanesimo e la 'Cioceria'* (Trani, 1912), 53: '*Tu enim primus Tragoediae, quam nos juventutem excitandi gratia et agere et cantare primi hoc aevo docuimus (nam eius actionem jam multis saeculis Roma non viderat) in medio foro pulpitum ad quinque pedum altitudinem erectum pulcherrime exornasti. Eamdemque, postquam in Hadriani mole, vivo Innocentio spectante, est acta, rursus intra tuos penates, tamquam in media circi cavea, toto consessu umbraculis*

This text shows that Pomponio's productions really did take place, and in a strikingly novel way. The audience, used to the free motion of outdoor religious pageants, was confined to a fixed, covered space, before a fixed stage. And this in turn was 'decorated' – probably, though the text is too brief for us to be certain, with a colonnade of gilt and elaborate pilasters and doorways (this seems to have been what the best antiquarians took as the standard Roman stage setting).[20]

The student actors, then, were caught up in an event that was elegant, fashionable and even avant-garde. Joining such impressive productions must have given them unusual feelings of intimacy with the Roman world – or at least with the spoken use of classical Latin. And these feelings would have been reinforced by other aspects of the productions – for example, by the verse prologue that one of them, Tommaso Inghirami, was made to speak before performing the title role in Seneca's *Phaedra*, which hammered home the novelty of Pomponio's neo-classical staging:

> We who intend to play a tragedy
> Of heroes' sufferings for you today
> Beseech the gods in all humility
> That no real tragedy may come our way,
> And that they keep you safe from every ill
> And make you prosper well in your affairs.
> We ask, also, that you who watch be still
> And quietly attend the youthful players;
> You too, O Raphael, who are the bright
> Adornment of the Church's holy Senate.
> For you will see here something that's not trite,
> A story various and grave, and with that
> Most lamentable. We make bold to say
> You'll not be sorry that you're here today.[21]

---

tecto, admisso populo et pluribus tui ordinis spectatoribus honorifice excepisti. Tu etiam primus picturatae scenae faciem quum Pomponiani Comoediam agerent nostro saeculo ostendisti.'

[20] There has been much controversy about the nature of these settings; see in general M. Dietrich, 'Pomponius Laetus' Wiedererweckung des antiken Theaters', *Maske und Kothurn* 3 (1957), 245-67.

[21] Pecci, *L'umanesimo e la 'Cioceria'*, 57 (freely translated):
> *Tragoediam acturi quoniam hodie sumus,*
> *Quae continet heroica infortunia,*
> *Primum rogamus prece pia cunctos deos,*
> *Tragoedia ut vobis nihil dignum accidat;*
> *Sed procul omnibus repulsis tristibus,*
> *Vos augeat magnis et domi et foris opibus.*
> *Post id novis actoribus, qui usu abditos*
> *Revocant theatrales jocos et fabulas*
> *Ad vos juvandos; decus etiam poeticum*
> *Dive Raphael, optime, integer, sacri*
> *Lumen senatus, inclitum Ecclesiae decus,*

As a permanent contribution to the student's humanistic education, these performances had their intended effect, at least on some participants. Consider the case of Inghirami, whose performance as Phaedra won him the permanent nickname 'Thomas Phaedra' and was still being talked about when Erasmus came to Rome twenty years later. When the stage machinery broke down, we are told, Inghirami 'held the audience's attention with extemporaneous Latin verses until the machinery was repaired and the play could go on'.[22] Evidently, then, performing under Pomponio's direction really did make some of his students remarkably fluent and practised at producing authentic-sounding verse and speaking it expressively. True, some criticised Inghirami's earlier performance in Plautus' *Asinaria*, claiming that his gestures had been too flamboyant.[23] But even such criticism suggests that Pomponio's troupe had done much to create a public with sophisticated expectations about Latin verse and its proper delivery.

In the light of these successes, it is not surprising that Pomponio's classroom was sometimes overcrowded, or that his teaching produced so many original and influential writers of Latin verse. When Giovanni Gioviano Pontano inaugurated a fashion for writing verse in the form of inscriptions, and Jacopo Sannazaro created the neo-Latin pastoral, they were applying the lessons they had learned from Pomponio.

Yet Pomponio's teaching had its limitations, like that of his colleagues. He had little to say about the Greek background to Roman literature. More significantly, his innovations did nothing to overcome or correct the shortcomings of the Roman method of humanistic education: the absence of moral instruction, the unattractive and precocious air of knowingness and the hypocritical attitudes which it fostered in its students. In that respect he too fell short of the original ideals of such earlier teachers as Guarino.

Furthermore there is no sense in which the philological and stylistic novelties which Pomponio Leto and his contemporaries purveyed could plausibly be said to add up to a coherent education. True, they did not confine themselves to a narrow traditional curriculum in grammar and rhetoric. Marsi was not the only teacher to fill his lectures with archaeological and natural-historical discoveries. Pomponio Leto offered an incomparably full and orderly introduction to Roman civilisation. But they did not provide access to a clearly defined or clearly-presented set of disciplines; they did not use Valla's new brand of dialectic to give order and thought-content to their instruction; above all, they do not appear to have

---

Adeste placidi oramus et silentio
Nobis favete. Rem novam spectabitis,
Historiam variam, gravem, miserabilem
Cum fabula mistam. Pigebit neminem
Hic affuisse.
[22] W. Creizenach, *Geschichte des neueren Dramas* ii, 2nd ed. (Halle, 1918), 346-7.
[23] P. Cortese, *De cardinalatu libri tres* (Castrum Cortesium, 1510), Bk. ii, fol. 98[V].

made any attempt to offer texts of varying levels of difficulty to audiences at different stages of preparation. To this extent they did not offer an 'education' at all. What was the student supposed to know after he had attended three courses on Silius? The Roman teachers have little to say on this subject. And the fragmentation and duplication in their offerings was only made worse by the fact that the university offered so many opportunities for part-time lecturing on a small stipend that few professors felt it their duty to work up a coherent programme of instruction. As a result, like their predecessor Valla, they failed to produce a 'following'. The next generation of Roman students and teachers turned to new interests – including scholastic philosophy and Greek science – and to a new style, flawless Ciceronian prose, which was devoid of *hapax legomena* and obscurities. Raffaele Maffei and Paolo Cortese, the leaders of the new vogue, found their elders wanting as figureheads for a Roman humanist 'school', and exemplary only in their zealous desire to recover the treasures of ancient literature and art.[24]

It might be objected that the Roman situation was not representative – that the University of Rome, with its large number of jobs for humanists, was a special case (though in a sense each Italian university was a special case). But the evidence suggests that the experiences and efforts of the Roman teachers had parallels in other, quite different university settings. Bologna, for example, was a famous university long before Rome, with ancient traditions and strong connections with the Italian élite. From the twelfth to the fourteenth century, it had been the first and greatest school of Roman law; its teachers and pupils, who included Bartolus and Baldus, had been the most brilliant and effective lawyers in the highly litigious society of North Italy. More recently, its *universitas artistarum* had surpassed the law school. Medicine, with its concomitant preparatory fields of logic and natural philosophy, had become a Bolognese speciality. And from the early fourteenth century, the holders of the Chair of Rhetoric and Poetry had founded a strong tradition of formal lectures on literary texts.[25]

By the late fifteenth century the Bolognese teachers of humanistic subjects were as eager for the favours of the ruling family, the Bentivoglio, as the Romans were for those of popes and cardinals. They won them in much the same way. Filippo Beroaldo, the dominant Bolognese humanist, loved to lecture on the *Golden Ass* of Apuleius; Apuleius' references to Egyptian magic and religion were a pretext for unbelievably learned digressions into recondite areas of ancient life, and his rich diction led to careful discussions of many lexical points.[26] Beroaldo's learning and his inimitable Latin style, itself

[24] C. Dionisotti, *Gli umanisti e il volgare fra quattro e cinquecento* (Florence, 1968).

[25] P.O. Kristeller, 'The University of Bologna and the Renaissance', *Studi e memorie per la storia dell'Università di Bologna*, new ser., 1 (1956), 313-23.

[26] K. Krautter, *Philologische Methode und humanistische Existenz: Filippo Beroaldo und sein Kommentar zum Goldenen Esel des Apuleius* (Munich, 1971); M.T. Casella, 'Il metodo dei commentatori umanistici esemplato sul Beroaldo', *Studi medievali*, 3rd ser., 16 (1975), 627-701.

studded with inkhorn terms, gained him rich rewards. He served on the city's council of Anziani, went on a mission to Pope Alexander VI and wrote propaganda and panegyrics on demand for official circulation (even though he had little interest in political life).[27] Like the Romans, he explicitly defended the richness and preciosity of his diction as a sign of true learning:

> If my words seem difficult to you, the fault is yours, not mine. You never read anything rich or out of the ordinary. Content with two or three works, you ignore the rest and think that nothing is Latin unless it is found in your standard books. But we too write Latin, and take our words from the most Latin of authors. You who are toothless should not envy those with teeth: you that are blind should not despise those with eyes. That the blind man does not see the light is the fault of his eyes, not the sun; that you do not understand our works and therefore attack them is the fault of the reader, not the writer ... We like a learned, not an everyday style ...[28]

In Bologna, as in Rome, the pressure for novelty produced students inclined to make wild claims to precocious learning and ingenuity. The inaugural lectures of Beroaldo's friend and rival Antonio Codro Urceo portray an unpleasant world of academic one-upmanship. He shows us students trying desperately to outface one another on the most minute and technical points of textual criticism and interpretation:

> 'Hah, hah.'
> 'What are you laughing at, you fools, morons, owl-faced halfwits, who eat up other people's bread as if you were mice?'
> 'At your stupidity. You'll soon be claiming that you know everything, and that you can criticise Homer himself.'
> 'I do claim that, and now.'
> 'That you can criticise Homer, the greatest poet among philosophers and philosopher among poets?'
> 'Homer, I say, in the first line of the Iliad:
>
> *Mênin aeide thea Pêlêiadeô Achilêos*
>
> (Sing, goddess, of the anger of Achilles, son of Peleus);
>
> I say there are three mistakes there. The first mistake is that he put an iamb in the third foot, which the dactylic hexameter does not allow. The second mistake is that he did not use a synaloephe in the fifth foot, which is very common in Greek, but made a rough synaeresis in the scansion. The third mistake is that in the same foot he treated as short a syllable which is long by its position [before] a double *l*. For Achilles is written with a double *l*, as Homer himself wrote it correctly elsewhere.'
> 'O heavens, o earth, o seas of Neptune; he is clearly possessed by a devil. Shut up, you pedant.'
> 'Shut up, all of you, you ignoramuses, or defend Homer.'
> 'You are looking for trouble if you go on with this slander.'

[27] Krautter, *Filippo Beroaldo*, ch. 1.   [28] Quoted ibid., 86-7 n. 58.

'You'll get into trouble even if you're not looking for it ...'[29]

Even the details of a lecturer's style could come in for savaging:

> 'Let's examine our commentaries and introductory lectures, [and see] how
> poorly and absurdly they are put together. "The present work is divided into two
> parts, into the proemium and the treatise. Then the proemium is divided into
> three parts; the first there, the second there, the third there." What sane man
> would not find this comic?'
> 'Tell us, you paragon of eloquence; if you were going to lecture on Virgil's
> *Aeneid*, how would you begin?'
> 'I would begin thus: I believe, gentleman that it is worthwhile for me to
> divide my prolegomena to Virgil's *Aeneid* into two parts.'
> 'Shut up, shut up, my good man, that's all I need to know. While you babble
> and brag about "its being worthwhile" and "prolegomena" you've commited a
> solecism.'
> 'What solecism are you babbling about?' ...[30]

Florence resembled neither Bologna nor Rome as an institution. Lorenzo de'
Medici officially transferred the university to Pisa in 1472, leaving only a few
chairs for humanists in Florence itself.[31] But their holders too had to fight for
Medicean favour. We saw at the beginning of the last chapter that such
struggles could take the form of debates over the proper method of teaching
literary texts. In the 1480s such debates became even more acute.

Politian, who had been tutor to Lorenzo's children and a sort of court poet
avant la lettre, became professor of poetry and rhetoric at Florence in 1480. He
was to teach 'at a different hour from master Cristoforo Landino', the
reigning master of the old school, whose lectures on Cicero and Virgil had
won him a salary of 300 florins, three times what Politian received.[32]
Politian immediately set out to expose Landino. Instead of Cicero or Virgil,
he chose difficult texts – Statius' *Silvae*, which had also been one of
Calderini's favourites, and Quintilian's *Institutio*. In his inaugural lecture he
distinguished between the sort of technical knowledge he could provide and
the traditional glossing of texts offered by Landino. Exuding false modesty,
he explained that his listeners 'had always had with them in abundance'
those who were willing to teach the central authors; he, on the other hand,
was willing 'to humble himself' and teach the second-rate (though, as he also
pointed out, Statius and Quintilian were not actually second-rate at all,

[29] A. Codro Urceo, *Opera, quae extant, omnia* (Basel, 1540), Sermo I, 48-9 (the Greek text of
Iliad I.1 is as printed here).

[30] Ibid., 19.

[31] A. Gherardi, *Statuti della Università e Studio fiorentino dell'anno MCCCLXXXVII* (Florence,
1881), 273-6.

[32] A.F. Verde, *Lo Studio fiorentino, 1473-1503*, ii (Florence, 1973), 27 ('*alia hora quam dns
Christophorus Landinus*'); for Landino's salary, see ibid., 174.

merely exponents of a different sort of style from Golden Latin).[33] And in the commentary proper he happily plunged into Statius' biography, definitions of poetic genres, Greek and Roman sources, parallels and echoes of individual lines, and vast quantities of antiquarian and mythological details – as well as more conventional matters such as the rhetorical function of individual lines and sections.[34]

Politian took special pleasure in attacking Calderini's printed commentary on Statius. He claimed that this was an intellectual exercise – so that students would not be misled by Calderini's great reputation into trusting him uncritically:

> Since I gather that some claim that I am undutiful and immodest in departing so often from Calderini's view, let me briefly explain my reasons. It is my opinion, students and colleagues, that nothing is so harmful to our wits and studies as the habit of following authority rather than reason. For we cease to apply our judgment and accept the view of the scholar whom we believe in. And we often fall into that worst of all faults: agreeing with opinions that are false or that we have not examined.[35]

Calderini's works were spoilt, according to Politian, by their arrogance, their unnecessary attacks on better scholars and their over-hasty solutions to hard problems. Their true nature had to be exposed to the public. After all – so Politian argued, following Valla – in attacking Calderini he was doing no more than the ancients had done to one another:

> Study the grammarians, the dialecticians, the orators, the doctors, the astrologers, and other authors in the liberal arts; you will find much more in their books directed against others than in their own favour. For as Aristotle says, stubborn debate greatly sharpens the wits. Hence Aristotle attributed much to his teacher Plato, but much more to truth; and Theophrastus, according to Quintilian, disagreed boldly with his teacher Aristotle.[36]

The arguments sound plausible (indeed they are the same as Valla used in defence of his own polemical and critical approach); but they were probably no more important to Politian than the fact that Calderini had made a name and a career in the same way – and that he had turned against the Medici in the last years of his life. Attacking him was therefore simply a way of currying

[33] L. Cesarini Martinelli, 'In margine al commento di Angelo Poliziano alle "Selve" di Stazio', *Interpres* 1 (1978), 101-2.

[34] A. Poliziano, *Commento inedito alle Selve di Stazio*, ed. L. Cesarini Martinelli (Florence, 1978). For further records of Politian's practices as a teacher see his *Commento inedito all'epistola ovidiana di Saffo a Faone*, ed. E. Lazzeri (Florence, 1971), his *La commedia antica e l'Andria di Terenzio: appunti inediti*, ed. R. Lattanzi Roselli (Florence, 1973), and the review of these last two editions by S. Rizzo in *Annali della Scuola Normale Superiore di Pisa*, Classe di lettere e filosofia, 3rd ser., 4 (1974), 1707-11.

[35] Poliziano, op. cit., 90.

[36] Ibid., 92.

favour with powerful patrons and of staking a claim to the same sort of learning as had made Calderini famous.[37]

Politian was, of course, far more than a hanger-on of the Medici. An innovative poet in both Latin and Italian, he studied the form and content of the *Silvae* with unremitting attention to detail. And he tried to pass on his skills as well as his animus against Calderini. Consider his clever, if wrong-headed, argument that Statius married Martial's widow, Polla:

> In the letter that precedes Book II of this work we find this:
> *Genethliacon Lucani, quod Polla rarissima uxorum, cum hunc diem forte consideraremus, imputari sibi voluit*
> (The birthday poem for Lucan, for which Polla, rarest of wives, wished to be held accountable when we by chance considered this day).
> Smell these words one by one. You will see that they are too familiar to fit another man's wife. He says 'rarest of wives' – 'wives', not 'women' – 'wives', because she both venerates the memory of her dead husband and sweetly loves her living one. 'When we by chance considered this day' – both the adverb 'by chance' and the plural number of the verb 'we considered' clearly have a certain familiarity to them. 'To be held accountable' – the poem was to be written for her sake, to be given to her; here you can entirely recognise the wife in his words. Nor should you worry because he calls her Claudia in a letter ...[38]

The argument is wrong: the attempt to explain away the other text in which the name is given as Claudia is unconvincing. But Politian's terrier-like inspection of the text, point by point, represents a novel and intensive training in close reading – something far removed from the long learned digressions, often loosely related to real problems in the text, that the Romans went in for.[39] His work – though created to meet conditions similar to those that shaped Calderini's – reached a far higher level of seriousness and remains a useful guide to Statius' text.[40]

By the end of his life Politian was challenging the scholastics as well as his fellow humanists. He studied natural philosophy and dialectic, he gave private lectures on the central scholastic texts – Porphyry's *Isagoge*, Aristotle's *Posterior Analytics*, Euclid's *Geometry* – and he claimed that his direct access to the Greek text of Aristotle and his original Greek commentators enabled him to deal far more competently with philosophical problems. As one of his students reported (a self-satisfied young man named Girolamo Amaseo, who left Padua for Florence in 1493 in the hope of learning Greek, and stayed to

---

[37] Cesarini Martinelli, 'In margine al commento di Angelo Poliziano alle "Selve" di Stazio', 103-13.

[38] Poliziano, op. cit., 7.

[39] Cf. D. Coppini, 'Il commento a Properzio di Domizio Calderini', *Annali della Scuola Normale Superiore di Pisa*, Classe di lettere e filosofia, 3rd ser., 9 (1979), 1119-73, esp. 1126-33.

[40] See esp. Cesarini Martinelli, 'In margine al commento di Angelo Poliziano alle "Selve" di Stazio', 115-24.

work with Politian after being promised that 'when I go back to Padua I shall make a great name both for him and for myself'):

> He is lecturing on Book I of the *Prior Analytics*. I have been occasionally. He lectures splendidly and solves the technical problems that the barbarians don't understand. This isn't surprising; it is on the basis of his Greek scholarship that he is so daring.[41]

Politian's combination of skills stood him in good stead in establishing and sustaining his prominent position with the Florentine élite. The university authorities tried to hold him in check; in 1482 they repeated their admonition that he must teach at a different time from Landino, 'so that it cannot be said implicitly or explicitly that he is a competitor of the aforesaid Cristoforo'.[42] Others on whose territory he encroached, notably Bartolomeo della Fonte, also complained bitterly of his tactics.[43] But his friendship with Lorenzo proved proof against all such assaults, and he really could correct and explain harder Greek and Latin texts than anyone else. When he died in 1494 he had reached a position of considerable eminence. He was receiving the very high salary of 450 ducats a year – more normal for a jurist than a humanist – while Landino was still making do on 300.[44]

The situation in Rome, in short, was not far different from elsewhere in Italy. Politian, Barbaro and Leto had different sets of interests and values; yet they recognised one another as the heads of their respective schools and the possessors of distinctive technical skills. All competed for reputation; all (with the exception of Leto, with his ostentatious austerity) vied for the highest salary. No one has ever evoked the atmosphere of rivalry and ambition in which they flourished more powerfully than Gregorio, another member of the Amaseo family, in a letter of 1499:

> And so that you may see some examples of the fame that humanistic studies still enjoy in our time: Platina was head of the papal library with a salary of 700 ducats; not to mention Leonardo Bruni, Gregorio Tifernate, Lorenzo Valla and other early examples, Pomponio was famous throughout the world; Angelo Poliziano had eight hundred ducats at Florence and left immortal fame; Beroaldo has three hundred ducats at Bologna and more fame than any lecturer in that *studio* and more students ... Giorgio Merula had four hundred ducats at Milan, Francesco Filelfo eight hundred, and he went about dressed

---

[41] G. Pozzi, 'Da Padova a Firenze nel 1493', *Italia medioevale e umanistica*, 9 (1966), 195: '... *legit primum Prioris; audivi interdum, legit optime et m[in]utias illas barbaris non intellectas resolvit; nec mirum: graecis praesidiis audet tot et talia.*'

[42] Verde, *Lo Studio fiorentino*, ii, 27 ('*alia hora quam dns Christophorus Landinus, ita ut nec tacite nec expresse dici possit ipsum esse concurrentem dicti dni Christophori*').

[43] Cesarini Martinelli, 'In margine al commento di Angelo Poliziano alle "Selve" di Stazio', 103-4, n.13.

[44] Verde, *Lo Studio fiorentino*, ii, 26, 28.

entirely in cloth of gold, since he was one of the Duke's highest-ranking courtiers.[45]

Amaseo's figures are often inaccurate; but his emphasis on 'fame', salary and social mobility is extremely to the point.

When Northern humanists began to master and imitate the culture of Italian humanism, their idols were Leto, Beroaldo and Politian. But these men's almost obsessively learned, contentious and competitive brand of humanism did not fit Northern tastes and Northern conditions. As the Northerners strove to emulate the new learning from the South, they found the comprehensive reformed educational programmes of humanists like Valla more relevant to their needs. Humanism was metamorphosed once again as it made the transition from Italy to the Low Countries, but before we follow that story, there is another strand of Italian humanism that we must consider.

[45] Pozzi, 'Da Padova a Firenze nel 1493', 223-4.

CHAPTER FIVE

The New Subject:
Developing Greek Studies

So far we have been concerned with general patterns of educational practice. We have traced them in the work of famous individuals, treated synthetically and placed in broad contexts. What we have not done is to follow one element of the humanist curriculum through several generations. A good way to do this is to ask how successive humanist teachers tried to build new subjects into the old structure, and a fruitful answer to this question is to be found in the tools they forged in the course of their work – the textbooks they wrote and the texts they edited for the printers who came down into Italy and spread across Europe during the 1460s. Such a study will enable us to continue checking the humanists' claim to be radical innovators in teaching. At the same time, a whole series of new problems will be raised: above all, the problem of the relations between scholars and the businessmen who reproduced and distributed their works.

The humanists' favourite new subject was Greek. Medieval schools and universities had long offered courses in Latin grammar and rhetoric and the reading of Latin texts. As we have seen, the early humanists often took far more of their teaching materials from medieval sources than they would willingly have admitted in public. But medieval education did not include literary Greek at any level. Anyone who wished to learn or teach it had to begin from scratch.[1]

Moreover of all the subjects omitted by medieval education Greek was the one most urgently needed. Cicero, Quintilian and Gellius had firmly stated that it was essential for the writing of serious history, poetry and oratory in Latin – or even for an appreciation of the Latin classics. Cicero could not even be read in full by those unable to understand the Greek words and phrases he had liked to use. But one could not learn Greek in Italy. True, some south Italians wrote and spoke Greek of a sort. Petrarch had had a few lessons from the Calabrian monk Barlaam. But he had made little progress, and reported that he could only caress, not read, the Greek manuscripts of Plato and

---

[1] See in general R. Weiss, *Medieval and Humanist Greek* (Padua, 1977), chs. 1-8.

Homer that he owned. Barlaam's pupil Leonzio Pilato taught Greek publicly for a few years in Florence and produced an unattractive, word-for-word Latin version of Homer. Petrarch used and criticised Pilato's translation and notes. But by and large the south Italians disappointed the humanists. They did not get on well with Tuscans and Lombards; and they seem to have been pedestrian teachers at best. The humanists had to look elsewhere.[2]

By the 1390s everyone recognised that Constantinople was the only place to look. There the tradition of studying Greek literature had never died. In court and church circles it had even remained normal to write and speak a highly literary, classicizing form of Greek. Formal prose stuck so closely to classical norms that it often became vague and unwieldy. Historians had to refer to all barbarian opponents of the Empire, whether Avars, Goths, Huns, Arabs or Turks, as 'Scyths'; for that was the only ancient word that came close in meaning.[3]

Since the Palaeologan restoration of 1261, when the Byzantines had recovered Constantinople from its Western conquerors, scholars had become even more devoted to their classical Greek heritage. Earlier Byzantine intellectuals had proudly described themselves as 'Romans'. Now, resenting the sack of Constantinople by Western Crusaders in 1204 and the weakness of their church and empire, they insisted that they were 'Hellenes' – not pagans, certainly, but heirs to the literary culture of the Greek church fathers, who had themselves been steeped in the classics, and this heightened self-confidence bore fruit in intensive scholarly work of high quality.[4] Demetrius Triclinius, for example, became the first scholar since antiquity to master the complex metrical patterns of Greek verse. He corrected the texts of Pindar, Aeschylus, Sophocles and Euripides; he collected and studied the less famous works of ancient authors, which were not taught in Byzantine schools and therefore were not much copied, thus saving about half of the plays of Euripides that now survive; and he compiled from the remains of ancient scholarship full school commentaries on his favourite texts. These reached a wide public as marginalia in the manuscripts that he and his pupils prepared. Triclinius was far from isolated: other fourteenth- and fifteenth-century scholars produced teaching materials that ranged from a carefully bowdlerized recension of the *Greek Anthology* to model letter-collections in Attic prose. Consequently when the humanists turned east they encountered a scholarly tradition very similar to their own.[5]

[2] A. Pertusi, *Leonzio Pilato tra Petrarca e Boccaccio* (Venice and Rome, 1964); Weiss, *Medieval and Humanist Greek*, chs. 10-12.

[3] A. Garzya, *Introduzione alla storia linguistica di Bisanzio* (Naples, 1972).

[4] On Palaeologan culture see S. Runciman, *The Last Byzantine Renaissance* (Cambridge, 1970); A.E. Vacalopoulos, *Origins of the Greek Nation: The Byzantine Period, 1204-1461*, transl. I. Moles (New Brunswick, NJ. 1970); *Art et Société à Byzance sous les Paléologues* (Venice, 1971).

[5] L.D. Reynolds and N.G. Wilson, *Scribes and Scholars: A Guide to the Transmission of Greek and*

Most Palaeologan scholars were professional teachers of grammar and rhetoric. They therefore had experience of a problem that the Italians also faced: the teaching of *classical* Greek to pupils for whom it was not a native language. Byzantine boys grew up speaking not pure Attic but the vastly different popular language of medieval Byzantium – which had lost the classical dative case, had undergone drastic changes in such vital words as the verb 'to be' and had freely admitted neologisms of all kinds. Even aristocratic boys had to purify their diction artificially if they were to join the élite in court or church. To help them, the Palaeologan teachers compiled an impressive range of teaching devices. Some were new, and others went back to the second century when there had been a widespread movement to restore an earlier form of literary Greek. They included grammars in the form of catechisms, annotated excerpts from classical and modern model texts, systematic exercises for the inflection of nouns and verbs, and elaborate lexica of the ancient dialects. (The parallel between this work and that of Valla and Guarino will by now be clear.) All these devices could suit Italians as well as their original Byzantine clientèle.[6]

But there was more than one disadvantage. In the first place, it was almost impossible to gain access to Byzantine teachers. An Italian could go to Constantinople, as did Guarino, Francesco Filelfo and a few others. There he could learn not only from university lectures but from a Greek-speaking culture. Filelfo found that aristocratic women spoke a very pure Greek as a result of their sheltered life which had preserved them from exposure to neologisms. He married one, who helped him immensely. As he later recalled with admiration, she and her friends had been able to decline nouns and even use the proper moods and tenses of verbs as well as any man. The fluency he gained from her he later applied effectively in his Greek letters, which still make lively reading.[7] Guarino, as we have seen, also mastered classical Greek during his stay in the Levant. But this course was not always practicable. The journey out and back was expensive and dangerous, and at best it meant a long postponement of one's career as a teacher. Hence few even attempted it.

The second problem was even more difficult. The Palaeologan teachers had been accustomed to dealing with native speakers of a form of Greek. Hence – like a modern university lecturer teaching Middle English – they could expect their pupils to know most words and forms even before they began to study the strictly classical language. Moreover they only aimed to

Latin Literature, 2nd edn.. (Oxford, 1974), 58-69; on Triclinius see esp. H. Hunger, *Die hochsprachliche profane Literatur der Byzantiner* II (Munich, 1978), 73-6.

[6] See in general Garzya, *Introduzione alla storia linguistica*; Hunger, *Die hochsprachliche profane Literatur*, 3-83.

[7] V. Rotolo, 'L'opinione di F. Filelfo sul greco volgare', *Rivista di studi bizantini e neoellenici* 10-11 (xx-xxi) (1973-4), 85-107. The most detailed study of how an Italian humanist learned Greek in Constantinople is M. Cortesi, 'Il "Vocabularium" greco di Giovanni Tortelli', *Italia medioevale e umanistica* 22 (1979), 449-83.

make a few boys fully fluent. Given these advantages, they could require their students to master the full and bewildering richness of the ancient language. A simple example comes from the tradition of grammar teaching. Following ancient precedent, they grouped the nouns by their nominative endings into no fewer than 56 declensions – 35 masculine, 12 feminine and 9 neuter. A student had to reproduce any or all of them on demand in paradigms. This mass of information must have been daunting even for a native Greek; its impact on a speaker of Latin or Italian can be readily imagined.

Just before 1400 one Byzantine scholar set out to solve both problems. Manuel Chrysoloras was a man of high birth and great charm, who taught in Constantinople during the 1380s and 1390s. He understood clearly that Byzantium could not withstand the attacks of Mongols and Turks without substantial help from the Western powers, and he decided that one way to win such help was to attract the sympathy of powerful Western intellectuals for Greek culture. He learned Latin – an unusual step for a Byzantine intellectual – and he established contact, through intermediaries, with the Chancellor of Florence, the humanist Coluccio Salutati, who was a great dispenser of cultural patronage. Salutati desperately wanted direct access to Greek literature and philosophy and brought Chrysoloras to Italy. Chrysoloras taught in Florence and elsewhere for some years after 1397, and enabled a substantial number of Italians to read Greek prose. Wisely, he emphasised the importance of translating from Greek into fluent classical Latin. Some pupils produced versions of Greek texts, ranging from short tracts by Plutarch to Plato's *Republic*. Some began to revise the medieval translations of Aristotle, correcting them against the Greek and polishing their diction, and some – above all Guarino – continued to give Greek lessons after Chrysoloras left. Competent instruction was therefore now available in Italy.[8]

Chrysoloras also set out to equip Italians with a Greek grammar which was really suited to their needs. Like earlier Palaeologan scholars, he chose the form of a catechism (hence the standard title, *Erôtêmata*, i.e. 'Questions'). But if the form was traditional, the content was new. It had long been known that the Greek nouns could be grouped into far fewer than 56 declensions, if they were arranged by their genitive rather than their nominative endings. But earlier grammarians had made nothing of this principle. Chrysoloras built his grammar upon it. He reduced the nouns to ten classes: four of nouns that did not receive extra syllables in the genitive (parisyllables) and six of those that did (imparisyllables). He thus produced a less comprehensive but far more accessible textbook, which was more than adequate for the needs of the

Italian pupil, Jacopo Angeli da Scarperia, for whom he composed it in Constantinople. He brought the work with him to Italy. His pupils not only read but copied it, which helped them to master its contents. Guarino later made an abridgment that proved even more popular than Chrysoloras' already short original.[9]

Chrysoloras' political efforts, like those of his imperial masters, failed. Constantinople fell in 1453. But paradoxically the fall only heightened the success of his cultural initiative. The supply of men and books in Italy was greatly increased. Byzantine émigrés took posts at Padua, Ferrara and elsewhere. Two of them, Constantine Lascaris and Theodore Gaza, composed elementary grammars of their own on the lines laid down by Chrysoloras. By the 1470s, therefore, it was not hard to find a textbook, and in three or four Italian cities one could even hope to find a teacher.

But the provision of reasonable textbooks and a few teachers was only half the battle. Consider the character of the early textbooks. Highly compressed in style, composed in Greek and available only in manuscript, they offered little more than definitions of the parts of speech and endless paradigms. They presented no general rules to account for the radical changes in the stems of nouns and verbs in the course of declension. They taxed the reader's skill and patience with their script, which bristled with abbreviations and contractions. And they said nothing whatever about syntax. Few pupils could build on such meagre foundations. In fact the authors of *Erôtêmata* did not intend their works to be complete and sufficient introductions to Greek. Lascaris explained that his own *Epitomê* had been designed only to meet the needs of Italians, who, 'since they are Latin-speaking, and, being grown up, have to live with their fellow-countrymen, cannot learn our language from the ancient grammars'.[10] To fill a few of the gaps that the *Epitomê* left, he composed brief supplementary textbooks on the rules for the behaviour of nouns and verbs and on syntax. Gaza, similarly, included a treatment of syntax in his grammar.

From the standpoint of pupils, however, what mattered was not just that such supplementary works should be composed but that they should be fused with the introductory grammars into self-sufficient, widely-available textbooks. This fusion did take place. But it was less the work of scholars than of Greek, Italian and German printers. If we follow the development of one grammar – Lascaris' – over its first fifty years in print, we can observe the growth of a coherent first course in Greek in one volume, and thus some of the changes experienced by students. In particular, we learn that short-term

[9] We follow the fundamental article by A. Pertusi, 'ERÔTÊMATA. Per la storia e le fonti delle prime grammatiche greche a stampa', *IMU* 5 (1962), 321-51. See also S. Bernardinello, 'Gli studi propedeutici di greco del grammatico padovano Pietro da Montagnana', *Quaderni per la storia dell'Università di Padova* 9-10 (1976-7), 103-28.

[10] Constantine Lascaris, *Peri onomatos kai rhêmatos* (Vicenza, 1489), *epilogos*; reprinted by R. Proctor, *The Printing of Greek in the Fifteenth Century* (Oxford, 1900), 207-8.

changes were not always for the better. For close attention to the texts reveals not so much a march forwards as a perverse minuet for salesmen and scholars, liars and braggarts, danced to the tune of 'two steps forward, one step back'. We will not be inclined to exaggerate the speed with which students' lives were actually made easy.

Here are the main points, presented schematically:

1476   D. Paravisinus published the first edition of Lascaris' *Epitomê*. He wisely chose a clear type with almost no abbreviations. But he added no translation, explanatory notes, or supplementary material.[11]

1480   Bonus Accursius, a Milanese entrepreneur, reprinted the Greek *Epitomê*. He also induced a friend, Giovanni Crastone, to translate it into Latin, and printed original and translation in parallel columns, making the text accessible to anyone literate.[12]

1489   A Vicenza printer repeated Accursius' edition, adding the Greek text of Lascaris' short work on nouns and verbs (but not translating it, and producing a text full of blunders).

1495   Aldus Manutius, a teacher turned printer who was soon to become the most original and ambitious of all scholar-publishers, published his first version of Lascaris. From the standpoint of completeness he moved backwards, for he omitted the textbook on nouns and verbs. But from a student's or a reader's point of view his version is much improved. First, he added a brief introduction to the Greek alphabet, which explained the sounds of the Greek letters, tabulated their forms, and showed how to transliterate them into Latin: 'A α makes an *a* as ʼΑΛΛΑ᾽ ἀλλὰ *alla*; ʼΑΓΑΘΟΣ ἀγαθὸς *agathos*; Β β makes a *v* as ΒΑΡΒΑΡΟΣ βάρβαρος *varvaros*'.[13] Secondly, he added a selection of simple Greek texts with Latin translations – enough, at any rate, to give the buyer some practice in applying his new knowledge (though the grammatical section of the work did not explain how to construe or to construct an ordinary sentence). The reader was to start with short, simple passages, whose Latin versions he already knew: the Lord's Prayer, and the beginning of the Gospel of John. Then he should advance to the longer, highly moral poems traditionally attributed to Pythagoras and Phocylides. Aldus claimed to base the Greek text of his grammar on a manuscript specially corrected by Lascaris; in fact he followed Accursius' text for the most part. He claimed to have added a Latin translation 'on his own initiative'; in fact he reproduced a slightly altered version of Crastone's Latin – and omitted any mention of Crastone.[14]

[11] Lascaris, *Epitomê* (Milan, 30 January 1476; repr. Amsterdam, 1966); cf. the introduction by J.J. Fraenkel to the reprint.

[12] *BMC* vi, 756. Accursius writes: '*cum mea opera et studio vir Venerabilis et graece et latine doctissimus Iohannes monachus Placentinus verterit in latinum Erotemata Constantini Lascaris, rem mea sententia iis perutilem, qui graecae litteraturae peritiam assequi cupiunt ...*'. On Accursius see Proctor, *The Printing of Greek*, 59 ff.

[13] *Constantini Lascaris Erotemata cum interpretatione latina* (Venice, 1494-5), *Alphabetum Graecum cum multiplicibus literis*, fol. A iiii[r].

[14] Aldus claims that his text is improved '*in locis circiter centum et quinquaginta*' thanks to his

1502 Aldus filled the main gap in his earlier Lascaris by bringing out a second edition which included the short works on nouns and verbs and on syntax, both with Latin translations facing the Greek. The treatise on syntax was especially helpful. It was not brilliant or original; like most others, it organised the verbs not by their functions but by the cases of the nouns that preceded and followed them. But it did at least provide simple sentences as illustrations: 'The second form of active verbs requires before it a subject in the nominative and after it an object in the dative, as: *ho sophos Aldos ta megista boêthei tois philellêsin entupôn ta biblia.* ('Aldus the wise greatly benefits lovers of Greece by printing books.')'[15] At last teachers and students had a stock of phrases on which to ring changes as their classes progressed.

1510 Now that Aldus had arrived at a coherent and almost self-contained textbook, the Ferrarese publisher Maciochus entered the field with a competitive version, one which combined willingness to pilfer useful matter with total blindness to the needs of beginning students. On the one hand, Maciochus kept all the Greek texts and Latin versions that Aldus had assembled. On the other, he omitted Aldus' brief and well-organised introduction to the alphabet and put in its place a much longer treatise full of whimsical rhapsodising about the mystical powers of the Greek letters.[16]

1512 Aldus came out with a still larger corpus, which included everything his earlier editions had contained and, in addition, three Greek treatises on the ancient dialects (one of which was given twice over by mistake). In an interesting additional note he pointed out that the Byzantine pronunciation – the one followed in his own treatment of the alphabet – was quite different from that described by ancient scholars.[17] This insight he did not develop in the body of the work, which still followed traditional principles.

1515 The Giunti reprinted Aldus' final version. B. Giunti noted in the forward that '*We added* the golden verses of old Pythagoras, which deserve to be taken deeply to heart ... nor *did I hesitate to insert* the lovely poem of Phocylides'. This edition was reprinted at least once.[18]

'*emendatum manu ipsius Constantini librum*'. As to the translation, he writes '*Interpretationem vero latinam e regione addidimus arbitratu nostro, rati commodius utiliusque futurum graece discere incipientibus.*' Cf. M. Lowry, *The World of Aldus Manutius* (Oxford, 1979), 224-5, for the true story. For the full texts of Aldus' prefaces – and a very important introduction to his work by C. Dionisotti – see *Aldo Manuzio editore*, ed. G. Orlandi (Milan, 1976).

[15] *Constantini Lascaris Byzantini de octo partibus orationis* (Venice, c. 1502), De constructione liber, fol. A ii[v].

[16] *Constantini Lascaris Institutiones universae cum plurimis auctariis nuperrime impressae, tanta diligentia et rerum copia quanta nunquam alias* (Ferrara, 1510); the treatise on the alphabet is by Baptista Piso.

[17] *In hoc libro haec habentur. Constantini Lascaris de octo partibus orationis lib. I ...* (Venice, 1512); for Aldus' views on pronunciation see I. Bywater, *The Erasmian Pronunciation of Greek and its Predecessors* (Oxford, 1908).

[18] Giunti wrote in his ep. ded. to P. Vettori: '*Addidimus his quoque antiquissimi Pythagorae aurea*

1516   Th. Martin of Louvain printed a Greek-Latin Lascaris that omitted all the supplementary material Aldus had assembled.

1521   M. Sessa reprinted the final Aldine edition. In a preface he noted that 'We have added a splendid little work on dialects'.[19]

From 1521 the final Aldine corpus was the normal Lascaris, and from then on most standard Greek grammars – both reprintings of Byzantine ones and original works by Europeans – followed the same pattern, including treatments of syntax and basic reading passages as well as parts of speech and paradigms.

From the story of Lascaris' *Epitomê* three conclusions can be drawn. First, as printers and scholars collaborated, they did manage to produce a comprehensive, structured and accessible Greek course in one volume. Any determined student who knew Latin could read and understand the final version, if not necessarily master it. And, being the fittest, it outlived its less well-equipped rivals – for example, the 1510 edition with its paens to α and β. Secondly – and here it becomes possible to draw an interesting analogy with modern practices – neither printers nor scholars were satisfied with the modest improvements that were made in any single edition. Instead, they made wild claims to originality, mingling hyperbole with open untruth. Aldus, in the preface to his 1495 Lascaris, claimed that his Greek text had been improved by the use of Lascaris' own manuscript and that his Latin translation was original with him; as we saw, both claims were untrue. In 1515 his rivals the Giunti repaid him in the same coin. They claimed to have 'added' the poems of Phocyclides and Pythagoras to the grammar proper; in fact they were merely reprinting the reading selections which Aldus had already put together. Sessa's claim in 1521 to have 'added a splendid little work on dialects' was equally empty; the new 'work' was nothing more than the old treatises on dialects that Aldus had already inserted into his corpus. Neither Giunti nor Sessa mentioned Aldus' name, though both retained the tell-tale sample sentence about 'wise Aldus' in Lascaris' syntax. Like modern publishers, then, the pioneers of textbook marketing were not above selling their works over blurbs which made extravagant claims. Clearly we should not regard their aims as wholly idealistic.

The third conclusion is even more negative. It is simply that the utility of a survey like this is necessarily limited. We have seen a good textbook take form. But we still do not know how it was used in the classroom. After all, an ingenious teacher can make almost any book perform an astonishing array of tricks while a mediocre teacher can find even the best book hopeless. To know what it was really like to learn Greek from such books we must turn to more

---

carmina, intimis prorsus cordis penetralibus reponenda ... Neque etiam Phocillidis pulcherrimum inserere poema, dubitavi.'

[19] Sessa wrote in his ep. headed '*Studiosis*': '*Addidimus etiam de linguis aureum sane opusculum ...*'

direct products of school life.

One surviving commentary on a Greek grammar seems to be a very frank record of classroom practice; though it was printed, its spontaneity and lack of polish strongly suggest that it resembles a stenographic transcript. This is the work of the Ferrarese humanist L. Ponticus Virunius – who, as a good citizen of Ferrara, chose to lecture on Guarino's version of Chrysoloras' grammar. A few passages of his commentary will reveal something of the alchemy which transformed textbooks into usable instruction:

> The *Erôtêmata* of Chrysoloras. Into how many categories are the twenty-four letters divided? Into two: into vowels and consonants. There are seven vowels: *a e ê i o u ô*. Of these two are long, that is *ê* and *ô*. How many are short? Two, that is, *e* and *o*.[20]

Virunius takes this section as a whole and translates it word for word. Then he explains it, informally, and at great length:

> *eis* (into). It is the teacher who is speaking here. *diairountai* (are divided). Be of good cheer and do not ask me right now how this is declined; you will know how to do it yourselves later on. You should note that whenever *n* falls before *t* then the *t* is pronounced as *d* to make a sweeter sound – for example *antônios* [is pronounced] *andognios* … *ta* (the) has no meaning. The Greeks use articles for this reason: just as we say in the genitive *poetae del*, in the dative *poetae al* [using the Italian articles to distinguish between the identical genitive and dative of Latin *poeta*], the Greeks use the articles that mean *el, dal, al*. It also sometimes means 'some' as in *ta men philô, ta de kai kataleipô* that is, 'Some I love, but some I abandon'. *eis duo* (into two). This is the answer of the student who does not waste time in school when his teacher is lecturing, but takes notes, writes everything down very carefully, and therefore, being well taught, answers questions very well.[21]

Virunius keeps up this discursive, even logorrhoeic style throughout the series of lessons, even when dealing with the most important technical points. Here, for example, is Guarino/Chrysoloras on the distinction between parisyllables and imparisyllables:

---

[20] *Erotemata Guarini cum multis additamentis, et cum commentariis latinis* (Ferrara, 1509), fol. A iii^r.

[21] Ibid., *Pontici Virunii declarationes quaedam*, fols. 14^v-15^r: 'TRADVCTIO *ad verbum*. Eis posa. *In quot dividuntur viginti quattuor litterae? in duo, in vocales, et in consonantes, vocales quidem sunt septem*, a e ê i o *parvum*, u *tenue, et* ô. *magnum, ex quibus duae quidem sunt longae sicut* ê *et* ô *magnum, breves autem duae sunt* e *tenue et* o *parvum*. eis *est autem praeceptor, qui nunc loquitur*. diairountai, *esto bono animo, et noli nunc quaerere quomodo declinatur, quoniam postea scies per te ipsum. est advertendum quotiens* n *est ante* t *tunc pronunciatur pro* d, *ad sonum dulciorem, ut* antônios, andognios, *immo sono medio inter* d *et* t *meditare, ut* pente legontai.ta *nihil facit, nam graeci ponunt articulos propter has causas, sicuti dicimus in genitivo poetae del, in dactivo poetae al, graeci ponunt illos articulos, qui* el, del, al *significant, et aliquando partim significat, ut* ta men philô, ta de kai kataleipô, *id est, partim quidem amo, partim autem etiam relinquo*. … eis duo. *est responsio discipuli, qui non nugatur in schola, quando praeceptor legit, sed notat, scribit diligenter omnia, et ideo doctus doctissime respondit* …'

Of nouns, some are declined as parisyllables, such as *Aineias, Aineiou*. Others are imparisyllables, such as *Aias, Aiantos*.[22]

And here is Virunius:

> The Greeks considered that all nouns that exist in the entire world can be divided into two categories: for they either grow in the genitive or do not grow. Therefore they put all the nouns that do not grow into four declensions. Those that grow in the genitive, however, they put into one declension, namely the fifth. And each declension resembles a monastery of friars, so well are they ruled.[23]

The language of this passage is typical. Virunius thought by association of striking images. His expositions, accordingly, swarm with lively metaphors. He kept up the metaphor of the monastery throughout his explanations of the individual declensions:

> The first declension, like a sort of monastery, has its own constitutions and privileges. The first is that all must be masculine who enter this declension. For only masculines are declined here; this is Mount Athos, in Italian, *monte sancto*, the community where no female creature is found. They probably have an inscription over the gate: 'Let no female cross our threshold.' The second privilege is that they do not grow in the genitive, since that is their primary badge of rank. Third, that their genitive singulars always end in *ou*. Fourth, that they have only two endings, *as ês*, because those friars don't want much work ... In the second declension only female nouns are declined. For the women are angry with the men, because the men threw the women out of the first declension, saying, 'Let no female cross our threshold.' And the women say 'No men allowed here. *Procul ite profani.*' But they steal their husbands' endings.[24]

What Virunius was trying to do is quite clear. In the first place, he expounded every point at great length, returning over the same ground two or three times. Thus the clipped Greek of the original becomes discursive and

---

[22] *Erotemata Guarini*, fol. A iii[v]:

[23] Ibid., *Pontici Virunii declarationes quaedam*, fols. 31[v]-32[r]: '*Quare graeci contemplantes, quod omnia nomina, quae sunt in toto mundo, dupliciter habentur, nam vel crescunt in genitivo, vel non crescunt, cum ita sit, ea quae non crescunt omnia in quattuor regulis locaverunt. Quae autem nomina in genitivo crescunt, in una tantum regula posuerunt, scilicet in quinta, et una quaeque regula videtur esse unum monasterium fratrum, tam bene regulantur*'.

[24] Ibid., fols. 32[v]-33[r], 37[r]: '... *Ista igitur prima declinatio tamquam quoddam monasterium habet suas constitutiones et privilegia; primum est, quod omnes sint masculi, qui debent ingredi hanc primam declinationem. Nam non declinantur hic, nisi masculina, est mons Athos, vulgo monte sancto, istud coenobium, ubi foemineum nullum animal reperitur. Habent fortassis carmen supra portam. Nostrum non intrat foemina limen. Secundum privilegium est quod non crescunt in genitivo, quoniam ista est prima eorum dignitas. Tertio quod eorum genitivi singulares semper terminantur in* ou. *Quarto quod habeant nisi duas terminationes quia volunt paucum officium isti fratres, as* ês ... *In hac ii. decli. declinantur solummodo nomina foeminina. Sunt enim mulieres viris iratae, quia viri pepulerunt eas de prima decli., dicentes, nostrum non intrat foemina limen, et mulieres dicunt, hic non licet esse mares, procul ite profani. Tamen furantur maritorum suorum terminationes* ...*'

accessible in a way that the straight printed text could never be. Where Guarino/Chrysoloras merely stated the difference between parisyllables and imparisyllables, Virunius explained the point at length and took care to show that it could serve as the basis for mastering the Greek nouns. In the second place, he used the Greek text of the grammar itself as the basis for teaching a vast number of points that Guarino/Chrysoloras omitted. Complex problems such as the parsing of the verb *diairountai* he postponed. But every conceivable simple point of pronunciation, grammar or syntax, the different sounds of *n*, the different functions and meanings of the article, he took up at length, so that the bare rules of Greek grammar served as model sentences in their own right, teaching the student far more than their author had intended. Thus a year's reading of a grammar became a year's introduction to syntax as well. Finally, he spiced this already rich stew of facts and principles with far-fetched metaphors and comic patter, which not only kept the students' attention but also fixed salient points in their memories. The student who worked through a grammar with Virunius really did learn much more than he could have done by simply reading the printed text on his own.

Whether Virunius' tricks were normal – in so far as any teaching method can be described as 'normal' in the period – is not clear. He himself boasted that 'nobody ever made more jokes while teaching' than he did.[25] But we suspect that his manipulation of the Greek text of his grammar was not unusual. Clenardus, the author of the standard sixteenth-century grammar, advised teachers to use their texts in this way, and a copy of Book I of Theodore Gaza's grammar, now in the Gennadius Library in Athens, contains two sets of marginal notes that follow exactly the same pattern. Even the title becomes grist for the commentator's mill. On the words:

> Of Theodore's grammatical introduction, of the (books divided) into four, the first

a reader has written:

> In accordance with the norms of Attic, the dialect in which Theodore is writing, by the article 'the' we should understand the substantive 'books' and the adjective 'divided'. For the Attics frequently understand the substantive from the article.[26]

Gaza's account of the article (literally, 'It does not have no vocative'; properly, 'It has no vocative') provoked another excursus into syntactical teaching, also recorded in the margin: 'Note here that the Greeks use two negatives to form

---

[25] Ibid., fol. 34^r: '.*Nemo unquam fuit, qui maiores sales, et maiores facecias loquatur docendo.*'

[26] Theodore Gaza, *Grammaticae institutionis liber primus* (Basel, 1516): MS note in Gennadius copy: '*Intelligitur ex articulo more attico in qua lingua scribit iste theodorus substantivum librorum et adiectivum divisorum. nam hoc frequens est atticis ut ex articulo substantivum intelligant.*'

a negation.'[27]

Greek grammar as taught in the West, then, was the Byzantine version of the subject made more compact and less rigorous. For a century after Chrysoloras began it, the process of dilution was continued by scholars, teachers and printers. By 1510, when Aldus was printing and Virunius was teaching, they combined – in practice if not in theory – the separate fields of grammar and syntax, excised hundreds of unnecessary details and distinctions, and applied a sugar-coating to the material that remained.

But naturally grammars were not enough, however intensively teachers used them. To learn Greek the student had to read Greek texts. These too had to be selected, printed and provided with an apparatus that would make them accessible.

The range of Greek texts fit for teaching was not large. Most of them had been favourites in the Byzantine schools, which relied on anthologies of short 'teachable' works – a book of Homer, one play each by Sophocles, Euripides and Aristophanes, some Pindar and Theocritus.[28] Especially in the sixteenth century, the student often began with the Greek New Testament. Then he might read Aesop; then simple prose passages from the *Moralia* of Plutarch, the dialogues of Lucian, the speeches of Demosthenes and Isocrates, or simple verse from Homer, Hesiod or Theognis. Aristophanes would be his introduction to Greek drama; sometimes he might also read bits of tragedy, and sometimes a bit of Theocritus or Pindar. Often he would read epigrams from the *Anthology*.

These, at all events, are the authors who recur in our sources. When Demetrius Chalcondyles began to teach Greek at Padua – so Hartmann Schedel's notes tell us – he chose Hesiod as the first text to follow the *Erôtêmata*. When Varino Camerte taught at Florence in the 1490s, he used Homer and Aristophanes as basic readings. And when François Tissard put out the first Greek texts ever printed in France, in order to provide a basis for his own lectures *c.* 1507, he printed the mock-Homeric *Battle of the Frogs and Mice*, Hesiod's *Works and Days* and Chrysoloras' grammar.[29]

What is less clear is the effect of printing on the choices and methods of teachers. We know that a large number of ephemeral editions, pamphlet-sized and unpretentious, were run off to meet students' needs. But we also know that supply and demand were by no means in balance. Camerte's students at

---

[27] Ibid., fol. I 3ʳ: MS note in Gennadius copy: '*Hic adverte grecos duabus negationibus negare.*'

[28] On late Byzantine school anthologies see R. Browning, 'Homer in Byzantium', *Viator* 6 (1975), 15-33; 16-18.

[29] On Chalcondyles see D.J. Geanakoplos, *Interaction of the 'Sibling' Byzantine and Western Cultures in the Middle Ages and Italian Renaissance* (New Haven and London, 1976), 296; on Camerte see G. Pozzi, 'Da Padova a Firenze nel 1493', *Italia medioevale e umanistica* 9 (1966), 193; on Tissard see J. Paquier, *Jérôme Aléandre* (Paris, 1900), 36-7.

Florence did not all have copies of his texts.[30] As late as 1524 Philip
Melanchthon had to make his Wittenberg students write out copies of his
own printed Demosthenes before he could begin to lecture on it.[31] And as
late as 1572 students in the Collège de Reims in Paris were trying to follow
Claude Mignault's lectures on Demosthenes on the basis of printed texts that
disagreed with the one he was using, so that his parsings did not fit the verbs
in front of them;[32] Evidently, then, printers did not always provide teachers
and students with the texts they wanted. Given that the available evidence is
spotty – and that much of it has not been studied – we cannot say for certain
whether the balance of successes and failures changed over time.

Yet we can point to some central features of the situation. In the first place,
it was not the great critical editions of Greek authors – the Aldine Aristotle
and the like – that students bought. These vast series were a drug on the
market. What students could afford and understand were small-format,
Greek-Latin editions of short texts. And these were the staple of university
Greek printers from Bonus Accursius – who pioneered in this field with a
bilingual Aesop – onwards.[33] Tissard, running off texts for his Greek lectures
in Paris, naturally chose the *Battle of the Frogs and Mice* and Hesiod's *Works
and Days*. Only texts like these were appropriate to Gourmont's printing-shop,
which could only provide Greek letters with accents and breathings by placing
them on a separate line above, and only texts like these were appropriate to his
students, who had not even read a basic grammar when he began to lecture
on easy texts.[34] Girolamo Aleandro, following Tissard as both teacher and
printer of Greek, ordered some Lucians from Aldus and printed a few tracts of
Plutarch on his own. The limit of his ambition was to print and lecture on
selections from each of the major Greek authors; and this he never carried
out.[35] Other printers concentrated on anthologies of easy reading: a few
fables, Hesiod and the *Frogs and Mice*. One could not wax fat on this diet.
Most students could hardly have carried away much sense of the range,
diversity and historical development of Greek literature. Many of them read
little more than the basic texts appended to their grammar; the texts required

[30] Camerte's student R. Amaseo heard lectures on Aristophanes' *Plutus* and Homer; of the
former he writes (Pozzi, 'Da Padova a Firenze', 193), '*tot autem versus exaravimus quot per aliquot dies
mihi suppeditarentur ad auditionem*'; of the latter, '*iam autem viginti dies sunt transacti quibus in audiendo
Homero sine libro consumo, adhaerens in ludo aliis auditoribus.*'

[31] U. Schindel, *Demosthenes im 18. Jahrhundert* (Munich, 1963), 9.

[32] A.T. Grafton, 'Teacher, text and pupil in the Renaissance class-room: a case study from a
Parisian college', *History of Universities* 1 (1981), 37-70; 67 n. 49.

[33] Proctor, *The Printing of Greek*, 61 and plate XVIII.

[34] F.R. Walton, 'The Greek book, 1476-1825', *Dixième congrès international des bibliophiles*
(Athens, 1979), 31-2.

[35] See Aleandro's ep. ded. in *Quae hoc libro comprehensa sint: Plutarchi Chaeronei de virtute, et vitio ...*
(Paris, 1509), unpag.: '*Huius [= Aldi] praeclaris inventis haec quae faciunt impressores nostri non adsurgant
modo velim, verum etiam eo a nobis animo suscepta credantur, ut haec ad ea, quae apud Aldum imprimuntur,
facilius evolvenda rudibus quasi viam substernant.*' A long extract is translated in Paquier, *Jérôme
Aléandre*, 65-6.

by the statutes of many English grammar schools are those found in snippets in the appendices to Clenardus.[36] The main effect of printing, then, was to make a very small range of texts available to a great many student readers.

In the second place, pagan texts continued to form the centre of most courses. A few teachers tried to change this emphasis. Clenardus produced as an appendix to his grammar a set of *Meditationes Graecanicae* in which he subjected a Christian text – a letter of the Church Father Basil – to word-by-word parsing, analysis and literal and literary translation; this was meant to be a Christian basis for Greek teaching.[37] But his zeal had little reward. He himself imagined his students as complaining that he 'taught nothing but grammatical rules and something from Chrysostom, on whom he lectured as if he were not teaching but giving a sermon'.[38] And a French scholar soon provided an appendix of secular texts – snippets from Homer, Aristophanes, Hesiod, Euripides, Theocritus and Pindar, to accompany Clenardus' *Meditationes* for the benefit of those unwilling to submerge themselves in Christian Greek.[39]

In the third place, teachers chose among the available pagan texts on highly pragmatic grounds. To read the educational theorists, one would think that teachers chose the books that would make their students Christian activists and, at the same time, introduce them to the ancient world *as it really was*. To watch a teacher looking for appropriate texts is to enter quite a different world. When a friend of Clenardus, teaching Greek at Salamanca, wrote that he was thinking of teaching Demosthenes *On the Crown*, Clenardus urged him to reconsider.

> The speech is long, and there are others that you might be able to teach without boring the students so much. They do like short texts. I cannot understand why you do not teach Plato's *Laws*, since you have fifty copies of it. It is easier, and more fun, and would get you more students. Besides, I do not think that you have fifty copies of the Demosthenes there. Do not worry about the size of the work. You only have to teach one or two books of it.[40]

[36] M.L. Clarke, *Classical Education in Britain, 1500-1900* (Cambridge, 1959), 19 and 186.

[37] N. Clenardus, *Meditationes Graecanicae, in artem Grammaticam* (Louvain, 1531); there were several subsequent editions, which are normally bound with copies of Clenardus' grammar, *Institutiones in linguam Graecam* (Louvain, 1531), which was also often reprinted.

[38] N. Clenardus, *Epistolarum libri duo* (Hanau, 1606), 152-3 [= *Correspondance*, ed. A. Roersch, 3 vols. (Brussels, 1940-41), I, 39]: '*Fuerat hic nuper Clenardus, et suspicabamur principio mira, sed nihil contulit praeter Grammaticos canones, et nescio quid ex Chrysostomo, quem sic interpretabatur, ut concionem potius habere videretur, quam professorum munus agere ...*'

[39] We consulted the edition of 1564: P. Antesignanus [Davantes], *Praxis seu usus praeceptorum grammatices Graecae* (Lyons, 1564), bound with the Lyon 1564 edition of Clenardus' *Institutiones*.

[40] Clenardus, *Epistolae*, 176 [= *Correspondance*, I, 73]: '*Oratio longa est, et alias forte minore discipulorum taedio queas enarrare: amant enim opuscula parva. Sed hic mirari subit, cum habeas Platonis in legibus quinquaginta exemplaria, cur non eum potius interpretaris, qui et facilior est, et iucundior, et auditorium redderet frequentius: neque enim puto illic quinquaginta esse Demosthenes. Nec tamen libri magnitudine absterreri debes, cum satis fuerit unum atque alterum librum exponere.*'

This is the language of classroom pragmatism with which any practising teacher would be familiar. The choice of texts should reflect the tastes of one's students ('they do like short texts') and the resources of one's university bookseller ('I do not think that you have fifty copies of the Demosthenes there'). Anyone who advises a friend to teach Plato's *Laws* because it is easy, fun and a good draw is not seriously worried about the content of his texts. Yet, as we have seen, Clenardus showed more concern with content than many of his rivals.

If teachers chose their texts on practical grounds, they were still free to interpret them as they liked in class. Most courses began with a brief 'argument', or summary of the text in question. Here some teachers took the time to infer moral or prudential lessons from their texts. But many of them contented themselves with giving the student a glimpse of the general drift of the text. Even the most scandalous myths were often summarised without comment. Here, for example, is how a French teacher (in the 1550s) dealt with Lucian's dialogue between Hermes and Pan:

> Pan was born of Mercury and Penelope. Mercury violated her when she had come to Taioeta to see to her father's flocks. When he saw her, he was inflamed with love. Transformed into a goat, he had his way with Penelope. That is how Pan was born. Others claim that Pan grew from the seed of all of Penelope's suitors. That is why Theocritus calls him *apatora* – that is, 'fatherless' – in the *Syrinx*; for he was born of an unknown father.[41]

Renaissance mythographers usually extracted a seemly allegorical kernel from such stories of goats and semen; in the case of Penelope and her suitors, they tended to argue that the story was both scientifically implausible and morally uncharacteristic of Penelope. What is revealing about this teacher is precisely that he did not resort to allegory or denial. Others plumped with equal decisiveness for a moral or allegorical reading: so Dorat, for example, elaborately analysed the Odyssey as the story of man's search for wisdom and happiness.[42]

Allegorists and literalists alike had to spend far more of their time on the text proper than on these general introductions. The best way to approach their work is through a sample: some notes on the first lines of the *Iliad*, dictated in Florence by Andronicus Callistus and probably taken down by

---

[41] MS note by M. De Garaud of Toulouse (probably entered after 1555) in his copy of *Luciani Samosatensis Dialogus de Sacrificiis* [*Dialogi deorum*, etc.] (Paris, 1550), British Library C.45.e.16(3), 33: '*Pan e Mercurio et Penelope natus est, cui stuprum optulit cum ad Taioeta progressa esset ut pecora paterna inviseret. Eam cum conspexisset Mercurius amore exarsit et in hircum mutatus cum Penelope rem habuit. Inde natus est Pan. Alii volunt crevitum eum esse ex semine omnium procorum Penelopae. Vnde eum Theocritus in fistula appellat eum apatora, id est sine patre, quod incerto patre natus sit.*' Cf. N. Comes, *Mythologiae sive explicationis fabularum libri decem* (ed. Padua, 1637), Book V, chapter 6, 242-8.

[42] P. de Nolhac, *Ronsard et l'humanisme* (Paris, 1921), 71-2.

Bartolomeo Fonzio. They begin with a word-for-word translation of the traditional heading of *Iliad* I:

> Alpha. Preces Chrisae. Pestem exercitus. Odium regum.

> (Book I. The prayers of Chryses; the plague of the army; the hatred of the kings)

along with the Greek original:

> ἄλφα λιτὰς Χρύσου λοιμὸν στρατοῦ ἔχθος ἀνάκτων

This is followed by a literal translation into Latin of the first eight lines of the text. Then comes the exegesis proper:

> This work is called a *rhapsôdia*, from *rhabdos*, the staff which the singers of Homer's verses used, or from *rhaptô*, 'sew' and 'assemble', because Homer's verses, which were scattered, were assembled and made into a coherent body by Peisistratus.

ἄλφα	is from *alphô* 'invent'.
λιτή-ῆς	prayer. We also call goddesses *litas*. Hence
λίσσομαι	the poetic word for 'pray'.
λοιμός-οῦ	plague.
ἔχθος-εος	hatred.
μηνίω	I hate. Hence
μῆνις	Lasting anger; it takes the accusatives *mênida* and *mênin*.
μηνύω	Make known and accuse. Hence
μηνυτής	informer and accuser.
ἀείδω	Sing, sometimes know.
Πηληίδης-ου	*o* and *u* are transformed into *eô*, the Ionic form, and an α is inserted, and the result is *Pêlêiadeô*. It is a patronymic from Peleus.
Ἀχιλεύς	Achilles is written with one l. For it is derived from *a* and *chilos*, that is, 'food', because he went without food, or from *achos*, that is, care.
ὄλλυμι	Destroy; the future is *olesô*, the Aorist middle is *olomên*; in Ionic, however, it is *oulomên*. The participle is *oulomenos-menê-on*, that is, 'destructive', though it can properly be both active and passive.
μύρια	Ten thousand.
μυρία	Innumerable.[43]

The direction of Callistus' efforts is clear enough. What interests him is teaching Greek. That is why he spends as much time on the words of the prose summary of the Homeric text as on the text proper; that is why his notes are

---

[43] Callistus taught in Florence *c.* 1471-5. These notes are reproduced from Florence, Bibl. Laurenziana, MS 66, 31, fol. 7ʳ by I. Maïer, *Ange Politien: la formation d'un poète humaniste* (Geneva, 1966), 58; we have used Maïer's transcription, ibid., 59, correcting it against her reproduction of the MS.

almost exclusively linguistic, concerned not with Homer's story but with the etymology of the name Achilles and the patronymic 'son of Peleus', the principal parts of the verb 'to destroy' and the range of meanings and derivatives of every word in the text. Even a fairly elementary set of lectures on a Latin text (such as Guarino's lectures on the *Ad Herennium* which we discussed in Chapter One) clearly presupposed much more knowledge and aimed to satisfy more elaborate needs.

The source of this method is equally clear. It is the direct descendant of the standard Byzantine exercise, the *epimerismos* or parsing, in which teacher and student paraphrased, parsed and etymologized every word of a short text.[44] Byzantine teachers took care, as Callistus does here, to make each text the basis for lexical instruction by piling up lists of all common words related to any word that crops up in the text proper.

What Fonzio's notes do not reveal is how Callistus went about conveying all this information to the student. But a collateral text enables us to reconstruct his manner as well as his matter. In 1493 (as we saw in Chapter Four), Girolamo Amaseo left Padua to study Greek in Florence. He learned the elements from Varino Favorino Camerte, who had studied with Politian, who in turn had studied with Callistus – and who thus probably followed a method like Callistus'. In an unusually vivid letter to his brother, Amaseo describes his Greek classes:

> This is how Varino sets out to instruct us. First he sets out the meaning of the passage briefly, clearly and elegantly [this is the literal translation with which Fonzio's notes on Callistus begin]. After the initial translation he works out the inflexion of the verbs and nouns, if it is difficult. He also deals with the etymology and the other figures. Then he goes through the reading again, and confirms and tests us all, so that we do not forget what he said before. And immediately after the lesson one of us explains the reading. We are made to give declensions, and we do not mind (for every study has its rude beginnings). He teaches the *Odyssey* in the morning, thirty verses; after lunch Aristophanes, only twenty verses; at the twenty-second hour the *Iliad*, forty verses ...

Amaseo's testimony shows that Callistus did not dictate his lesson without a break. Like Ponticus Virunius, though with less picaresque humour, he would have gone through the day's lesson two or three times. He would have asked questions and conducted drills. Thus his lessons would have been less uniform and dull than Fonzio's bare notes suggest. But they would have been almost entirely grammatical and lexical in content. For Amaseo's own boastful testimony shows that students received their teachers' implicit message clearly. A mechanical facility at construing was what they wished to attain:

---

[44] See e.g. Hunger, *Die hochsprachliche profane Literatur*, 22-9.

I understand Aristophanes so well that those who have been following the course for six months are not ashamed to consult me and have me explain the lesson we have heard, translating word for word.[45]

In the course of the sixteenth century the diffusion of printed texts changed the manner in which teachers carried on lessons and students recorded them. More students came to take their notes in printed copies of the texts they studied, entering translations in the spaces between the lines of Greek and scribbling the teacher's discursive remarks in the margins. The results, like the following example, taken down by J. Hager at Freiburg in 1559, have the look of polyglot hieroglyphs when first confronted:

                                           navigium
Exordium   Τί γελᾷς ὦ Χάρων, ἢ τί τὸ πορθμεῖον

                relinquens   rediisti   praesentem
ex abrupto   ἀπολιπών, δεῦρο ἀνελήλυθας ἐς τὴν πάρουσαν

                lucem
                ἡμέραν;

                        per   Iovem   chare Mercuriale
Antonomasia   ἀλλὰ πρὸς τοῦ πατρός, ὦ φίλτατον Ἑρμήδιον,

                deseras   expone
Atticismus   μὴ καταλίπῃς με. Περιήγησαι δὲ τά ἐν τῷ βίῳ

                                               scilicet ad
                        videns redeam   stygiam paludem
                ἅπαντα ὥς τι καὶ ἰδὼν ἐπανέλθοιμι ὡς ἦν με σὺ

---

[45] Pozzi (n. 29 above), 193: '*Hanc autem curam Guarinus ipse in nobis instruendis impendit: primo sententiam lectionis paucis et dilucide eleganterque colligit, post interpretationem primam verborum et nominum inflectionem, si duriuscula est, reperit, etimologiam non tacet et figuras reliquas; secundo eam ipsam lectionem percurrit et, ne quae prius dixerat obliviscamur, confirmat examinatque nos omnis et, post ipsam statim lectionem, aliquis e numero nostrum eam exponit: cogimur declinare, nec displicet (omnia enim studia suam habent infanciam). Legit mane Odysseam, versus autem triginta; post prandium Aristophanem, versus saltem viginti; vicesima secunda hora Iliadem, versus quadraginta.*' '*Aristophanem sic percipio ut qui iam sex menses audierunt se ad me conferre non erubescant: ut interpreter et auditam lectionem verbum e verbo transferens enucleem.*' Most lectures on Greek texts in the Renaissance seem to have been similarly restricted to lexical, etymological, syntactical and rhetorical analysis; cf. e.g. those of Marcus Musurus (a student of the Byzantine exile Lascaris) on the *Greek Anthology* (discussed by J. Hutton, *The Greek Anthology in Italy to the Year 1800* (Ithaca, NY, 1935), 156); those of the Parisian *lecteur royal* J. Toussaint on Musaeus, preserved in a copy of the Paris 1538 edition (Bibliothèque Nationale, Paris, shelf-mark Rés. Yb. 2200-2202); those of the greatest of the French Greek scholars, Jean Dorat, on the *Greek Anthology* and on Pindar (the former are discussed by J. Hutton, *The Greek Anthology in France and in the Latin Writers of the Netherlands to the Year 1800* (Ithaca, N.Y., 1946), 111-12; the latter are published by P. Sharratt, 'Ronsard et Pindare: un écho de la voix de Dorat', *Bibliothèque d'Humanisme et Renaissance* 39 [1977], 97-114). But this generalisation is highly tentative, and will have to be confirmed or refuted by far more detailed studies than are presently available.

dimiseris   a caecis   differam
a simili ἀφῇς, οὐδὲν τῶν τυφλῶν διοίσω. Καθάπερ γε ἐκεῖνοι

impingunt titubantes   tenebris   sane
σφάλλονται διολισθαίνοντες ἐν τῷ σκότῳ, οὕτω δὴ

hallucinor
caecus fio ad conspectum lucis

κἀγώ σοι πάλιν ἀμβλυώττω πρὸς τὸ φῶς. [46]

But decipherment reveals fairly meagre contents. In this case, Lucian's *Charon* – a dialogue in which Charon comes up from Hades to inquire why the souls he ferries are so sorry to leave the world above, and asks Hermes for guidance – is being dealt with much as Callistus dealt with Homer. The teacher, Th. Miileskius, translated the text. Hager clearly took down only the renderings of slightly difficult words, not those of the particles and conjunctions that he already knew. Hence the gaps in his Latin. Miileskius paraphrased where the meaning was not obvious. Where Charon asks Hermes to lead him 'so that I have seen something when I return', Miileskius expanded on the phrase: 'return, that is, to the Stygian swamp.' Finally, Miileskius subjected the piece to a rhetorical analysis, as if it were a speech or a student exercise. He identifies the opening ('Why are you laughing, Charon, and why have you left your ferry ...?') as an abrupt exordium; he calls attention to the figure of antonomasia ('by the father', for 'by Zeus') and to a simile ('just as [the blind] trip and stumble in the darkness, so I am blinded by the light'). Such were the tools – however blunt-edged they may seem – with which most Greek teachers attacked their materials. Even *The Battle of the Frogs and Mice* received this treatment, rhetorical analysis and all. Evidently, then, wider availability of texts did not result in more sophisticated methods of exegesis.

Naturally, teachers could expatiate and disagree on specific points. To N. Girard, teaching *Iliad* I in the 1560s, Hera's epithet 'golden-throned' in line 611 ('Then Zeus went up and slept, with Hera of the golden throne beside him') was not to be taken literally in that context:

Golden-throned: having a golden throne, that is, a powerful queen. Gold signifies elegance; the throne signifies royal power. Clearly those who are going

---

[46] Text and notes are reproduced from a Cologne, 1544 edition of Lucian's *Charon* now in the Gennadius Library, Athens (GC 4049-50). The passage quoted means: 'Hermes: "Why are you laughing, Charon, and why have you left your ferry and returned to the light of day?" ... Charon: "But by the father, dear Hermes, don't leave me. Explain to me the affairs of the living, so that I'll have seen something when I return. If you send me away, I'll be just like the blind. For as they trip and stumble about in darkness, so I am blinded [or dazed] by the light." '

to bed had no immediate use for a throne.[47]

An anonymous French teacher ten years later saw the same line as an elaborate physical allegory:

> Iuno means the air, Jupiter fire. But because the highest part of the air is near the aether, Juno is here called 'golden-throned'. Gold is here used for 'fire', because of the similarity of colour.[48]

But for our purposes what matters is that neither of them raised the level of his teaching above the level Callistus had already reached: a somewhat dilute version of what Byzantine masters had done. Indeed the allegory that the anonymous master found in line 611 was not his own discovery but that of the Byzantine scholar Eustathius of Thessalonica, from whose vast commentary on Homer it was doubtless quarried, and Girard's explanation is no more than an obvious back-formation from the text. Real learning continued to be imparted in comments on Latin texts.

As one would expect, Renaissance teachers tried to emulate their Byzantine predecessors in yet another respect: they tried to give their pupils an active command of classical Greek. To do so they printed and revised the late Byzantine lexica of acceptable words and phrases. Guillaume Budé produced an original and vastly influential treatise on Greek prose usage.[49] Johannes Posselius brought out detailed handbooks for Greek syntax and metre, illustrating every rule with copious examples, and giving Greek translations for every phrase that could imaginably form part of a composition.[50] Some even tried to teach their pupils to speak classical Greek. Reuchlin and others saw to the printing of the *Hermeneumata Pseudo-Dositheana*, the ancient bilingual schoolboy dialogues.[51] And Posselius wrote dialogues of his own with phrases to deal with all the trials of Renaissance school life:

> Boy: Reverend professor, teach me how to say in Greek, 'John gave me a beating.'
> Teacher: This is how to say it: *Iôannês etupte me.*

---

[47] N. Girard, *Meditationes in librum primum Iliados Homeri* (Paris, 1566), 104: 'Chrusothronos: chrusoun thronon echousa, *aureum thronum habens, id est, regina potens. Aurum elegantiam, thronus regiam dignitatem notat. Alioqui sane dormituris in lecto nullus est usus throni.*'

[48] Anonymous marginal note in the British Library copy of *Homeri Ilias, id est, de rebus ad Troiam gestis* [*Iliad* 1-3] (Paris, 1575), shelf-mark G 8633. 1, 23: '*Iuno aerem significat, Iupiter ignem; propter autem vicinitatem illam supremae aeris partis cum aethere, Iuno hic appellatur* chrusothronos, *aureum thronum habens. Aurum autem pro igne accipit propter coloris similitudinem.*'

[49] G. Budé, *Commentarii linguae Graecae* (Paris, 1529).

[50] J. Posselius, *Syntaxis ... Graeca* (Wittenberg, 1582); Posselius, *Calligraphia oratoria linguae Graecae* (Frankfurt, 1594).

[51] Cf. M. Anthon Jul. von der Hardt, *Ineditum Joannis Reuchlini ... Colloquium Graeco-Latinum, Anno 1489 Stutgardiae concinnatum* (Helmstadt, 1729); the colloquy – attributed in MSS to Julius Pollux, 2nd century A.D. – is printed in the 1516 Basel edition of Book I of Gaza's grammar.

Boy: Please, teacher, write down the forms of the Greek letters for me, so that I can imitate them by copying them.
Teacher: What did you do with the original that I wrote for you a few days ago?
Boy: I lost it carelessly. John tore it up.
Teacher: Look, here is another one. Take care that you do not lose it as well.[52]

Oddly enough, however, these expedients seem to have had little positive effect. At the beginning of the fifteenth century, the pioneers of Greek in Italy managed to write novel and distinctive works in their new language. Leonardo Bruni's Greek description of the Florentine constitution was both more penetrating and more frank than his works in Latin on the same theme.[53] Politian wrote elegant Greek epigrams, and Budé, some decades later, wrote learned Greek letters. But as Greek became a more regular part of the curriculum such original works ceased to be written in it. One might do short set pieces: the Tübingen MA candidates of the 1580s produced short essays in Greek on philosophical subjects, which they read aloud at their passing-out ceremony – no doubt to the unutterable boredom of their audiences.[54] But nothing like Bruni's essay on Florence was written once the lexica and grammars were widely available.

Greek, in short, ended the Renaissance in the position in which it first entered Italy: as a new subject, something on the margins of the curriculum. Individual Western scholars mastered Greek to a high level. But in the schools it never took the position that Salutati or Chrysoloras had hoped for. It remained an extra subject, something to be studied in one's spare time. This intellectual position is reflected in the institutional situation. Even at the height of enthusiasm for Greek philosophy in later fifteenth-century Italy few schools and universities offered continuous, coherent programmes of Greek studies. In 1493, Amaseo had to leave Padua if he wanted to learn Greek. And even in Florence he found a highly mixed group of fellow students:

> There are sixteen of us students, including the poet Naldi, who is fifty years old
> ... others forty years old, others thirty, others younger, others who are
> teen-aged ...[55]

This passage shows that even in Florence the demand for Greek was not enormous, and that even there no regular tradition of teaching existed (hence the wide variety of ages in one class). Aleandro felt that he would need only a

[52] J. Posselius, *Familiarium colloquiorum libellus* (London, 1660).

[53] N. Rubenstein, 'Florentine constitutionalism and Medici ascendancy in the fifteenth century', *Florentine Studies*, ed. N. Rubenstein (London, 1966), 447-8.

[54] Some examples in M. Crusius, *Germanograeciae libri sex* (Basel, 1586), Book III, 89-110. Greek plays were also performed by students on occasion; see e.g. Politian's description of a performance of Sophocles' *Electra* in 1493, starring Alessandra Scala (*Opera omnia*, ed. I. Maïer, III (Turin, 1971), 539-40, and chapter 2 above).

[55] Pozzi (n. 29 above), 193: '*Discipuli autem sedecim audimus, inter quos poeta Naldius, quinquagenarius ...; alii autem quadragenarii, alii triginta annorum, alii iuniores, alii ephebi ...*'

dozen copies of Lascaris for his Greek classes in Paris.[56] And even in the great grammar schools of mid-sixteenth-century France and England, Greek received far less time and far less rigorous treatment than Latin.

Yet in one respect Greek studies proved more fruitful than might be expected from their unfavourable position. Many teachers did enable their students to write, if not classical Greek, at least elegant Latin translations and adaptations from the Greek – works that could find a far readier market among patrons and professors. Guarino, for example, evidently taught his pupils to paraphrase Greek texts, piling up synonyms and making much play with elegant variation. The British Library has a set of translations from Aesop, made by his pupil Ermolao Barbaro in 1422 when he was twelve years old (BL MS Add. 33782).[57] Here the very schematic originals are transmuted into florid and eloquent set-pieces, as one sample will show:

> A fox that had never seen a lion, when by chance it met one, was at first so frightened that it almost died ... [Aesop]

Barbaro's paraphrase:

> A fox that had never seen a lion, and then by chance and the will of fortune met one, was at first so overcome with fear and terror that its soul almost fled with a wail to the realm of darkness ...[58]

By the end of the fifteenth century, the favourite exercise had become the translation and adaptation of Greek verse. The *Greek Anthology*, with its hundreds of lyrics and epigrams on every conceivable subject, was as appropriate a school text in the West as it had been in Byzantium. The émigré Janus Lascaris lectured on the *Anthology* and edited the text itself in 1494. Some shortened selections from it came into being, in which each Greek epigram might be accompanied by dozens of translations, adaptations, replies, and even paraphrases in Greek.[59] The most popular of these was Henri Estienne's *Epigrammata selecta* of 1570. Here (to give but one example) *AP* 11.431 ('If you are slow to run and fast to eat, run with your mouth and eat with your feet') is accompanied by a word-for-word Latin translation and no fewer than ten Latin versions by Estienne and others, which apply every possible resource of language – first strong active verbs, then adjectives, then

[56] Paquier, *Jérôme Aléandre*, 39. Aleandro also asked for six copies of a lexicon and six Lucians.

[57] Barbaro described his versions as done '*sub expositione* ... *Guarini*' (fol. 39ᵛ); according to Cencio de' Rustici, Chrysoloras used the word *exponere* to refer to the making of a loose paraphrase (R. Sabbadini, *Il metodo degli umanisti* (Florence, 1922), 23-4).

[58] London, British Library, MS Add. 33782, fols 7ᵛ-8ʳ: '*De Vulpe et Leone: Vulpes cum nondum leonem conspicata esset/deinde forte/et fortuna ita volente cum ipsi se obviam fecisset/primo quidem visu adeo timore et pavore confecta est/quod ferme eius vita cum gemitu fugit indignata sub umbras:* ...'

[59] See in general J. Hutton, op. cit.

compound nouns – rendering the same rather undistinguished witticism.[60]

It is not surprising that such exercises in Alexandrianism proved popular. By learning to adapt a Greek original in Latin the student picked up a socially and politically useful talent. When his sovereign died or his teacher published a book he could produce an epigram for the occasion that would be out of the ordinary – not because it was original, but precisely because it was conventional in an unusually stylish way. This sort of exercise became a most effective means (especially in England) to catch the attention of rulers and their classically-educated ministers.

Teachers of Latin texts whose pupils could read Greek did find their teaching opportunities enlarged. For they could teach the best Latin texts not only as rhetorical set-pieces but as masterpieces of imitation from the Greek. Emphasis on Virgil's imitation of Homer or Cicero's of Demosthenes helped one's pupils in their efforts to become stylish Latinists. And the teacher who could identify the more obscure Greek sources on which Roman poets and orators had drawn had yet another way of proving his superiority to the competition. Thus Politian, struggling to prove his excellence to his patrons the Medici, emphasised in his lectures his great skill at unravelling the tangled web of Roman allusion to Greek sources.[61] To that extent at least, the original hopes of Salutati and Chrysoloras were fulfilled. Greek learning was preserved and adapted to fill the needs of a predominantly Latin culture.

[60] H. Estienne, *Epigrammata Graeca selecta ex Anthologia* (n.p., 1570), 274-5;

INTERPR. AD VERBVM

Si celer ad comedendum et ad cursum tardus es,
Pedibus tuis comede, et curre ore.

Estienne's versions:

Quum pedibus tardus, quum sis celer ore vicissim,
Ore tuo curras, at pedibus comedas.

Si tarde curris, sed edis velociter, ore
Curre tuo posthac, at pedibus comede.

Tu qui currendo segnis, non segnis edendo,
Fac currant dentes, fac comedantque pedes.

Quum cursor sis tardus, edo sis impiger idem,
Os tibi fac cursor, fac tibi pes sit edo ...

Dens tibi sit cursor, sit pes edo. nanque remissus
Pes tibi, dente autem quadrupedante voras ...

Tardipes es nimium, nimiumque es dentibus acer:
Tardivorus pede sis, denteque tardigradus.

Similar efforts were made to naturalise some of the peculiar devices of Greek prose composition in Latin; see M. Baxandall, *Giotto and the Orators* (Oxford, 1971), 78-96, for a detailed case study.

[61] See e.g. his *Commento inedito alle Selve di Stazio*, ed. L. Cesarini Martinelli (Florence, 1978), 135-6, 183-4, etc.

CHAPTER SIX

Northern Methodical Humanism:
From Teachers to Textbooks

We argued in our opening chapter for a more considered assessment of the actual impact of the humanism of the school of Guarino on culture and society of the early fifteenth century. We suggested that in spite of the high ideals of individual figures associated with the humanist movement in Italy, fewer people were directly affected by those ideals than modern scholars have claimed. The direct impact of humanism, we argued, was in producing growing numbers of people fluent in the ancient languages, rather than in any perceptible results of the 'moral training' or 'preparation for life', supposed to be provided by humanism. In this chapter we shall argue from almost exactly the opposite point of view for the widespread influence of the works and reputations of Rudolph Agricola and Desiderius Erasmus.[1] We shall observe how certain names are used to recall entire sets of pedagogic and ideological commitments, and give rise to such ultimately vague notions as 'Erasmian method' or 'Agricolan dialectic'.

The different approach in this chapter is dictated by the altered circumstances of humanism and its influence on education in the late-fifteenth and sixteenth centuries. It is also a consequence of the different nature of the impact on the *secondary* literature on humanism (now labelled 'Christian humanism') of the charismatic individuals of this period.

---

[1] On the Europe-wide dissemination of the works and reputation of Agricola, see W.J. Ong, *Ramus, Method, and the Decay of Dialogue* (Cambridge, Mass., 1958) and *Ramus and Talon Inventory* (Cambridge, Mass., 1958), 534-58; C. Vasoli, *La dialettica e la retorica dell'Umanesimo: "Invenzione" e "Metodo" nella cultura del XV e XVI secolo* (Milan, 1968), 147-82; *Profezia e ragione: Studi sulla cultura del Cinquecento e del Seicento* (Naples, 1974), passim. Erasmus' enormous reputation and influence are at once generally acknowledged and (because his theological works were placed on the Index) often unascribed in works emanating from Catholic territories; in Protestant countries like England, however, his influence is quite apparent. See R.R. Bolgar, *The Classical Heritage and its Beneficiaries: from the Carolingian Age to the end of the Renaissance* (Cambridge, 1954), 321; M. Mann Phillips, 'Erasmus in France in the later sixteenth century', *Journal of the Warburg and Courtauld Institutes* 34 (1971), 246-61; T. Cave, *The Cornucopian Text: problems of writing in the French Renaissance* ((Oxford, 1979), 9; J.K. McConica, *English Humanists and Reformation Politics under Henry VIII and Edward VI* (Oxford, 1965); 'The fate of Erasmian humanism', in *Universities, Society, and the Future*, ed. N. Phillipson (Edinburgh, 1983), 37-61.

Guarino's is a shadowy presence behind the impressive claims for early Italian humanism made in the influential works of Garin and Baron: Erasmus' is a name confidently associated with an entire European 'mentality' (and, as we shall suggest, Agricola's has to be yoked with that of Erasmus). While we were able to provide a comprehensive bibliography on Guarino and his school, it would be quite impossible to offer more than a sample (selected from a single point of interest) of the vast bibliography relating to the fortunes of Erasmus and 'Erasmianism'. The present chapter is largely concerned with this very issue: how does there come to be a general consensus on 'Erasmianism' as a major force for change in Europe, without there being any consensus on the nature of the Erasmian 'method' which reshaped the hearts and minds of generations of arts students?

Publishing – the emergence of the printed text – clearly had a great deal to do with the 'fame' of Agricola and Erasmus. School curricula, university statutes, probate book inventories, letters of advice to students (whether princes or commoners), and the various ephemera of sixteenth-century pedagogic activity are all permeated by Agricola's and (above all) Erasmus' presence.[2] We only begin to comprehend the altered nature of 'influence' as such once that influence is both substantial (Erasmus' staggeringly prolific body of printed pedagogic treatises and editions) and vague, since Erasmus' own accounts of the methods for using his works are evasive (sometimes defensive).

It is particularly difficult to unravel the educational consequences of Erasmianism since reverence for Erasmus' *dicta* coincides with a general move among teachers to replace individual classroom example (such as Guarino's) by a generalised humanist curriculum. The individualism, verging on hero-worship, of early humanism gave way in the early sixteenth century to an ideology of routine, order and, above all, 'method'. Early humanism had shifted the emphasis from the formal and artificial disputation within the schools to the oration as a personally tailored means of persuasion, and to mastery of language as a desirable accomplishment for the urbane member of a civilised community. With the goal of the individual performer prominently in mind, the *process* whereby the uninitiated might achieve such mastery was lost to view. It was left to the next generation of humanistically trained teachers to point out that this concentration on ends at the expense of means was socially and intellectually exclusive (in marked contrast to Aristotelianism).[3]

The urge to organise humanistic teaching seems to precede a clear

[2] The most conveniently accessible source of all these types of surviving trace of Agricola and Erasmus is T.W. Baldwin, *William Shakespere's Small Latine and Lesse Greeke*, 2 vols. (Urbana, 1944).

[3] Although social exclusivity is not explicitly considered, the desire to make humanistic education more widely available implies a desire to release it from the tight aristocratic circles in which it hitherto flourished.

understanding that the problem is the absence of a structured programme.[4] Although Guarino's son Battista called his textbook (based on his father's inspirational classroom teaching) *De ordine docendi et discendi* ('Concerning the *order* [or organisation] of teaching and learning'), the *content* reproduces Guarino's personal classroom practice.[5] But by the early sixteenth century it is a common complaint that current teaching is 'indigestible', i.e. that only those with access to the exceptional teacher, or those exceptionally well-prepared themselves, stand to gain from current humanistic teaching practices:

> But today our masters distinguish neither time nor age nor methodical order. They mix everything up, confuse it all, teach everything at the same time. Greek, Latin, orators, poets, historians, dialecticians, philosophers, come at the same time, on the same day, at the same hour, to fill the minds of the students with confusion, overwhelmed beneath this indigestible mass of knowledge.[6]

Such critics take the view that the treasury of ancient learning uncovered by the brilliant classical scholars of an earlier generation is not being made available in a form in which it can be absorbed by less dedicated (and perhaps less gifted) students. And it is surely true that until humanists had devised a curriculum and an order or method for progressing through its bewilderingly rich resources, humanism was bound to remain the preserve of a small number of dedicated (and leisured) specialists.

'Method' was the catchword of promoters of humanist education from the 1510s onwards.[7] This practical emphasis on procedure signals a shift in intellectual focus on the part of the pedagogic reformers, from the ideal end-product of a classical education (the perfect orator, perfectly equipped for political life), to the classroom aids (textbooks, manuals and teaching drills) which would compartmentalise the *bonae litterae* and reduce them to system. It marks a genuinely transitional stage in the institutionalising of Renaissance humanism. It is part of the gradual shift from humanism as the practice of an exemplary individual, to humanism as an institutionalised curriculum subject – a distinctive discipline in the arts. However awkwardly characterised by its practitioners, it represents a fresh trend in contemporary thinking, one which takes into account the manner of transmitting

---

[4] If indeed this was ever clearly formulated as the problem. Perhaps this is the reason for the 'method' vogue. On the Renaissance 'method vogue' in general see N.W. Gilbert, *Renaissance Concepts of Method* (New York and London, 1960). For a recent comprehensive survey of varieties of 'method' in the sixteenth century as they culminate in the pedagogic treatises of Peter Ramus see N. Bruyère, *Méthode et Dialectique dans l'oeuvre de La Ramée* (Paris, 1984), 65-201.

[5] See above, Chapter One.

[6] Claude Baduel (1491-1561); cit. Gilbert, *Renaissance Concepts of Method*, 72.

[7] See Gilbert, *Renaissance Concepts of Method*; L. Jardine, *Francis Bacon: Discovery and the Art of Discourse* (Cambridge, 1974), 17-65; *Distinctive Discipline: Rudolph Agricola and Modern Methodical Thinking* (in preparation); A. Crescini, *Le origini del metodo analitico: il cinquecento* (Udine, 1965).

information from teacher to student as part of the 'study' with which humanism is concerned.[8]

In this chapter we examine textbook claims for *ordo* and *methodus* in arts teaching, and we relate these to an uneasiness in relation to 'discipline' in teaching during the early sixteenth century, as humanism was changed from an active emulation of great scholarly teachers (like Guarino) into a 'liberal' arts course – an all-purpose substitute for other forms of basic education.[9] We shall look in particular at the work of two pedagogic reformers who were influential in forming the ideals of humanists of the south into a programme of education suitable for the pragmatic north: Rudolph Agricola and Desiderius Erasmus.[10] Both were drawn to humanism by the propaganda claims of Italian teachers like Guarino. Both believed humanist *educatio* to be intrinsically morally regenerative and conducive to the formation of a true Christian spirit: a methodical programme for the moral regeneration of European civilisation and culture.

Agricola exerted a far-reaching personal influence in the Low Countries during his lifetime as an inspirational teacher and a man of integrity. A close friend of Alexander Hegius, headmaster of Erasmus' school at Deventer, he was associated by Hegius with the school's avowed purpose of forming students according to the tenets of the *devotio moderna*; Erasmus was at the school when Agricola visited in 1484.[11] Agricola's role as a 'living example' of a humanist-inspired life of lay piety is made explicit in an early life of Agricola, written by a friend of Erasmus' who had been present when Hegius read out to his school with great emotion a letter bearing news of Agricola's death in 1485.[12]

None of Agricola's works on education was publicly available during his lifetime,[13] and his influence derived solely from his exemplary life. Posthumous publication of his *Oratio in laudem philosophiae* and his seminal

---

[8] Gilbert treats humanist methodical teaching as one among a range of 'job-specific' methods (*Renaissance Concepts of Method*, ch. 3). We suggest that 'method' is more of a catch-all word in the sixteenth century, which is used whenever an author feels under pressure to provide some attempt at system.

[9] On *ordo* and *methodus* and other synonyms like *via ac ratio* see Gilbert, *Renaissance Concepts of Method*.

[10] We are particularly conscious in this chapter of the fact that other figures, notably Melanchthon and Sturm, might usefully have been made part of the discussion. We remind the reader that the present study is of necessity *partial*, and hope that our remarks on 'influence' might be extended to discussion of other important teachers and thinkers in northern Europe in the sixteenth century.

[11] R. Pfeiffer, *History of Classical Scholarship 1300-1850* (Oxford, 1976), 69; P.S. Allen, *Opus Epistolarum*, 12 vols (Oxford, 1906-58), I,106 (for Erasmus' own reference see I,2); J.E. Sandys, *A History of Classical Scholarship*, 3 vols (Cambridge, 1903-8), II, 129, 253.

[12] *Commentarii seu index vitae Rudolphi Agricolae Phrisii ...*, ed. P. Pfeifer, *Serapeum* 10 (1849), 97-107; 113-19; P.S. Allen, 'The letters of Rudolph Agricola', *English Historical Review* 21 (1906), 302-17; 303.

[13] In fact, even his reputation as a teacher was based on a very brief period in which he was able to put his own educational ideas into practice. See Vasoli, *La dialettica e la retorica*, 163-4.

letter *De formando studio* by Peter Gilles, with Erasmus' encouragement, gave the public a taste of his urbane eloquence.[14] But Agricola's most original (and ultimately most important) pedagogical work, the *De inventione dialectica* (*c.* 1480) appears to have influenced the 'methodical' school of Erasmian pedagogical humanism initially by its reputation alone. We certainly find it hailed as an exemplary work of methodical humanistic practice before we have any account of the *manner* in which it is radically innovative. The story of the recovery and publication of this work is a revealing example of how prior assumptions on the part of intellectuals and teachers colour their perception of the importance of a single specified text, and shape its subsequent reception and interpretation.

Agricola died in Heidelberg, where he had gone to teach in 1484, at the invitation of Dalberg, Bishop of Worms.[15] On his death-bed he appointed a Strasburg physician, Adolphus Occo, as his literary executor. All such papers and manuscripts as were in Heidelberg passed into Occo's possession, while others were scattered, remaining in the hands of friends and correspondents, like his devoted admirers the brothers Theodoric and Johannes von Plenningen (who put together their own manuscript collection of letters and *opuscula*).[16] It was nearly forty-five years before committed disciples of Agricola's approach to teaching the liberal arts, like Erasmus himself and Alardus of Amsterdam (who ultimately edited the collected works), tracked down uncorrupted copies of the seminal works they knew he had left in manuscript.[17]

The story of how the key treatise, the *De inventione dialectica*, was retrieved is characteristic. Agricola was known to have left a work on humanist dialectic in three books: Erasmus inquired after its whereabouts in the *Adagia* of 1508. After Agricola's death it circulated in manuscript, though it is not clear what the provenance of such manuscripts was, nor how accurate they were. In a letter to Budaeus (Budé) of 1516, Erasmus regrets that he did not have access to the *De inventione dialectica* before the publication of his *De copia* (1512).[18] In any case, the text appears to have caused enough problems to make Agricola's numerous admirers look for an intact original. When, around 1514, Jacobus Faber in Deventer announced that he possessed a complete manuscript containing six books rather than the familiar three, Alardus rushed to Deventer, only to find that it consisted of the standard three books and was, moreover, a faulty copy of the original.[19] Nevertheless he negotiated a deal with Faber, and

[14] *Rodolphi Agricolae Opuscula* (Louvain, 1511). See Allen, 'The letters of Rudolph Agricola', 304, and passim.
[15] Sandys, *A History of Classical Scholarship*, II, 253-4.
[16] *Unedierte Briefe von Rudolf Agricola: Ein Beitrag zur Geschichte des Humanismus*, ed. K. Hartfelder, *Festschrift der Badischen Gymnasien, gewidmet der Universität Heidelberg* (Karlsruhe, 1886); Allen, 'The letters of Rudolph Agricola', 303.
[17] Allen, 'The letters of Rudolph Agricola', 303-5.
[18] Allen, *Opus Epistolarum*, II, 363 (letter 480).
[19] Alardus recounts the incident in a note to Agricola's influential 'De formando studio' letter; R. Agricola, *Lucubrationes* (Cologne, 1539), 203.

the *De inventione dialectica* was published for the first time, from this manuscript, in Louvain, in 1515.[20] This version of the text was widely reprinted, epitomised and commented on over the next twenty years, during which time fragments of Agricola's other writings appeared in publications by other humanists associated with the northwards spread of classical learning.[21]

Erasmus, however, continued publicly to express interest in acquiring fair copies of Agricola's surviving works with a view to publishing a collected edition, and he kept in touch with the equally eager Alardus. On 11 November 1516 Alardus wrote to Erasmus informing him that a large collection of Agricola's papers had turned up in Amsterdam, in the possession of Pompeius Occo (who had inherited them from his uncle, Agricola's physician).[22] Unfortunately it appeared that Occo had lent the manuscript of the *De inventione dialectica* to a Danish nobleman at about the time that Alardus had set out on his wild goose chase to acquire Faber's manuscript of the same work. This manuscript was finally returned to Occo in 1528, whereupon Alardus set about editing and commenting on it so as to be able to publish it as a companion volume to the *Lucubrationes* which he was already in the process of preparing for the press.[23] Because of difficulties in finding a publisher, however, the two volumes did not appear till 1539, by which time Erasmus was dead (and was himself the object of a Europe-wide pedagogic cult).[24]

Meanwhile, Erasmus' public interest in Agricola's works, and his tributes to the great teacher's posthumous memory, meant that a readership was eagerly awaiting the opportunity to consult Agricola at first hand.[25] Within

---

[20] Ong, *Ramus and Talon Inventory*, gives a chronological list of editions of Agricola's *De inventione dialectica* which is extremely valuable. Inevitably, however, some items in this list are plainly misdated or misplaced, if one is more familiar with the known fortunes of the various editions. Thus items i and ii should be ignored (as Ong himself suggests), while item v must be later than 1539 and is clearly related to item xlv (1552).

[21] Allen, 'The letters of Rudolph Agricola'.

[22] Allen, *Opus Epistolarum*, II, 375-8 (letter 485).

[23] Allen, 'The letters of Rudolph Agricola', 308; Agricola, *Lucubrationes*, fol. *3^V.

[24] Erasmus died in 1536.

[25] For Erasmus' public praise of Agricola before the appearance of his works see *Adagia* (1508) No. 339, where he inquires about the whereabouts of the *De inventione dialectica* (cit. Allen, 'The letters of Rudolph Agricola', 304); in the version of *Adagia* (1536) I.iv.39 (*Quid cani et balneo?*), Erasmus gives a long eulogy of Agricola as teacher, thinker and musician, and bewails the non-availability of his works, before using Agricola's use of the adage as his key example. Margaret Mann Phillips' note says that the text already appears in roughly this form (with a briefer eulogy) in the 1500 *Collectanea* 25. *Collected Works of Erasmus* vol. 31, ed. M. Mann Phillips (Toronto, 1982), 348-51. At the end of the *Ciceronianus* in 1528 Erasmus printed the *Oratio in laudem Matthiae Richili*, 'with a note to express [his] earnest desire that more of Agricola's work should be brought to light' (Allen, 'The Letters of Rudolph Agricola', 307); in the 1514 preface to a new edition of the *De copia* he calls Agricola 'Homo vere diuinus', and hopes his works will become available (reprinted in Allen, *Opus Epistolarum*, II, 32). There are repeated references in Erasmus' letters: Allen, *Opus Epistolarum*, I, 2 (*Catalogus omnium Erasmi Lucubrationum*, 1523); 1,106 (letter 23, <1489>); I,414 (letter 185, 1505); II, 350 (letter 471, <1516>) (published in

months of the publication of the first (1515) edition of the *De inventione dialectica*, John Fisher wrote excitedly to Erasmus to tell him how greatly he had benefited from reading it, claiming that he would have forfeited his bishopric for an opportunity to have been taught by the great man.[26] In 1523 Johannes Phrissemius published an edition of the 1515 *De inventione dialectica* with his own substantial commentary (this influential book went through nearly twenty editions in the next twenty years). By the time the definitive 1539 version of the text appeared, with Alardus' own commentary, Agricola's dialectic treatise had become the standard curriculum work on the subject, wherever humanism had gained a foothold in education in northern Europe.

Agricola's *De inventione dialectica* was thus associated with his more famous disciple (or at least, admirer), Erasmus, before it was generally available as a teaching text. When it did appear, first as a separate text, and then (in 1539) in a somewhat motley collection of works by Agricola (no 'collected works' as such was ever produced), offered as a 'methodical' introduction to the liberal arts, the reader's reaction to it was conditioned by the dense commentary surrounding each section or chapter. (The chapter breaks themselves had apparently been inserted by the two early commentators, Alardus and Phrissemius.)[27] The first edition of Phrissemius' commentary on the text of the *De inventione dialectica* which had come to light in 1515 appeared in 1523;[28] Alardus' commentary on the text finally located in 1528 appeared first in 1539.[29] We know that Alardus was closely involved with Erasmian humanism throughout the period of gestation; and since Phrissemius himself urged Alardus to produce his edition of Agricola's literary works we may take it that their approaches were in sympathy.[30] In other words (as P.S. Allen long ago recognised), the recovery of Agricola's works takes place within a

---

Illustrium virorum epistolae … ad Ioannem Reuchlin Phorcensem, 1519); VII, 368 (letter 1978, 1528); VII, 533 (letter 2073, 1528, in which Agricola is once again called 'diuinus'). A letter from Faber to Erasmus extolling Agricola is printed by Allen I, 385 (letter 174, 1503); it was published in *Alexandri Hegii … carmina* (Deventer, 1503). Erasmus' admiration for Agricola is explicitly linked by him with his admiration for his own teacher Hegius, a link which ensures that the *spiritual* aspects of education are always prominent.

[26] Allen, *Opus Epistolarum*, II, 70.

[27] Ong, *Ramus and Talon Inventory*, 534-5.

[28] See Allen, *Opus Epistolarum*, VII, 368; Ong, *Ramus and Talon Inventory*, 540 (item ix). Phrissemius' commentary acknowledges that the version of the text with which he is working is corrupt.

[29] Allen, 'The letters of Rudolph Agricola', 309; Ong, *Ramus and Talon Inventory*, 548 (item xxix). For Alardus' own account see Agricola, *Lucubrationes*, fol.†1ᵛ. It has been suggested that Alardus' edition with commentary appeared earlier than this (e.g. by M. Cogan, 'Rudolphus Agricola and the semantic revolutions of the history of invention', *Rhetorica*, II (1984), 163-94; 163). It cannot have appeared before 1532: in December 1531 Erasmus writes to Goclenius that Alard is negotiating with Frobenius for publication, but wants his fare paid to Basle! Allen *Opus Epistolarum*, X, 407 (letter 2587). In his first edition of the Agricola Aphthonius in 1532 he promises the two-volume edition of Agricola's works as forthcoming (Allen, 'The letters of Rudolph Agricola', 309). Ong has no edition before 1539.

[30] For Phrissemius' letter see Agricola, *Lucubrationes*, fol. †2ᵛ.

cultural context already steeped in Erasmus' distinctive brand of humanism.[31]

Agricola's published *oeuvre*, in the canonical form established by Alardus in his two-volume Cologne edition of 1539, comprises a series of teaching works associated with a graded programme of instruction in the liberal arts.[32] Following the first bulky volume of the *De inventione dialectica*, with its extensive commentary, we have Agricola's version of Aphthonius' *Progymnasmata*, with a commentary by Alardus which ties it closely with the first volume. To this Alardus appends Priscian's Latin version of Hermogenes' work of the same title, again with his own commentary, and a prefatory indication that Agricola considered the two works as belonging together.[33] The volume also contains fragments of a commentary by Agricola on Seneca's *Declamationes*,[34] and some of Agricola's elegant and influential orations and letters, including the important essay-letter *De formando studio lucubrationes*. (This last was used by Alardus in his commentary to structure yet more explicitly an Agricolan programme of learning.) The *De formando studio* was widely believed by contemporaries and by later scholars to have provided a sketch or blueprint for humanistic teaching practice (including such 'Erasmian' features as commonplaces and notebooks), and with coining the phrase *philosophia Christi*, for a particular brand of linked pagan and Christian letters and learning.[35]

Like the classical prototypes which it emulates (Cicero, Quintilian, Seneca, Aphthonius), this collection represents the *practice* corresponding to a theoretical position towards which the accompanying letters and prefaces gesture. That position is not made explicit, because (as we have suggested) the editor had already committed himself to such an approach when he undertook the publishing project – and his readership (as we have also suggested) was eagerly awaiting the textual remains of the teacher Erasmus regularly referred to publicly as 'divine' ('*quid Rodolpho Agricola diuinius?*' [Allen, VII,533]). As far as Agricola's published oeuvre is concerned, it is Erasmus' expressions of admiration for, and indebtedness to, Agricola which ensure that the reader already knows where the *Progymnasmata* (say) fits into a humanistic programme of learning. We, from our remote point in time, must self-consciously place the contents of Agricola's *Opera* in their appropriate intellectual milieu, if we are to appreciate their pedagogic *sense*, let alone their innovative force.

[31] Both Phrissemius' and Alardus' commentaries are packed with cross-references from Agricola's works to equivalent works of Erasmus. See, for example, both commentators on *De inventione dialectica* III, 5 (*De copia in dicendo quomodo paretur*).

[32] As Alardus makes explicit in his prefatory letters to volume II, the *Lucubrationes*.

[33] Agricola, *Lucubrationes*, fol. L1^r-v.

[34] On Seneca's *Declamationes* see J. Fairweather, *Seneca the Elder* (Cambridge, 1981). For the importance of the *declamatio* as a replacement for the scholastic disputation in humanist-inspired curricula see, e.g, McConica, 'The fate of Erasmian humanism', 43 and passim.

[35] See Pfeiffer, *History of Classical Scholarship*, 70-1; Bolgar, *The Classical Heritage and its Beneficiaries*, 272-4, 305.

In a letter to the grammarian Clenardus which prefaces the second volume of Agricola's *Opera*, Alardus suggests that if one is seeking a 'methodical' way of instilling the precepts of rhetoric (and we note that Alardus takes it for granted that such 'methodical' or ordered teaching is indeed the project in hand), there is no better text with which to begin than Aphthonius' *Progymnasmata*:

> In Ennius, Neoptolemus says that he must play the philosopher, but only a little way, because he did not approve of doing it constantly. The same goes for us with regard to the practice of rhetoric. For I would be most unwilling to draw on the dregs or follow out the streams, but would want to see the sources from which everything is derived, and to fetch what I wanted from near the fountainhead. No methodical way of proceeding seemed more solid than to give first a careful edition of the rhetorical *Progymnasmata* of the Sophist Aphthonius. In translating these Rudolph Agricola gave a first specimen of his brilliance. By means of this I could provide, as it were, a ramp leading up to the more subtle precepts of rhetoric.[36]

He reinforces this opinion in a further prefatory letter, addressed this time to a former pupil of his at Alcmar, Peter Nannius – a letter both more didactic and more hortatory, as befits one penned by teacher to student:

> One can hardly express how distinguished a practitioner of the liberal arts Aphthonius the Sophist is, who attracts and entices the reader with his fitting brevity, his clarity, his orderliness, and with other synoptic aids of this kind. Who manages matters with the student with no less diligence than conviction, not constantly striving so that he appears learned, but so that he causes the reader to become learned. In these *Progymnasmata*, with what brilliant conciseness, with how admirable a method [*ordo*], with what simplicity is the whole sum of rhetoric comprehended, as if some clear image were drawn out before us?[37]

The emphasis is here clearly laid on the provision of a coherent, graded and comprehensive introduction to speaking and writing Latin: an introduction which is consistent with the ideals of humanism (the desire for Latin eloquence as identical with moral rectitude and worth), but which is structured in terms of the *practical* problems of inculcating the requisite skills. Where Guarino, say, offered a model for emulation in the classroom,

---

[36] '*Quemadmodu[m] enim Neoptolemus apud Enniu[m] philosophari sibi ait necesse esse, sed paucis, nam omnino haud placuit: Ita & nobis quidem rhetoricari. Neq[ue] tamen uel de fece haurire uel riuulos uellem sectari, sed fontes unde omnia manant uidere, iuxtaq[ue] a capite quod optarem arcessere. Nulla certior occurrebat methodikê, quam si Aphthonii Sophistae progymnasmata Rhetorica, in quibus uertendis, primum ingenii sui specimen aedidit Rodolphus Agricola uir plane diuinus primu[m] dilige[n]ter excuterem, ut hisce quasi gradum aditumue facerem ad reco[n]ditiora rhetorices praecepta*' (Agricola, *Lucubrationes*, fol.*3ᵛ).

[37] '*Non potest dici quam sit insignis artifex Aphthonius Sophista, ut qui lectorem alliciat, inescetq[ue] commoda breuitate, luce, ordine, aliisq[ue] id genus epitomis: quiq[ue] non minore diligentia, quam fide discentis agit negotium, non id statim captans, ut ipse doctus appareat, sed ut lectorem doctum reddat. In hisce progymnasmatis, quam scito compe[n]dio, quam miro ordine, qua simplicitate rhetorices summam co[m]plexus est, ceu simulacro quodam nobis deliniato?*' (Agricola, *Lucubrationes*, fol.A2ʳ).

Agricola's Aphthonius offers a programme, and a systematic classroom practice, available to the teacher of modest ability.

In giving prominence to Apthonius' role in *structuring* the transmission of the rhetorical skills required to produce active and influential members of the community, both Agricola and Alardus are associating the liberal arts with *discipline*, as an essential requirement of a self-sufficient programme of education, in a formula which was to take a firm hold throughout sixteenth-century Europe. They also follow the impeccable (for fifteenth-century humanists) example of Quintilian, and (by implication) mature Roman education.[38] Roman rhetorical education modelled itself self-consciously on the Greek prototype, using Aphthonius' framework to take the student through a meticulously graded programme in the *ars disserendi* (the art of discourse) which culminated in *declamatio* (the declamation) – the formal lawcourt or exhibition debate on a set theme – the acme of intellectual achievement in the late Roman Empire.[39] Alardus, ardent disciple of Agricola, and mediator of Agricola on behalf of Erasmus, makes this goal explicit in his commentary. His full annotations to Agricola's Aphthonius open with a brief, accurate synopsis of the relation between ancient *progymnasmata* and declamation (taking Seneca as the mature example of the latter), and cross-reference Agricola's *De inventione dialectica* for a theoretical position which maintains that there is no essential difference between *display* – rhetorical – declamation and serious oratorical ratiocination. 'Rhetoric' as a systematic training, in other words, will be the core of Agricola's educational programme, because oratory (the art rhetoric teaches) is the basis of all civilised discourse. This is Cicero's position, as it is Quintilian's. It is not that of late medieval education: in calling his work on ratiocination *de inventione*, Agricola aligns his educational approach squarely with the Roman orators, and breaks decisively with scholastic training in language use, directed as it is at the formal language-game of the disputation.[40] The ability to perform outstandingly in *declamatio* shows that the student has absorbed his *moral* as well as his intellectual lessons, has acquired a set of values as well as a set of argument techniques. It marks a man out as having 'leadership quality'.[41]

The idea of the exercises in Aphthonius is to produce a total routineness of imaginative writing by reducing its variety systematically to a sequence (graded according to difficulty) of specified (and supposedly key) types of verbal composition, including both narrative forms and argument forms. Each type is expected to become second nature to the student, so that his public utterances will be pre-shaped to the requirements of public debate – the

[38] For Quintilian on *progymnasmata* see A. Gwynn, *Roman Education from Cicero to Quintilian* (Oxford, 1926); S.F.Bonner, *Roman Declamation in the late Republic and early Empire* (Liverpool, 1949; reissued 1969); *Education in Ancient Rome: from the elder Cato to the younger Pliny* (London, 1977), ch. 21 ('Declamation as a preparation for the lawcourts'). See above, Chapter Three for Valla's commitment to Quintilian.

[39] See below, and Bonner, *Roman Declamation*, chs 1 and 2.

[40] On the difference between medieval and humanistic conceptions of 'invention' and its relation to dialectic see Cogan, 'Rudolphus Agricola and semantic revolutions'.

[41] On the historical coincidence between an emphasis on *declamatio* and élitism in education, see J. Chomarat, *Grammaire et rhétorique chez Erasme*, 2 vols. (Paris, 1981), II, 1001.

lynch-pin skill for social and political life.[42] While we are concerned here with the large-scale impact of such 'system' on arts education, it is to be readily detected in the occasional detail of Renaissance literary composition (*litterae*). Specifically, the prominence of worked examples in the text means that there is a particular quality of almost banal familiarity about the subsequent use of (or reference to) the *same* examples by writers for whom they had formed part of an intensive classroom-drilling. Two examples taken from the work of William Shakespeare (a product of humanistic pedagogy whose works continue to be 'popular', that is, read by non-specialist readers) will, we hope, make this point clearly.[43]

The second exercise in Aphthonius is the imagined narrative with illustrative point – *narratio*. The example given in the text is a narrative consideration of the way in which the beauty of the rose brings to mind the 'wound' of Venus – her love for Adonis and her subsequent grief at his death:

> If anyone marvels at the beauty of the rose, let him consider with me the wound of Venus. The goddess loved Adonis, while Mars loved the goddess; and the goddess was struck with love of Adonis as was Mars with love of Venus. The god burned with desire for the goddess; the goddess pursued the man. Both loved similarly, though their loves differed in nature as gods and men differ. Mars, in envy of Adonis, decided to kill him, thinking that his death would be the only remedy for [the goddess's] love. When Adonis was struck down, and the goddess had learnt of this, she rushed to his aid; and having in her haste chosen a path that led through rose bushes, she encountered their thorns, and grazed her heel. The blood which flowed from the wound changed the colour of the rose. That is how the rose – initially white – was transformed in colour to that which we now know.[44]

Succinctness, simplicity and emotional compactness are here made textually concrete; and in case there is any doubt about this, Alardus adds in his commentary Politian's yet more compact version of the same *narratio*. In Politian's version, the rose, Venus' flower, is emblematically changed from white to red in the moment of Venus' intense grief for Adonis: 'Mars wounded Adonis; Venus rushed to his aid; she ran into roses and was caught by the thorns, wounding her foot. The blood which flowed from the wound gave the rose its own colour.' In the opening stanzas of his narrative poem,

---

[42] For a sixteenth-century example of Agricola's Aphthonius being used for just this purpose, see Edward VI's student exercises, as reproduced by Baldwin, *William Shakspere's Small Latine and Lesse Greeke*.

[43] On Shakespeare's humanistic education see Baldwin, *William Shakspere's Small Latine and Lesse Greeke*.

[44] '*Si quisquam est qui rosae decorem miratur, is animo mihi Veneris reputet uulnus. Amabat enim dea Adonidem, contra Mars ipse deam amabat, pariq[ue] dea Adonidis amore, quo Mars Veneris tenebatur. Flagrabat deae desiderio deus: dea sequebatur hominem, similis utrorumq[ue] ardor, tametsi natura inter se ut dii homoq[ue] differre[n]t. Inuidens Mars Adonidi, perimere ipsum decreuit, unicum abolendi amoris remedium, mortem ipsius arbitratus. Percusso demum Adonide, quum rem dea accepisset, ut succurreret festinabat: raptoq[ue] properanter inter rosaria cursu, spinis incidit, calcemqu[ue] pedis perstrinxit. defluens autem ex uulnere sanguis, rosae colorem in nouam facie[m] mutauit. Sicq[ue] rosa quae initio fuerat alba, in hunc quo nunc aspicitur tra[n]siit colore[m].*' (Agricola, *Lucubrationes*, 10).

Venus and Adonis, the textbook familiarity of the white rose turned red in Aphthonius' *narratio* on Venus' doomed love allows Shakespeare to produce a frisson of anticipation of disaster – the white of the rose already tinged with red:

> Even as the sun with purple colour'd face
> Had ta'en his last leave of the weeping morn,
> Rose-cheek'd Adonis hied him to the chase;
> Hunting he lov'd, but love he laugh'd to scorn.
>   Sick-thoughted Venus makes amain unto him,
>   And like a bold-fac'd suitor 'gins to woo him.
>
> 'Thrice fairer than myself,' thus she began,
> 'The field's chief flower, sweet above compare;
> Stain to all nymphs, more lovely than a man,
> More white and red than doves or roses are:
>   Nature that made thee with herself at strife,
>   Saith that the world hath ending with thy life.'[45]

'Purple-colour'd' ('In Elizabethan English "purple" often meant a colour ruddier and brighter than in modern usage ... Shakespeare often uses it of blood'),[46] 'rose-cheek'd', 'More white and red than doves and roses',[47] must surely remind the sixteenth-century schoolroom product, drilled on Agricola's Aphthonius, that Venus' infatuation is doomed, just as her rose is doomed to change from white to red. The kind of 'readiness' these exercises give the student is readiness of expression, and readiness of expectation: the ability to select, and to anticipate the right turn of phrase, the appropriate commonplace reference point for a given (typical) occasion. 'Exemplary', in this context, takes on the specific meaning of 'forceful and emotionally compelling because all-too-well-known'.[48]

Or again, the worked example given in the Aphthonius/Agricola text of a highly emotionally-charged, imagined first-person speech (*ethopoeia* or *allocutio*) is Niobe's lament for her slaughtered children (a disaster brought about by her own pride). The lament of Niobe passes into European literature as a commonplace of rhetorically intensified, pre-packaged emotion, most memorably, surely, in Hamlet's (equally highly-wrought) lament over his mother's lack of constancy:

> Let me not think on't – Frailty, thy name is woman –
> A little month, or ere those shoes were old
> With which she follow'd my poor father's body,

---

[45] *The Poems*, Arden edition, ed. F.T. Prince, 11. 1-12.

[46] Arden, note 3.

[47] The dove is, of course, Venus' other traditional attribute.

[48] For another example of the way in which a reconstruction of the *banality* of the source allows the modern reader to reconstruct the tone of Shakespeare's poem see W.J. Ong on Shakespeare's sonnet 129 and Textor's *Epitheta*: 'Commonplace rhapsody: Ravisius Textor, Zwinger and Shakespeare', in *Classical Influences on European Culture, AD 1500-1700*, ed. R.R. Bolgar (Cambridge, 1976), 91-126.

Like Niobe, all tears – why, she –
O God, a beast that wants discourse of reason
Would have mourn'd longer – married with my uncle,
My father's brother – but no more like my father
Than I to Hercules. Within a month,
Ere yet the salt of most unrighteous tears
Had left the flushing of her galled eyes,
She married.[49]

'Like Niobe, all tears' calls upon the audience to shape their response to a shamelessly derivative classroom example ('most unrighteous tears').[50]

Our scrutiny of the extraordinarily far-reaching European 'influence' of Agricola and Erasmus has thus far concentrated on what amounts to the Agricolan *mystique*: the way the textually unsubstantiated word-of-mouth reputation of Agricola as a crucially significant humanist pedagogue was painstakingly reconstructed under the patronage of Erasmus into a collection of key teaching texts. The point we are making is that the real importance of Agricola's textual remains is in part historical accident – only such imperfect texts as the personal admirers of Agricola could eventually lay their hands on become *the corpus*. However, in part also (to give those admirers their due) Agricola's surviving works do indeed capture the great teacher's flair and originality – as long as the reader is already alerted to the kind of altered perspective on the *studia humanitatis* that Agricola is trying to give. This understanding, as we have already suggested, is provided by the explicitly Erasmian pedagogic context for which all the edited texts of Agricola's works (issuing as they do from thirty to fifty years after Agricola's death) are explicitly intended (as the commentaries readily explain). (For instance, by 1523 Phrissemius' commentary to the *De inventione dialectica* confidently refers the reader of III,5 ('*De copia in dicendo quomodo paretur*') to Erasmus' *De copia* for a full and thorough treatment; while Alardus opens his commentary on Aphthonius' example of the penultimate exercise in *Progymnasmata*, the *thesis* (in which he argues the case for and against marriage), with a check-list of those of Erasmus' works in which the student will find 'everything you need to know regarding matrimony'.)[51]

But the problem of converting Agricola's reputation into a concrete body of teaching texts is only one of those which Phrissemius, Alardus and Erasmus (among others) faced. The other concerns Agricola's failure, anywhere in his surviving *opera*, to explain how a training in rhetoric on the ancient model is elevated into a spiritually enlightening *educatio*. Alardus appears to resolve this issue (in his prefatory letters and thereafter in his commentaries) by

---

[49] *Hamlet*, Arden edition, ed. H. Jenkins, I.ii. 146-56.

[50] One might equally well have taken Hecuba's lament (Aphthonius' other example of affective *ethopoeia*), and Hamlet's 'What's Hecuba to him, or he to her,/That he should weep for her?' (II.ii.553-4). And of course, Lucretia's distraught confession of her rape before her suicide (another favourite classroom example of this exercise) finds its way into Shakespeare's *The Rape of Lucrece* (see, for comparison, Salutati's *Declamatio Lucretiae*).

[51] The Phrissemius comment is cited by Cave, *The Cornucopian Text*, 17-18. For the Alardus comment see Agricola, *Lucubrationes*, 66.

maintaining that *because* Agricola's programme is supremely 'methodical', the pursuit of Agricolan method of itself moulds the student, morally and spiritually. According to Alardus, in Agricola's Aphthonius (and the commented Seneca *Declamationes* which follow it) we have in embryo that 'discipline', that curricular version of the *bonae litterae*, which enables the humanist teacher to turn his students into well-trained specialists, reliably and with confidence: or, as Alardus put it, allows a teacher not to teach by 'constantly striving so that he appears learned' (inspirationally), but 'causes [the student] to become learned' (systematically). His commentary on the *De inventione dialectica*, and the persistent cross-referencing of the works in the *Lucubrationes* volume to precise points in this work, is then used to suggest that the *De inventione dialectica* provides the programme with that manifest rigour which guarantees its intellectual and moral stringency. As Alardus explains to Clenardus (himself an educator of repute),[52] it is the *De inventione dialectica* which upgrades rhetorical fluency into learning:

> [After Aphthonius] I thought it best to peruse Agricola's remarkably complete books on Dialectical Invention, because perfect, or at least reliable indications of every art are found in him, and because he is unrivalled in his diligence in invention, in his acuity and precision in judgment, his fulness in discourse, and his purity in explication. So that since the golden age of Cicero there has been no one else whom we could produce as an example of the fulness of real learning, and who – as Octavius Augustus declared of the orator Vatinius – 'had his wits in ready cash', except Agricola.[53]

When Alardus offered the *De inventione dialectica* as the key to the 'discipline' of the *ars disserendi* he was already following an established humanist intellectual tradition. As we saw earlier (in Chapter Three), Lorenzo Valla initiated (or at least elegantly and influentially developed) a movement among professors of the *studia humanitatis* to provide some kind of substitute within the *studia humanitatis* for the rigorous programme in logic of the scholastic training, whose iron grip on general education they challenged.[54] What could not have been forseen was the way Agricola's idiosyncratic 'dialectical method' would be seized upon by educators and students as *the* answer to the problem of how to give humanism a rigorous profile. Assisted by its association with

---

[52] See this chapter, below; above, Chapter Five; Sandys, *A History of Classical Scholarship*, II, 158-9.

[53] '*Deinde absolutissimos Rhodolphi Agricolae de inuentione dialectica libros accuratius expenderem, & ob id expenderem quod in eo uiro nullius non artis aut perfecta aut certe non dubia uestigia reperiantur, quodq[ue] nihil eo in inueniendo diligentius, nihil in iudicando acrius, aut exactius, nihil in trade[n]do plenius aut uberius, nihil in explicando castius aut politius, ut prorsus alterum ab aureo illo Ciceronis seculo proferre non possimus, qui omnes iustae eruditionis numeros impleuerit, quiq[ue] (ut de Vatinio oratore pronunciauit Octauius Augustus) ingenium in numerato habuerit nisi Rodolphum*' (Agricola, *Lucubrationes*, fol. *3^v).

[54] See L. Jardine, 'The place of dialectic teaching in sixteenth-century Cambridge', *Studies in the Renaissance* 21 (1974), 31-62; 'Humanism and dialectic in sixteenth-century Cambridge: a preliminary investigation', in *Classical Influences on European Culture, AD 1500-1700*, ed. Bolgar, 141-154; 'Lorenzo Valla and the intellectual origins of humanist dialectic', *Journal of the History of Philosophy* 15 (1977), 143-63.

Erasmian pedagogy (an association only further strengthened, as we shall see, by Erasmus' own evasiveness on the question of *what* procedure he had in mind in his recurrent appeals to 'method' as animating the *philosophia Christi*), Agricola's dialectical 'method' was adopted almost unscrutinised as the backbone of humanist 'discipline'.

The 'method' of Agricolan dialectic is largely organisational – it organises conveniently entirely traditional material on the *topics*. So Alardus' commitment to Agricola's 'method' produced a commitment on the part of generations of humanist teachers to an ingenious set of readily transmitted routines for classifying the accumulation of matter for debating or declaiming (or composing poetry or fiction) by 'commonplaces'. It also appears to have produced a passionate commitment on the part of educators loyal to the Agricolan tradition (like Ramus) to the view that these routines provide a pathway to truth, rather than a rhetorical technique. Grouping by headings was not in itself the invention of the methodical humanists.[55] When Agricola combined 'grouping by headings', as a means of ordering the fruits of one's reading, with a set of simple rules for generating propositions which could be relied on to convince any auditor out of the contents of those *loci*, he was broadly following Boethius. But packaged by Alardus, and marketed by Erasmus, the *De inventione dialectica* swept the educational board as the *system* which would transform the by now familiar process of collection and accumulation of 'matter' into a pathway to truth and salvation.[56]

We suggest that the reconstruction of the *artes sermocinales* as 'textual matter' and 'method' dominates sixteenth-century pedagogy, particularly under the influence of Erasmus (whose admiration for Agricola was open and undisguised). Two original areas of textbook development preoccupy Erasmus: the manual of 'copie', *de copia*, the rich and ready accumulation of matter for discourse, drawn from the best of the classics, and the treatise on method, the orderly and convincing deployment of matter for use. Agricola had ultimately laid emphasis on the 'method' as a neutral shell or skeleton for more or less loaded material: Erasmus' temperament seems to have led him to favour techniques for developing 'copiousness' itself, and to treat 'method' as somehow guaranteeing that the subsequent deployment of the material will not be just aesthetically pleasing, but morally sound.[57] His reticence on method, we suggest, leaves Agricolan method the only contender in the field. The fact remains that insofar as this system is 'methodical' it is clearly a systematic training in rhetoric – in our terms, a *literary* training – however much first Agricola and then Erasmus are at pains to insist that their

---

[55] As Robert Bolgar points out, *The Classical Heritage*, 272 and note, this was already a technique used by preachers.

[56] On the technical detail of Agricola's topical dialectic see Jardine, *Francis Bacon*, 29-35; Cogan, 'Rudolphus Agricola and semantic revolutions'.

[57] On Agricola and Erasmus and 'copia' see Cave, *The Cornucopian Text*.

methodical practice is no mere drilling in the art of public speaking, but the means of making significant intervention on the most challenging intellectual issues of the day, both temporal and spiritual.[58] In the rest of this chapter we shall look at how Erasmus puts 'humanist method' (Agricolan method, in fact) into practice, so as to convey an impression of 'discipline', while always, in the end, relying on the good will, or faith of the reader to carry him through the process.

It should be made clear at this point, however, that Erasmus is not alone in requiring such an 'act of faith' from his audience. The difficulty in establishing a clear 'order' or 'system' in humanist pedagogy is endemic to the liberal arts.[59] Arts teachers regularly invoke the notion of 'rigour' or 'method' to establish the seriousness and systematic nature of their subject, while at the same time not wishing thereby to restrict their subject to the kind of mechanical regularity expected of 'hard' sciences.[60] In the teaching of the arts from antiquity onwards, textbook prefaces have insisted on the systematic nature of what is taught, while remaining vague as to whether it is the subject or its presentation which is 'disciplined'.[61] In the preface to his *The Living Principle: 'English' as a Discipline of Thought*, for example, F.R. Leavis is at once typically vague and typically precise as to the 'disciplined' nature of his kind of arts training:

> I have intimated something, then, about my reasons for insisting that the critical discipline – the distinctive discipline of university 'English' – is a discipline of intelligence, and for being explicit and repetitive in associating the word 'intelligence' with the word 'thought'. As for 'discipline', I am sure that that is the right word, though the training that justifies it in the given use is a training in delicacy of perception, in supple responsiveness, in the wariness of conceptual rigidity that goes with a Blakean addiction to the concrete and particular, and in readiness to take unforeseen significances and what is so unprecedented as to be new. By way of emphasising that 'discipline' is the right word I will sum up by saying that it is a training in responsibility ... Having said this, I will go on to say further that the discipline is a training in fidelity to – which must be delicate apprehension of – the living principle.[62]

[58] On Erasmus' use of rhetorical procedures in scriptural investigation see Chomarat, *Grammaire et rhétorique chez Erasme*; J.K. McConica, 'Erasmus and the grammar of consent', in *Scrinium Erasmianum*, ed. J. Coppens, 2 vols (Leiden, 1969), II, 77-99; J.B. Payne, 'Towards the hermeneutics of Erasmus', *Scrinium Erasmianum* ed. Coppens, II, 13-49; Cave, *The Cornucopian Text*.

[59] Those scholars who have attempted to deal with the extraordinarily varied types of arts 'method' in the sixteenth century have on the whole been reluctant to tackle the enormous question of whether teachers of the arts have *always* claimed their procedures as 'methods', while avoiding being pinned down to precise taxonomies or pseudo-scientific systems. See e.g. Gilbert, *Renaissance Concepts of Method*.

[60] See e.g. I. Gregor, 'English, Leavis, and the social order', *Twentieth Century Studies* 9 (1973), 22-31.

[61] See M.I. Finley, 'The heritage of Isocrates', in *The Use and Abuse of History* (London, 1975), 193-214.

[62] *The Living Principle* (London, 1975), 13-14.

By adroit play on the word 'discipline' – a word which connotes both a
stringency of moral address to the subject and a regulated procedure which
does not depend on the caprice of the individual reader – Leavis is enabled to
go on to use the terms 'method', 'logic', 'argument' very much as Erasmus, or
Sturm, or Agricola or Melanchthon might have, to allude to an ambition for
rigour, while separating off the *kind* of rigour they are after from that of
'philosophy' or 'science':

> I bring in the word 'logic' here as part of my insistence on the propriety of my
> way of using the word 'thought' and on the cogency I aspire to in my mode of
> argument. The mode is not, it seems to me, philosophical; it would be
> misrepresented by calling it that ... I am left, then, insisting on the 'other
> discipline'. What I find it relevant to say immediately is that the mode of
> argument by which I endeavour to explain and enforce that insistence seems to
> me decidedly not a philosopher's. Its affinity is rather – and appropriately – with
> the other-than-philosophical discipline for which I aim at getting recognition. I
> have to justify my contention about the humanly necessary kind of thought that
> is hardly recognised at all as that, and, in doing so, to communicate to others
> my firm belief that something relevant can be done; that is, I am concerned –
> inseparably – with practicality and with persuasion to directed energizing.[63]

Whenever the teaching of the arts becomes a crusade, as it does for Leavis
and as it does when northern humanists counter the accusation that they
teach 'mere' rhetoric, mere play with words, we get this urgency of tone and
this insistence on 'discipline' in competition with, but in distinct contrast to,
philosophy, or science. It is a training – but it is a training in 'delicacy of
perception, in supple responsiveness', in unquantifiables, to be opposed to
'conceptual rigidity'. It is a training useful for life, but 'useful' here means
permeating every aspect of human activity, and transcending anything so
mundane as the providing of teachable skills.

We should not be surprised, therefore, to find that there is no
straightforward answer to the question 'What was Erasmus' spiritual
method?'. The piety which marks his moralising treatises is conventionally
homiletic and parochial in character, elevated perhaps by the characteristic
flair and virtuosity with which Erasmus handles the Latin language. The
pedagogic treatises, on the other hand, comprise a lively collection of drills
and routines, copiously and often ingeniously illustrated, which offer an
orderly and methodical route to a solid grounding in the humanities. What
part the meticulous training in eloquence actually plays in the spiritual
preparation of the 'Christian soldier' is left deliberately vague (indeed,
Erasmus had to defend himself against the charge, levelled by devout
colleagues, that some of these works were essentially 'trivial').[64] So that the

---

[63] Ibid., 16-17.
[64] See for instance the letters exchanged between Erasmus and Budé in 1516. Allen, *Opus
Epistolarum*, II, 272-6 (letter 435) and II, 362-70 (letter 480) (part of a longer sequence of letters,

question 'What then is the theological method of Erasmus?' tends to produce on the one hand reconstructions of Erasmus' own (only partially systematic) ways of handling scriptural text after the manner of secular text criticism, on the other an elaborate theory (nowhere confirmed by Erasmus himself) of the 'stages' of ascent from mastery of Latin and Greek to self mastery. (A third possibility is to abandon the published 'systems' altogether and reconstruct Erasmus' model Christian life from his homiletic writings, as the true goal of his pedagogy – his own passionate interest in secular eloquence notwithstanding.)[65]

Whenever the topic is raised in the prolific correspondence he conducted with scholars and clerics across Europe, Erasmus maintains that there is an intimate and vital relationship between the piety of his intentions (his explicit goal always being the education of the devout member of the Christian laity) and the systematic works on humanistic eloquence, however apparently secular the latter may appear. The subject was a sufficiently important one to produce more than one carefully crafted epistolary 'apologia' among the letters whose publication Erasmus authorised (not to say, stage-managed) in the early decades of the sixteenth century. If we assimilate thoroughly such exchanges of letters, as they are collected in P.S. Allen's monumental *Opus Epistolarum Des. Erasmi Roterdami*, it is easy to convince ourselves that a work like the *De copia* (a highly popular and much reprinted elementary manual on ways of enlarging and enriching the student's mastery of classical Latin) is self-evidently part of a systematic programme of spiritual development.[66] In other words, in spite of there being no explicit link between the influential textbooks of Latin eloquence and any moral or devotional meta-system, Erasmus' extremely public personality (priest permanently occupied with lay piety) and the letters conveniently available to 'gloss' a work like the *De copia*[67]

published during Erasmus' lifetime, offering a justification of the Erasmian programme for the secular classics as an intrinsic part of a training in piety).

[65] See, for example, C.G. Chantraine, S.J., 'The *Ratio verae theologiae* (1518)', in R.L. DeMolen (ed.), *Essays on the Works of Erasmus* (New Haven, 1978), pp. 179-85, p. 179: 'What, then, is the theological method of Erasmus?' See also the collection of articles grouped as 'La théologie Erasmienne: principes et méthode' in *Scrinium Erasmianum*, ed. Coppens, II: J. Etienne, 'La médiation des Ecritures selon Erasme' (3-11); J.B. Payne, 'Toward the hermeneutics of Erasmus' (13-49); G. Chantraine, 'L'Apologia ad Latomum. Deux conceptions de la théologie' (51-75); J.K. McConica, 'Erasmus and the grammar of consent' (77-99); C.J. de Vogel, 'Erasmus and his attitude towards Church dogma' (101-32).

[66] On the *De copia* in particular, and its popularity as a classroom text see H. Rix, 'The editions of Erasmus' De Copia', *Studies in Philology*, University of North Carolina Press 43 (1946), 595-605; Bolgar, *The Classical Heritage*; M. Mann Phillips, 'Erasmus and the art of writing', in *Scrinium Erasmianum*, I, 335-50; Baldwin, *William Shakspere's Small Latine and Lesse Greek*; Cave, *The Cornucopian Text*.

[67] Chomarat argues that Erasmus' letters are not simple bits of textual evidence concerning his life and thought, but were (as we might well expect) carefully constructed exercises, along the lines laid down in Erasmus' own *De conscribendis epistolis* (Chomarat, *Grammaire et Rhétorique chez Erasme*, II, 1039-1052). If so, they beg the question as to whether a link is actually established between upright behaviour and exemplary Latin. Important letters used by Erasmus scholars as

enable the Erasmus scholar to graft piety on to *litterae*.[68]

The sixteenth-century public certainly seems to have been convinced. In a northern European religious climate sympathetic towards the idea of an educational programme which promised to produce a laity educated to a personal understanding of Sacred Scripture, this package of *bonae litterae* and individual piety was greeted enthusiastically. It is hardly necessary to dwell here on the remarkable success of Erasmus' programme of education in the liberal arts in educational institutions, from the *gymnasia* and the grammar schools, to the Royal Colleges at Oxford and Cambridge. We may take as typical a single piece of contemporary evidence (available in a printed source), testifying elegantly to the permeation of the arts curriculum by Erasmus' textbooks and editions by the 1530s. Alexander Nowell kept a notebook during the years 1535 to 1540, while he was studying for his Master of Arts degree at Brasenose College, Oxford. In 1539 he records a gift of books, left with him by his friend Thomas Bedel, who had just graduated Bachelor of Arts. The list of titles runs as follow:

bookes wych Thomas bedle left wyth me att his departyng	
orationes longolii	Virgilius versum
explanacio dominicae precationis	*copia verborum
R. Agricola ii papre bokes	*libellus de constructione erasmi
Vergill	
Valerius maximus †terentius	Vulgaria terentii
tulii exempla	*erasmi paremia cum aliis
†tragediae Senecae	theodori grammatica graeca
ovidii opera ii voluminibus	bene loquendi institutio
*erasmus de conscribendis epistolis	cum aliis
Horatius	
*adagia erasmi	Justinus
*enchiridium ad copiam	dialogi mosellani
Plinii epistolae	dialectica melanchthonis
tullii epistolae	*similia erasmi
†officia ciceronis	grammatica latina
Vivis opera aliquot	elucidarius poeticus
dati elegantiae	*erasmi epistolae aliquot
de ratione carminum	reuclin epistolae
	methodus conscribendi epistolarum
*paraphrasis in elegantias Vallae	grammatica cleonardi

evidence certainly were published (and made popular and influential reading) in his lifetime. For the publishing history of Erasmus' letters see Allen, *Opus Epistolarum*, Appendix VII, I, 593-602.

  [68] Curious things happen when a modern 'post-structuralist' critic takes on this problem, as Terence Cave does in *The Cornucopian Text*. The difficulty in locating Erasmus' (or Agricola's) moral doctrines, compared with the obviousness of their systematic *rhetorical* practice, tempts Cave into attributing to these authors a modern Barthesian notion of 'le plaisir du texte': a kind of sensual enjoyment as the goal of Agricolan and Erasmian 'method' and 'copie'. While this is certainly not a sixteenth-century response to Erasmus' pedagogy (because the moral was so deeply *assumed*, as we continually stress), it is a reading to which these authors are vulnerable,

institutiones Iuris civilis
†novum testamentum
*colloquia erasmi

The ten asterisked works in this list are all by Erasmus; in addition, a further four items (marked †) are probably edited by Erasmus.[69] And this testament to the Erasmus publishing boom can be matched in many of the book lists which survive in probate inventories for the plague-ridden years of the mid-sixteenth century in England.[70] Even if Nowell didn't read through all the books he acquired, they show, at the very least, that having a lot of Erasmus on your desk was the appropriate thing!

When cultural and intellectual historians talk of the impact of humanism on sixteenth-century European life and thought, it is generally Erasmian influence in educational establishments that they have in mind. In the case of England, in particular, where Henry VIII's quarrel with the canon lawyers in the 1530s made a replacement curriculum an urgent necessity, an Erasmian liberal arts programme was seized upon by the Tudor Establishment (with the support of Thomas Cromwell) as a politically appropriate substitute for scholasticism in the statutes of Oxford and Cambridge.[71] And this should remind us of a further important feature of Erasmian educational reform: it is extremely difficult to disentangle political from 'intellectual' motives in the tale of the curricular impact of Erasmian studies in the classrooms of northern Europe. Both Agricola and Erasmus were publicly associated with a particular brand of Christian lay piety. Agricola was Alexander Hegius' friend and intellectual example (as Erasmus' public commendations frequently remind the reader), and Hegius was head of the Deventer school at which Erasmus gained his grounding in the lay piety of the Brethren of the Common Life. Erasmus' association with Luther and the moderate liberal wing of the Catholic Church (he remained an Augustinian monk on permanent leave of absence from his monastery throughout his public career)

---

and that vulnerability is symptomatic of the failure ever to voice crucial but tacit assumptions about the sense in which the *bonae artes* are 'good' – the subject of this book.

[69] We take this list from Baldwin, *William Shakspere's Small Latine and Lesse Greeke*, I, 174, expanding contractions for easier identification by the reader.

[70] See L. Jardine, 'Humanism and the sixteenth-century Cambridge arts course', *History of Education* 4 (1975), 16-31.

[71] On Erasmus and sixteenth-century English education, see Bolgar, *The Classical Heritage*; 'From humanism to the humanities', *Twentieth Century Studies* 9 (1973), 8-21; 'Classical reading in Renaissance schools', *Durham Research Review* 6 (1955), 1-10; J.K. McConica, *English Humanists and Reformation Politics under Henry VIII and Edward VI* (Oxford, 1965); Joan Simon, *Education and Society in Tudor England* (Cambridge, 1966; reissued 1979); Baldwin, *William Shakspere's Small Latine and Lesse Greeke*. For some reservations about the actual extent of Erasmian influence in the Tudor universities see J.M. Fletcher, 'Change and resistance to change: a consideration of the development of English and German universities during the sixteenth century', *History of Universities* I (1981), 1-36. See M. Mann Phillips, *Erasmus and the Northern Renaissance* (New York, 1950) for general European influence.

inevitably coloured the reception of his pedagogy.[72]

The very success of the institutionalising of the Erasmian classroom timetable makes it tempting to look for a recognisable 'method' in Erasmus' traditional pietistic works, to enable us to pin down 'Erasmianism' to concrete evidence and quantifiable influence. McConica's influential work on Erasmianism and the English Reformation has the following to say about the crucial (and enduringly popular) *Enchiridion*:

> To read this once-famous work is perhaps initially to be disappointed. It would be difficult to regard it as a treatise of profound spirituality, and it is impossible to overlook its loose and repetitious construction. Yet its once phenomenal popularity throughout Europe challenges the imagination of the modern reader.[73]

His sense of not getting to the bottom of the work is shared by Bolgar, who turns to it as he traces the emergence of the concept of the Christian hero in the Renaissance (a theme to which the *Enchiridion* obviously contributed):

> The *Encheiridion militis Christiani* – the Christian knight's handbook or mirror (the Greek word has both meanings) – is a gummy, diffuse piece of writing. We miss the irony, the sharp insights that distinguish the best productions of Erasmus. If the men of the sixteenth century valued the *Encheiridion*, which they seem to have done, it must have been for its general thesis. Its attacks on sensuality, maliciousness, pride, avarice and violence appear no more than the commonplaces of medieval satire until, coming to know the book better, one realises that they mask a positive ethic.[74]

Erasmus himself, meanwhile, tells Martin Dorp that 'in the *Enchiridion* we have straightforwardly presented a model for the Christian life' (*in Enchiridio simpliciter Christianae vitae formam tradidimus*).[75] For the 'positive ethic' – the explicit insistence on a procedure and a method – we have to turn to the poised pedagogic works like the *De pueris instituendis*. And in order to regard *their* method as the backbone of Erasmus' personal piety, it is necessary to make the crucial assumption of equivalence between humanistic discipline (the habits of systematic use of language inculcated by the humanistic programme of education) and moral probity. So we are back with a situation in which it is *Erasmus himself* (his personal reputation for Christian devotion and probity of character) who validates the equation 'competence in the ancient languages is equivalent to a preparation for Christian piety', a validation which, we would maintain, was so successful as to leave its mark on institutional

---

[72] See R.H. Bainton, *Erasmus of Christendom* (New York, 1968).

[73] McConica, *English Humanists and Reformation Politics*, 17.

[74] R.R. Bolgar, 'Hero or anti-hero? The genesis and development of the *miles christianus*', in N.T. Burns and C.J. Reagan (eds.), *Concepts of the Hero in the Middle Ages and the Renaissance* (Albany, 1975), 120-46, 134-5.

[75] Allen, *Opus Epistolarum*, II, 93 (letter 337, 1515).

attitudes towards a liberal arts education right down to the present day.

In a recent article entitled 'The fate of Erasmian humanism', McConica captures succinctly the submerged assumptions in the Erasmian programme:

The most crucial single change was the replacement of medieval grammars with those of humanist grammarians, and the corresponding displacement of logic and dialectic by the early study of grammar and rhetoric; in the latter were found, of course, poetry and history as well as the art of persuasive speech. It was to be an education in virtue as well as knowledge, and the conduct of the child was to be as much a part of discipline as the languages it would learn. In the title of his *De pueris statim ac liberaliter instituendis* every word was made to count. The education of the child should begin without delay, and the design should be 'liberal' – that is, on the lines of the *bonae litterae*. Latin and Greek must begin it: first speaking, then reading and writing. The child was to be drilled in grammar in the strict sense – syntax and the parts of speech – then encouraged to acquire the formidable command and ease of manner in which Erasmus himself was preeminent by the constant practice of rhetorical variation, by the assiduous study of terms, especially the vivid vocabulary of everyday objects and events, and by immersion in the best stylists of the ancient world. Aphorisms, those memorable bearers of distilled wisdom, would instruct in ethics, as would proverbs and the sayings of ancient men – *parabolae* and *adagia*. Any natural bent to the artistic, or to the study of nature, or mathematics, or geography, should be encouraged. It was of prime importance that study should be attractive, combining instruction with enjoyment: what he disparaged was the abstract, the formal, the purely logical. The implicit aim was an international society of men – and of women – clerical and lay, who were steeped in a common cultural discipline derived from the ancient world, divorced from the arid, exclusive, dialectical technicalities of the Schools, and bound together essentially by Latin eloquence, although Greek too was to play its part: hence the *De pronunciatione*. It was an alternative culture of formidable pretensions, well aware of the threat it posed to the established intellectual disciplines, as it was aware equally of being excluded from the citadels in which those disciplines held sway.[76]

'It was to be an education in virtue as well as knowledge, and the conduct of the child was to be as much a part of discipline as the languages it would learn' – that, indeed, is the promise held out to parents and prospective patrons. It is a formula endorsed by teachers like Sir John Cheke and Roger Ascham eager to gain employment in the Courts of Europe educating the Christian Prince. Indeed by the time Roger Ascham describes the education of his royal pupil Elizabeth I, in a letter written to Sturm in April 1550, it has become curiously difficult to disentangle her grasp of religion and morals from her polished mastery of Latin and Greek – grammatical competence is proudly offered as virtual proof of the integrity and moral probity of the young King Edward's Protestant sister:

---

[76] J.K. McConica, 'The fate of Erasmian humanism', in N. Phillipson (ed.), *Universities, Society, and the Future* (Edinburgh, 1983), 37-61, 41-2.

She had me for her tutor in Greek and Latin for two years ... She has often talked to me readily and well in Latin, and moderately so in Greek. When she writes Greek and Latin, nothing is more beautiful than her hand-writing. She is as much delighted with music as she is skilful in the art ... She read with me almost all Cicero and great part of Titus Livius; for she drew all her knowledge of Latin from those two authors. She used to give the morning of the day to the Greek Testament, and afterwards read select orations of Isocrates and the tragedies of Sophocles. For I thought that from those sources she might gain purity of style, and her mind derive instruction that would be of value to her to meet every contingency of life. To these I added Saint Cyprian and Melanchthon's Common Places, &c., as best suited, after the Holy Scriptures, to teach her the foundations of religion, together with elegant language and sound doctrine. Whatever she reads she at once perceives any word that has a doubtful [forced] or curious meaning. She cannot endure those foolish imitators of Erasmus, who have tied up the Latin tongue in those wretched fetters of proverbs. She likes a style that grows out of the subject; chaste because it is suitable, and beautiful because it is clear. She very much admires modest metaphors, and comparisons of contraries well put together and contrasting felicitously with one another. Her ears are so well practised in discriminating all these things, and her judgment is so good, that in all Greek, Latin, and English composition, there is nothing so loose on the one hand or so concise on the other, which she does not immediately attend to, and either reject with disgust or receive with pleasure, as the case may be. I am not inventing anything, my dear Sturm; it is all true.[77]

'Chastity', 'modesty', 'discriminating' are unselfconsciously deployed here by Ascham so as to imply that Elizabeth's Protestant devotion and female decorum are directly linked to her outstanding ability in humane letters.

The fact that Erasmus returns again and again in his letters to the connection between his publishing activities in the secular sphere and his scriptural and doctrinal studies suggests that the welding of profane learning to lay piety requires a certain amount of intellectual sleight-of-hand. In a letter of 1514 to his old friend Servatius Roger, Prior of the monastery at Steyn (to which he remained technically attached throughout his life), he justifies his literary activities by juxtaposing their success and virtuosity with his personally pious intentions:

To say a word about my writings. I think you have read my *Enchiridion*, which many persons say has inspired them to a life of piety. I am not taking any credit for that, but am grateful to Christ if, through my efforts, some good has been accomplished as a result of his gift. I am not sure if you have seen the Aldine edition of my *Adagia*. The contents, of course, are secular, but it is a very useful work for any kind of learning. At any rate, it cost me an inestimable amount of toil and sleepless nights. I have published my *De rerum verborumque copia*, which I dedicated to my friend Colet; it is a very helpful work for those preparing to preach. But such things are despised by men who despise good learning. During the past two years, in addition to many other things, I have emended the text of

[77] Cit. Baldwin, *William Shakspere's Small Latine and Lesse Greeke*, I, 259. See Chapter Seven.

St. Jerome's Epistles. I have indicated the corrupt and spurious passages, and have explained the obscure ones in the notes. By collating the old Greek manuscripts I have emended the entire [Latin] text of the New Testament, and have annotated more than a thousand passages, not without benefit to theologians. I have begun to do commentaries on Paul's Epistles, which I shall finish after publishing this other material. For I am determined to live and die in the study of Sacred Scripture. To these tasks I am devoting both my free and my working hours. Men of importance say that for these tasks I have an ability which others lack. Were I to live your way of life [in the monastery] I could accomplish nothing.[78]

The textual evolution of the *Colloquies* – which went through more than a hundred editions in Erasmus' lifetime, and a further hundred before the turn of the century – supports the view that Erasmus sometimes felt obliged to make the relationship between Latinity and piety more explicit. What began as a (pirated) manual on correct 'table' Latin (formulae of address, variations of expression, and felicitous phrases along the lines of the *De copia*) became in the course of successive substantial revisions a collection of exemplary tales (still in exemplary Latin) illustrating the morally upright life in the form of entertaining and elegant dialogues.[79] In other words, to establish the integrity of the project, the *content* of the exercises is made more explicitly moralistic. In the process (as the apt phrase is fleshed out into the exemplary moral tale), Erasmus' moral lessons become extremely local and specific: the tales caution against the ordinary misdemeanours of society (for example, the demands of clever daughters and reluctant wives).[80]

It is when Erasmus applies the tools of humanistic textual exegesis directly to Scripture, to develop a new theological framework based on 'close reading', that he is necessarily most explicit about the interdependence of profane humanistic arts education and Erasmian lay piety. His model is Lorenzo Valla's uncompromisingly lexical and philological annotations on the New Testament, which he defended publicly as exemplary humanistic scriptural exegesis.[81] In his *Methodus*, one of the treatises that accompanied and defended his new Latin translation of the New Testament, the *Novum Instrumentum* of 1516, he himself adopted an equivalent approach. Examination of this text reveals at once the immense flexibility of the *studia humanitatis* in the hands of a master humanist, and, at the same time, the ultimate vagueness of the Christian humanists' claim that their art of reading and composition builds on solid spiritual foundations.

[78] Allen, *Opus Epistolarum*, I, 570 (letter 296, 1514).

[79] See F. Bierlaire, *Erasme et ses Colloques: Le livre d'une vie* (Geneva, 1977).

[80] See Chomarat, *Grammaire et Rhétorique chez Erasme*, II, 849-930.

[81] For Erasmus' public admiration of Valla's method of scriptural textual exegesis see his prefatory letter to Christopher Fisher, in Erasmus' 1505 edition of Valla's annotations on the Latin text of the New Testament, *Laurentii Vallensis ... in Latinam Noui Testamenti interpretationem ex collatione Graecorum exemplarium Adnotationes* (Paris, 1505); reprinted in Allen *Opus Epistolarum*, I, 406-12 (letter 182).

The *Methodus* runs over much familiar ground. Erasmus begins with a reference to the definitive treatment of the liberal studies appropriate to a theologian – Augustine's four 'precise and copious' books *De doctrina Christiana*.[82] He reviles scholastic theology. Far from preparing the young student to understand the Bible, this actually distracts him from piety, which should be his central aim in life. It makes him contentious, and gives him a taste for the elaborate analysis of issues alien to the biblical text and irrelevant to his own or anyone else's salvation:

> The quality of foods does not exert so strong an influence on the condition of one's body as one's reading does on one's mind and character. If we frequent barren, flat, artificial, rebarbative and quarrelsome writers, we must come to resemble them. If we frequent those who truly express Christ, who burn, who live, who teach and display true piety, we must resemble them at least to some extent. 'But,' you will object, 'if that is the whole of it, I shall be ill prepared for the scholastic prize-ring.' But it is our purpose to train a theologian, not a boxer – and a theologian who would rather express his theology in his conduct than in syllogisms.[83]

The true theologian should study that which can make him like his model, Christ – the Bible itself, and the eloquent works of the Fathers of the Church, which will make him want to be a good Christian himself, and equip him to make good Christians of others: 'The profession of theology is founded more in the emotions than in technicalities.'[84] Here, as consistently in Erasmus' works, sensitive and attentive reading of Scripture is contrasted with 'philosophical' theology – the arid (in Erasmus' view) debating of knotty technical issues drawn from isolated texts.[85]

In the *Methodus* Erasmus lays careful emphasis on the proper procedure for 'disciplined' reading. He argues in detail that the only way to draw the true message from the Bible is to read it as a good humanist would read a classic pagan text: as the record of Christ, that incomparable orator, and Paul, that incomparable theologian, addressing specific audiences and dealing with specific issues. By keeping the context always in view, by bearing in mind the speaker's and writer's situation, the student will be able to avoid the doctrinal

[82] Erasmus, *Methodus*, ed. and tr. G.B. Winkler, in Erasmus, *Ausgewählte Schriften*, ed. W. Welzig, III (Darmstadt, 1967), 38-77; 38.

[83] '*Neque enim perinde ciborum qualitas transit in corporis habitum ut lectio in animum ac mores. Si in ieiunis, in frigidis, in fucatis, in spinosis ac rixosis scriptoribus assidui simus, tales evadamus oportet. Sin in iis, qui vere spirant Christum, qui ardent, qui vivunt, qui veram pietatem et docent et praestant, hos saltem aliqua ex parte referemus. At dices, si nihil accesserit, parum instructus fuero ad palaestram scholasticam. Neque vero nos pugilem instituimus, sed theologum, et eum theologum, qui quod profitetur malit exprimere vita quam syllogismis*' (72).

[84] '*Et quoniam professio theologica magis constat affectibus quam argutiis …*' (50).

[85] See e.g. Erasmus' long 'apologia' letter to Martin Dorp; Allen, *Opus Epistolarum*, II, 90-114 (letter 337, 1515), and the coresponding 'apologia' letter from Thomas More to Dorp (partially reprinted in *Juan Luis Vives Against the Pseudodialecticians: a Humanist Attack on Medieval Logic*, ed. R. Guerlac (Dordrecht, 1979), 166-95).

errors and evasions that the scholastics – those insensitive readers – have committed:

> Now there is a less perceptible, but on that account a more harmful kind of corruption, which takes place when we abuse the words of holy scripture and make 'Church' mean 'priests', and 'world' mean 'Christian laymen'; when we make what is said of 'Christians' apply to monks alone ...[86]

To avoid such mistakes in reading, which, Erasmus implies, will be symptomatic of mistakes in theology, the young student must always read as a philologist would:

> Let him not consider it adequate to pull out four or five little words; let him consider the origin of what is said, by whom it is said, to whom it is said, when, on what occasion, in what words, what precedes it, what follows. For it is from a comprehensive examination of these things that one learns the meaning of a given utterance.[87]

And in order to reduce the results of his reading to order, the student of theology must do to the Bible what he has done in school to the secular classics: cut it into properly interpreted gobbets and arrange these into categories appropriate to theological discourse.

> Make for yourself or take over ready-made from someone else some theological *loci* [places], in which you can organise everything you read, as if they were pigeon-holes: thus it will be easier for you to find what you want to retrieve.[88]

Erasmus gives examples of the proper heading for theological commonplaces or *loci*: 'faith', 'fasting', 'bearing evils', 'helping the infirm'.[89] He insists that such a supply of ordered material will be all the theologian needs to carry out his task:

> If you need to discuss something, the matter will be ready and accessible; if you need to explicate something, the comparison of passages will be easy.[90]

[86] '*Iam est occultius quidem, sed hoc ipso nocentius depravandi genus, cum abutentes divinae scripturae vocabulis ecclesiam interpretamur sacerdotes, mundum laicos Christianos, interim, quod de Christianis dictum est, monachis accommodantes ...*' (64).

[87] '*Idque quod certius fiat, non sat habeat quattuor aut quinque decerpsisse verbula, circumspiciat, unde natum sit quod dicitur, a quo dicatur, cui dicatur, quo tempore, qua occasione, quibus verbis, quid praecesserit, quid consequatur. Quandoquidem ex hisce rebus expensis collectisque deprehenditur, quid sibi velit quod dictum est*' (64).

[88] '*Id est huiusmodi, ut locos aliquot theologicos aut tibi pares ipse aut ab alio quopiam traditos accipias, ad quos omnia quae legeris veluti in nidulos quosdam digeras, quo promptius sit, ubi videbitur quod voles depromere ...*' (64).

[89] Ibid., 66.

[90] '*Sive quid erit disserendum, aderit ad manum parata supellex, sive quid explicandum, facilis erit locorum collatio*' (66).

And he explicitly draws the analogy between his theological and humanistic textbooks and methods:

> Once you have ordered the *loci* by difference or similarity of content, you should put into them in an orderly way everything of any importance in the Old Testament, in the Gospels, in the Letters of the apostles, everything that corresponds or disagrees, as we showed once before in the *Copia*.[91]

What Erasmus does not explain (what from his point of view as a humanist pedagogue requires no explanation) is how the young theologian can be sure that simple, straightforward reading will produce guaranteed right doctrine. He does admit that the *tirunculus* could use a simple and straightforward manual of doctrine based on the gospels and epistles to help him master the necessary doctrinal points;[92] but by his own account such a manual would itself have to be produced, without elaborate theological preamble, by the very process of reading that it was meant to guide. Erasmus sees no problem here – and in this context the assumption is a clear one – because for him the secular humanist's method of close reading in context is itself an enterprise of evident moral value. The mere exercise of reading the text as it really is will make the reader moral and wise in a direct way that no systematic body of dogmatic teaching can rival. Accurate reading is not only a necessary but a sufficient training for the theologian because accurate reading is itself a morally-loaded act. Naturally Erasmus hopes that the humanist theologian will practise biblical scholarship at a higher level than the scholastics had; that he will be able to recognise the tropes and poetic quotations in the Bible and to explicate the things it mentions without falling into the banality of the traditional commentators, 'who either make impudent guesses or consulting vile reference works make trees into four-legged beasts, and jewels into fish'.[93] But scholarship of this sort is merely a by-product. The real point of close reading is that it produces the right sort of person – a person of evident worth.

Agricola and Erasmus together provided the sixteenth century with a promise that the humanist education they promoted and developed would make its recipients better people, and they provided the pedagogic tools to make that education accessible to the many: synthetic accumulations of matter and graded and systematic procedures for employing that matter. The tacit assumption is that the two things *necessarily* go together: that successful

---

[91] '*His in ordinem compositis iuxta rerum pugnantiam aut affinitatem, ut in Copia quoque nostra quondam indicavimus, quicquid usquam insigne est in omnibus veteris instrumenti libris, in evangeliis, in litteris apostolorum, quod vel conveniat vel dissonet, ad hos erit redigendum*' (66).

[92] Ibid., 58.

[93] '*... adeo ut nonnunquam vel impudenter divinantes vel sordidissimos consulentes dictionarios ex arbore faciant quadrupedem, e gemma piscem. Abunde doctum videtur, si tantum adiecerint: est nomen gemmae, aut species est arboris aut genus animantis. Atqui non raro ex ipsa rei proprietate pendet intellectus mysterii*' (50).

drilling in *copia* and *methodus* will guarantee a classroom product of moral uprightness and good character.

Coda: Erasmian tutors – proof of the pudding

In his own manual describing how such an education is achieved, Erasmus himself preferred to entrust the mysterious process of making the boy 'good' by programmatic arts teaching to the private tutor, and reinforced parental confidence in the inevitable transformation of the child into the upright man by characterising that tutor as having a rare combination of qualities: the youthfulness to enjoy dealing with children, the playfulness to make his lessons enjoyable and the adaptability to dilute difficult subjects to the point where children could grasp them: 'How do you teach a child to walk? By bending over and shortening your steps to match his childish abilities.'[94] Above all the tutor must be a good psychologist, one who can fit both the content and the presentation of his lessons to the interests and capacities of his pupil, which will vary widely from age to age and child to child:

> Now infants themselves sometimes show a clear aptitude for a given discipline, such as music or arithmetic or cosmography. For I myself have encountered some who are remarkably slow at mastering the rules of grammar and rhetoric, but very apt at learning those more subtle disciplines. One must help nature to move in the direction in which she herself is inclined to go; the work is always easier on a slope.[95]

Such tutors, Erasmus assured his public, will do more than any classroom teacher to bring out their charges' innate abilities, mitigate their weaknesses, and entice them to hard work with jokes and kindness.

We have argued throughout this chapter that the development of a systematised programme of arts training in northern Europe out of the cumulative and unstructured educational practice of early Italian humanism, in conjunction with a marketing drive which insisted that that training would produce good Christians, led to a convenient confusion of the 'methodical' with the 'morally sound'. As a coda to this chapter, therefore, we offer the reader some documented examples of private tutoring, which show all too clearly the gap between the ideals and practicalities of providing the young with a 'humane' education.

Between 1552 and 1555 three sons of Julius Caesar Scaliger, the Aristotelian philosopher, doctor and literary critic, studied with tutors to guide them at the Collège de Guyenne, perhaps the most famous municipal school in France. They had three tutors in three years: Girard Roques,

---

[94] Erasmus, *De pueris statim ac liberaliter instituendis*, ed. J.-C. Margolin, in Erasmus, *Opera omnia*, I, pt. 2 (Amsterdam, 1971), 65.
[95] Ibid., 67.

Simon Beaupé and Laurens de Lamarque. But this rapid turnover in personnel had little apparent ill effect. All three kept up a lively correspondence with the boys' brilliant and opinionated father, the surviving passages of which shed a vivid light on all parties to the relationship. The tutors rendered the father a detailed accounting of the money he sent them, assured him that the boys were being reared in the strictest Catholic orthodoxy even if they occasionally had to use textbooks by Protestants, and sent him uncorrected samples of the boys' writing so he could judge their progress directly:

> Sir: if you find errors in the children's letters, I am leaving them there so as not to mislead you in your assessment of them. I swear that I would not add or remove anything.[96]

They gave him sound advice on how to endear himself and his sons to the Collège's official teaching staff:

> Sir: at the Feast of St Remy your children will have to move to another class. It seems to me that it would not be a bad idea for you to give a silver coin of some sort to the regents who will have to supervise them.[97]

And they supplemented the Collège's official teaching with their own. Julius' instructions in this crucial area sometimes lacked the desirable precision. 'You instruct me,' wrote Laurens de Lamarque in April 1555,

> to introduce the children to Aristotle's works. I don't know which works you mean. Do you want me to lecture to them on the dialectic, the ethics, the physics, the metaphysics, the politics, and other books composed by Aristotle, in my view the prince of all philosophers?[98]

But another letter soon cleared the difficulty up in much the way one would expect. Within a month de Lamarque was teaching the elements of dialectic from Porphyry and planning to continue with Aristotle's *Categories*. And even as he dictated his own introduction to this advanced subject, he continued to review the boys in their literary 'lectures communes'. By mid-June he reported with satisfaction that 'two of your children, Joseph and Leonard, already know more Aristotle than I did after I had heard the whole course on him'.[99]

All three tutors showed their ability in other ways as well. All noticed the precocity of the oldest boy, Joseph, 'who hears nothing that he does not understand immediately', and who proved able to produce compositions not merely by the mechanical recombination of characters and events he had

---

[96] J. de Borrousse de Laffore, 'Jules-César de Lescale (Scaliger)', *Recueil des Travaux de la Société d'Agriculture, Sciences et Arts d'Agen*, ser. II, 1 (1863), 54.
[97] Ibid., 58.   [98] Ibid., 62.   [99] Ibid., 63.

read about in classical texts but by extempore improvisation.[100] Their perceptions were borne out in the event, for he was to become the greatest classical scholar of the later sixteenth century. True, even these three conscientious and hardworking tutors could not do everything Scaliger asked for his three clever sons. Despite the principal's promises, the Collège proved unable to offer them a serious Greek course. All Beaupé could do was to give Julius a frank prediction:

> Your children have made good progress in Latin, but in Greek they know only a very little. You must not hope that they will learn much Greek in Bordeaux, for they teach it less seriously than I would like to put in writing.[101]

But even Julius could hardly blame the tutors for the defects of the Collège. On the whole this was tutoring at its most effective, so far as the participants were concerned: conscientious, systematic, attentive to parents' desires and children's abilities. No classroom teacher could have hoped to offer such intimate attention to individual boys.

Our second case reveals a strikingly different picture: the parents out of reach, the tutor out of his depth and the pupil in the throes of adolescent rebelliousness. Ten years after the young Scaligers went to Bordeaux, the young Julius Schlick came to Paris from Prague with his tutor Simon Wirt. Like Roques and company, Wirt tried to see to his charge's life and studies, and recorded his zealous efforts and their pitifully meagre results in a detailed diary. He drew up daily timetables:

> Monday and Tuesday: you will rise at five o'clock, and after spending the proper amount of time on your toilet you will strengthen your piety by reading a chapter of the New Testament.

> VI. After saying your prayers you will hear an exposition of Cicero's *Oratio pro Archia poeta*, which will do you some good.

> VII. You will repeat and memorise what you have heard.

> VIII. You will eat breakfast.

> IX. Let this be preparation for the next lesson and your exercises.

> X. After an explanation of the most commonly applied rules in law and morals you will study etymology.

> XI. Lunch.

> 1. To work on learning to read and write French.

> 2. You will learn the rules of syntax and grasp everything to be taken down from the lecture on Terence.

[100] Ibid., 60, 55.   [101] Ibid., 60.

3. Drill on Terence and syntax.

IX. o'clock in the evening will be the time for a test on your whole day's work.

Then you will go to bed.[102]

Here was individual attention with a vengeance; and Wirt accompanied it by threats, cajolings and moral lectures:

> When you go out be sure that there is a particular place that you mean to go to, so that you do not have to indulge in your habit of wandering about the streets.[103]

Wirt insisted more than once that he was going to break off their connection entirely, hoping that this would persuade Julius to bring his behaviour into line with his tutor's requirements.

But no exhortation Wirt could muster was powerful enough to overcome Julius' resistance to discipline. He went on inviting home disreputable friends (one apparently had a venereal disease that had grossly disfigured him) and then leaving Wirt to deal with them. He went on spending his time at feasts and tournaments and demanding that he be allowed to spend his time learning to fight rather than learning to write Latin. Even when he did some work he refused to do it on the text Wirt had assigned:

> In the morning, when I was to hear Julius' Horace, he recited a letter of Cicero's by heart, insisting that it would be of no use to him to read Horace. He was hurrying to learn to speak Latin as quickly as he could. Then he asked to be given leave to go to the Palace. When this was denied him he took it badly, and made me this reproach among others: 'You are doing me harm by preventing me from seeing the foreign people and gentlemen.' To this I said: 'Be patient. If God wills I will not prevent you for long.'[104]

Meanwhile Julius kept his tutor baffled to the point of paralysis by pouring over him a flood compounded of abuse and adulation in equal proportions. After being scolded he cried: 'I shall see that I go with a fine man like Lazarus Schwendi [as tutor]', injuring Wirt's feelings deeply; but after his tutor threatened to wash his hands of him, he proclaimed his loyalty and affection as winningly as if he had been a model pupil.

Clearly even the best humanist – and Wirt was a good one, well-trained and long-suffering – lacked any pedagogical theory that could account for, or any rhetorical armament that could help him to deal with, adolescent rebellion. Wirt could only confide his failed plans and ineffectual speeches to

---

[102] S. Proxenus (Wirt) a Sudetis, *Commentarii de itinere Francogallico*, ed. D. Martínková (Budapest, 1979), 51-2.
[103] Ibid., 41.
[104] Ibid., 32.

his diary, and pray for deliverance. We must sympathise with the tutor, forced to keep his whole cargo of grammar and rhetoric aboard, despite his desperate attempts to unload it. But we must also feel something for Julius, a square aristocratic peg who simply did not want to be rounded off with Latin rhetoric and fitted into a neat hole in the government apparatus he was intended to join.

Nor (as we might guess) was such a case unique – gifted academic tutors are by no means the most competent guardians of teenage boys. For another example of a tutor's inability to cope with his young charges we may turn to the letters exchanged between John Amerbach, the Basle printer, and John Blumenstock of Heidelberg, who tutored Amerbach's two older sons, Bruno and Basil, during the years they spent away from home studying at the University of Paris. Blumenstock complains to Amerbach that the boys make fun of him, that they accuse him of keeping them with too tight a hand, that he has trouble making them work, and that once in his absence they disgraced him by running from one College to another dressed only in doublet and hose without a belt.[105] In this case, however, unruly behaviour was not a mark of any intellectual stupidity, nor did it ultimately impede the students' education; these are the boys whose abilities in Latin, Greek and Hebrew – testimony to their father's admirable care with their education – Erasmus praised to Leo X in a letter of 1515.[106]

An even more exacting and strenuous experience than that of the young Scaligers fell to the lot of the young Henri de Mesmes in the 1540s:

My father gave me as tutor J. Maludan, a Limousin and pupil of Dorat's, a scholar chosen for his blameless life and himself of a suitable age to guide me in my youth until I knew how to rule myself. This he did. For he worked so incredibly hard at his studies that he was always as far ahead of me as he had to be in order to teach me, and he did not give up his responsibility until I took up my office. With him and my next younger brother J.J. de Mesmes I was sent in 1542 to the Collège de Bourgogne [at Paris], to be in the third class. Then I was in the first class for just under a year ... I find that my eighteen months in the Collège did me quite a bit of good. I learned to answer, dispute, and speak formally in public; met honourable boys, some of whom are still alive; and learned the frugal life of the scholar and how to use my time effectively. When I left, in fact, I gave several speeches in Latin and Greek of my own composition in public, and I offered a good many Latin verses and 2000 Greek verses done as my age allowed; recited Homer by heart from one end to the other. That was why the best men of the time thought well of me, and my tutor sometimes took me to see Lazare de Baïf, Toussain, Strazelius, Castellanus, and Danès; ... in September 1545 I was sent to Toulouse to study law with my tutor and my brother ... At Toulouse we were students for three years, leading a pinched life and performing terribly hard work of a sort that they could not stand nowadays.

[105] P.S. Allen, *The Correspondence of an Early Printing House: the Amorbachs of Basle* (Glasgow, 1932), 17-20.
[106] Allen, *Opus Epistolarum*, II, 88 (letter 335).

We rose at four and, after prayers, went to work at five, our big books under our arms and our candles and writing-desks in our hands ... After dinner we read Aristophanes or Sophocles or Euripides for fun ... We often had Adrien Turnebus, Denys Lambin, Honoré Chatelain with us ...[107]

In this case the tutor not only oversaw the boys' work and leisure but passed on to them the classical skills he had learnt from Dorat and introduced them to some of the brightest stars of European humanism. Pupils like the young Amerbachs probably did not receive this high a polish.

But the most celebrated documented example we have of a pupil on whom seemingly endless amounts of tutorial care were lavished between the ages of seven and fifteen is that of Henry VIII's cherished son Edward, later Edward VI of England. Edward was tutored by Richard Cox and John Cheke, two of the most distinguished humanists and Greek specialists Cambridge produced in the sixteenth century (a third, Roger Ascham – like Cheke a product of St John's College, Cambridge – tutored Edward's sister Elizabeth, as we saw above).[108] After only five months under the tutorship of Cox (with Cheke as junior 'supplement'), the seven-year-old's progress is described by Cox to Sir Richard Paget as follows:

[Edward] hath expugned and utterly conquered and [sic] great nu[m]b[er] of the captayns of ignorance. The eight parts of speche he hath made the[m] his subiects and servaunts, and can declyne any man[ne]r latyne noune and coniugate a v[e]rbe p[er]fectly onlesse it be anomalu[m]. These parts thus beten downe & conquered, he begynneth to buylde the[m] vp agayn and frame the[m] aft[e]r his purpose w[ith] dew ordre of construction, lyke as the Kyngs mai[es]ti[e] fframed vp Bullayn when he had beaten it downe. He undrestondeth and can frame well his iii concordes of gram[ma]r and hath made all redy xl or l prety latyns and can answere welfavourdly to the parts, and is now redy to entre in to Cato, to so[m] p[ro]pre & p[ro]fitable fables of Esops, and othre holsom and godly lessons [that] shall be deuised for hym. Every day in the masse tyme he redeth a portion of Salomon's p[ro]v[e]rbs for the exercise of hys reding, wherin he deliteth muche and lerneth ther how good it is to geve eare vnto dyscipline, to feare god, to kepe godds com[m]aundme[n]ts to beware of straunge and wanton wome[n], to be obedieint to fath[e]r and mother, to be thankfull to the[m] [that] telleth hy[m] of his fawtes &c.[109]

And he kept up this relentless pace. By 1546, at the age of nine, he is citing Erasmus' *Colloquies*, by 1547 his *De copia*.[110] Somewhere around the same time he began seriously to study Greek. We should not forget that, in the midst of all his gruelling schoolwork, in 1547 Edward also succeeded Henry VIII as King of England.

---

[107] H. de Mesmes, *Mémoires inédits* (Paris, n.d.), 135-42.
[108] On Edward VI's education and his tutors, see above all Baldwin, *William Shakspere's Small Latine and Lesse Greeke*, I, 200-56.
[109] Baldwin, *William Shakspere's Small Latine and Lesse Greeke*, I, 203-4.
[110] Ibid., I, 215-16.

In 1548 we find Edward using Agricola's translation of Aphthonius' *Progymnasmata* to learn methodical Latin composition,[111] and by 1549 he is producing fully-fledged orations according to Aphthonius' schemata, drawing additional material from precisely the range of classical texts we find specified in the curriculum of the great Tudor grammar schools.[112] His orations also make it clear that he had learnt to structure his orations with the pseudo-Ciceronian *Ad Herennium* beside him:

> [In] an exercise which he dates July 28, 1549 on the subject *Dulce Bellum Inexpertis*, a subject which is to be found in the *Adagia* of Erasmus treated at great length ... Edward labels his parts, *Exordium a re et adversariorum contemptu, Narratio, Divisio, Confirmatio a testimonio, ab experientia, Distributio, Peroratio primae partis, Belli fructus, Confutatio, Conclusio*. Here are in order the six parts of an oration *à la Ad Herennium*, with certain telltale, descriptive additions. For instance, in *Ad Herennium* the various forms of exordium are classified. So Edward uses two of these classifications in his exordium *a re* and *a ... adversariorum contemptu*. Narratio, Divisio are the next in order and are not further described by Edward. The *Ad Herennium* points out that Confirmatio and Confutatio form the heart of the oration. These sections, therefore, receive detailed treatment. Edward has added *a testimonio* and *ab experientia* to show the particular varieties of Confirmatio he is using. Similarly in the first part of his Confirmatio he uses Distributio and ends with a Peroratio. Next he turns in the second part of his Confirmatio to the *Belli fructus*. The third part of his Confirmatio he does not label. He is then ready for the fifth and sixth parts of the oration, the Confutatio and Conclusio ... The whole oration observes and ties together these parts with the utmost precision.[113]

The twelve-year-old King's surviving classroom orations bring home clearly to us the amount of arduous and repetitive drilling he was subjected to by his teachers – eager to prove the worth of their pupil (and ensure their own renown as teachers) by the mastery of Greek and Latin he could display in his weekly exercises. They also make it plain that while the themes chosen by Edward's teachers are gravely moralistic, the exercises he performs are meticulous, dutifully imitative rhetorical compositions, in which the balanced phrase has clearly occupied the pupil's mind, rather than the weightiness of the issue. For one short period Edward produced carefully competent and utterly soulless orations, crafted out of Cicero's and Erasmus' borrowed phrases, on topics ranging from 'The performance of virtue is more admirable than an inclination towards it', 'A king ought to rule with gentleness and clemency (Isocrates)', 'The most beautiful of deaths is to die for one's country in war', to 'All adulterers should be ruthlessly put to death' and 'War ought to be waged against the Turks, on religious grounds' (on which theme

---

[111] Ibid., I, 222-3.

[112] For the grammar-school curricula see Baldwin, *William Shakspere's Small Latine and Lesse Greeke*, I.

[113] Ibid., I, 233-4.

Edward produces orations in both Latin and Greek).[114] Preserved for posterity, they are a monument to the child King's endurance. We may ask with T.W. Baldwin whether it might not have been Edward's superior but relentless schooling which drove him to an early grave![115]

The varied, if fragmentary, testimony available to us, concerning tutoring on the Erasmian model, suggests (as we might expect, away from the overawing context of 'Christian humanism') that its products were as varied, and as variable in their moral outlook, as the products of any other educational system. We may tentatively draw a few conclusions from our small survey. The first is that tutoring had little effect on the rebellious and incompetent. If anything, the sound moral principles and calls to piety which were all a tutor could use to soften the heart of his young charge – who was usually his social superior and well aware of the fact – must often have been counter-productive. The second, which is not unrelated to the first, is that if tutor/pupil relations varied greatly, the criteria by which the parties to them assessed their success or failure hardly varied at all. The ability to jump the highest academic hurdles with apparent ease, the self-discipline to follow a killing regimen without protest – these were the attributes which great French lawyers like de Mesmes, cosmopolitan scholars like Scaliger, successful commercial men like Amerbach and Bohemian nobles like the parents of Julius Schlick all wished to see instilled in their sons. To that extent the variation in individual cases is a matter of means not ends. The tutor might recognise that each child differed from all others in aptitude; his aim was not to create different adult individuals but to use different means to bring different children to the same final condition: the predetermined humanist ideal of eloquence and erudition. (Not all *tutors*, of course, were in the same mould: the future Marshal de Bassompierre had to cut his college career short in 1591 after five months, when his tutor murdered his dancing-master.)[116]

We close with a curious anecdotal example of tutoring, involving another Erasmian Hellenist, Clenardus, whom we have come across before, seriously involved in developing humanistic pedagogy. As an educational experiment Clenardus undertook the tutoring of three slaves whom he had bought in order to train them as amanuenses – and whom he had named, with startling lack of sensitivity, Carbo, Dento and Nigrinus (Coal, Toothy and Blacky). Unlike Cheke and Cox's royal charge, Clenardus' slaves had no advantages at all, no access to books, no prior knowledge; he overcame these deprivations in a brilliant experiment in direct-method teaching, immersing them in

[114] J.G. Nichols, *Literary Remains of King Edward the Sixth*, 2 vols. (London, 1857), I, Table of Contents.

[115] Baldwin, *William Shakspere's Small Latine and Lesse Greeke*, I, 256. In an appendix to this chapter we reproduce in its entirety one of Edward's exercise orations, so that the reader can judge for himself.

[116] P. Ariès, *Centuries of Childhood*, tr. R. Baldick (New York, 1962), 319.

spoken Latin whenever they were together and making them fluent speakers of the language even before they could learn to read or write it. Clenardus evidences no humanity whatsoever towards his slaves – he appears to have regarded *them* as less than human:

> Others who wear purple take great delight in monkeys: I, when tired of study, enjoy my monkeys, who have the power of reason. They learn Latin whether they want to or not, for that is all they hear from me ...[117]

But he made his exotic pupils literate. For all the difference in execution, the ends in view are recognisably the same as those enthusiastically pursued by Cox and Cheke as they groomed and put through his paces the sickly boy King. Moor or monarch, slave or prince, the boy entrusted to an able humanist tutor emerged at the end of his schooling linguistically and rhetorically fluent and therefore, in the eyes of a community which attached *value* to the acquisition of such a grooming, a credit to his parents (or in the case of Clenardus' Nigrinus, his guardian). We leave the reader with Erasmus' eulogy of the Amerbach brothers, in which well-taught pupils are elevated effortlessly into exemplary invididuals:

> Their father, best of men, saw to it that his three sons were thoroughly instructed in Greek, Hebrew and Latin. On his death he committed that application to learning to his children's cares as a kind of inheritance, bequeathing whatever resources he had to this enterprise. And those best of young men zealously perform that most glorious/illustrious charge, enjoined upon them by that best of parents.[118]

---

[117] *Correspondance de Nicolas Clenard*, ed. A. Roersch (Brussels, 1940-1), I, 115; not surprisingly the passage is bowdlerized in the translation, III, 67. See the indices s.nn. Carbo, Dento, Nigrinus.

[118] '*Pater, vir omnium optimus, treis filios in Graecis, Hebraeis ac Latinis litteris curarat instituendos. Ipse decedens liberis suis studium hoc velut hereditarium commendauit, quicquid erat facultatum huic negocio dedicans. Atque optimi iuuenes pulcherrimam prouinciam ab optimo parente mandatam gnauiter obeunt*' (Allen, *Opus Epistolarum*, II, 88).

Appendix

Exercise oration of Edward VI

Amor maior causa obedientiae quam timor

Outline:

Exordium ab utilitate qu[a]estionis. Enarratio meae sententiae. Confirmatio per uxoris amorem. timor deterret a malo, non hortatur ad bonum. quid amor fecerit in Alexandro Seuero, quid timor in Heliogabalo. Tyrannorum exitus. quid amor in Themistocle, Epaminonda, Scipione, Metello, Cicerone et &. Confutatio. 1. Rat. Bruta animantia timent, non amant. Nego 2. Sunt gradus amoris. Quid tum. 3. Leges sancitae indicant metum uehementiore[m] esse amore. 4. Metus trahit nole[n]tes/1. Tyrannis obeditur magis amoris causa quam/sed non bonis regib[us]/2. Amor non satis potest/3. Fateor sed & timor non sufficit, neutru[m] malu[m] amor praestantior.

Development:

Cum nulla natio bene institui possit, nisi inferiores superiorib[us] obtemperent, cum nulla ciuitas ciuiliter gubernari, nisi subditi magistratib[us] obediant, cum nullus exercitus possit esse accommodatus ad pugnam, nisi milites pareant uoci ducum, & imperatoris, ita ut eorum nutu in ordines se redigant, parent ad pugnam, & castra metant, necessarium est & ualde utile omnib[us] iis qui aliquam curam habent, aut nationis, aut ciuitatis, aut exercitus, cognoscere quo modo possint & hominum me[n]tes attrahi ad bonum, & deterreri a malo. Hi enim gubernatores qui habe[n]t ciues, huic regulae pare[n]tes, sunt omnium foelicissimi. De hac igitur re, hoc tempore constitui disserere, & meam sententiam patefacere, in hoc ut ueritas ex orationibus utrinque habitis excussa, sit dilucida, & uobis facile uideatur. Duo autem sunt modi, quib[us] solent plerunque uulgi animi adduci ad obedientiam, quorum alter est timor alter amor. Timor eos cogit ad benefaciendum & parendum, idque ui; Amor eos allicit ad pare[n]du[m] idque uoluntate. Quanquam enim utrunque coniunctu[m] multum ualeat, neque boni gubernatores solo amore aut solo timore in eorum gubernaculis utantur, tamen mente iam separata, uter maior sit causa & uehementior obedientiae iam est qu[a]estio. Ego quidem puto amorem esse maiorem causam, idque facilius perspicietis, qua ratione p[er]suasus, teneam, si prius quae sit natura horum affectuum, quae partes, quae uis, quod robur, denique quinam & quales sint, uelitis perpendere, & animo uestro penitus & integre reuoluere. Amor est animi affectus, qui oritur, ex bona aliqua opinione de aliquo concepta, aut ex familiari consuetudine inter homines, qui extenditur erga eum qui amatur sui causa, non alicuius lucri causa aut uoluptatis eius qui amat. Si enim talis sit affectus, insimuletur, in hoc ut quis decipiatur & sua spe penitus frustretur, non amor est dicendus sed qu[a]edam assentatio, aut adulatio, inter malos maxime existens, etiam max[im]e inimicos. Timor est autem animi quidam impetus, excitatus ex repentino aliquo malo futuro, uel imminenti, quo quis deterretur a male agendo, & ueretur, ne si quid malum perpetret, statim supplicio afficiatur. Hinc s[a]epe pallor, exanimatio, c[a]eteraque similia oriuntur. Ex his igitur perspicere quis potest amorem esse in homine illius causa qui amatur, timorem supplicii imminentis causa, unde et uideri potest, amorem tam diu permanere posse, quamdiu ille qui amatur existit, timorem solum manere ad tempus, quamdiu quis habeat supplicium & malum imminens pr[a]e oculis. Nam quamdiu causa manet tam diu plerunque effectus manet, diutius autem non potest quia nihil fit sine causa. Igitur cum ille qui amatur causa sit amoris, supplicium timoris, necesse est timorem non diutius manere quam pro occulis habeat supplicium, amorem autem tam diu quam cogitat de amato. Veheme[n]tia autem plerunque diutius permanent quam ea quae leuia sunt, quia unumquodque tam diu permanet, quamdiu habet uim & robur. Adh[a]ec si tales debent esse reges erga subditos, quales patres erga filios, ut eodem genere officii gubernatores, quo patres, & subditi, quo filii, tum certe alterutra debent uti, sed magis amore. Nam patres, (dico autem naturales & honestos) semper afficiuntur amore erga filios, & filii, qui ad aliquam aetatis maturitatem peruenerint, patribus, max[im]e amoris causa obediunt. Cum autem filius peccauerit, uel in aliquod graue crimen sit illapsus, tum terret eum pater minis, & interdu[m] supplicio, quanquam adhuc eum amare non desinat. Hoc autem indicat amorem in patre maiorem locum obtinere, quod amor sit ipsa causa efficiens eum terrere filium, ueritus ne alias in grauia crimina labatur. Si igitur principes his similes esse debent tum & illos summa ope niti oportet, ut amore parent beneuolentiam ciuium, maius quam supplicio faciant eos timere. Vnde & hoc bene mihi dictum uidetur, quem metuunt oderunt, quem oderunt eum periisse cupiunt. Quanquam enim coguntur timore, ad tempus obedire, tamen si aliquam sint nacti omnino occasionem uolunt omnib[us] uiribus ei resistere, qui hoc modo eos in timorem coniicit. Huius rei multa possumus pr[a]eclara exempla proferre, & inter Athenienses & Romanos. Erat quidem inter Athenienses in primordiis ciuitatis nomine Codrus uir admodum pr[a]eclarus, cui cum indicaretur auspiciis eo mortuo in pugna Athenienses uicturos, quamprimum hostes conspexit in eorum se medium coniecit, & ibi fortiter pugnans pro patria mortuus est. Hic uir clarissimus amoris causa concitatus erga patriam in non dubiam mortem se coniecit. Timoris autem causa neminem unquam audiui morti se tradere, quia supplicii solum est timor, & cum mors extremu[m], & omnium maximum sit, tum omnem timorem mortem euitare, & non patriae causa eam oppetere necesse est. Simile etiam existit inter Romanos exemplu[m] illius uiri nobilissimi Curtii, qui ciuitate multum oppressa peste quadam, ita ut pene deuastaretur natio Romana, cum oraculis traderetur pestem cessatam fore, cum in puteum quendam max[im]e horrendum coniiceretur optima & preciosissima gemma ciuitatis armatus insidens equo optimo, & gemmis adornato se coniecit in illum profundissimum ubi statim expirauit. Sed quid qu[a]eram externa & antiqua exempla, cum & hic satis eorum habeamus domestica? Nonne magis efficiebat amor erga Henricum septimvm eius nominis, insitus in animis populi, quam timor ille quo crudelissimus tyrannus Richardus eos cohibebat? Nonne semper uidemus populum sua sponte, cum aliqui de regno certarent, ei adh[a]esisse quem max[im]e amauerant eum odisse quem max[im] e timebant? Alterum enim uoluntate suscipitur alterum inuitus. Ex his itaque est manifestum amorem esse maiorem & uehementiorem causam obedienti[a]e quam metus. Dixi. Finis. Eduardus Rex.

(B.L. Add. MS. 4724, 74^r ff. Erasures etc. not indicated. Reprinted in T.W. Baldwin, *William Shakspere's Small Latine and Lesse Greeke*, 2 vols. (Urbana, 1944), I, 251-3)

CHAPTER SEVEN

Pragmatic Humanism: Ramism and the rise of 'the Humanities'

There is a kind of double inevitability about our concluding this book with a treatment of Ramism. In the first place, no study with claims to get to grips with humanist *practice* rather than its theoretical and idealistic promises could fail to tackle that most pragmatic and 'applied' of arts educationalists, Petrus Ramus (Pierre de la Ramée). There is, indeed, general agreement within the extensive secondary literature on Ramus that the impact and importance of Ramism lies within the classroom. So that although we have claimed that historians have not, on the whole, given enough of their attention to what actually went on in the Renaissance classroom in the name of humanism, in the case of Petrus Ramus they have done little else. Since W.J. Ong's pioneering bibliographical work on Ramus, historians of sixteenth-century France have taken account in various ways of the impact on thought and letters of Ramus' substantial contribution (in bulk and in notoriety) to arts education of the period.[1] It is widely agreed that while intellectually many of Ramus' works are muddled and derivative,[2] Ramist textbooks were a runaway printing and teaching success: traces of Ramist habits of mind have

---

[1] For recent bibliography on Ramus see P. Sharratt, 'The present state of studies on Ramus', *Studi Francesi* 47-8 (1972), 201-13. The essential works are C. Waddington, *Ramus: sa vie, ses écrits et ses opinions* (Paris, 1855); W.J.Ong, *Ramus, Method, and the Decay of Dialogue* (Cambridge, Mass., 1958; reprinted New York, 1972); R. Hooykaas, *Humanisme, Science et Réforme: Pierre de la Ramée (1515-1572)* (Leiden, 1958); J.J. Verdonk, *Petrus Ramus en de wiskunde* (Assen, 1966) (English synopsis in Sharratt, 'The present state of studies on Ramus', 205-6). See also C. Vasoli, *La dialettica e la retorica dell'Umanesimo: "Invenzione" e "Metodo" nella cultura del XV e XVI secolo* (Milan, 1968), 333-601; W. Risse, *Die Logik der Neuzeit* I (Stuttgart, 1964), ch. 3; 'Die Entwicklung der Dialektik bei P. Ramus', *Archiv für Geschichte der Philosophie* 42 (1960), 36-72.

[2] See e.g. E.J. Ashworth, *Language and Logic in the Post Medieval Period* (Dordrecht, 1974); C.B. Schmitt, *John Case and Aristotelianism in Renaissance England* (Kingston and Montreal, 1983), ch. 1; N.W. Gilbert, *Renaissance Concepts of Method* (New York and London, 1960; reprinted in 1963), chs. 5 and 6; W.S. Howell, *Logic and Rhetoric in England, 1500-1700* (Princeton, 1956); L. Jardine, *Francis Bacon: Discovery and the Art of Discourse* (Cambridge, 1974), 41-7. On the other hand, for evidence of Ramus' original intellectual contributions in specialist fields such as mathematics see Verdonk, *Petrus Ramus en de wiskunde*; N. Jardine, *The Birth of History and Philosophy of Science* (Cambridge, 1984), 234-5, 267-9.

been found in the works of contemporary figures as diverse as Francis Bacon and the Pléiade poets.[3]

It is also inevitable, however, that we turn to Ramus in pursuit of that crucial moment of transition when (we maintain) 'humanism' became 'the humanities'. We shall argue in this chapter that it is only possible to make sense of the *succès fou* of Ramism within arts institutions across Europe if one concedes that by 1550 'humanism' as an identifiable movement had become 'the humanities' (and their teaching). It is with their treatment of Ramus and Ramism, we suggest, that traditional historians of humanism fail in the end to give a satisfactory account as a result of their own prior assumptions. For they have inadvertently consented to the view that humanism as an ideal declined, and to the view that humanism triumphed as a curriculum practice. They insist on the banality and triteness of Ramus' intellectual contribution to the liberal arts which, they are committed to maintaining, is a travesty of the high ideals of true humanism. But the fact is that that *is* the version of liberal arts teaching that 'caught on' and left its indelible trace on western European thought. For historians of humanism Ramus is a blot on the sixteenth-century intellectual landscape; for historians of education he heralds the age of standardised classroom teaching and the best-selling textbook. But our argument throughout this book has been that these two facets of intellectual life cannot, in fact, be separated. If Ramist 'method' was a pedagogic success story, but the theoretical underpinning offered by Ramus fails to convince the intellectual historian, we should ask ourselves why. To find an answer we continue our case-study approach and offer three documented examples of Ramism in action: Petrus Ramus himself; Claude Mignault, humanities teacher active in Paris during the years immediately before and after Ramus' death; and Gabriel Harvey, briefly acting Professor of Rhetoric at the University of Cambridge, during the same period (1573-5).

Petrus Ramus rose to notoriety during the 1540s in Paris because he advocated the union for teaching purposes of philosophy and eloquence and challenged the authority of Aristotle.[4] From the perspective of our present study it is not difficult to see that this is a position which belongs to the tradition of Valla and Agricola – that is, to a tradition of humanist pedagogy concerned to frame a coherent programme of arts education, heavily directed towards Cicero and Quintilian and independent of the traditional curriculum. Indeed Ramus was himself eager publicly to establish this

[3] For Ramus' influence on the poets of the Pléiade see P. Sharratt, 'Peter Ramus and the reform of the university: the divorce of philosophy and eloquence?', in *French Renaissance Studies, 1540-70: Humanism and the Encyclopedia*, ed. P. Sharratt (Edinburgh, 1976), 4-20; G. Castor, *Pléiade Poetics* (Cambridge, 1964). For Ramus' influence on Francis Bacon see Jardine, *Francis Bacon: Discovery and the Art of Discourse*.

[4] For details of Ramus' career see P. Sharratt, 'Nicolaus Nancelius, *Petri Rami vita*, edited with an English translation', *Humanistica Lovaniensia* 24 (1975); Waddington, *Ramus*; Ong, *Ramus, Method, and the Decay of Dialogue*; Sharrat, 'Peter Ramus and the reform of the university'.

particular pedigree for his proposed shift in emphasis from formal logic and the Theology Faculty towards Agricolan dialectic and eloquence. In 1569, in the course of revising his writings for a possible 'collected works', Ramus recalled that 'Johannes Sturm first brought these remarkable and pleasing dialectical fruits to Paris from the school of Agricola', and that this had enabled him first to taste the 'abundant' riches of humanist dialectic.[5] In his colleague Omer Talon's edition with commentary of the *Dialectica* which Ramus saw through the Basle press in the same year, a crucial dialectical distinction is glossed as follows:

> Rudolph Agricola made this distinction in the first book of his *De inventione dialectica*, and Ramus follows him in this, to the extent that he came to rival Agricola's achievement in this art especially, whom Ramus himself was wont to rank in logical studies immediately after the ancient school of Socratic logic (in which the practical application of that art is handled, as much as the science), and ahead of all subsequent logicians. And he used to say publicly that thanks to Agricola the true study of genuine [*germana*] logic had first been established in Germany [*Germania*], and thence, by way of his disciples and emulators, had spread throughout the whole world. The Academy at Paris first received that fruit with the arrival of Jacobus Omphalus and Bartholomaeus Latomus, but above all with the arrival of Johannes Sturm, by whom the utility of the art of Logic has been most fully and copiously set out.[6]

This particular set of loyalties makes it natural for Ramus to make his practical interventions into contemporary intellectual debate in the form of a revised programme of education – one centred on grammar and dialectic (probabilistic argument), and aimed at proficiency in that range of arts skills which will make the product of his school an able and active member of contemporary society. The 'new philosophy' of the school of Agricola and Erasmus makes *utility* its main criterion for success: utility being taken to mean, productive of the kind of competence which will make an individual a

[5] 'Hos dialecticos tam insignes tamque amabiles fructus Ioannes Sturmius ex Agricolae schola Lutetiam Parisiorum primus attulit ... Illum logicae facultatis usum ... logicam istam ubertatem primum degustavi ...' (*Scholae in liberales artes* (Basle, 1569), preface, 3); cit. N. Bruyère, *Méthode et Dialectique dans l'Oeuvre de La Ramée* (Paris, 1984), 305. On Sturm's dialectic teaching see A. Schindling, *Humanistische Hochschule und freie Reichsstadt: Gymnasium und Akademie in Strassburg, 1538-1621* (Wiesbaden, 1977). On the Basle publishing project of a collected works see Bruyère, *Méthode et Dialectique dans l'Oeuvre de La Ramée*, 19-22.

[6] 'Hanc differentiam Rodolphus Agricola docuit 1. lib. de Inventione, quam P. Ramus sequutus est, sic ut aemulatus in hac arte inprimis industriam illius viri, quem in studio logico, post antiquam illam Socraticorum Logicorum scholam (in qua non minus usus artis, quam scientia tractabatur) omnibus postea natis Logicis anteponere solitus est, dicereque palam ab uno Agricola verum germanae Logicae studium in Germania primum, tum per ejus sectatores et aemulos, toto terrarum orbe excitatum esse. Percepit autem Parisiensis Academia primo fructum illum adventu Jacobi Omphalii, Bartholomaei Latomi: sed in primis Joannis Sturmii, a quo Logicae artis utilitas plenius et uberius est exposita' (*Dialectica A. Talaei praelectionibus illustrata* (Basle, 1569), 95; cit. Bruyère, *Méthode et Dialectique dans l'Oeuvre de La Ramée*, 305-6). As Bruyère points out, this edition of Talon's commentary of Ramus' *Dialectica*, revised well after Talon's death, by Ramus, during his stay at Basle, undoubtedly reproduces Ramus' own views on his works and their intellectual origins. See also Ong, *Ramus and Talon Inventory*, 190-1.

responsible, moral and active member of the civic community. In his *Pro philosophica Parisiensis Academiae disciplina oratio* of 1551 (at the high point of his career), Ramus sets out and defends the detailed timetable he has introduced at the Collège de Presles, to achieve just these ends (we use Sharratt's synopsis of this account):

> The pupils were taught five hours in the morning and five in the afternoon, in each case made up of one hour's lecture on classical literature, two of '*ediscendi*', that is studying or memorising, and two more of debate and practice (pp. 26-7). Behind this procedure lies his theory of analysis and genesis leading to original composition (pp. 28-43). The course lasts seven and a half years (from the age of seven to fifteen): in the first three years there is a graded study of grammar and syntax, in the fourth year rhetoric, and then begins '*tempus philosophicum*' starting with logic in the fifth year, ethics in the sixth (the first four books of Aristotle) and mathematics, that is arithmetic and geometry, music and optics. The final year is devoted to physics (the first eight books of Aristotle) including meteorology and some astronomy – '*Physicam veram, mathematicis rationibus fundatam*' he calls it, though his own *Scholae physicae* (1556) fall far short of this. As in all the other subjects, physics would be studied through literature, in this case Virgil's *Georgics*, Ovid's *Metamorphoses*, and some Lucretius, Seneca and Pliny (pp. 44-5), a union if you like of science and poetry, but poetic science rather than scientific poetry. At the end the student graduates master of arts, 'not just in name but in truth' says Ramus, already, at the ripe age of fifteen years prepared to teach other people, or to study law, medicine or, theology and ultimately to play a useful part in society (p.49).[7]

This manifesto of Ramus' polemical teaching practice (and we suspend judgment for a moment on *why*, in 1551, it should be viewed as polemical) was published in the very year in which Ramus was appointed Professor of Philosophy and Eloquence at the Collège Royal in Paris. By good fortune we have a record, in an assiduous student's manuscript notes, of the lecturing with which Ramus began his tenure of this illustrious post. Surely Ramus must have considered this lecturing as representative of his whole approach to education? His professorship had, after all, been created for him, to fulfil his original claim (on the strength of which he had been banned from teaching philosophy for a number of years) that philosophy and eloquence go hand in hand, and that Aristotelian philosophy is unnecessarily technical and quibbling.[8]

François Chambut (Franciscus Chambutus) who attended Ramus' earliest course at the Collège Royal, beginning with his inaugural address, bound up his manuscript notes on the specified texts with the subsequent

---

[7] Sharratt, 'Peter Ramus and the reform of the university', 7-8.

[8] For these and other biographical details see Ong, *Ramus, Method, and the Decay of Dialogue*; Sharratt, 'Peter Ramus and the reform of the university'.

published versions of texts with Ramus' commentaries.[9] The volume (now in the library of the Free University of Amsterdam)[10] contains the following texts:

Audomari Talaei Praelectiones in partitiones Ciceronianas (missing title page, 1 and 2) 4°, 19 pp.

M. Tul. Ciceronis Oratio pro C. Rabirio perduellionis reo, Argumento illustrata. Parisiis, ex typographia Matthaei Davidis Via Amygdalina, ad Veritatis insigne, 1551, 4°, 16 pp. With Chambut's manuscript commentary in the margins, written between a double ruled margin, and bearing the date of the beginning of Ramus' course.

M.T. Ciceronis pro Caio Rabirio perduellionis reo Oratio, Petri Rami Regii Eloquentiae et Philosophiae professoris praelectionibus illustrata, Lutetiae, ex typographia Matthaei Davidis, via Amygdalina, ad Veritatis insigne, 1551 4°, 41 pp. + 1 p. s.n. and 1 p. bl.

M. Tul Ciceronis de Lege Agraria contra P. Servilium Rullum Tribunum plebis in Senatu Oratio I. Parisiis, Ex typographia Matthaei Davidis, via Amygdalina ad Veritatis insigne, 1551, 4°, 14 pp and 1 p. bl. With manuscript commentary without place or date, in the same hand as the commentary on the *Pro Rabirio,* also written in the margins between two ruled margins, and on the final blank page.

M. Tul. Ciceronis de Lege Agraria contra P. Servilium Rullum Tribunum plebis ad populum .Oratio II. Parisiis. Ex typographia Matthaei Davidis, via Amygdalina, ad Veritatis insigne, 1551, 4°, 50 pp. and 1 p. bl. With a manuscript commentary, without place or date, in the same hand as the preceding volume, and similarly placed.

M. Tul. Ciceronis de Lege Agraria contra P. Servilium Rullum Tribunum pleb. ad populum Oratio III. Parisiis, Ex typographia Matthaei Davidis, via Amygdalina, ad Veritatis insigne, 1551, 4°, 8 pp. With a manuscript commentary, without place or date, in the same hand as the preceding volume, and similarly placed.

M. Tullii Ciceronis de Lege Agraria contra P. Servilium Rullum Tribunum plebis orationes tres, Petri Rami Veromandui eloquentiae et philosophiae professoris Regii praelectionibus illustratae, ad Carolum Lotharingum cardinalem. Lutetiae, Apud Ludovicum Grandinum, e regione Gymnasii Remensis, 1552, *Cum privilegio,* 4°, 8 ff. s.n. + 131 pp.

M. Tullii Ciceronis in L. Catilinam Orationes III, Petri Rami, Eloquentiae et philosophiae professoris Regii, praelectionibus illustratae. Ad Carolum Lotharingum Cardinalem. Lutetiae, apud Ludovicum Grandinum, e regione Gymnasii Remensis. M.D.L.III., 4°, 141 pp. + 2 pp. s.n.

M. Tullii Ciceronis Paradoxa ad Marcum Brutum, Audomari Talaei commentationibus explicata, ad Carolum Lotharingum Cardinalem. Lutetiae, cura et diligentia Caroli Stephani, M.D.L.I., 4°, 52 pp.[11]

---

[9] See R. Barroux, 'Le premier cours de Ramus au Collège Royal d'après les notes manuscrites d'un auditeur', *Mélanges d'histoire littéraire et de bibliographie offerts à Jean Bonnerot* (Paris, 1954), 67-72.

[10] We are extremely grateful to Peter Sharratt for drawing the present location of these volumes to our attention.

[11] Ibid., 68-9.

Here, in miniature, as it were, is Ramus' teaching practice. A modest collection of elementary works by Cicero is discussed line by line, and passage by passage, the student annotating his specially printed 'bare' text. The comments are carefully grammatical and rhetorical:

> *Perduellionis reo. Perduellis* [fighting enemy] was the word formerly used for what was afterwards called *hostis* [enemy, also foreigner], 'the mildness of the expression relieving the harshness of the fact'. As Cicero says in the first book of the *Officia*: Hence *perduellio* [hostile conduct against one's country], the indefensible crime of treason [Chambut heard *magistratus* instead of *maiestatis*], or one accused of that crime who was incited to hostility against the state or the head of state.[12]

Or, alternatively, they provide a dialectical analysis of the passage's argument, in a recognisably 'Ramist' manner:

> The causes which move Cicero to defend Rabirius are the same as must move the Quirites to acquit him;

> But Cicero is moved by friendship, by honour, by humanity, by custom, and above all, in his capacity as consul, by the welfare of the State;

> Therefore the Quirites must be moved to acquit him for the same causes.[13]

In either case, Ramus apparently dictated his comments slowly enough for the dutiful student to record them exactly as he heard them: the printed commentaries which Chambut bound with his classroom notes are strikingly close to his own – apart from what he had misheard. In the first note above, Chambut misheard *hostis* as *hostes* (and got his grammar wrong); he misheard *maiestatis* as *magistratus* (and presumably lost the full force of the 'treason' example); and he attached 'as Cicero says in the first book of the *Officia*' to the following quotation (in fact from the *Digest*), rather than the preceding one. In other words, the printed texts capture to the letter the experience of the controversial teacher at work; what they do not capture is the student's vain attempts to follow the teacher in action.[14] Indeed the extraordinary closeness between the printed *praelectiones* and the class as delivered by the master suggests that one of Ramus' aims, in his publications, is to capture his teaching 'on the run', just as it happened, 'in the flesh', in a way which

---

[12] '*Perduellis a veteribus dicebatur qui postea hostes [sic] dictus est, lenitate verbi tristitiam rei mitigante. Ait Cicero Officiorum primo: hinc perduellio crimen immunitum magistratus [sic] vel criminis hujus reus qui hostili animo adversus rempublicam vel principem animatus fuit*'. Cit. Barroux, ibid., 70.

[13] '*Summa huius exordii complexca [sic] syllogismo. Quibus caussis Cicero mouetur ad defendendum Rabirium hiisdem Quirites moueri debent ad absoluendum. Atqui amicitia, dignitate, humanitate, consuetudine, salute rei publice officio consulatus Cicero mouetur. Hiisdem igitur Quirites commoueantur.*' Cit. Barroux, ibid., 71.

[14] For the printed versions of these two notes see Barroux, ibid., 70-1.

dictation in the classroom actually made impossible. This would go some way towards explaining why almost every university session saw a fresh 'version' of Ramus' key works, especially the *Dialectica,* issued from the printing presses.[15] It is supported by Ramus' care when dealing with his publishers, to see to it that the text is perfectly 'representative' of his practice.[16]

In keeping with the pragmatism of his publishing efforts, Ramus constantly stresses the appropriateness of his approach to learning (and his manner of teaching) as a preparation for public life: *'in forum, in Senatum, in concionem populi, in omnem hominum conventum.'*[17] Meanwhile, however, his adversaries stressed its derisory shallowness. Petrus Gallandius opposed Ramus' 1551 teaching manifesto with a vigorous denunciation of the new Regius Professor's opportunistic popularising, claiming:

> Most of those who read your rubbish, Ramus (and don't let their number go to your head) do so not to derive any profit from them, but as though they were French books about the ludicrous Pantagruel, as a game and for amusement.[18]

(Rabelais responded by proposing, as the only solution, the total 'petrification' of both these 'Petruses'!)[19]

Galland makes it clear that he regards Ramus' approach to arts education as *seditious,* and his attempts to yoke philosophy and eloquence as misleading and vague:[20]

> He holds that philosophy is far better taught from poets than from philosophers. In this obscure conjunction of philosophy with eloquence, he teaches no Aristotle, no philosophy, but pretty much poetry alone. He claims that Aristotle – whom he contends is in part stuffed with impiety, in part with captious and irrelevant matter – should either be entirely left alone or read through compendia and outlines, or should be relegated to that part of the work which

---

[15] See Ong, *Ramus and Talon Inventory*; Barroux, ibid., 70; Sharratt, 'The present state of studies on Ramus'.

[16] On Ramus' stay at Basle, supervising Basle printings of his works, see P.G. Bietenholz, *Basle and France in the Sixteenth Century: The Basle Humanists and Printers in their Contacts with Francophone Culture* (Geneva, 1971), 153-63, 304-7.

[17] P. Ramus, *Pro philosophica Parisiensis Academiae disciplina oratio* (Paris, 1551), 50-1, cit. Sharratt, 'Peter Ramus and the reform of the university', 8.

[18] *'Melior Pars eorum qui hasce tuas nugas lectitant Rame (nec hinc tibi nimium placeas) non ad fructum aliquem ex iis capiendum, sed ueluti uernaculos ridiculi Pantagruelis libros ad lusum et animi oblectationem lectitant'* (P. Gallandius, *Pro schola Parisiensi contra nouam academiam Petri Rami oratio* (Lutetiae, 1551), fol. 9ᵛ). Cit. Sharratt, 'Peter Ramus and the reform of the university', 8; the 'Ramus Galland curriculum dispute, with commentary by Rabelais' is detailed in W.J. Ong, *Ramus and Talon Inventory* (Harvard, 1958), 496-8; Rabelais' treatment of the dispute is briefly discussed by T. Cave, *The Cornucopian Text: Problems of Writing in the French Renaissance* (Oxford, 1979), 214-15. For treatment of the substantial philosophical criticism made by Galland – that Ramus is an Academic sceptic – see C.B. Schmitt, *Cicero Scepticus: A Study of the Influence of the Academica in the Renaissance* (The Hague, 1972), 92-102.

[19] Ong, op. cit., 498.

[20] Sharratt, 'Peter Ramus and the reform of the university', 8.

the student does without his tutor. He confuses the gospel with philosophy, and taints the minds of inexperienced and ignorant adolescents with quite unnatural views.[21]

At the same time, he tries to discredit Ramus' originality on the grounds of his indebtedness (acknowledged as we saw by Ramus himself) to an earlier humanistic tradition:

> What have you said or written which has not previously been taught or made a subject of enquiry by Lorenzo Valla, Rudolph Agricola, Vives, Melanchthon or Agrippa?[22]

We began this chapter by suggesting that it will not do to take such accusations of 'shallowness' and 'derivativeness' at face value. What, we should ask ourselves, is Galland really objecting to (since competitors always accuse successful teachers of being unoriginal and 'mere' popularisers)? A number of Galland's phrases are verbally telling: thus '[Ramus] confuses the gospel with philosophy, and taints the minds of inexperienced and ignorant adolescents with quite unnatural views.' The words hint at impiety, corruption and 'unnaturalness'. Behind them seems to lie an uneasiness about the *disruption* Ramus is causing to the educational system.[23] We have to ask ourselves why this should be. What was there about Ramus' approach that so threatened established teachers that they dismissed it as 'freak', 'unnatural', 'seditiously disturbing'? Our first tentative answer must be that the threat was institutional: Ramus deliberately discarded the difficulty and rigour of high scholastic schooling and thereby attracted those who regarded education as a means to social position rather than as a preparation for a life of scholarship (or of theological debate). In so doing he explicitly (though not necessarily deliberately) achieved the final *secularisation* of humanist teaching – the transition from 'humanism' to 'the humanities'. He proposed as a test of an education that it should prove 'useful' – that it should repay those who undertook it with skills applicable outside the universities. He thereby won the approval of a mercantile class determined to get value for money from their 'investment' in their sons' education (and who continued to support

---

[21] '*Ex poetis philosophiam quam ex philosophis multo melius doceri contendat: in hac umbratili philosophiae et eloquentiae coniunctione, non Aristotelem, non philosophiam, sed poetas fere tantum doceat; Aristotelem partim impietatis plenum, partim rerum captiosarum et inutilium, vel non attingendum, vel per compendia quaedam et summa tantum capita legendum, vel etiam discipulis citra praeceptoris operam committendum esse affirmet; evangelium cum philosophia confundat prodigiosisque omnino opinionibus imperitos et incautos adolescentes imbuat*' (ibid., fol. 3^r); cit. Schmitt, *Cicero Scepticus*, 93.

[22] '*Quid a te dictum scriptumue, quod non ante a Laurentio Valla, Rudolpho Agricola, Viue, Melanchthone, Agrippa, uel traditum sit, uel in disquisitionem reuocatum?*' (Gallandius, *Pro schola Parisiensi contra nouam academiam Petri Rami*, fol. 9^r).

[23] The various specific controversies are catalogued in Ong, op. cit., 492-533.

Ramus when the university establishment tried to remove him).[24]

Ramus consistently objected to the tendency of traditional teaching to confuse the student who was trying to reach a level of intellectual competence short of true scholarship:

> At present my arguments bear not on order but on usefulness. Is it not far easier for a boy to learn and memorise an art from a few precepts than to make excruciating efforts to pursue it as it lies scattered and diffused in a great many books?[25]

The machinery of scholastic philosophy is wholly unsuitable for the instruction of students whose aim is ultimately to engage in polemic in the public arena, rather than to solve weighty analytical problems in philosophy:

> This confusion, these sophisms, these enigmas, these chimerical dream-charms have robbed you of your judgment and your reason. Take counsel sometime with yourself, if you can, and ask yourself what good this work does you. Because I have learned to unsettle my students (and myself above all) with a thousand arguments concerning the noun, the verb, 'finite propositions', 'infinite propositions' and modals, have I therefore learned anything whatsoever worthy of mankind? Will I be able to use this rubbish to advise rash friends, to relieve the afflicted, or to hold the unrestrained in check? On the contrary. Will I be able to try cases in court, to indict the wicked, to arouse judges by unravelling crimes, or to defend the innocent and free them from punishment? Hardly ... What good then does it do? Issue forth from your school, which no useful consideration has ever been allowed to enter, and look for fruits in proportion to all the time you have wasted here so miserably.[26]

Ramus offered an *all-purpose* technique for transmitting knowledge (the

---

[24] It is generally acknowledged that the composition of university students changed in universities throughout Europe during the sixteenth century. For an account of the numbers and class backgrounds of university students in Oxford in the latter half of the sixteenth century see L. Stone, 'The size and composition of the Oxford Student Body 1580-1909', in *The Universities in Society*, vol. I, *Oxford and Cambridge from the 14th to the Early 19th Century*, ed. L. Stone (Princeton, 1974), 3-110 ; J.K. McConica, 'Scholars and commoners in Renaissance Oxford', in *The Universities in Society*, ed. Stone, 151-81. On changing patterns of endowment see V. Morgan, 'Cambridge university and "the country" 1560-1640', in Stone, op. cit., 183-246.

[25] '*De ordine iam nihil disputo; de utilitate disputo; an non est longe, multoque facilius puero paucis monitis artem discere, memoriaque complecti, quam tot libris dissolutam, dissipatamque laboriosissime, et molestissime persequi?*' (*Aristotelicae animadversiones* (Paris, 1543), fol. 26^v); cit. Vasoli, *La dialettica e la retorica*, 358.

[26] '*Haec confusio, haec sophismata, haec aenigmata, haec chimericae somniorum fascinationes rationem, iudiciumque vobis eripuerunt, adhibete aliquando vos in consilium, si potestis et vosmetipsos sic interrogate, quid me labor hic adiuvat? An quia de nomine, verboque, de pronunciatis finitis, infinitis, modalibus, discipulos meos mille argumentis perturbare, et meipsum in primis didici, ideo dignum homine quicquam didici? At his adiutus nugis potero vel amicis inconsideratis consilium dare, vel afflictos molestia levare, vel affrenatos reprimere? nihil minus. An in foro caussas agere, improborum nomina deferre, sceleribus explicandis iudices commovere, an innocentes tuere et supplicio liberare? Nihil simile ... Quid ergo est? Egredere e schola tua, in quam cogitatio utilitatis nulla unquam ingressa est, require tanti temporis quantum hic misere consumis, fructum*' (ibid., fol. 37^r-37^v); cit. Vasoli, *La dialettica e la retorica*, 360.

infamous *unica methodus*) in place of the detail and complexity of traditional teaching. His 'one and only method' was a suitable vehicle, he claimed, for transmitting the content of any discipline. Let us leave aside the question of whether or not this is a valid notion (or even a sensible one), since it has received persistent attention in recent years.[27] It opened the prospect that the purpose of education was to purvey information and skills, not to be morally improving: Ramist teaching might make you a good grammarian or a good mathematician; there was no guarantee that it would make you a good person. In other words, Ramist method had implications for the *ideology* of arts teaching, which went far beyond the trivial details of 'ascent' and 'descent' in the method itself. But since this is necessarily speculative, let us take a look at another example of a Ramist teacher in action, to see whether we can detect traces of any such break with traditional moral teaching.

In 1978 Princeton University acquired a *Sammelband* of pamphlet editions of classical texts published in Paris between 1550 and 1572, all of them festooned – between the lines, in the margins, and on interleaved pages – with a student's notes on lectures given in the University of Paris in the early 1570s.[28] The lecturer was Claude Mignault – better known, perhaps, by his Latin name, Claudius Minos.[29] Born near Dijon in about 1536, he spent seven years in what he called 'the unbearable condition of a *paedotriba* (schoolmaster)'.[30] By 1567 he had contributed liminary verses to a local doctor's book on the plague; in the summer of the same year he came to Paris.[31] A hard-working student of Greek and philosophy, by 1570 he had become a teacher of humanities in the Collège de Reims at Paris where he completed a meticulous commentary on Alciato's emblem-book.[32] In 1572

[27] On Ramus' 'method' see the bibliography above, notes 1 and 2.

[28] For a good brief description of the collection, see William Salloch, *Catalogue 353: The Classical Heritage, Part I*, 9-10. Another brief description and a reproduction of a page appear in the *Princeton University Library Chronicle* 41 (1979), 76-8. For a full list of the books in the collection see Appendix 1, below, pp. 201-2.

[29] On Mignault, see the article from Papillon in Niceron, *Mémoires pour servir à l'histoire des hommes illustres dans la République des lettres*, 14 (Paris, 1731), 81-99, and the articles in the *Biographie Universelle* and *Nouvelle Biographie Générale*.

[30] 'Minos lectori', in *Omnia Andreae Alciati V.C. Emblemata cum commentariis, quibus Emblematum omnium aperta origine mens auctoris explicatur, et obscura omnia dubiaque illustrantur per Claudium Minoem Divionensem* (Antwerp, 1577), 17 (... *ad miseram paedotribae conditionem*').

[31] For Mignault's liminary verses, see Claude Fabri, *Paradoxes de la cure de peste* (Paris, 1568), sigs. [*vii^v-*viii^v]; the privilege is dated Paris, 30 May 1567; the preface, Dijon, 1 September 1567; and the volume itself was, according to a legend on the verso of the title page, 'Achevé d'imprimer pour la premiere fois le 29. d'Octobre 1567'. For Mingault's move to Paris, see Mignault to Philibert Colin, 3 August 1567, in Pierre Palliot, *Le parlement de Bourgongne* (Dijon, 1649), 187-8.

[32] The first edition of Mingault's commentary was published in 1571 by Du Pré, who also published several of the pamphlets in the Princeton collection. See Henry Green, *Andrea Alciati and his Books of Emblems: A Biographical and Bibliographical Study* (London, 1872), 92-3, 195-6, 216-17; George Boas, tr. *The Hieroglyphics of Horapollo* (New York, 1950), 36-40; A. Camarero, 'Teoría del símbolo, empresa y emblema en el humanismo renacentista (Claude Mignault, 1536-1606)', *Cuadernos del Sur* 11 (1972), 63-103.

and 1573 he delivered lectures on classical texts so varied in genre, style and historical context as to fill a modern teacher with both pity and terror: Cicero, *De optimo genere oratorum, Topica, De finibus* I, *Academica* I, *Somnium Scipionis, Philippics* I-II, *Catilinarians* I-II; Pliny, *Natural History* VII: Justin, *Epitome of Pompeius Trogus* I; Horace, *Odes* II-IV, *Ars Poetica, Epistles*; Ausonius, *Griphus Ternarii Numeri*; Lucian, *On Not Believing Calumny Rashly*; Plutarch, three short treatises from the *Moralia*; Demosthenes, *On the Peace*, with the *argumentum* by Libanius; Isocrates *Against the Sophists*; a manual of Roman antiquities, and a manual of dialectic.

From the outset Mignault was faced with a fundamental problem. He had to supply his students with the texts he wished to teach, for it would have been inconceivably tedious to dictate them all as well as lecture on them.[33] Accordingly, it seems, he had several printers – most often Du Pré or Brumen – run off pamphlet editions of the individual texts. Where such editions already existed, as they often did, his students could simply buy them.[34] These were not critical editions. Their anonymous editors were not bothered with textual problems and rarely recorded a variant reading. But they were not bare texts either, for most had brief running notes. One example will suffice. For *Odes* 3.1, which is 48 lines long, our student's anonymous editions gave two notes. The first introduced the poem as a whole:

> In this Ode, which may serve as a preface for the book, he instructs youth in holy precepts. For men, he says, have different conditions and desires. But all strive for happiness, and all are fated to die. Hence rulers are no luckier than ordinary men, however well they live. For happiness lies not in things of that sort, but in security and peace of mind, which are usually the lot of ordinary men, not the great. Nor do they profit by the buildings they raise over the oceans, which only raise their cares. Finally, he says that if purple and fine

[33] In cities where the printing trade was not well developed, dictation of every text long remained necessary. See e.g. Jean de Gaufreteau's description of the situation in Bordeaux, where until 1578 '... les escoliers escrivoyent leurs textes, ce qui leur estoit une grande peyne'. Quoted in Louis Desgraves, *Elie Vinet, humaniste de Bordeaux (1509-1587): vie, bibliographie, correspondance, bibliothèque* (Geneva, 1977), 24n. 159. On the production of editions for the student market in sixteenth-century France, see also Ong, *Ramus and Talon Inventory*; M. Mund-Dopchie, 'Le premier travail français sur Eschyle: le Prométhée enchaîné de Jean Dorat', *Les lettres romanes* 30 (1976), 261-74, a useful case study.

[34] It is not possible to determine which of the texts in the Princeton collection were definitely printed at Mignault's behest. He had come into contact with Paris printers and learned to detest their greed by 1567, when he wrote as follows to Colin, for whose poems he had tried to find a publisher: '*Vt autem me apud te promissis exolvam, bonam partem typographorum qui hic agunt iam agnovi satis, qui nihil eiusmodi excudunt, nisi numerata pecunia, videoque apertis oculis eos maxime et praeter modum rei familiari esse deditos. Continuo enim videre est eos Doctorum precibus vix aut rarissime flecti posse ...*' (Palliot, *Parlement de Bourgongne*, 188). It is thus possible that any of the works printed after 1567 – e.g. the Ausonius of 1569 – were done for him. It seems quite likely that he is responsible for several of the items printed by Brumen and Du Pré in 1570 and after. And it seems quite clear that he did not have the items printed that appeared before 1567. At least some of the books – e.g. the *Somnium Scipionis* of 1565 – were reprints of well-established teaching editions and could have been commissioned by almost anyone.

clothes do not drive off sorrow, there is no reason for him to exchange his Sabine farm for them.[35]

The second printed note treats the phrase in line 41:

> *Phrigius lapis*: Synnadican marble, so the commentators take this, from Synnada, a city in Phrygia. But Pliny seems to have a different view about that stone in 36.19.[36]

Neither note is original. The first is the standard *argumentum* to the Ode, which the editor – very likely Mignault himself – could have found in any earlier edition. As to the second, here is what the Swiss scholar Glareanus had to say on the same line:

> Both Acro and Porphyrio [the 'commentators'] take Phrygian stone to be Synadican marble, from the city of Synada in Phrygia, mentioned by Strabo and Ptolemy ... But Pliny seems to have a different view about that stone in 36.19, at the very end of the chapter. I only wanted to point this out to the reader and leave it to him to judge, as I have done elsewhere.[37]

The editor clearly took Glareanus' note and boiled it down. He did not even bother to read Pliny 36.19 to see what Pliny's deviant opinion was, but simply copied out Glareanus' reference and passed on. Throughout this edition of the *Odes*, in fact, we find exactly the same combination: the traditional *argumenta* with a number of specific notes by Glareanus. Presumably the editor simply took a copy of Horace with the standard *argumenta*, wrote in digests of what he found and liked in Glareanus, and sent it to the printer. Mignault and his colleagues seem to have done much the same for the other editions, ranging from Cicero to Ausonius.

A good deal of Mignault's time, then, was spent producing these small-scale editions, which must have necessitated a search for copy-texts and constant running back and forth to the printers – much as a modern teacher

---

[35] Printed *argumentum* to *Odes* 3.1; *Q. Horatii Flacci carminum liber III* (no publishing information given; cf. Appendix 1 below, no. 14), fol. 31^{r-v}: '*Hac Ode quae prooemii vice in sequentem librum esse possit, sanctissimis praeceptis teneram aetatem imbuit. Nam quum, inquit, variae sint hominum conditiones: alii aliis studiis, sed omnes ad felicitatem contendant, et aequa sit omnibus mortis conditio, privatis nihilo sunt feliciores satrapae, quamlibet laute pascantur: felicitatem non in eiusmodi sitam, sed in securitate et animi tranquillitate, quae plerunque mediocrium fortunam comitatur, extreme potentium non ita: neque prodesse, quod in mar[i] aedificent, quo aeque ascendunt curae. Demum ait, si purpura et vestes splendidae dolores non pellunt, non est quod illas velit permutare cum fundo suo Sabino.*'

[36] Printed note to *Odes* 3.1.41; ibid., fol. 31^{v}: '*Phrygius lapis) Synnadicum marmor, Commentatores intelligunt, a Synnada urbe Phrygiae. At Plin. lib. 36. c. 19. aliter de eo lapide sentire videtur.*'

[37] '*In Q. Horatium Flaccum Henrici Glareani Helvetii, Poet. Laureati Annotationes*', in *Quinti Horatii Flacci Poemata omnia* (Freiburg i. B., 1549), separately paginated, 35: '*Per Phrygiam lapidem et Acron et Porphyrio Synadicum marmor intelligunt, ab urbe Synada Phrygiae. Cuius urbis Strabo lib. xii. meminit, non ita longe a fine: meminit et Ptolemaeus. At Plinius lib. 36. cap. 19. aliter de eo lapide sentire videtur, ad finem prorsus eius capitis. Quod lectori indicare duntaxat volui, ac ipsum suo relinquere iudicio, ut in aliis plerisque facimus.*'

might spend time producing and reproducing syllabuses and extracts from primary sources. Du Pré and Brumen were the sixteenth-century equivalent of the xerox machine and the offset press.[38]

Mignault taught the 'first class' (*primus ordo*): that is, the highest form of the Collège de Reims.[39] But he did not assume that they had learnt to read texts competently in the lower forms. This was probably wise, since some students took as little as a year to reach the top form.[40] He began by making sure that they had an understanding of the literal meaning of each text. Whether a work was in prose or verse, in Latin or Greek, about warfare or theology, Mignault started by paraphrasing it *in toto*, word for word, in Latin. The student who recorded his lessons, Geraldus de Mayres, meticulously wrote out his paraphrases in tiny script between the lines of his printed texts. We can go back to *Odes* 3.1 for an example of Mignault at work. Lines 37-40 read (in the text used by Mayres):

> *sed timor et minae*
> *Scandunt eodem quod [sic] dominus: neque*
> *Decedit aerata triremi et*
> *Post equitem sedet atra cura.*

(But fear and threats scale the same heights as the master: black care does not leave the bronze ship and sits behind the horseman)

Between these lines Mayres wrote:

> *metus perturbationes*
> *sequuntur quocunque eum qui est animo perturbato*
> *relinquit hominem in navi*
> *sequitur hominem quantumvis equis instructum tristis*
> *solicitudo.*

Evidently Mignault dictated a continuous prose paraphrase in complete sentences. His students could not take notes as quickly as he spoke. So they omitted obvious words selectively. Here, for example, lines 38-9 are clearly

---

[38] One qualification should be made. Evidently Mignault did not see to it that his pupils always had the same printed text before them as he did – at least when it came to Greek, for which he used very short texts printed on one or two leaves. For in a comment on Demosthenes, *On the Peace* 7, he parses the verb *ēkousate* ('*a verbo akouō*') as first aorist; but his student's printed text in fact read as *ēkouete* which is imperfect. On the whole, one suspects that such discrepancies were more common in Greek teaching than in Latin; but it would be useful to have more information.

[39] The place and times of Mignault's lectures are specified in a number of subscriptions by the student who took the notes in the Princeton volume, Geraldus de Mayres; for these see Appendix 2 below. The form most of them take ('*Annotationes ... datae* [or *dictatae*] *a domino Minoe ... in primo Rhemensium ordine*') seems to indicate that the notes were taken by a student at public lectures. So do a large number of slips in the notes proper.

[40] R. Chartier, D. Julia, and M. Compère, *L'éducation en France du XVIe au XVIIIe siècle* (Paris, 1976), 172-3.

negative: fear does *not* leave the bronze ship. Mignault's paraphrase must also have been negative. Mayres, however, left out *non* or some other simple replacement for *neque* because he knew that he could trust himself to understand the line without it. Hurried note-taking of this kind must have been a major part of the pupil's activities.

Not all Mignault's paraphrases were merely literal. Sometimes they take flight to a level of banality unimaginable outside the classroom, as here, where Horace's unforgettable image, *Post equitem sedet atra cura*, 'Dark care sits behind the horseman', is transmuted into 'Sad care follows a man, however many horses he owns'. Sometimes, too, the paraphrase serves to make a grammatical point as well as to open up the text. Libanius' *argumentum* to Demosthenes *On the Peace*, for instance, begins *Mêkunomenou tou polemou* ('the war being prolonged'). This Mignault rendered *prorogato bello cum bello prorogaretur* – 'the war being prolonged, since the war was prolonged'.[41] One hears the faint echo here of a lost lesson on the Greek genitive absolute and its Latin equivalent. But for the most part, baldness was the order of the day.

Paraphrase too was only a beginning. By long-standing tradition the teacher had to do much more. Like Guarino and Erasmus before him, Mignault had to present the text as a whole: to identify its author, describe the circumstances which had called it forth, and define the genre into which it fell. And he had to select for particular discussion a number of interesting points: edifying anecdotes that would help to form his students' characters, novel facts that would make them properly well-informed, elegant phrases and neat imitations that would serve to adorn their styles.[42] Let us watch Mignault do this to *Odes* 3.1. He begins soundly, with a general summary which is also a nice piece of moralising rhetoric, full of the highest sentiments and more than a little obtuse:

> Horace plans to discuss the blessed life, which all desire to attain, but ignore the road that leads to it. First he warns off from this study men who are impure or depraved in their opinions, as profane men from sacred mysteries. Then he shows that the various conditions of men are all under the control of God, and that all are equally fated to die. This one thought should restrain all raging emotions and wild desires. Finally, by a comparison of unlike things through a fine induction, he shows that one attains the blessed life not through wealth or honours or possessions or other things subject to chance, but only by tranquillity of spirit.[43]

He then proceeds to extract for conventional comment the points that were conventionally seen as worthy of discussion. He finds more pretext for moral

---

[41] Mayres's note actually reads '*progoraretur*'.

[42] For a good summary of what was expected, see Erasmus, '*De ratione studii*', in *Opera omnia Desiderii Erasmi Roterodami* (Amsterdam, 1969-), I.2, 136-46; see also above, Chapter 6.

[43] For Mignault's comments on *Odes* 3.1 and their sources, see Appendix 3 below, where they are reproduced in their entirety.

discourse in Horace's *Virginibus puerisque canto* 'I sing to girls and boys':

> It is very important that boys be first trained in good actions and disciplines.
> They tend to hold most closely to what they have learned in their early years.

He discovers historically interesting matter about Roman institutions in stanzas three and four: 'By *campus* Horace means the Campus Martius, where the Romans normally held meetings and *comitia* to choose magistrates.' Lines 27-8 are used as a pretext for a brief disquisition on the names and properties of stars, and line 35 as the springboard for a digression into the 'three types of stones from which buildings are made'. Finally, in line 2, he finds justification for a conventional linguistic comment on the phrase *favete linguis*, which he illustrates with parallels from Ovid. Here, indeed, as so often happens in a commentary, Mignault's discussion broadens out into an excursus that establishes the religious origins of Horace's phrase as well as its place in the Roman literary tradition.

Such use of the text as an armature on which the teacher may hang whatever useful matter comes to mind is entirely traditional, as we have seen. So is Mignault's heavy dependence on earlier commentators. In this case Mignault is chiefly exploiting Denys Lambin's great edition of Horace, which had appeared in a revised form only five years before; that is clear, for example, in his introductory note, in his discussion of *favete linguis*, and in his treatment of the Campus Martius, where he has simply abridged or extended what he found in Lambin, often using exactly the same words. And both the habit of digression and the habit of dependence characterise Mignault's other lectures as well. His lessons on Cicero *De optimo genere oratorum*, for example, begin with long etymological and literary explanations of the terms 'tragedy', 'comedy' and 'dithyramb', all used by Cicero.[44] These summarise what Ramus had said about the same words in his ampler and much more learned commentary on the same text.[45] No blame, of course, can be attached to

---

[44] Here, for example, is Mignault's gloss on the word '*tragici*' in *De optimo genere oratorum* 1.1: '*Tragici poetae res tristes et calamitosas quae magnis et sublimibus personis feruntur accidisse, tractant, nomenque habent* apo tou thragou *hoc est ab irco. Quo pertinet illud Horatii: carmine qui tragico vilem certavit ob ircum …*' Verso of title page, *M.T. Ciceronis Liber de optimo genere oratorum* (App. 1 below, no. 1).

[45] Here is Ramus' gloss on the same word: '*Tragici*] *Tragoedia fabula est regum et principum mores exprimens: et miserabiles exitus habet, ut caedes, exilia, ruinas civitatum: dicta* apo tou tragou kai tês ôidês, *ab hirco et cantu, quia praemium erat huic carmini hircus: vel* apo tês trugos *a faece, quia actores hujus fabulae, faece perungerentur: de quo utroque sic Horatius in Arte: Carmine qui tragico vilem certavit ob hircum.*' Peter Ramus, *In Ciceronis orationes et scripta nonnulla, omnes quae hactenus haberi potuerunt praelectiones* (Frankfurt, 1582) 671 (the commentary on the *De optimo genere oratorum* first appeared in 1557). The line from Horace is *Ars poetica* 220. Admittedly Mignault could have found his definition and etymology of tragedy elsewhere (e.g. in the scholia of Porphyrio and Pseudo-Acro *ad loc.*), but the consistency with which his notes resemble Ramus' suggest that he was boiling the latter down. Ramus' source on tragedy may well have been Ioannes Britannicus' comment on *Ars* 220, for which see *Horatius cum quinque commentis* (ed. Venice, 1527), fol. CXLIIII[r].

Mignault for his borrowings, as they were absolutely normal practice. After all, how else could an arts teacher give two or three lectures a day on as many different texts?

Yet in one sense Mignault is an extremely selective plagiariser. He is pillaging Lambin, but he is careful with what he borrows and what he chooses to discard from his source. Consider their respective notes on the phrase *favete linguis* (*Odes* 3.1.2). Mignault took from Lambin both his explanation of the phrase and his evidence for it, a quotation from Paulus Diaconus' epitome of Festus. But he omitted what was most characteristic of Lambin's method: namely, the sugestion that a Greek term, *euphêmeite*, exactly parallels the Latin *favete linguis*. Throughout the ode, in fact, he has failed to take over the Greek parallels that were Lambin's special gift to readers of Roman poetry – most conspicuously, perhaps, in the case of line 8, where Mignault has nothing at all to say about Lambin's point that the phrase *cuncta supercilio moventis* (Jupiter 'who moves the world with one eyebrow') is adapted from a well-known Homeric passage. And this is no accident. Even a brief comparison reveals that throughout his lectures on Horace Mignault omitted the great majority of Lambin's comments on matters of style and diction – above all those that seek to place some Latin word or phrase in a Greek literary tradition. One very striking example comes from another text. At *Ars Poetica* 136 ff. Horace instructs the poet on how to begin his work. As an example of the proper way to do so he cites a couplet:

> *Dic mihi, Musa, virum, captae post tempora Troiae,*
> *qui mores hominum multorum vidit et urbes*

(141-2: Tell me, Muse, of the man, who, after Troy was taken, saw the cities and customs of many men).

As Horace himself makes clear, he is translating the beginning of the *Odyssey*. One would certainly expect any self-respecting Renaissance teacher or commentator to quote the original Greek – and, perhaps, to point out that Horace left out about a line of it.[46] Lambin not only quoted part of the Greek but made the line the occasion for quoting parts of Ronsard's *Franciade*, in both French and Latin, in order to show that France now had an epic poet fit to stand comparison with Homer.[47] Here is all Mignault found to say:

> *Dic mihi*: This is the beginning of Homer's *Odyssey*, and states the purposes of the

---

[46] See e.g. *Francisci Luisini Vtinensis in librum Q. Horatii Flacci De arte poetica commentarius* (Venice, 1554), fol. 33[r]; *In Q. Horatii Flacci Venusini librum De arte poetica Aldi Manutii Paulli F. Aldi N. Commentarius* (Venice, 1576), 34 (both handily reprinted in one volume as *Poetiken des Cinquecento*, vol. 19 (Munich, 1969)); E. Jacobsen, *Translation: A Traditional Craft* (Copenhagen, 1958), 47-51.

[47] *Q. Horatius Flaccus*, ed. Denys Lambin (Paris, 1567), 2, 359-61.

whole work; in it Ulysses is described in terms of his attributes and experiences.[48]

At this point – and there are a great many others like it both in his lectures on Horace and elsewhere – one must suspect that Mignault is deliberately avoiding the sort of stylistic commentary in which (from the cases we have so far looked at) we would expect such a teacher to engage.

Why did Mignault ruthlessly prune the stylistic portions of Lambin's commentary? Was it because his pupils at the Collège de Reims did not know Greek? Apparently not. He lectured on Greek texts as well as Latin, and his pupils – or at least Mayres – knew enough Greek to follow and copy down whole sentences. Nor was Mignault blind to the merits of Lambin's method. In fact, he was an expert on Latin adaptations of Greek poetry. His whole commentary on Alciato, as he explained, aimed 'to identify the source and origin of each emblem, gathering relevant passages from Greek and Latin'.[49] Hence his avoidance of Greek parallels in teaching must have been the result of a conscious pedagogic choice. And an explanation of that choice will bring us close to the heart of his personality, and point to those features of his method as a teacher that were genuinely distinctive.

Mignault's lecture on *Odes* 3.1 contains one category of material quite different from those we have so far discussed; and it was apparently because he wanted to make room for that material that he omitted excess historical and linguistic matter. Take, for example, his note on line 5:

> *Regum timendorum* begins a *gradatio* through an obscure *prolepsis* which can easily be resolved as follows: Someone will say that kings and princes are more blessed than the others inferior to them – those, that is, whom they rule and to whom they present themselves as terrifying figures. In fact, says Horace, kings and tyrants, however ruthless, are ruled by almighty God, and cannot free themselves from His rule. He proves this by an induction of one example, namely, that of the giants.

What Mignault is doing here (and in his notes on 9, 17 and 41, and in most of his other lectures) is to concentrate his attention on the formal structure and argument of the poem. He tries to identify the points that Horace is out to make, and to classify the types of argumentation that he uses to make them. In the passage just given, for example, what catches Mignault's eye is Horace's use of rhetorical induction: the weak form of argument that does

---

[48] Mignault, note on *Ars poetica* 141; *Q. Horatii Flacci De arte poetica liber* (App. 1 below, no. 16), fol. 5ʳ: '*Dic mihi. Odysseas homericae principium est et propositio totius poematis qua ex adiunctis et effectis Vlysses describitur.*'

[49] *Omnia Alciati emblemata*, 22: '*Id vero* [Mignault's skill] *maxime, nisi fallor, perspicuum erit in observando fonte et origine cuiuscunque Emblematis, in comparandis utriusque linguae auctoribus, qui magnum videbantur adferre adiumentum ad singulas notas et explicationes, ut denique in cumulandis iis locis, qui sparsim apud Alciatum in scriptis aliis prolixissimis habeantur.*'

not prove a thesis, but makes it more probable by supporting it with several cases in point. Line 9, similarly, interests Mignault not because it contains a Grecism, *Est ut viro vir* – that is what Lambin had noticed – but because it too uses a formal device to prove a moral point: 'He criticises the insatiable and purblind greed of men who cling so strongly to things subject to chance ... He proves this by an induction of four characters, from the adjuncts of those who wear themselves out on these things.' His final comment on the poem also deals with its argumentative or dialectical strategy, rather than its literary beauties. And the great majority of his other lectures also aim to extract the formal principles of argumentation from finished literary works. For Mignault, then, the central interest of literary texts lay in their application of the principles of dialectic. To analyse them was to receive not only a lesson in good writing but instruction in reasonable argument.

Here a striking example will suggest the consistency of focus of his interest. Perhaps the most-quoted line from Horace's much-quoted Roman Odes is 3.2.13: *Dulce et decorum est pro patria mori.* As Lambin pointed out, this line alludes to a good many similar Greek passages, the most striking parallel being in Tyrtaeus.[50] For Mignault, however, the line is less a thing of verbal beauty than an argumentative tactic, the refutation of a possible objection:

> *Dulce et decorum*: Horace supports what he has said and at the same time refutes the objection which could be raised by those who might say that they would rather avoid death by fleeing than meet it by fighting hard.[51]

At this point, Mignault's dialectical method of commentary is insistently predictable: whatever goes in, however rich and varied, emerges in a neat, uniform and constricting package. Mignault wants his exegetical method to be seen as a Method with a capital M – or, as he puts it in an inaugural lecture, flinging all his metaphors into one basket with splendid abandon: 'It provides a star to light our way across the ocean of the liberal arts and an Ariadne thread to lead us out of the labyrinth of confusion.'[52]

For a teacher active at Paris in the 1570s, these tactics represent more than a general choice of method; they are a statement of allegiance to Ramus and a Ramist educational system. The assumption that there is one and only one form of true and natural dialectic, and that this true dialectic is employed not

---

[50] *Q. Horatius Flaccus*, ed. Lambin, 1, 145.

[51] Mignault, note on *Odes* 3.2.13; *Horatii Carminum liber III*, fol. 32$^\mathrm{r}$: '*Dulce et decorum. Reddit rationem dicti et eadem opera occurrit obiectioni quae moveri posset ab his qui dicerent se malle vitare mortem fugiendo quam eam acriter pugnando oppetere.*'

[52] '*Oratio prima, De studio literarum recte instituendo, deque Academia Parisiensi ... Habita in schola Marchiana 6. Kalend. Octobris 1574*', in Mignault, *De re literaria orationes tres, habitae in Academia Parisiensi* (Paris, 1576), 17-18: '*Equidem AVD., methodum rem non tam levem aut exilem esse puto, in qua pene una studiorum omnium liberalium fructum iure statuo: ea enim efficit ut tenebras animo expellamus, et ordinem nobis certissimum proponamus, qui in hoc vasto disciplinarum liberalium Oceano nobis tanquam stella quaedam benigna praeluceat: aut ut filum Ariadnes, quo nos e labyrintho rerum implicatarum extricemus.*'

only by philosophers but also by orators and poets is a key Ramist one.[53] And given this ideological commitment to the identity of philosophy and eloquence, it was a point of Ramist principle to teach the elements of dialectic by showing how the great ancient writers had employed them, even when writing verse.[54] At the heart of Mignault's pedagogy lies his adherence to Ramus – his *way* of teaching, rather than any polemical manifesto or pronouncements, commits him to a Ramist view of the liberal arts. (Lecturing as he does in the tense months before the Protestant Ramus' murder in August 1572, Mignault might well be reluctant to draw attention to his name rather than his method.[55] As late as 1599 Ramus' biographer, Nancel, wrote that it was 'neither permissible, nor desirable to speak more fully' of his murder, since the scar has still barely healed on the incident, nor should memory of the political motives be revived.)[56]

Mignault's method of teaching is characteristically 'Ramist', then, though largely following conventional patterns of grammatical and historical exegesis. It is, in fact, very like the sort of teaching we saw Ramus himself doing in his earliest course at the Collège Royal. Mignault also made his own contribution to the Ramist publishing boom: in 1577 he published an edition of a major Ramist work, Omar Talon's *Rhetorica*, for which he provided the first detailed commentary. In his Prooemium Mignault argues the Ramist line that rhetoric should consist only in its traditional third and fifth parts, elocution and pronunciation, since invention and disposition are properly parts of dialectic (the general art of reasoning).[57] And he explicitly says that one

---

[53] For a pointed analysis of the earlier secondary literature on Ramus, see P. Rossi, 'Ramismo, logica, retorica nei secoli XVI e XVII', *Rivista critica di storia della filosofia*, 12 (1957), 357-65; on more recent works see Sharratt, 'The present state of studies on Ramus'. The present account follows for the most part W.S. Howell, *Logic and Rhetoric in England, 1500-1700* (Princeton, 1956); Jardine, *Francis Bacon*.

[54] Ramus describes his method as follows: '... *eademque et analyseos et geneseos exercitatione, Demosthenis, Homeri, Virgilii, Platonis, Aristotelis dialecticum et ex argumento consilium, et ex syllogismo iudicium, et ex ordine universae collocationis complexum interpretando, meditando, scribendo, declamando perpendimus, imitamur ...*'. *Pro philosophica Parisiensis Academiae disciplina oratio* (Paris, 1557), fol. 17[r]. And he explicitly argues that a child will find it easier to learn dialectic from the literary texts that he already knows than from Aristotle's rigorous, formal terminology ('*Omne b est a*' and the like): '*Virgilianis igitur et Ciceronianis, id est, humanis et popularibus exemplis idem facientibus potius, quam illis abecedariis figmentis utar*' (ibid., fol. 27[r]).

[55] On Ramus' death, and the political climate surrounding it, see Waddington, *Ramus*, 243 ff.; Ong, *Ramus, Method, and the Decay of Dialogue*, 28-9.

[56] Cit. P. Sharratt, 'The present state of studies on Ramus', 201.

[57] Mignault, '*Prooemium in hanc Technologiam Rhetoricam*', in *Audomari Talaei Rhetorica e P. Rami praelectionibus observata, una cum facillimis ad omnia praecepta eiusdem artis et exempla illustranda, commentationibus, per Claudium Minoem* (Frankfurt, 1582), 12: '*Nam praeter ornatum verborum et pronunciationem, nihil est ad artis hujus perfectionem somniandum. Quas partes duas ita commode parique brevitate digessit [scil. Talon], et postremo exemplis tam selectis et elegantibus illustravit, ut veram hanc et propriam, universalem inquam, et Philosophica descriptam methodo artem ausimus appellare. Neque vero fuit, cur in artis confectione (quam propriis et naturalibus praeceptionibus instituebat) de Inventione, deque Dispositione quicquam praeciperet: has enim partes esse Dialecticae proprias intelligebat, quae sua in arte, non in aliena, docendae potius, quam confusa quadam praeceptionum farragine permiscendae videbantur.*'

who has 'to discuss the parts of a poem, or disputation, or history, and the arrangement of the contents in part or in whole', should use 'the dialectical sources of disposition'.[58] And at the end of the work he provides a typical Ramist device: a folding chart of the art of rhetoric and its subsections, neatly arranged in bracketed dichotomies.[59] There is further evidence of Mignault's affiliation to the Ramist camp in direct borrowings from Ramus' own commentaries, imported into his lectures. At the beginning of his lecture on Cicero's *Catilinarian* I, Mignault observes:

> But we must first point out that the general topic of this oration is whether Catiline should be expelled from the city or put to death. This is argued out as follows, from the baneful adjuncts and effects on the state:
>
> > The pernicious citizen is to be killed.
> > But Catiline is pernicious.
> > Therefore Catiline is to be killed.[60]

Here is the beginning of Ramus' commentary on the same oration, itself derived from lectures:

> A summary of the proemium, cast in this syllogism from the adjuncts of the person, contains this *sententia*:
>
> > Pernicious citizens are to be punished with death.
> > Catiline is a pernicious citizen.
> > Therefore Catiline is to be punished with death.[61]

---

[58] Ibid., 18: '*Nam si de poematis cujusdam vel disputationis, aut historiae partibus tractandum sit: earumque rerum omnium oeconomia et dispositio ex partibus aut integris (ut nominantur) aut etiam universis examinanda sit, non erit ars quaedam nova fingenda. Etenim Dialectici fontes de disponendo sunt puriores et aptiores ad intelligentiam memoriamque juvandam, quam rivuli excogitati a Rhetoribus: quos quanquam non penitus aspernemur, eos tamen non eo habemus in numero, ut cum fontibus illis doctrinae generalis et universae conferamus.*'

[59] Ibid., ad fin.: '*Tabula in Aud. Talaei Rhetoricam, studio ac labore Claudii Minois conscripta.*' This divides *Rhetorica* into *Elocutio* and *Pronunciatio, Elocutio* into *Tropus* and *Figura*, etc. On the origin and spread of the vogue for such tables see K.J. Höltgen, 'Synoptische Tabellen in der medizinischen Literatur und die Logik Agricolas und Ramus', *Sudhoffs Archiv für Geschichte der Medizin und der Naturwissenschaften*, 49 (1965), 371-90. On Mignault's edition of Talon see also L. Terreaux, 'Claude Mignault, commentateur de la 'Rhetorica' d'Omer Talon', *Acta conventus neo-latini turonensis, Université François-Rabelais, 6-10 Septembre 1976*, ed. J.-C. Margolin (Paris, 1980), 2, 1257-67.

[60] Mignault, introductory note to *Catilinarian* I; *M.T. Ciceronis in L. Catilinam Invectiva oratio prima* (App. 1 below, no. 8), verso of title page: '*Sed primum debemus observare quae sit generalis quaestio huius orationis nimirum utrum Catilina eiciendus sit ab urbe vel necandus quae ex effectis adiunctisque reipublicae pestiferis hoc modo disseritur. Pernitiosus civis occidendus est. Catilina est pernitiosus. Catilina itaque necandus est …*'.

[61] Ramus, *In Ciceronis Orationes praelectiones*, 233 (a commentary first published in 1553): '*Summa prooemii in hunc ex adjunctis personae syllogismum inclusa, sententiam hanc continet: Perniciosi cives sunt morte multandi:*'

By now, then, we can form a fairly clear picture of Mignault's 'method'. The focus of his teaching interest as he stood before his *primus ordo Rhemensium* was dialectic, the sixteenth-century art of convincing and reasonable discourse. This he presented to his pupils as a universal skeleton key, showing again and again that it would open any lock if properly applied.[62] And before we are too disparaging about the intellectual possibilities of such an approach to textual analysis, we should recognise that Mignault's Ramist method displays a number of virtues which more traditional methods lacked.

In the first place, it was a training in orderly thinking rather than in what Bolgar has encouraged us to call 'bricolage': the stringing together of elegant phrases and stereotyped headings, which, as we showed in the last chapter, came to characterise the humanists' arts teaching.[63] Hence it was a sensible preparation for a variety of careers in the public sphere, for which a clear head and a quick mind counted for as much as pure Latin eloquence. Mignault's students presumably became priests, *officiers* and teachers. His selective teaching technique prepared them to stand up and argue a case in public, to compose a sermon or draft a government memorandum, to think a situation through and devise a course of action to meet it, just as they were trained to think through a work of literature. To that extent, the loss in Mignault's commentary of any treatment of finer literary points may well have been seen by his customers – students, and prospective employers of his graduates – as their gain.

In the second place, Mignault's method differed from the traditional one in that the lectures it generated could be systematically and coherently reissued

---

Catilina perniciosus est civis:
Catilina igitur morte multandus.'

[62] Like Ramus himself, Mignault does in fact make it clear that this approach to logic is specifically tailored to arts teaching, and that although he believed that there was a single true 'ars disserendi', philosophers do in fact argue more rigorously than poets. His lectures on the *Compendium in universam dialecticam, ex Rivio aliisque recentioribus collectum* (App. 1 below, no. 26) cover syllogistic as well as enthymeme and induction (though the figures of the syllogism are not treated in much detail). Cf. his introductory remarks: '*Quid sit discriminis inter dialecticam et logicam. Vniversa disserendi ars apud Aristotelem instruit ad tractationem quaestionum singularum omnisque doctrinae perpetuitatem quae propria methodi indeque ab interpretibus organum logicum itemque ars artium nominatur. Et quoniam quaestionis cuiuscunque tractatio ac methodi perpetuitas in omni re duplex esse potest, una popularis ad eorum cum quibus agitur imbecillitatem accommodata, altera exacta philosophorum propria, idcirco huius artis (si modo haec una ars apud Aristotelem vere dici potest) duae partes ut novae artes extiterunt, una Topica, altera Analytica, quae multa quidem inter se habent communia, sed finibus ita distinguantur ut illa opinionis effectrix, haec vero scientiae procreatrix esse dicatur: utraque tantum communis quia usu suo per omnia rerum genera diffunditur, etiamsi in argumentis hoc intersit quod Topica sit eorum probabilium ad disserendum in partes contrarias, Analytica (cui demonstrandi ratio est subiecta) necessariorum tantum et eorum quae uni parti quaestionis sunt addicta, et denique propria ut philosophus arte Analytica instructus ex propriis agere dicatur, dialecticus vero ex communibus ... quanquam utraque ars communiter sit omnium quaestionum tractandarum, quia tamen non est in omnibus idem tractationis modus, idcirco ab Aristotele in utraque arte quaestionis divisio est ut eius formis distinctis accommodaret etiam distinctum tractationis modum.*'

[63] R.R. Bolgar, 'From humanism to the humanities', *Twentieth Century Studies* 9 (1973), 8-21; L. Jardine, 'Humanism and the sixteenth-century Cambridge arts course', *History of Education* 4 (1975), 16-31.

with the growth of the teacher's knowledge and experience. When, previously, a traditional teacher, interested chiefly in the diction, allusions and other literary aspects of a text, wished to improve a set of lectures, he could only do so by accumulation: by citing more Greek and Latin parallels, by making each definition into a full-scale dictionary article, by discussing every point of syntax and prosody exhaustively, and the like. In the course of such treatment, as we have seen, the text itself is lost completely from view: it becomes less a work of literature than a pretext for the composition of a non-alphabetical ency-clopedia.[64]

On the other hand, Mignault's strategy of showing that his method *fits* the text he applies it to means that he is obliged to test his application of it each time he lectures; and the resulting process of cross-checking and correlation can and does lead him to sharpen and refine the analysis itself to make it an increasingly close fit for the text before him. To give one example – in his lecture on Horace *Epistles* 1.20 Mignault applied his method with breathtaking obtuseness:

> This describes Horace's modesty and humility through a *prosopopoeia* of his book, which he rebukes because it wants to be published ...[65]

This is to take Horace's affected scepticism about his book's reception entirely seriously. And Mignault himself clearly realised this in later years. For in a later version of this lecture he added:

> This seems to be an effort to dissuade his book from wishing to be published ... But he does this rather slyly. For when he later warns the book that if it is asked about Horace it should describe him as he is, he wants precisely to be praised and to receive the applause he deserves.[66]

Here the additional gloss contextualises that argument in a way which certainly enhances the reading. The fact that in the case of Ramus' own lectures on Cicero's *Pro Rabirio* the printed commentary shows a similar sharpening and improving of focus over the student notes suggests that this is indeed an intrinsic feature of the Ramist exegetical method.[67]

---

[64] Cf. A. Grafton, 'On the scholarship of Politian and its context', *Journal of the Warburg and Courtauld Institutes* 40 (1977), 152-5.

[65] Mignault, introductory note to Horace, *Epistles* 1.20; *Q. Horatii Flacci Epistolarum libri duo* (App. 1 below, no. 17), fol. 19ᵛ: '*Modestia pudorque Horatii describitur per prosopopoeiam ad librum quem obiurgat, quod cupiat in lucem emitti, simulque adiungitur Horatii descriptio ex variis adiunctis.*'

[66] *Q. Horatii Flacci Epistolarum libri duo*, ed. Mignault, (Paris, 1584), 117: ('*In epistolam vicesimam Methodus*'): '*Videtur esse dehortatio ad librum suum, qui in lucem edi cupiat: pericula enim recenset, quae editionem sequi possunt. Id tamen caute admodum facit. Nam cum subinde monet, ut si rogetur liber de conditione personae Horatianae, describat eum uti sit: nihil aliud vult quam seipsum tacite commendari, et meritis ornari laudibus. Ad eum pene modum alii quidam poetae, sed Ovidius et Martialis imprimis, libros alloquuntur suos, vel uti se tecte laudent, aut etiam vindicent a contemptu vel odio invidorum.*'

[67] For the parallel account of the development of Ramus' commentaries see Barroux, 'Le premier cours de Ramus'.

The documents in Princeton provide a tiny local sample: the year's work of a young man in a relatively insignificant college. In 1574, however, possibly irked by his principal's criticism of Ausonius' *Griphus* as too frivolous a text for proper arts teaching, Mignault moved to the better known Collège de la Marche.[68] There he seems to have spread himself a bit more. At all events, he later recalled that he had discussed the 'copious and useful' question of selecting books profitable to students 'when I gave public lectures on Basil's oration *Ad adulescentes* in the Collège de la Marche' – a description that suggests more elaborate lectures on a Greek text than those he had given at Reims.[69] And when, in 1575, he rose to the *splendor* of the *regia Burgundionum schola*, he went even farther.[70] His lectures on Ausonius' *Protrepticon*, taken down in 1575 and later published by his students, show an unwonted fullness of detail in all respects. Mignault derived from Joseph Scaliger's very recent edition the discovery that Ausonius' *innumeros numeros* (line 48) are 'the free verses of comedy, which proceeds, to be sure, by feet, but loose ones'.[71] Verbal and other parallels are now heaped on with a lavish hand. After using some eleven quotations to show that Ausonius was rather vain about his consulship, Mignault goes out of his way to defend his display of erudition as good pedagogy:

I fear that my careful citation of these passages may irritate some self-styled

---

[68] The date of Mignault's move is determined by the 'Oratio' cited in note 52 above. For Mignault's problems with his principal at Reims see his '*Appendix apologetica pro Ausonii Gripho*', dated Paris 1575, in Mignault ed., *D. Magni Ausonii Griphus ternarii numeri* (Paris, 1583), fols. 26^r (misnumbered 29)-29^r.

[69] *D. Ausonii Burdegalensis, Viri consularis, Eidyllia duo; unum, Protrepticon ad nepotem Ausonium, De studio puerili; alterum, De ambiguitate eligendae vitae; Quibus adiecta est facilis et aperta explicatio, ex praelectionibus quotidianis Claudii Minois. Excepta omnia ex ore docentis, a studiosis aliquot adolescentibus in Academia Parisiensi, anno MDLXXV*, ed. Mignault, (Paris, 1583) [The title is given in full because it is unusually informative], fol. 12^{r-v} *ad Protrepticon* 45: '*Sunt enim veteres in primis deligendi, non quidem omnes, sed probatissimi, ex quibus solida paratur eruditio. Ex recentioribus sunt nonnulli minime aspernandi, sed ii maxime qui foeliciter veteres illos aemulantur. Quod argumentum certe copiosum et utile admodum studiosis, quia memini me pluribus tractasse, et illustrasse anno superiore, cum in Marchiano publice orationem Basilii magni pros neous explicarem, hic non ero longior.*'

[70] For Mignault's move to the Collège de Bourgogne see his '[*Oratio*] *Altera. De causis quibus maxime Parisiensis Academia periclitetur; et qua via imprimis eidem subveniri posse videatur. In regio Burgundionum gymnasio, pridie Kalend. Octobris 1575*', *De re literaria orationes* 42-75, esp. 72-3.

[71] *Ausonii Eidyllia duo*, ed. Mignault, fol. 13^r: '*Innumeros numeros) solutos Comoediae versus: quae quidem pedibus incedit, sed solutioribus, neque lege vinctis adeo severa, ut sunt alia poematum genera. Quam explicationem debeo Iosep. Scaligero viro doctissimo ...*'. The relevant passage from J. Scaliger, *Ausonianarum lectionum libri duo* (Lyon, 1574) is: '*Intelligit enim solutos comoediae versus: qui sunt quidem numeri: nam suis pedibus incedunt, sed non veri numeri: quia legibus soluti. Ita Horatius cum scribit: numerisque fertur Lege solutis: intelligit haud dubie innumeros numeros Pindari. Eiusmodi autem est, imo liberior comica poesis. Quare et in Epitaphio Plauti per innumeros numeros Comoedia intelligitur, Nam quid aliud scripsit Plautus praeter Comoediam* [cf. Aulus Gellius, *Noctes Atticae* 1.24 for Plautus' epitaph]? ... *quod dictum est Graecanice. ut* numphê anumphos, gamos agamos.' (2.17, 134).

opponent of excessive diligence. But this is what the teacher's office requires of him.[72]

He even finds time to mention his manuscript of the Persius scholia, written in 'fading script'.[73] And, while even in his courses at the Collège de Bourgogne he paraphrases his texts and sometimes sums them up in neat dialectical formulae, he tries to pass on much more information, often of a quite recherché kind, and takes for granted his audience's ability to follow an argument.

Mignault had no doubt read much more by 1575 than he had in 1572; his audiences in the larger colleges may well have wanted more in the way of Greek quotations and references to up-to-date scholarship and out-of-the-way texts; and he himself was moving towards a career decision (which he took in 1578) to leave arts teaching and become a canon lawyer.[74] Yet, even at his most learned, Mignault never quite abandoned his Ramist habits. He certainly did not bombard his students with all the dense information Scaliger had provided about Ausonius' rich and curious language, nor did he ever entirely abandon a structured and argument-based method of analysis.[75]

Claude Mignault was a teacher in the Ramist mould, whose teaching, we have suggested, shows little of the revolutionary fervour or intellectual iconoclasm that we might expect from a follower of a supposedly 'radical' and disruptive pedagogy. Our last Ramist is a rather more flamboyant character.

Gabriel Harvey was born in 1550 at Saffron Walden, near Cambridge, the eldest son of a prosperous burgher family.[76] He died in 1631, having become, apparently, a pillar of the Saffron Walden community. But in the 1570s he appeared to have more prestigious, gentrified prospects as a senior academic member of the University of Cambridge: a member of the Tudor Establishment, and a social cut above his Saffron Walden origins. The social mobility promised by Harvey's successful academic career has been all too vividly captured by his adversary in print, Thomas Nashe, in his polemical

---

[72] *Ausonii Eidyllia duo*, ed. Mignault, fol. 19^r: '*Quos studiose locos adducenti mihi vereor ne quis succenseat, ut qui non probet nimium diligentem: sed hoc tamen exigitur docentis officio.*'

[73] Ibid., fol. 10^r ad *Protrepticon* 30: '*Ego quidem habeo penes me commentarium anonymi cuiusdam in Persium membrana descriptum litteris certe fugientibus, ex quo didici ad Satyram 5. scuticam fuisse olim corrigiam, quae habebat in summitate nodos quosdam in modum fabae.*'

[74] See Mignault's letter '*lectori studioso et candido*', in *Horatii Epistolarum libri duo*, ed. Mignault, sig. Y iii^r.

[75] Cf. the passages quoted in n. 71 above.

[76] For Harvey's biography see V.F. Stern, *Gabriel Harvey: His Life, Marginalia and Library* (Oxford, 1979), which replaces earlier sources. See, however, W.G. Colman's review article, *English Studies* 64 (1983), 169-74, for serious reservations about the accuracy of Stern's study of Harvey's marginalia.

pamphlet, *Have with you to Saffron-walden:*[77] all too vividly, because it is difficult for the modern reader (difficult, indeed, even for Harvey's twentieth-century editors) not to be distracted by Nashe's lively portrayal of the posturing 'upstart' courtier from the Elizabethan class conservatism which motivates it.[78] But Nashe's attack, and the attempts of a number of Harvey's colleagues at Cambridge to block his rise up the academic promotion ladder, should alert us to the fact that excelling in the liberal arts or *bonae artes* in sixteenth-century England signifies more than simply academic distinction.[79] It is recognised as a means of access to prominent civic position, to the Elizabethan court, to power and influence.[80] In other words, the equivalence between humanistic learning and suitability for public office has apparently become an official reality in sixteenth-century England. Harvey believes (as we shall see) that by excelling in the arts he will become a member of the Tudor ruling élite; opponents like Thomas Neville, who tried to block his academic promotion, clearly express their social and political prejudices in their objections.[81]

As he read, Harvey wrote extensive notes in the margins and blank pages of each volume he owned, thus providing us with a clear picture of the way he went about his studies. When he worked on a number of volumes together he cross-referenced one book in the pages of the other (in the process of which he was not above filling the margins of borrowed books with notes!). These annotations are a rich source of information on how an ambitious arts student (and subsequently teacher) approached his education.[82] In particular

[77] For an excellent account of the Harvey/Nashe quarrel, as well as the printed text of *Have with you to Saffron-walden* (1596), see *Works of Thomas Nashe*, ed. R.B. McKerrow, 5 vols (London, 1904; reprinted New York, 1966).

[78] Grosart, who edited Harvey's works, both assents to Nashe's version of Harvey's personality, and makes it clear that he himself is out of sympathy with it. A. Grosart, *Works*, 3 vols (London, 184-5). See also *Pedantius: A Latin Comedy formerly acted in Trinity College, Cambridge*, ed. G.C. Moore Smith (London, 1905).

[79] On the attempts made first to prevent Harvey from taking his M.A. degree, then to block his fellowship at Pembroke, his appointment to the Greek lectureship at Pembroke, to the Professorship of Rhetoric, and finally to a college Mastership, see Stern, *Gabriel Harvey*.

[80] For a short while it looked as if Harvey's academic success would gain him a coveted secretaryship to the Earl of Leicester. On Harvey's limited successes in the court sphere see Stern, *Gabriel Harvey*.

[81] For the details of Neville's opposition to the award of Harvey's M.A. see Stern, *Gabriel Harvey*, 16-25. For an interesting recent account of the relationship between Harvey's studies and his aspirations to high Tudor office see F. Wigham, *Ambition and Privilege: The Social Tropes of Elizabethan Courtesy Theory* (Berkeley and Los Angeles, 1984), 22-6.

[82] On the Harvey marginalia see the following: G.C. Moore Smith, *Gabriel Harvey's Marginalia* (Stratford-upon-Avon, 1913); 'Printed books with Gabriel Harvey's Autograph or MS. notes', *Modern Language Review* 38 (1933), 78-81; 39 (1934), 68-70 and 321-2; 30 (1935), 209; H.S. Wilson, 'Gabriel Harvey's method of annotating his books', *Harvard Library Bulletin* 2 (1948), 344-61; Stern, *Gabriel Harvey*; 'The *Bibliotheca* of Gabriel Harvey', *Renaissance Quarterly* 25 (1972), 1-62; W.G. Colman, 'Gabriel Harvey's holograph notes in his copy of *Gnomologiae*', *Renaissance Quarterly* (in press); J.-C. Margolin, 'Gabriel Harvey, lecteur d'Erasme', *Archivos do Centro Cultural Portugues* IV (1972), 37-92 (with plates).

they enable us to see how Ramus' and Talaeus' pedagogic works were used in practice (in private study, and as preparation for university teaching at Cambridge), and to draw some tentative conclusions about the 'impact' of those works, as opposed to any internal reading we may choose to give of individual texts like the *Dialectica* in isolation.

We start from Harvey's copy of Quintilian, now in the British Library in London (*M. Fabii Quintiliani oratoris eloquentissimi, Institutionum oratoriarum libri XII*. Parisiis. Ex officina Rob. Stephani Typographi Regii. M. D. XLII. class mark C.60.1.11), together with Harvey's copy of Cicero's *Topica*, with Talaeus' *praelectiones*, now in All Souls College Library in Oxford (*M. Tul. Ciceronis ad C. Trebatium Iurisconsultum Topica; Audomari Talaei praelectionibus explicata*, ... Parisiis, Ex typographia Matthaei Dauidis ... 1550. class mark a-11-4(3)).[83] We take these two volumes and their marginalia together in the first instance because Harvey cross-refers between them and refers in both to other reading in common.

A number of inscriptions in these volumes tell us when Harvey read them and what he read alongside them. On the title page of the Quintilian we have Harvey's signature twice, and two dates: 'mense Martio. 1567. precium iij^S vj^d' and '1579'. At the end of Book 10 (fol.M.viii^r)[84] we have another signature and the words 'Rhetoricus Professor Cantabrig. 1573. 1574. 1575'. After the printed 'FINIS' (fol. T.vii^r) we have a further signature, and the following:

> *Relegi ab jnitio: Mense Septembri. Anno. 1579. unaq[ue] Ciceronis Oratorem ad M. Brutum, cum Quintiliani Oratore comparaui: ut utrumq[ue] ita collatum, Ramaeis demu[m] Rhetoricarum scholarum ponderibus examinaui.*[85]

(I reread [this work] from the beginning in September 1579, and I compared Cicero's *Orator* with Quintilian's *Orator*. And when I had thus compared them, I weighed each of them up against Ramus' *Scholae rhetoricae*.)

At the end of the dedicatory epistle in the *Topica* he writes:

> *Ad ciuilem Topicorum vsum, forensemq[ue] argumentoru[m] praxim, malim Ciceronem topicum doctorem, quam ipsum Aristotelem, aut alium aliquem illius temporis magistrum, seu Graecum philosophum, seu Latinum scholasticum. ... gabriel harueius, 1579.*[86]

(For civil use of Topics, and for public application [*praxis*] of arguments, I prefer

---

[83] W.G. Colman, University of Ghent, has transcribed all the marginalia which have currently come to light in British libraries, and intends to publish a complete edition in due course. We are extremely grateful to Mr Colman for having generously made his transcripts of selected marginalia available to us.

[84] We give folio numbers for the Quintilian because Harvey's copy is wrongly paginated at the top of the pages.

[85] Fol. T.vii^r.   [86] 5 (fol. A.iii^v).

the *Topica* of learned Cicero to those of Aristotle, or of any other master of that period, whether Greek philosopher or Latin scholastic ... Gabriel Harvey, 1579.)

At the end of the book he writes after his signature:

Calendis Februar. 1570. *Multo etia[m] diligentius,* 1579. *jamtum aliquanto studiosius iuri Ciuili incumbens.*[87]

(First February 1570. Much more thoroughly in 1579, already at that time exerting myself somewhat more studiously in the Civil Law.)

What this establishes is the following: Harvey read the Quintilian for the first time in 1567, and '*releg[it] ab initio*' in 1579. In between he probably used Book 10 for his public lectures as Professor of Rhetoric in the three years in which he held that office (1573, 1574 and 1575).[88] He read the Cicero in 1570, but this work also he read 'much more thoroughly' in 1579. Since there are extensive collations and cross-references between the two volumes we suggest that the bulk of the marginal annotations (certainly the ones we shall be interested in) date from the 1579 reading, and that Harvey had the two books before him for study together.[89]

Harvey's annotations show that in 1579 he had beside him Talaeus' *praelectiones* on Ramus' *Dialectica* (*Petri Rami ... Dialecticae libri duo, A. Talaei praelectionibus illustrati,* probably in the 1569 Basle edition, or one of its reprintings),[90] and on Cicero's *De oratore* (*M. Tullii Ciceronis De oratore ad Quintum fratrem dialogi tres, Audomari Talaei explicationibus illustrati. Parisiis:*

---

[87] 74 (fol. E.v^v).

[88] The character of some of the notes to Book 10 tends to confirm the view (suggested by the inscription at the end of the book) that these notes are preparatory to lecturing on it as a set text. The notes are characteristically complete sentences rather than jottings or page references, and they are highly 'occasional' (suitable for a lecture to a Tudor audience). They include allusions to (and suggestions of comparison with) a wide range of humanistic works which a good student might be expected to consult, from Agricola's *De inventione dialectica* and his translation of Aphthonius' *Progymnasmata* (several times) to Angelus Decembrius' *De politia literaria,* Lorenzo Valla's *Elegantiae* and *Dialecticae disputationes,* Paulus Manutius' commentaries and Erasmus' *Ciceronianus.* There are also 'local' references in the form of laudatory references to commentaries by eminent English pedagogues: Cheke, Carr and Ascham.

[89] Other corroborating evidence can be derived from the fact that Harvey is using an edition of Ramus' *Dialectica* from after 1569 (we have checked all earlier editions, and the page numbers of Harvey's citations fail to match the appropriate passages in these editions).

[90] For a clear description of the various versions of these *Praelectiones* see N. Bruyère, *Méthode et Dialectique dans l'Oeuvre de La Rámee* (Paris, 1984), 19-22. The editions which it is possible Harvey used all date from 1569 or later; see W.J. Ong, *Ramus and Talon Inventory* (Harvard, 1958), 190-3, entries 245-9. These are the only editions substantial enough (i.e. with enough pages) to match Harvey's pagination. They are all extremely rare (see Ong). We are extremely grateful to W. Risse who has notified us of a number of editions of the *Praelectiones* not listed in Ong or Bruyère (personal communication, Paris, December 1985); the one which is of interest to us in the present case is a 1567 Cologne edition, now in Amsterdam University Library. Since we were not able to consult any of these we have used the 1566 Paris edition in Trinity Hall Library, Cambridge, and the 1583 Frankfurt edition in the University Library, Cambridge.

Carolus Stephanus, 1553), and Ramus' own *Praelectiones* on Cicero's *De optimo genere oratorum* (*M. T. Ciceronis De optimo genere oratorum praefatio in contrarias Aeschinis et Demosthenis orationes, P. Rami, regii eloquentiae et philosophiae professoris, praelectionibus illustrata* (Paris, 1557)). The nature of the annotations in both the Quintilian and the Cicero suggest that it was the sixteenth-century works that Ramus perused in depth, and that he turned to the classical texts to elucidate technical or polemical points in Ramus (and Talaeus). This is a crucial point. Precise page references to Ramus' *Dialecticae libri duo, A. Talaei praelectionibus illustrati* appear in the margins throughout both the Quintilian and the Cicero *Topica*. The vast majority of marginal references link a passage in the Quintilian or Cicero with a verbatim quotation of that passage in the Ramus *Dialectica*. In our view the only way Harvey could have picked up these cross-references was by pausing in his reading of the *Dialectica* as he encountered them, turning up the passage in the original text (usually accurately cited in Talaeus' commentary) and marking the appropriate *Dialectica* reference there. A further set of cross-references similarly picks up technical terms in the *praelectiones* (often Greek ones) attributed to Quintilian by Talaeus, which can be found in the index to the Paris edition of Quintilian. Again, we think that as Harvey encountered the term in the Talaeus commentary he turned up the index in his Quintilian, found the appropriate passage and marked the *Dialectica* reference.

What this tells us is that Harvey's intensive study of Quintilian and Cicero takes place *via* – that is, literally *by way of* – Ramus and (particularly) Talaeus; and this in turn gives us an important insight into Harvey's study of 'the classics', or *studia humanitatis*. He absorbs Quintilian and Cicero as they agree with, or differ from, Ramist dialectic. Dialectic is certainly the focus of his attention: Book 5 of Quintilian and the technical sections of the Cicero *Topica* are the most closely annotated and the most thoroughly collated with the Ramus *Dialectica*. It is, however, a study of dialectic enriched to the point of unrecognisability by the wide-ranging and imaginative Greek and Latin classical material which Talaeus brings to bear on Ramus' rather meagre text in his *praelectiones* and which absorbs some of the key themes concerning ancient eloquence that are to be found in Talaeus' commentaries on Cicero.

Throughout his marginal jottings Harvey is deeply involved in characterising a particular type of 'perfect orator': the Elizabethan lawyer or diplomat – a pragmatic version of the Roman orator.[91] Book 12 of Quintilian (the book summing up and describing the qualities of such a perfect orator) is also heavily annotated. Above the key chapter (entitled in Harvey's edition,

[91] 'Pragmaticus' is a term taken from the Greek and used by Quintilian to refer to the person who provides the concrete facts which are the orator's ammunition when arguing any case. See e.g. 12.3.4: *neque ego sum nostri moris ignarus oblitusve eorum, qui velut ad arculas sedent et tela agentibus subministrant, neque idem Graecos quoque nescio factitasse, unde nomen his pragmaticorum datum est.* (See also 2.21.3; 3.6.35,57-9; 3.7.1). Harvey's emphasis on *this* facet of the 'perfect orator' shows clearly his practical, law-court bias.

'Non posse Oratorem esse nisi virum bonum') Harvey writes; '*Quinctiliani ORATOR*' (Quintilian's definitive Orator)[92] and at the end of the book he transcribes large extracts from Cicero's *Orator* and *De oratore* for comparison. These passages pick out particularly vivid descriptions of the practical qualities the orator must display if he is to be a successful public figure and 'man of action'. Drawing together the marginal notes in these volumes and the Ramist passages to which they refer, it is possible to suggest that Harvey's reading produces a highly idiosyncratic version of humanism – *pragmatic* humanism; and we suggest further that a centrally subversive feature of Ramus's approach to the arts, whose implications Harvey fully draws out, is that it offers just this possibility of separating oratorical practice from any moral underpinning. In other words, a committed Ramist finds himself free to pursue the *ars disserendi* simply as a route to high government office, without worrying about being *vir bonus* (a good man).

To pursue this theme of the 'perfectly pragmatic orator' we need to return to the inscription at the end of the Quintilian, to pick up a crucial work by Ramus which Harvey had before him. That inscription tells us that Harvey returned to this text in 1579 equipped with Ramus' *Scholae rhetoricae* and Cicero's *Orator*. The first thing to point out is that this was an eminently sensible thing for a committed Ramist to do. Ramus' *Scholae rhetoricae* appeared under that title for the first time in 1569, published in Basle as part of the collection of works Ramus himself saw through the Basle press.[93] It consists of the eight books of the *Brutinae quaestiones* (Ramus' praelectiones on Cicero's *Orator*), together with the twelve books of the *Rhetoricae distinctiones in Quintilianum*. In other words the obvious way to study the *Scholae rhetoricae* is to read it together with Cicero and Quintilian's primary texts.

The notes which refer directly to this comparison of Cicero with Quintilian occur largely in Books 11 and 12 of the Quintilian (there are further, obviously contemporary, notes comparing the two in the margins of the Cicero *Topica*). On Quintilian 11.3 ('De pronuntiatione'), for instance, Harvey writes:

Vide 65. *Confer, quae breuiter, et summatim Cicero, jn Oratore ad Brutu[m]; de singulari Actionis Vsu in Oratore,* 231. 232.[94]

(See page 65 [1.11 in the Loeb]. Compare what Cicero says briefly and compendiously, in the *Orator*, concerning the singular use of action by the orator, pages 231 and 232 [*Orator* 17.55-18.60 in the Loeb].)

[92] Fol. Q.viii[V].
[93] On Ramus' stay at Basle, supervising Basle printings of his works, see P.G. Bietenholz, *Basle and France in the Sixteenth Century: The Basle Humanists and Printers in their Contacts with Francophone Culture* (Geneva, 1971), 153-63, 304-7. For details of Ramus' career see P. Sharratt, 'Nicolaus Nancelius, *Petri Rami vita*, edited with an English translation', *Humanistica Lovaniensia* 24 (1975). See also footnote 1 above.
[94] Fol. O.v[V].

In addition, in available spaces within the Quintilian text and on the blank pages at the end of the volume Harvey copies out complete passages from Cicero's *Orator* and even more substantial passages from the *De Oratore*. On fol. S.vi^r, for instance, in the section of 12.10 on varieties of oratorical style, Harvey copies out a substantial part of *Orator* 29.100-30.106. This passage describes the styles employed by the 'perfect orator' in extremely succinct and practical terms – in stark contrast to the stylistic niceties with which Quintilian is concerning himself at this point in Harvey's text. Furthermore Harvey omits a passage from the Cicero which suggests that such a practical or pragmatic orator is not a reality but an ideal ('*Ego enim quid desiderem, non quid viderim disputo, redeoque ad illam Platonis de qua dixeram rei formam et speciem, quam etsi non cernimus tamen animo tenere possumus*'); and he generally tidies up his passage to provide a forceful, down-to-earth version of the man who 'can discuss trivial matters in a plain style, matters of moderate significance in a tempered style, and weighty affairs weightily'. In other words Harvey here counteracts the 'preciousness' (as we might consider it) of the Quintilian by juxtaposing the passage from the *Orator*.[95] The result is an extremely positive, and extremely practical, version of the 'perfect orator', which entirely supports the end-note in the *Topica* which tells us that Harvey was 'already inclined towards' the Civil Law (in which he subsequently took his Doctorate) at the time of reading.

It must already be apparent that in his enthusiastic and practical response to Cicero and Quintilian as exemplifying Ramus' dialectical precepts in the 'perfectly pragmatic orator' Harvey is heavily indebted to Talaeus. All his significant marginal comments are to the *commentary* on the *Dialectica* – his notes rarely refer to Ramus' actual text.[96] In his marginal response to Ramus' *Scholae rhetoricae*, by contrast, which he notes that he used extensively in his 1579 reading of Quintilian (and in which there is no collaboration with Talaeus), Harvey is clearly uneasy with Ramus' intransigence. There are in fact only two direct references to Ramus' *Scholae rhetoricae* itself in Harvey's Quintilian (there are actually rather more page references to it and the companion *Scholae dialecticae* from the same volume in the margins of the Cicero *Topica*). The most striking of these is the one we gave earlier, but which we gave only in part. The complete note after the 'FINIS' in the Quintilian runs as follows:

[95] The lengthy passages from the *De Oratore* which Harvey transcribes on the blank end pages of his Quintilian are (with one exception) Antonius', and describe the practical ways in which a forensic orator will sway the emotions of his audience to achieve agreement to a desired conclusion in arguing a difficult case. He also transcribes the appropriate sections of Talaeus' commentary on the text.

[96] Though Ramus did apparently have a large hand in Talaeus' commentary. On Ramus' close involvement in the preparation of the later editions of Talaeus' *praelectiones* on his *Dialectica* see Ong, *Ramus and Talon Inventory*, 189-91 and Bruyère, *Méthode et Dialectique dans l'Oeuvre de La Ramée*, 19-22.

Relegi ab jnitio: Mense Septembri. Anno. 1579. *unaq[ue] Ciceronis Oratorem ad M. Brutum, cum Quintiliani Oratore comparaui: et utrumq[ue] ita collatum, Ramaeis demu[m] Rhetoricarum scholarum ponderibus examinaui: Acute quidem Ramus atq[ue] uere artes distinguit: quas tamen oratorius, et forensis iste vsus coniungit: nec vero Oratorem suu[m] Cicero, et Quintilianus, vnius facultatis professorem, sed tanq[u]a[m] Artificu[m] Artificem esse uoluere; plurimis, maximisq[ue] Artibus; ijs praesertim, quarum summus esset in foro, inq[ue] Ciuium causis perorandis vsus; vndiquaq[ue] instructum, et armatum.*[97]

(I reread [this work] from the beginning in September 1579, and I compared Cicero's *Orator* with Quintilian's Orator. And when I had thus compared them, I weighed each of them against Ramus' *Scholae rhetoricae*. Ramus discriminates acutely and rightly between the arts: but they are run together in oratorical and public practice. Nor indeed do Cicero and Quintilian wish their Orator to be a professor of any one faculty, but rather a Craftsman of Craftsmen, equipped and armed at all points with most of the Arts, and above all those which rank highest for use in public life, and in pleading state cases.)

And he continues in English:

A *perfit Orator*: A most excellent Pleader, and singular Discourser in any Civil Court, or otherwyse: not A bare Professo[u]r of any one certain faculty, or A simple Artist in any one kynde: howbeit his *principall Instrumentes* ar Rhetorique, for Elocutio[n], and Pronunciation; and Logique, for Invention, Disposition, and Memory.[98]

Harvey here takes issue with Ramus' flamboyantly destructive *Scholae rhetoricae*, which launches a systematic attack on Cicero and Quintilian for failing to keep clear the essential Ramist distinction between the scope and function of the various individual arts. Harvey accepts that it is desirable to make clear distinctions for teaching purposes, but he maintains that Quintilian and Cicero have in mind a person who is to be equipped for the legal and diplomatic duties of civil life, and that such a person must indeed be skilled in a whole range of arts and sciences. In the only other explicit reference in the Quintilian to the *Scholae rhetoricae* Harvey again loyally cites Ramus, even though Ramus' negative treatment in that (in fact early) work contradicts the judgment which he has derived from Talaeus' largely enthusiastic citations of Quintilian in the *praelectiones* to Ramus' *Dialectica*:

[97] Fol. T.vii[r].
[98] Ibid.

Liber istorum omnium maxime singularis. Consulendus tamen scholarum rhetoricarum liber etiam 18⁴⁵. Ne asper aliorum Criticus, sine sui arguto Critico, nimis insolenter exsultet. Iuuat acerrima vtrinq[ue] Censura, sed maturima [sic].⁹⁹

(This book is the most singular of this entire work. However, one ought also to consult the eighteenth book [i.e. the commentary on Quintilian 10] of the *Scholae rhetoricae*. No severe critic of others should vaunt himself excessively and unacceptably without his own outspoken critic. The most abrasive censure is acceptable, as long as it is timely.)

Two pages later, against Quintilian 10.1 ('*De copia verborum*'), Harvey cites Talaeus' *praelectiones* on Ramus' *Dialectica* where '*hic locus laudatus ab A. T O*'.¹⁰⁰

Yet in crucial respects, we would argue, Harvey's 'pragmatic orator' would be impossible without Ramus at his most extreme. At the beginning of Book 9 of the *Scholae rhetoricae* (the first book of the commentary on Quintilian), Ramus takes up the crucial definition of the 'perfect orator', *orator est vir bonus dicendi peritus*, and argues abrasively for a total separation of the ethical from the linguistic in any definition of an orator:

Hunc oratorem Quintilianus nobis instituit, quem postea libro duodecimo viru[m] bonum bene dicendi peritum, similiter definit, & illas animi virtutes exponit, justitiam, fortitudinem, temperantiam, prudentiam: item philosophiam totam, legu[m] scie[n]tiam, & cognitionem historiarum, & alia pleraq[ue] laudum ornamenta. Quid igitur contra istam oratoris finitionem dici potest? Ego vero talem oratoris definitionem vitiosam mihi videri confirmo: quamobre[m]? quia supervacanea cujusvis artificis est definitio, quae plus complectitur, qua[m] est artis institutis co[m]prehensum.¹⁰¹

(Such is the orator as Quintilian instructs us, who afterwards in Book 12 he defines similarly as 'a good man, who excels in the art of discourse', and he sets out the virtues of his soul as justice, fortitude, temperance and prudence: as also the whole of philosophy, of the legal sciences, and a knowledge of history, and other and various praiseworthy ornaments. What then can be said against this definition? I maintain that such a definition of the orator seems to me entirely defective. Why? Because the definition of any profession whatever is redundant which involves more than is contained within the subject matter of that art.)

Accordingly Ramus rejects any definition of the 'perfect orator' which in any way implies ethical understanding or moral integrity on the part of the orator. And he claims that it is only because the orator is ultimately to play a prominent part in civic affairs that Quintilian feels that his training ought to have an ethical dimension. In other words, Ramus severs the *ars disserendi*

---

⁹⁹ Fol. K.iʳ.
¹⁰⁰ Fol. K.ii.ʳ.
¹⁰¹ *P. Rami Scholae in liberales artes* (Basle, 1569), fol. 0.2ᵛ.

from the ethical underpinning which for early humanists had justified the claim that the *studia humanitatis* were a training for civic life.

The copious marginal annotations to Book 12 of his Quintilian reveal the emphatically civic – and above all the emphatically *Tudor* – context within which Harvey locates his Orator. Severing the virtuous man from the accomplished public speaker (just as Ramus did, if less flamboyantly), Harvey makes it clear in his annotations that *his* version of the *vir bonus* is a 'great man' (not the same thing at all). Where Quintilian's text runs

> *Dicet idem graviter, severe, acriter, vehementer, concitate, copiose, amare, comiter, remisse, subtiliter, blande, leniter, dulciter, breviter, urbane, non ubique similis, sed ubique par sibi. Sic fiet cum id, propter quod maxime repertus est usus orationis, ut dicat utiliter et ad efficiendum quod intendit potenter, tum laudem quoque nec doctorum modo sed etiam vulgi consequatur.*[102]

([The Orator] will speak gravely, severely, sharply, with vehemence, energy, fullness, bitterness, or geniality, quietly, simply, flatteringly, gently, sweetly, briefly or wittily; he will not always be like himself, but he will never be unworthy of himself. Thus the purpose for which oratory was above all designed will be secured, that is to say, he will also win the praise not merely of the learned but of the multitude as well.)

Harvey reflects:

> *Omnes fere Megalandri, egregij erant vel natura, vel arte Oratores. Quales sub rege Henrico 8°. Cardinalis Volsaeus: Prorex Cromuellus: Cancellarius Morus: pragmaticus Gardinerus: quatuor heroici Consiliarij. Sub principe Edouardo 6to. Dux Northumbrius; archiepiscopus Cranmerus; secretarius Smithus; Checus paedagogus. Sub regina Elizabetha, Smithus Cineas; Cecilius Nestor; Baconus Scaevola; Essexius Achilles. Quot aulici, urbiciq[ue], Cicerones, et Virgilij: Columbi et Sfortiae!*[103]

(Well-nigh all the greatest men were outstanding Orators either by nature or by art. As, under King Henry VIII: Cardinal Wolsey; royal deputy Cromwell; Chancellor More; pragmatic Gardiner; four heroic counsellors. Under Prince Edward VI: the Duke of Northumberland; Archbishop Cranmer; Secretary Smith; educator Cheke. Under Queen Elizabeth: Cineas-like Smith; Nestor-like Cecil; Scaevola-like Bacon; Achilles-like Essex. How many courtiers and civic figures, Ciceros and Virgils, Columbuses and Sforzas!)

The implication here is that the perfect Orator is the Great Statesman, a view confirmed by a marginal note to 10.1. In Harvey's edition this chapter is headed '*De copia verborum*', firmly anchoring the text in Erasmian pedagogy

---

[102] *Institutio oratoria* 12.10.71-3, Loeb edn., ed. H.E. Butler. The Loeb translation tends to make the high moral tone of the Quintilian a good deal more obvious than it is in the original Latin.

[103] Fol. T.iii^v; cit. Stern, *Gabriel Harvey*, 153.

with its assumptions of the moral worth of eloquence.[104] But at the point in the text at which Quintilian eulogises Cicero, and prefers him to Demosthenes, as an outstanding individual, not merely as a great stylist, Harvey notes:

> *Nunquis hac aetate floret uel orator, uel aduocatus, uel aulicus concionator, uel politicus logodaedalus, vel regius consiliarius, vel legatus, vel ullius deniq[ue] facultatis professor, his eloquentior eloquentiss[im]is viris?*[105]

(Was there ever in our age a distinguished orator, or lawyer, or court spokesman, or politic speaker with finesse, or royal counsellor, or ambassador, or, finally, any professor of any faculty whatsoever more eloquent than these most eloquent men [the Roman orators]?)

The categories Harvey selects for possible success as an orator are those of public office within the Tudor élite: orator as public servant, rather than as intellectual, let alone as *vir bonus*. This is the goal which Harvey sees as the *real* object of higher education in the arts – the purpose for which that initiation into classical culture is intended.

Harvey's attitude towards the acquisition of eloquence – the becoming a 'perfect orator' – bears a family resemblance to Lorenzo Valla's or Rudolph Agricola's praise of true Latinity but, mediated *via* Ramus, it is in important respects distinctively Ramist. Elsewhere in his Quintilian, for instance, we find Harvey unconsciously using intellectual sleight-of-hand to make Valla's notion of *eloquentia* as 'philosophical understanding' or 'learnedness' into a much more banal kind of 'fluency' – in our modern sense of 'public speaking ability'. Against Quintilian's final eulogy of the Orator, Harvey has written:

> *Oratorem esse virum sapientem, quantum in hominem cadit: hoc est, plus esse, quam philosophum, et sophon. Vallae assertio in sua ad Pontificem Max. apologia: et in praefatione 1. 2.* [actually 1] *dialecticarum disputationum. vbi magnificum Oratoris praeconium.*[106]

(The Orator ought to be a wise man, insofar as it is possible for men to be wise: that is, beyond being a lover of wisdom he ought actually to be wise. As Valla maintains in his apologia and in Book 2 [actually Book 1] of his *Dialecticae disputationes*, where there is a magnificent celebration of the Orator.)

Harvey here quotes a crucial passage from the *Dialecticae disputationes* in which Valla prefaces his treatment of dialectic with a meticulous exploration of his attitude towards the acquisition of knowledge in general. For Harvey, Valla's logical and philosophical treatise is 'a magnificent celebration of the Orator',

---

[104] See above, Chapter 6.
[105] Fol. L.iii[r].
[106] Fol. T.vi[v].

a study of the art of speaking, rather than of knowing.

Harvey is open and ostentatious in his Ramism. His published works are as fulsome in praise of the controversial French Protestant and humanist as Mignault's are discreet.[107] It is probably fair to say that in the 1570s and 1580s in England it was a just-permissible sign of intellectual radicalism to profess Ramism – a somewhat voguish intellectual stance in keeping with Harvey's reputation for affecting Italianate dress and manners.[108] More tellingly, for our purposes, Harvey's marginal notes give evidence of a conscientious and meticulous use of Ramist texts to provide intellectual guidelines as he reads and then to shape the preparation of his lectures. In other words, Harvey is a Ramist in his reading practice, as much as in his proclaimed affiliations. And Harvey's Ramism manifests itself in a confident and self-conscious refocusing of the liberal arts training as a *pragmatic* training, a training for material success and public position. To return to the annotated Quintilian, in 12.11 where Quintilian writes

> *His dicendi virtutibus usus orator in iudiciis, consiliis, contionibus, senatu, in omni denique officio boni civis finem quoque dignum et optimo viro et opere sanctissimo faciet.*[109]

(After employing these gifts of eloquence in the courts, in councils, in public assemblies and the debates of the senate, and, in a word, in the performance of all the duties of a good citizen, the orator will bring his activities to a close in a manner worthy of a blameless life spent in the pursuit of the noblest of professions.)

Harvey adds:

> *Valde interest optimi Oratoris, maximum esse Pragmaticum. Vt apprime refert summi Pragmatici, praecellentissimum esse Oratorem.*[110]

(It is of the greatest importance to the best of Orators to be exceedingly 'Pragmatic'. As it especially profits the most distinguished 'Pragmatic' to be a superlative Orator.)

Or, as Harvey writes, in another marginal note, this time in his copy of *Ciceronianus Ioan. Thomae Freigii, in quo, ex Ciceronis monumentis, ratio instituendi locos communes demonstrata: et eloquentia cum philosophia coniuncta, descripta est libris decem* (whose very title may be read as a Ramist manifesto):

> *Cicero iamprimum methodicus, mnemonicus, pragmaticus. dignus, qui ad vnguem ediscatur.*

---

[107] See, for instance, Harvey's three published orations, in his *Ciceronianus* and *Rhetor* (London, 1577), and *A New Letter of Notable Contents* (London, 1593).

[108] Harvey's own marginal annotations regularly affect Italian views; see also Nashe, *Have with you to Saffron-walden* and the contemporary satirical play, *Pedantius*.

[109] Loeb 12.11.1.

[110] Fol. T.iii[v].

Nullum fere ulla aetate vel ingeniu[m] capacius, vel iudicium maturius, vel dicendi, agendiq[ue] facultas praestantior, vel efficacior in orbe Romano Experientia.[111]

(Cicero above all is methodical, memorizable, pragmatic. Worthy to be studied to perfection. For no one in any age has been more rich in ability, more mature in judgement, more outstanding in practice of action or of speech, nor more effective within the sphere of Roman practical affairs.)

Ramism, as exemplified by our three case-studies of Elizabethan Ramist practice, appears to lead us in the direction of 'the humanities', first as a programme of education in the arts which no longer carries with it its own guarantee that its products will of necessity be good and pious men, and then as an initiation rite for the Tudor administration. But this is not, in fact, the end of our third case-study. It remains for us to point out, as an important piece in our historical jigsaw, that Harvey's aspirations to high office *failed*. Harvey failed to follow in the footsteps of his patron Sir Thomas Smith, from academic brilliance in Latin, Greek and the higher faculty of jurisprudence to senior ministry in Elizabeth's government. Harvey was Greek lecturer at Pembroke in 1573 and Professor of Rhetoric from 1573 to 1575, and he obtained his Doctor of Civil Law degree at Oxford in 1585.[112] His academic credentials were on the face of it impeccable. Nevertheless the Professorship of Rhetoric proved to be the peak of his career. He failed in his bid to become Master of Trinity Hall in 1584; having qualified in Law, he apparently failed to make any impact on eminent legal circles in London or on the closely linked diplomatic service. In 1593 he returned to Saffron Walden, and the life of a prosperous country burgher – where in Elizabethan terms he belonged. If outstanding ability in the humanities was a ticket to preferment, it was only so, evidently, for those born within easy reach of office, those of gentle or noble birth.

*

Ramus and his followers, we have argued, reveal more clearly than any other group the direction in which humanism was moving in the later sixteenth century. But their actual successes in imposing their full programme were quite limited – especially in France, with its predominantly Catholic population. And even Ramus' supporters, as Kees Meerhoff has recently shown, modified central features of Ramist pedagogy, such as his emphasis on vernacular languages, even as they applied and defended others, such as his

---

[111] Marginal note in *Ciceronianus Ioan. Thomae Freigii, in quo, ex Ciceronis monumentis, ratio instituendi locos communes demonstrata: et eloquentia cum philosophia coniuncta, descripta est libris decem* (Basle, [1575]),fol.):(3^v.

[112] Three of Harvey's lectures are printed in his *Rhetor* (London, 1577) and *Ciceronianus* (London, 1577). On his LL.B. and Doctorship of Law see Stern, *Gabriel Harvey*, 75-7.

separation of dialectic and rhetoric.[113]

The crucial plank in the Ramist programme, in the end, is the one it shares with its most effective and popular competitors: its assumption that the aim of classical education is to produce effective writers and active participants in civic life, rather than original scholars and philosopher kings. To that purpose Ramus and his followers were willing to sacrifice the individuality of the ancient writers they studied – were willing, indeed, to ignore the contexts and intentions of the central classical texts – and we find this same instrumental and pragmatic brand of humanism in every flourishing school of the later sixteenth century, Protestant or Catholic.

Many cases could serve to illustrate this point: the Jesuit colleges, with their circumscribed canon of expurgated classics, their obsessive concern for rhetorical imitation, 'the soul of textual commentary'; the Protestant academies of Strassburg and Altdorf, with their encyclopaedic but elementary coverage of the arts and sciences; the Academia Julia in Helmstedt, far to the north.[114] But we concentrate on a single, uniquely prominent teacher and writer rather than an inevitably parochial institution.

Justus Lipsius (1547-1609) won world celebrity at an early age by the incandescent brilliance of his style, the astonishing rapidity of his climb to academic eminence and the terrifying elusiveness of his religious convictions. Educated in Louvain and given a high polish in Rome by private lessons from the French exile Marc-Antoine Muret, he pioneered one of the characteristic arts of modern academic life: changing places. Playing the Lutheran at Jena, the Calvinist fellow-traveller in Leiden and the ultra-orthodox Catholic in Louvain, he actually belonged to a heretical sect, the Family of Love, the members of which claimed to stand outside all established religions. Despite this liability – which could easily have been the death of a less adept academic politician – he won and held a dominant place in the European academic élite. For he developed a pedagogical programme even more adaptable than Ramus', and one even better suited to the needs of late sixteenth-century Europe.

Where Ramus had stressed the arts of reason and discourse, Lipsius stressed those of government and war. Developing Muret's pregnant hints, he argued that the ruling classes of his time needed an education that would equip them to cope with societies on the verge of dissolution – with an age, in short, in which mad tyrants and militant revolutionaries had replaced the virtuous kings and councillors dreamed of by Erasmus and More. The

---

[113] K. Meerhoff, *Rhétorique et poétique au XVIᵉ siècle en France: Du Bellay, Ramus et les autres* (Leiden, 1986).

[114] R.R. Bolgar, *The Classical Heritage and its Beneficiaries from the Carolingian Age to the End of the Renaissance* (Cambridge, 1954), 356-62; A. Schindling, *Humanistische Hochschule und freie Reichsstadt* (Wiesbaden, 1977); F.J. Stopp, *The Emblems of the Altdorf Academy* (London, 1973). For the wider background see also M. Fumaroli, *L'âge de l'éloquence* (Geneva, 1980) and W. Kühlmann, *Gelehrtenrepublik und Fürstenstaat* (Tübingen, 1982).

necessary skills were easy enough to isolate and describe: the self-control to endure religious war without despairing, the art of maintaining one's influence over subordinates and technical mastery of the most vital craft of all, the soldier's. Trained in these essential skills, the young aristocrat would be able to impose discipline on himself and his followers, serve his ruler efficiently and deal effectively with society's most pressing problem, the openly subversive, violent heretic. Order, so imposed, however tyrannical, was far preferable to disorder, of which Lipsius was openly fearful.[115]

Lipsius clearly held a Machiavellian concept of the true prince and aristocrat, but he did not tell his students to study Machiavelli. Instead he concentrated on classical authors who had inhabited and described a world like his own – above all Seneca and Tacitus, those pitilessly critical witnesses of the regimes of the mad emperors of the first century AD. But he was far too perceptive a scholar to believe that the classical texts were an adequate guide to *realpolitik* by themselves. He knew that ancient armies had had better discipline than modern ones – he advised the States General of Holland to make their soldiers dig their own ditches as the Romans had – but he also knew that modern military technology had made many ancient methods obsolete, and that ancient and modern authorities on war and government had often ignored the dictates of necessity in order to avoid infringing on traditional morality. Accordingly he provided his pupils with systematic manuals of the new amoral politics – manuals which drew profusely, but in a deliberately exploitative way, on ancient texts. His *Politica*, for example, presented itself as a *florilegium* of classical axioms on every question the young *politicus* would need answered. But Lipsius made no pretence that this classicizing work was faithful to its classical sources. Instead he described the work as a *cento*, in which the ancient *sententiae* had been deliberately taken out of context and given an up-to-date sense (just as the ancient poet Ausonius had twisted innocent lines from Virgil into an obscene *epithalamium*). This approach allowed him to offer out of Cicero a prescription for the proper way to deal with heretics: *ure et seca* (burn and cut), while insisting that he meant only that the problem required extreme measures.[116]

Lipsius' teaching attracted hundreds of students to Leiden, which became the largest and most advanced university in Europe even though it had been founded only in 1575. His book went through more than fifty editions in Latin and reached thousands of readers across Europe. The hard-bitten Spanish cavalryman Bernardino de Mendoza took time off between attempts to poison Queen Elizabeth in order to translate the *Politica* into Spanish; English courtiers and would-be courtiers like Harvey were as fascinated as their enemy by this supremely useful book; and both Protestant and Catholic

---

[115] M.W. Croll, *Style, Rhetoric and Rhythm* (Princeton, 1966); G. Oestreich, *Neostoicism and the Early Modern State* (Cambridge, 1982).

[116] See A. Grafton, 'A portrait of Justus Lipsius', *American Scholar* (in press).

teachers across Europe added a bit of Lipsius and Tacitus to their curricula –
not to mention a bit of drill and gunnery (at which the Jesuits excelled).[117]

This case is representative of both the achievements and the dilemmas of
late humanism. By the later sixteenth century humanist method could
achieve many striking results. It could provide novel, value-free forms of
knowledge and emotional distraction for great scholars like Joseph
Scaliger.[118] It could enhance man's power over the social world, as Lipsius
taught so effectively. It could enhance man's power over the physical world as
well, as John Caius and others showed when they applied the most up-to-date
methods of classical philology to clarifying and explicating the remains of the
ancient medical writers.[119] Philology was a powerful form of knowledge.
Humanist pedagogy, by contrast, could arm the young with exactly the
means they needed to arrive at positions of power in this world (if not the
next). But the once-tight bond that had held philology and pedagogy together
had been severed.[120] A Lipsius, who needed to make the ancient world look
useful, had to adapt and modernize its image. But a Scaliger, who insisted
that scholars should not teach practical politics, had to confine himself to
staggeringly complex technical problems which offered personal satisfaction
but no obvious practical rewards.

As philology became value-free and pedagogy became pragmatic, the larger
value of both enterprises was called into question. Why study the ancient
world if not to become more virtuous? But a training in virtue now seemed to
be one quality that neither scholars nor teachers could offer. Since
Montaigne – one of the first to offer these criticisms in a cogent form – the
claim that the liberal arts would produce 'new men', men of an enhanced
virtuous disposition, has often been repeated; and new generations of
believers in the ideals of early humanism have tried to show that some new
form of literary education could achieve this goal. For all their brilliance, and
for all their formative influence upon practitioners of the liberal arts, neither
Wilhelm von Humboldt nor Lionel Trilling, neither F.R. Leavis nor G.
Gentile has had an impact on anything but a small segment of élite education
in the West, or satisfied more than a handful of critics with the intellectual
centrality of their enterprise. Like them, we watch as our most gifted students
master the techniques and methods of textual analysis, the command of
ancient and modern languages (which they can transpose effectively to new
and developing disciplines), but in the main discard that over-arching

---

[117] See in general H. Wansink, *De politieke wetenschappen aan de Leidze universiteit 1575-±1650*
(Utrecht, 1980), with bibliography.

[118] See in general A. Grafton, *Joseph Scaliger*, i (Oxford, 1983).

[119] See the fine case study by V. Nutton, 'John Caius and the Eton Galen: medical philology
in the Renaissance', *Medizin historisches Journal* 20 (1985), 227-52.

[120] A more extended discussion of these issues appears in A. Grafton, 'Renaissance readers
and ancient texts: comments on some commentaries', *Renaissance Quarterly* 38 (1985).

framework of 'civilised values' by which teachers of the humanities continue to set such store. Whether we like it or not, we still live with the dilemma of late humanism: we too can only live in hope, and practise the humanities.

The books in Mayres's collection

1. M.T. Ciceronis Liber de optimo genere oratorum, cui accesserunt annotationes doctissimae, quae illum, alioquin multis in locis obscurum, clarum et fere omnino perspicuum reddunt. Parisiis, Ex Typographia Dionysii a Prato, 1570.
2. M.T. Ciceronis ad Trebatium iurisconsultum Topica. Cum enarrationibus Bartholomaei Latomi et Phil. Melanchthonis, ac Christophori Hegendorph. scholiis. Parisiis, Apud Michaelem Vascosanum, 1554. Cf. Paris, Bibliothèque Nationale, X.3122 (hereafter 'B.N.').
3. M.T. Ciceronis De finibus bonorum et malorum liber primus. Quibus in singulos accesserunt nunc primum argumenta, simul cum aliquot annotationibus, ad eos locos illustrandos qui obscuriores videbantur. Parisiis, Ex Typographia Dionysii a Prato, 1568.
4. M.T. Ciceronis Academicarum quaestionum liber primus. Illustratus scholiis Iacobi Camilli. Parisiis, Ex Typographia Dionysii a Prato, 1570.
5. M.T. Ciceronis Somnium Scipionis ex sexto libro de Republica, cum annotationibus Eras. Roterod., Petri Olivarii, Petri Rami, et doctissimi cuiusdam viri, margini adiunctis, ac suis numeris designatis. Parisiis, Ex officina Gabrielis Buonii, 1565. Ong. *Ramus and Talon Inventory*, 52 (first ed. 1556).
6. M.T. Ciceronis in M. Antonium Philippica I. Parisiis, Apud Andream Wechelum, 1572.
7. M. Tul. Ciceronis in M. Antonium Philippica II. Parisiis, Apud Andream Wechelum, 1559.
8. M.T. Ciceronis in L. Catilinam Invectiva oratio prima. Cum annotationibus Sylvii, Curionis, Rami, incertique cuiusdam authoris, margini adscriptis, ac suis numeris designatis. Parisiis, Ex officina Thomae Brumennii, 1571. Cf. Ong, *Ramus and Talon Inventory*, 208-9.
9. [M.T. Ciceronis in L. Catilinam, ad Quirites, Oratio invectiva secunda. No title page.]
10. C. Plinii Secundi Naturalis historiae liber septimus. In quo de homine agitur. Parisiis, Ex officina viduae Mauricii a Porta, 1551.
11. Iustini historici in Trogi Pompeii Historias liber primus. Veteris exemplaris beneficio repurgatus. Parisiis, Apud Gabrielem Buon, 1572.

12. Pomponii Laeti De Romanis magistratibus, sacerdotiis, iurisperitis, et legibus, ad M. Pantagathum libellus, cum annotationibus Richardi Gorraei Parisiensis. Parisiis, Apud Ioannem de Roigny, 1552. Adams P 1841.

13. [Q. Horatii Flacci Carminum liber II. No title page. This and items 14 and 15 were originally part – or meant to be part – of a complete edition of the *Odes.*]

14. [Q. Horatii Flacci Carminum liber III. No title page.]

15. [Q. Horatii Flacci Carminum liber IIII. No title page.]

16. Q. Horatii Flacci De arte poetica liber, ad Pisones. Cum scholiis brevibus, sed eruditis. Parisiis, Ex officina Thomae Brumennii, 1570. A reprint of B.N. Rés.p.Yc.1407 (also an interleaved and annotated copy); Paris: Buon, 1569.

17. Q. Horatii Flacci Epistolarum libri duo. Brevia, sed erudita, in eosdem scholia. Parisiis, Ex officina Thomae Brumennii, 1571.

18. Decii Magni Ausonii Burdegalensis Gryphus, sive ternarii numeri. Parisiis, Ex typographia Dionysii a Prato, 1569.

19. [*Loukianou peri tou mê radiôs pisteuein diabolêi*. Luciani de non temere credendo calumniae. Philippo Melanchthone interprete. Greek and Latin texts; no title page.]

20. [*Poteron ta tês psuchês ê ta tou sômatos pathê cheirona*. Plutarchi, utrum graviores sint animi morbi, quam corporis, Erasmo Roterodamo interprete. [Greek text and Erasmus's Latin; no title page.]

21. [*Libaniou hupothesis tou peri eirênês logou*. Libanii argumentum in orationem Demosthenis de pace. Greek text of both *argumentum* and oration; anonymous Latin version of the former. H. Wolf's of the latter; no title page.]

22. *Isokratous kata tôn sophistôn logos*. Isocratis Oratio contra sophistas. Parisiis, Apud Ioannem Bene-Natum, 1570. Greek only.

23. Isocratis Oratio contra sophistas, Hieronymo Vuolfio interprete. Colophon: Excudebat Guil. Morelius in Graecis Typographus Regius. M.D.LIX. B.N. Rés.X.1021 (8).

24. *Ploutarchou tou Chairôneôs hoti didakton hê aretê*. Plutarchi Chaeronensis, Virtutem doceri posse, libellus. Colophon: Parisiis, Excudebat Andreas Wechelus, 1569. Greek only.

25. [*Ploutarchou sunopsis tou paradoxotera hoi Stôicoi tôn poiêtôn legousin*. Quod magis inopinata magisque mirabilia a Stoicis quam Poetis adserantur, Plutarchi *sunopsis*, hoc est, brevis et compendiaria contemplatio, G. Longolio interprete. No title page.]

26. Compendium in universam dialecticam, ex Rivio aliisque recentioribus collectum. Parisiis, Ex typographia Matthaei Davidis, 1550. An earlier ed. of B.N. Rés.p.R.293 (Paris: Richard, 1558).

27. Naenia sive Prosopopoeia Scholae Rhemensis in obitum viri clarissimi D. Francisci A-Porta, in supremo Parisiorum Senatu causidici eloquentiss. et patroni celeberrimi. Parisiis, Ex typographia Dionysii a Prato, 1572.

The subscriptions in Mayres's books

The texts follow of the subscriptions so far found in the Princeton *Sammelband*; no doubt there are others to be turned up, as several of the volumes have not yet been gone through systematically. Suspensions and cropped letters have been silently filled in.

Cicero, *De optimo genere oratorum*
    ad init.: Annotationes in libellum Cic. de optimo genere oratorum dictatae a domino Claudio [?] Minoe in primo rhemensium ordine 19 cal. Febru: 1572.

Cicero, *Topica*
    ad init.: Annotationes in Ciceronis Topica datae a doctissimo viro domino Minoe in primo rhem. ordine Men. Martis 1572.
    ad fin.: 13° Cal. Maii 1572. Geraldus de Mayres.

Cicero, *De finibus* I.
    ad init.: Annotationes in primum Ciceronis librum de finibus bonorum et malorum datae a domino Minoe in primo rhem. ordine 4° Cal. Maii 1572.

Cicero, *Academica* I.
    ad init.: Consilium huius Academicae disputationis 1572.
    ad fin.: Hic pedem fixit Claud.

Cicero, *Somnium Scipionis*
    ad init.: Annotationes in Somnium Scipionis datae a domino Claudio Minoe 15° Cal. Iulii 1572, in primo rhemensium ordine.

Cicero, *Philippica* 2.
    ad init.: Haec oratio omnium praestantissima exposita fuit a Domino Minoe in primo ordine Rhem. 3. Cal. mart. 1572.

Cicero, *In Catilinam* I.
    ad fin.: Finis pridie Cal. decembris.

Pliny, *Naturalis historia* 7.
    ad init.: Annotationes in 7um Plinii librum de nat. historia datae a domino Minoe in primo rhem. 15° Cal. Iulii 1572.

Horace, *Carmina* 2.
    ad init.: 6° Cal. Martii 1572.

Horace, *Carmina* 3.

ad init.: Annotationes in tertium Horatii librum datae a domino Minoe in [MS: in in] Primo rhemens. ordine 4° Cal. Maii 1572.

Horace, *Ars Poetica.*

ad fin.: 6 Cal. Mart: 1572.

Horace, *Epistolae.*

ad 1. 4: 12 novemb.

ad fin.: xxvii Martii 1573.

Ausonius, *Griphus.*

ad init.: Annotationes in Ausonium magnum datae a Domino Minoe 18 Cal. Maii 1572 in primo ordine.

ad fin.: 6 Cal. Maii 1572.

Compendium in universam dialecticam.

ad init.: Explicatum fuit a doctissimo viro Cla: Minoe Idibus Augusti in primo rhemensium 1572.

ad fin.: xxii Septembris 1572. in collegio rhemensi.

Mignault's lecture on *Odes* 3.1

What follows is the text, reproduced with very slight changes in capitalization and punctuation, of Mignault's entire discussion of 3.1, from the blank leaf preceding the first page of Mayres's copy of *Odes* 3, recto and verso, and from the first leaf of the text proper (numbered 31), recto and verso. To make comparisons easier, we have inserted several notes from Mignault's principal source, Lambin's commentary on Horace, in square brackets at the appropriate places. These are taken from the second edition of Lambin's work, *Q. Horatius Flaccus* (Paris, 1567), 1, 141-3.

Annotationes in tertium Horatii librum datae a domino Minoe in primo Rhemensium ordine 4° cal. Maii 1572.

'Odi prophanum vulgus'

Dicturus aliquid de vita beata quam ut assequantur omnes optant sed ad eam accommodatum iter negligunt, primum quidem impuros homines et oppinionibus depravatos ab hac doctrina tanquam profanos a sacris quibusdam mysteriis arcet. Deinde sub dei unius arbitrio et nutu varias esse hominum conditiones et status sed aequam omnibus mortem propositam arguit. Quae una cogitatio motus omnes in animo tumultuantes et insanas [MS: insanes] cupiditates cohibere debet. Postremo dissimilium collatione per inductionem elegantissimam ostendit neque divitiis aut honoribus neque possessionibus aut rebus aliis fortuitis sed una animi tranquillitate vitam beatam parari.

'Vulgus et arceo'

Cum nimirum sit bellua multorum capitum [Horace, *Epist.* 1. 1.76] omne rectum iudicium corrumpit quod externis duntaxat capiatur ideoque a misteriis hisce philosophicis subducitur.

[Lambin ad 3.1.1:

Odi profanum vulgus] arcebantur non initiati, et profani a sacris quos Graeci *bebêlous kai amuêtous* appellant. Plato *Theaitêtôi: athrei dê periskopôn mêtis tôn amuêtôn epakouêi* id est, contemplare igitur circumspiciens nequis profanorum, et non initiatorum exaudiat (155 e). Theocr. in Amarillide. *zalô de, phila gunai, Iasiôna, hos tossôn ekurêsen, hos' ou peuseisthe bebaloi* id est, fortunatum Iasionem existimo, qui ea consecutus est, quae non audietis vos profani (3.50-51).]

1.2 'Favete linguis carmina'

Festus Pompeius scribit faventia bonam ominationem significare. Praecones enim clamantes populum sacrificiis favere iubebant. Favere enim est bona fari [Paulus-Festus 78. 14-16 L.] Sic Ovid. primo Fastorum: Prospera lux oritur linguisque animisque favete [71]. Sed et Metamorphoseon decimoquinto ubi verba facit de Aesculapio Romam advecto – En deus est deus est linguis animisque favete [677]. Imperabatur enim a sacerdote silentium ut sacrum rite peragi posset.

[Lambin ad loc:

Favete linguis *euphêmeite* ... Faventia (inquit Festus) bonam ominationem significant. Nam praecones clamantes populum sacrificiis favere iubebant. favere enim est bona fari.]

1.4 'Virginibus puerisque canto'

Nihil flexibilius aut tractabilius aetate tenera quae quocunque ducas facile sequi potest. Adeo a teneris assuescere multum est [Vg. *Georg.* 2.272, also quoted by Quint. *Inst. or.* 1.3.13]. Magni enim refert ut pueri optimis moribus et disciplinis primum informentur qui tenaciores esse solent eorum quae rudibus annis perceperunt.

1.5 'Regum timendorum in'

Instituit gradationem per obscuram prolepsim cuius ita facilis erit solutio. Aliquis dicet reges et principes aliis inferioribus beatiores esse, quibus nimirum imperent seque formidandos praestent. Immo vero inquit Horat: reges et tyranni quanquam crudelissimi domantur a supremo deo neque sese ab eius imperio vindicare possunt. Hoc autem probat inductione unius exempli nimirum Gigantum. Huc refert illud Ovidianum: Nihil ita sublime est supraque periculam tendit/Non scit ut inferius suppositumque deo [*Tris.* 4.8.47-8].

l.9 'Est ut viro vir latius'

Reprehendit insatiabilem et plane caecam hominum cupiditatem qui rebus fortuitis ita inhaerent ut quanquam omnes sciant aequam moriendi conditionem omnibus incumbere non desistant tamen relicta animi tranquillitate alios si possint pervertere in ambiendis honoribus et fortunis consequendis quae tamen omnia incerta sunt et brevi peritura. Hoc autem declaratur inductione quatuor personarum ex adiunctis eorum qui sese iis rebus excutiant.

[Lambin ad 3.1.8,9:

Cvncta svperc. mov.] Hom. *Il.* 1: *ê, kai kuaneêisin ep' ophrusi neuse Kroniôn.* id est, dixit, et nigris superciliis annuit Iupiter (1. 528). sequitur paullo post, *megan d'elelixen Olumpon*, id est, magnum autem commovit Olympum (1. 530). Et Virg. 9. totum nutu tremefecit Olympum (106).

Est vt viro vir] Sic loquuntur Graeci, *estin hôs*, vel *estin hopôs*.

l.11 'Descendat in Campum'

Intelligit campum Martium in quo comitia et cetus ad magistratus creandos Romani habere consueverant. Tanta autem fuit ambientium hominum cupiditas ut candidati vel prece vel pretio populum corrumperent vel sese quibusdam seditiosis adiungerent et sicariis vel uterentur quorundam potentia quo magistratum quem ambiebant, extorquerent.

[Lambin ad loc:

In Campvm] Martium, in quo comitia habebantur ...]

l.15 'Sortitur insigneis et'

Hoc ductum est a consuetudine veterum comitiorum in quibus centuriae vel tribus per sortes suffragia ferebant aut a iudiciorum calculis qui ab urna extrahebantur.

l.17 'Districtus ensis qui super'

Inductio est alius exempli per comparationem dissimilium ex adiuncto perpetuo metu qui tyrannos comitari solet. Dum enim maleficiorum conscientia iis terreatur qui perpetuo timet foelix esse non potest tametsi epulis opiparis et cantibus aliisque deliciis utatur quandoquidem vera foelicitas ab animo quieto et metu omnique perturbatione vacuo proficiscatur. At ea animi quiete non fere vacant qui mediocri et alioqui humili sorte contenti vivunt. Manifeste autem alludit ad Damoclis assentatoris historiam quam retulit uberrime Cicero 5. Tusculana [5.21.61-2, quoted in extenso by Lambin].

1.27 'Nec saevus Arcturi'

Arcturus sive Arctofilax stella post caudam Vrsae maioris cuius ortus et occasus gravissimas tempestates inducit. Hedi vero sydera sunt procellas et grandines inducentia ut notat Plinius [*Nat. Hist.* 18.278]. Sic autem Virgilius: Praeterea tam sunt Arcturi sydera nobis/Hedorumque dies servandi – [*Georg.* 1.204-5, also quoted by Lambin].

1.33 'Contracta'

Pergit insectari hominum inconstantiam quod superbis et insolentibus aedificiis frustra suas cupiditates sedare conentur.

1.35 'Caementa'

Tria sunt genera lapidum ex quibus aedificia conficiuntur. Nonnulli enim sunt quadrati et ad certam quandam normam incisi. Alii sunt impoliti et nulla arte constantes in ipsis aedificiis, cuiusmodi sunt caementa quibus operarii utuntur in infarcturis. Alii sunt quidem impoliti sed ordine quodam dispositi. Vide Budaeum in Pandectas. [G. Budé, *Opera* (Basle; repr. Farnborough, Hants, 1966), 3, 162: Structurae enim genera tria sunt: Quidam enim lapides quadrati vocantur, id est orthogoni, et ad normam respondentes, quos vulgo caesos vocamus. Sunt alterius generis lapides rudes et informes, quae caementa vocantur, quibus ad farcturas operum utuntur inter pilares vel quadratas eductiones, quas artifices gambas appellant. Vtuntur et his lapidibus ad parietes villaticos extruendos. Hoc genus structurae incertum est, et sine venustate, quasi lapide temere invento constructum. Est et tertium genus inter hoc et illud medium, ex lapide ordinario, nec temere congestum, nec ad perpendiculum respondens, sed tamen ordine coagmentatum.]

1.39 'Arata triremi'

Verisimile est aeratam triremem dici quae esset ornata aere vel auro quod veteres soliti essent ornare suas naves picturis ut intelligere licet ex decima quarta oda lib. primi ubi ait nisi pictis timidus navita pipibus fidit [1. 14.14-5].

1.41 'Quod si'

Traducto sermone ad thesim ad ipotesim suae personae concludit eum non esse beatum qui rebus praetiosis fruitur sed qui contentus est eo quod habet.

Conclusion: The Perfect Orator

To us belong – assuming that we are really orators, that is, persons competent to be retained as leaders and principals in civil actions and criminal trials and public debates – to us, I say, belong the broad estates of wisdom and of learning, which having been allowed to lapse and become derelict during our absorption in affairs, have been invaded by persons too generously supplied with leisure, persons who actually either banter and ridicule the orator after the manner of Socrates in Plato's *Gorgias*, or else write a few little manuals of instruction in the art of oratory and label them with the title of *Rhetoric* – just as if the province of the rhetoricians did not include their pronouncement on the subjects of justice and duty and the constitution and government of states, in short the entire field of practical philosophy.[1]

Throughout his oratorical and philosophical works Cicero insists on the self-evident identity of perfect oratorical competence and the ability to act wisely and with integrity – the identity of oratory and philosophy. Such is his commitment to the view that 'the man who sought perfection in oratory would take all knowledge, all *sapientia*, for his domain',[2] that there is hardly a point in his consideration of eloquence when he does not remind his audience of the congruence between his treatment of oratory and his treatment of philosophy. Yet that very insistence must in the end make us feel that the matter is not by any means as straightforward as the representation of *in utramque partem* debate as the backbone both of oratory and of philosophy tries to maintain. Or rather, the nature of the orator's *training* – the programme of arts education he is meticulously portrayed as following – cannot in the end manage to effect the elevation of the *ars disserendi* above the realms of rhetoric, and the virtuoso performance.

Cicero's early schooling was in Greek. He grew up with the belief that Greek teachers were more sophisticated and more able than their Roman counterparts, and that Greek education was the most carefully and

---

[1] Cicero, *De Oratore* 3.31.122. Cit. J.E. Seigel, *Rhetoric and Philosophy in Renaissance Humanism: The Union of Eloquence and Wisdom, Petrarch to Valla* (Princeton, New Jersey, 1968). For a general treatment which complements our own exploration of the long shadow thrown by the 'perfect orator' across Renaissance humanism and its educational aspirations see Seigel, *Rhetoric and Philosophy in Renaissance Humanism*, ch. 1 ('Rhetoric and philosophy: the Ciceronian model'). See also J.E. Seigel, ' "Civic humanism" or Ciceronian rhetoric?' *Past and Present* 34 (1966), 3-48; which is richly suggestive in directions which we hope perhaps we have managed to explore in detail in this book.

[2] Cit. Seigel, *Rhetoric and Philosophy in Renaissance Humanism*, 13.

systematically designed initiation into the culture of the civilised world currently available.[3] At the same time, Rome, by the first century BC, was culturally quite unlike the fifth-century Athens in which that education was rooted; and of this Cicero in his maturity was equally well aware. It is on account of this that Cicero shows himself so crucially preoccupied in his educational writings with the fundamental problem with which this study has been concerned – the problem of the inevitable discrepancy between an educational goal and the curriculum designed to achieve it.

When fifteenth-century humanists embarked on their reform of the liberal arts curriculum, what they envisaged as the 'rebirth' their Renaissance was to effect was a reborn Cicero. The ideal Cicero, the man of preeminent stature, was to be the model product of another bilingual educational system, this time imparted in Latin to those whose native language was (in the first instance) the Italian vernacular. And just as in Cicero's Rome, the distance between the foreignness of the erudite language and the nativeness of the culture whose institutions it was to mould and serve, makes itself felt in the uneasy and unspecific promises that mastery of the language is the same as becoming a model member of the community: eloquence is virtue (in the society's terms). So it is appropriate to conclude our exploration of that attempt at total reform of the arts education on which 'cultivation' in Renaissance Europe was to be based with a consideration of Cicero's own elegant examination (in dialogue form) of the relation between 'education' and 'civilisation', between the perfect orator and the good man, in the *De Oratore*.[4]

The goal Roman education set for itself was to produce cultured and articulate individuals who were prepared for active service in civic life. This meant that students were to be provided with a broad general training, coupled with intensive training in those skills appropriate for forensic debating purposes, or for legal pleading. It is with this goal in mind that Cicero takes as the ideal product of the well-conceived programme of education the *perfect orator*. The perfect orator is the man who can be relied upon to defend with integrity any cause, to justify any rightful course of action, draw on an almost limitless fund of detailed knowledge to support any just position. He is thus the pivot of the state; the man who can always be called upon when decisions have to be made, and above all when those decisions have to be communicated to the public at large.[5]

The *De Oratore* presents us at the outset with two such men, or rather two

---

[3] See E. Rawson, *Cicero: A Portrait* (London, 1975).

[4] There is confirmation of the fact that we are here on the right track, in our investigation of how the Renaissance thought about arts education, in the fact that Gabriel Harvey comments extensively on the *De Oratore* and its implications for the idea of the Perfect Orator in his marginal annotations, particularly in his copies of Quintilian, and of Cicero's rhetorical works.

[5] On the relation between eloquence and statesmanship in Cicero's writings in general see A. Michel, *Les Rapports de la Rhétorique et de la Philosophie dans l'Oeuvre de Cicéron* (Paris, 1960).

orators idealised to approximate to such perfection. Crassus and Antonius were both renowned orators of the generation before Cicero's. Cicero introduces them to his readers in full knowledge that their reputation for effective (yet individually distinctive) oratory, political and legal acumen, discretion, uprightness of character and general intelligence is still a lively one. And in his fictional debate (in which he himself is not a participant, as if to emphasise the ideal past in which Crassus and Antonius conduct their discourse) he faces them and his readers with the question: How do we create a programme of education to produce such individuals? How are perfect orators manufactured as the State requires them?

On the one hand we have a set of qualities: fluency, erudition, political and legal expertise, discretion, integrity, nobility of spirit, humility coupled with assurance. On the other we have a request on the part of the minor participants in the dialogue for an educational blueprint: a timetable of lessons and a course of study. The *De Oratore* explores the possibilities for matching, or even beginning to match, the one with the other.

In the first century BC in Rome there was a well-established traditional curriculum in the liberal arts. It derived self-consciously from the curriculum of the Greek schools (as we touched on in Chapter One), and it was taught by Greek émigrés. The programme covered the three central linguistic disciplines of grammar, rhetoric and dialectic, and the subsidiary disciplines music and mathematics (the latter comprising arithmetic, geometry and astronomy). These 'seven liberal arts' were regarded as essential preparation for all higher learning, and for all proficiency in any intellectual context whatsoever. Although the choice of emphasis within the programme varied, the seven liberal arts formed the basis of the general arts training during the entire period from the fifth century BC in Athens down to the fourth century AD.[6]

Grammar, rhetoric and dialectic are all studies concerned with the structure and use of language. And as such they can only be taught in conjunction with texts: with a body of material upon which their provisional rules can be tested, and from which further rules and procedures can be drawn. They cannot be taught as a system of rules alone, in particular because their acquisition is intended to prepare the student to write his own speeches, to compose his own prose works and poems, and to plead politically and in the law courts. Once the schoolboy Cicero had reached proficiency in the erudite language, Greek (acquired painlessly by the well-born from Greek nurses and slaves), he began his study of the major texts of Greek literature under a *grammaticus*.

The *grammaticus* (for whom we shall retain the Roman name) taught more than just grammar. He taught the *explication de texte*, the painstaking analysis of a major text by means of four techniques: *lectio, emendatio, enarratio, judicium*.

---

[6] See H-I. Marrou, *Saint Augustin et la fin de la culture antique* (4th edn., Paris, 1958), ch. 3, 'Les sept arts libéraux'.

The portion of the text – from Homer or Hesiod, Sophocles or Euripides – was first read aloud, which required the student to insert word divisions and punctuation in an undivided and unpunctuated text. It also required him to make decisions about delivery, resolving ambiguities of sense, deciding on breaks and transitions in argument. He also learned the passage by heart, to exercise his memory, test his powers of declamation and, in the process, provide himself with a future store of preprocessed literary material for his own compositions.

After *lectio* came discussions of authenticity, possible corrections of the passage, qualities and faults of diction and usage. This *emendatio* taught critical skills, and allowed the teacher to point out acceptable deviant usages (sanctified by their appearance in the works of the great Greek authors), and the margins within which a student could alter a text for sense and coherence. *Enarratio* extended this critical activity to the word-by-word and line-by-line commentary on the text, and the study culminated in *judicium*, the reaching of a decision on the aesthetic and literary value of the text under scrutiny.

The *enarratio* provided the grammaticus with the greatest scope for instructing his students in the whole range of observations which together were to provide them with 'facility' in the linguistic studies. He drew their attention to the rules which provided the groundplan for the work, the grammatical rules observed in the phrasing of individual sentences, the choice of words and their declension or conjugation. He further pointed out to them material drawn from specialist disciplines which the author had turned to literary advantage in his text, and drew out the moral and the argument. And he isolated and named the forms of argument and the types of ornament employed by the author, and assessed their effectiveness.

It is clear from this brief sketch (and by now the procedure is intriguingly familiar to us) that the grammaticus was responsible for awakening his students' awareness to the structure beneath the skin of the great works of the Greek heritage, at the same time as he conducted them through the canon of that literature. He introduced them to an entire culture – a foreign culture to which they were to gain privileged access – and via that culture he introduced them to the systematic skills of criticism and composition. Just as the infant Cicero had learned to read and write in a language which was not his mother tongue, so the adolescent Cicero learned to attach to each type of rhetorical ornament a Greek name, and to identify each device on the basis of Greek examples (our own surviving terminology – metaphor, metonymy, syllepsis, anaphora and so on – testifies to the strength and endurance of that early Greek hold on the subject). And when he came to *exercitatio*, his own student imitation of the classical techniques of composition, he did so once again in Greek.

It was at this point in his education, now steeped in Greek literature, and adept at identifying and imitating the literary techniques of Greek poets and dramatists, that the Roman student passed into the hands of the *rhetor*. And this is the point at which, in the *De Oratore*, Cicero's spokesmen in the dialogue take up the question of the education of the perfect orator.

The task of the rhetor was to teach the student eloquence. 'It was from the *rhetor* that the cultivated man received his essential formation; the *grammaticus* merely laid the foundations, prepared the materials; only the *rhetor* could complete the cultural edifice; it was on the strength of his teaching that a man could become what every man desired above all to be: an orator, *vir eloquentissimus*: the rhetor reduced the information gleaned by the student in the course of his analyses of specific texts to the format of the rule-book, explained its strategies, demonstrated and tested its applications.' It was from the rhetor that the student learned how each of the isolated rules of grammar, rhetoric and dialectic which he had identified in Homer or in Aristophanes fell into places within the systematic treatment of those studies. *Simile* (say) was no longer just one among many rhetorical tropes, identified and listed on the strength of examples carefully isolated during close reading of Homer. Now the student learned the general definition of the trope – a comparison with explanatory or amplifying force, signalled by the word 'like' –, its place in the classification of tropes, how the tropes differ from schemes, how embellishment in rhetoric relates to invention, disposition, memory and delivery. And instead of composing his own *exercitationes* by cunningly cobbling together passages learnt by heart from the texts he had read (with a few cautious transpositions and substitutions appropriate to his own theme), the student now learned how to structure each of the parts of an oration (introduction, statement of the case, narration, confirmation, refutation, summing up, conclusion), and how to construct valid argumentation (syllogism, induction, enthymeme and example), so that he was free to compose effectively and convincingly using his own original material.

It is at this point that the problems implicit in a liberal arts programme grounded in the heritage of a foreign language become explicit. For the model of an alien culture is just that: an ideal, an archetype. Its felt power is its suggestive aesthetic/moral content, its ability to inspire what is felt to be a more mundane culture by its shining example. But if this is the case, where is that 'original material' to come from, which the orator is to deploy astutely as the occasion demands, to win a legal case, to convince the State of the need to declare war on a neighbouring territory, or to defend or attack an intellectual thesis? What the student has so far is a solid grounding in Greek literature (including some Greek history and philosophy if his grammaticus has done his job well), and a sound grasp of the rules of grammar, rhetoric and dialectic, systematically organised and committed to memory. He has

---

[7] Marrou, *Augustin*, 47.

now to embark on the pragmatic business of tackling questions of the type orators must regularly deal with, from the resources of his own culture, his own experience.

In practice, the rhetor set his students questions of such a contrived and academic kind that he could cope with them by combining his rules and his reading with a restricted body of general knowledge drawn from the specialist disciplines. The student began with *progymnasmata* – preparatory exercises carefully graded so as gradually to increase the student's proficiency. He started with the simple exercise of retelling a classical myth, and graduated via narration of an incident from Homer, defence or opposition of a commonplace theme, praise of a classical hero, to dramatic monologue (once again drawing the theme from classic Greek epic or drama), and to the treatment of a case in law (once again we have seen that the *progymnasmata* were adopted by Renaissance humanists as part of an equivalent graded programme in creative writing).[8] He then graduated to 'imaginary' exercises, that is, exercises which do not depend for their material on the students' classical reading, but here the themes were carefully related to what the student had already learned: if he had to deliver an epideictic oration (a speech of praise), it would be set as a speech praising (say) a woman who had remained constant during the absence of her husband, despite failing hopes that he would return alive, and attractive alternatives, or threats, so that the student could use Penelope as his model. If (at the most difficult end of his *progymnasmata*) he was required to argue a case in law, it would be a case of the utmost contrivance, taxing his ingenuity rather than his technical grasp on the law and legal practice: the law of a city demands that a foreigner who mounts the ramparts is punished by death; during a war a foreigner saved the day from the ramparts; when peace has returned he is prosecuted; defend the man.[9]

According to Antonius and Crassus, in the *De Oratore*, there are only two possible ways of making the transition from this stage in one's education to the status of 'perfect orator' or 'ideal man of state'. One must either be extraordinarily widely read, or extraordinarily experienced.[10] Both orators are extremely reluctant (as the other participants in the debate repeatedly point out) to admit that *any* programme of study can shortcut or substitute for the slow process of gradually laying down knowledge in a wide range of areas

---

[8] E. Jullien, *Les professeurs de littérature dans l'ancienne Rome et leur enseignement depuis l'origine jusqu'à la mort d'Auguste* (Paris, 1885), summarises the *progymnasmata*, 293-331. For a valuable treatment of the whole question of the relationship between *progymnasmata* and an education in eloquence (including creative writing) see M. Roberts, *Biblical Epic and Rhetorical Paraphrase in Late Antiquity* (Liverpool, 1985). Unfortunately this came to our attention too late to incorporate its findings in our treatment of *progymnasmata* in Chapter Six.

[9] See the discussion of *controversiae* in Chapter One. See also D.A. Russell, *Greek Declamation* (Cambridge, 1983).

[10] *De Oratore* 1.

and disciplines on the basis of personal experience in an active public life. Yet the purpose of the *De Oratore* dialogue (the occasion for its taking place) is to press them individually to make a public statement on the kind of education aspiring orators should acquire; the kind of education a state which aims at producing a well-trained body of public servants ought to provide. The debate, then, is premised on the belief that education can only in a limited way fashion future orators; the question is, where should educational effort be concentrated. No education will mould an ideally cultured individual, but it can nurture growth and development in more or less profitable ways.

Now, once it is conceded that education is under no circumstances a blueprint for the *vir eloquentissimus* or *eruditissimus*, there are two separate strategies which may be adopted by an educator which will embark the would-be orator (the man aspiring to cultivation) in the right sort of direction. You may, like Antonius, favour a course of study which excerpts from the vast body of material the self-made 'man of experience' has read and assimilated a representative (manageably small) sample. This approach assumes that you give the student a taste for the various contributing fields of knowledge, and encourage him to continue to extend his grasp on the crucial works and areas of expertise beyond the training period. On the other hand you may, like Crassus, prefer a programme which drills the student unremittingly in the basic and systematic techniques for processing and assimilating any transmitted knowledge whatsoever. In this case your higher education will intensify the technical training in rhetoric, logic and mathematics, which provides regular procedures for taking *any* subject, breaking it down into its more and less important elements, committing these to memory, retrieving them for use, and incorporating them in your own compositions.

Antonius believes that being a statesman, being an orator, being the kind of man who can 'speak in a way calculated to convince' (in other words, being an educated Roman) is a matter of a broad grasp of learning, rather than a deep knowledge and expertise. The *vir eloquentissimus* can talk convincingly on any topic, sway his opponents, advise wisely, because he knows a wide range of the kinds of things useful for an active public life (but not necessarily the specialist knowledge and detailed arguments behind them). It is this line of thought which leads him to maintain that the best possible education is to take the student through a culturally ratified canon of reading; to make him read all the works which Rome values, from which her standards are drawn, from which she has derived her institutions, her procedures in the lawcourts and the forum, her beliefs and prejudices. Not surprisingly, it turns out that what Antonius really has in mind (he claims it as the pattern of his own self-education) is that the Roman student should read as widely as possible among the great Greek historians. (The suggestion comes, significantly, as a revelation to Antonius' admirers among his interlocutors, who claim they had always believed Antonius entirely ignorant of things Greek – it is part of Antonius' case that Greece should be plundered specifically for what is apt in a Roman context):

> When Antonius had finished Caesar exclaimed, 'What now, Catulus? Where are those who say Antonius does not know the Greek tongue? What a number of historians he has mentioned! With what insight and discrimination he has described every one!' 'Upon my word,' returned Catulus, 'in my astonishment at this I marvel no longer at something which had hitherto surprised me far more, I mean that our friend here, being all unversed in these matters, could speak so effectively.' 'And yet, Catulus,' rejoined Antonius, 'it is not because I am on the look-out for aids to oratory, but just for pleasure, that I make a habit, when I have time, of reading the works of these authors and a few more. To what purpose then? Well, I will own to some benefit: just as, when walking in the sunshine, though perhaps taking the stroll for a different reason, the natural result is that I get sunburnt, even so, after perusing those books rather closely at Misenum (having little chance in Rome), I find that under their influence my discourse takes on what I may call a new complexion.'[11]

From his reading 'for pleasure' Antonius will acquire simultaneously experience in social affairs, public life, politics, the lawcourts, and in fine style and diction. Antonius thus defines a type of 'higher education text': a non-technical treatise containing pertinent material for the man of the world. That material will in some cases still be relevant to Rome, in others it will provide precedents from the past, and in yet others it will suggest the development and evolution of Roman culture from its Greek prototype.

Having pursued such a course of reading, Antonius maintains that the student should set about emulating it. Practice in preparation for the real world is a matter of carefully choosing a model (an orator of distinction), and then following that model, not in pastiche, but 'in such a way as to strive with all possible care to attain the most excellent qualities of his model'.[12] By matching the living example with the absorbed textual model, the student hones his own performance into optimal shape:

> 'Why now is it, do you suppose, that nearly every age has produced its own distinctive style of oratory? Of this truth we can judge less easily in the case of our own orators, since they have left but very few writings on which a judgment could be based, than as regards the Greeks, from whose works the method and tendency of the oratory of every generation may be understood ... Let him, then who hopes by imitation to attain this likeness, carry out his purpose by frequent and large practice, and if possible by written composition'.[13]

The assumption strongly made by Antonius throughout his discussion of the passive and active stages in becoming a perfect Roman orator is that there exists, in the written accounts of Greek life and culture, a model for all that is

[11] Ibid. 2.14. 59-61.
[12] Ibid. 2.22. 90.
[13] Ibid. 2.22. 92-6.

best in the Roman state. By steeping himself in the Greek historical classics,
the Roman student is well on the way to matching their excellence.

Crassus, on the other hand, is much more technically exacting and
ambitious in his requirements for the orator. The perfectly cultured and
educated Roman must be an expert in every field of human knowledge. He
must not simply share the common popular sum of widely held learning, but
must have deeper resources. A man can only speak well and convincingly on
any topic if his grasp of the knowledge on which discussion is based is total.
All knowledge is interrelated, and any gap in his learning will reveal itself as a
non sequitur or *lacuna* in his argument. The only way that a man can have this
complete grasp of knowledge is to have a *method* for assimilating new facts to
his existing experience. And a method of this kind means in effect a school of
philosophy – a system of belief into which information can be fitted for
processing.[14] Again it is to the Greek schools of philosophy that Crassus turns
in search of a suitable unifying method, and again this is hailed as
astonishing by the other participants in the dialogue, who believe Crassus to
be quintessentially Roman, and unschooled in things Greek. The reason for
this (as in the case of Antonius) is that the foreign system of thought must be
so apt to the native culture that its very presence as a structuring framework
goes undetected. The system is an aid to learning, and a guide to practice, not
an end in itself.

Just as Antonius put together his orator's performance (down to the jokes
and illustrations) from Greek historical sources, so Crassus produces an
all-purpose armature for learning from the philosophical approach of the Greek
Academy. What the orator then develops is a mastery of the wide range of
strategies for arguing *in utramque partem*, for and against, on any topic (as we
saw Lorenzo Valla advocating, in his own system of oratory, in Chapter
Three). He must learn how to choose material, how to weigh it, the forms of
persuasive argumentation which will clinch points, or undermine the points of
his opponents. He must enlarge the body of rhetorical training he acquired in
boyhood with further refined procedures for embellishing and amplifying to
desired effect. He will then draw on a large fund of specialist and detailed
knowledge which he does not make the focus of his educational energies, but
which he treats as ammunition on which he can draw for polemical use.
Specialist knowledge for his purposes is a matter of convenient up-to-date
reference books, summarising progress in the field to date – what the expert
knows, digested into accessible form.

Throughout the *De Oratore* the distinguished practising orators attempt to
relate the standard banalities of curriculum teaching to the ideals of
oratorical competence as an activity meshed with, and vital to the civilised
status of the community. Neither Antonius nor Crassus really succeeds in
making the transition from familiar Roman classroom detail (with which the
dialogue is liberally peppered) to the 'perfect orator' (any more than
Decembrio succeeded in bridging the same divide in his discussion of
fifteenth-century classroom practice and oratorical ideals, as we discussed in

[14] Ibid. 3.6. 21-2.

Chapter One). The *De Oratore* offers us as an elegant and compelling literary version of the problem for real-life teachers on which this book has centred – the problem of matching education in the humanities to a belief in and commitment to 'humanism' as the necessary intellectual underpinning of a civilised society.

An education incorporates three distinct things: a conscious cultural tradition, an educational ideology, and a curriculum. The cultural tradition is present in the educational theory of a period as the canon of key texts to which the community defers.[15] For Rome in the first century BC this canon was uncompromisingly Greek, and established by the Greeks (although within a century of Cicero's death the Romans had framed their own Latin canon which remained fixed in its turn, down to the seventeenth century in Europe and beyond). To the educator the canon defines the cultural ideal: the man immersed in these classics will inevitably become the ideal spokesman of his community. To the student they are a set of tasks to be mastered, hurdles to be crossed, and there is no apparent reason why mastering Homer (or Virgil, or Shakespeare) will yield any further fruit than attaining the required standard in some final examination.[16] As far as Cicero was concerned, the form of the curriculum was fixed as received from Greece, and this once again is characteristic of pedagogic practice in all periods. The curriculum is resistant to change; it depends upon educational assumptions no longer articulated, state requirements and cultural attitudes long discarded, but survives because it is set up in continuously operating institutions. Teachers give up only with reluctance the programme in which they were themselves trained, and when they do make changes they tend to do so piecemeal. The programme of the seven liberal arts which Cicero takes for granted staked the boundaries of western education for more than two thousand years, and educational reform was bound to take place within its contours.

The most elusive factor in any education is the ideology on which it depends. The educational ideology contains the rarely articulated beliefs of the community about the functioning of the educational system: why this particular set of aptitudes has been selected for teaching emphasis; how these aptitudes are most effectively taught; and to what and whom the theoreticians believe an education ought to be directed. Much of the *De Oratore* is taken up with Cicero's efforts, via his main speakers, to reach some stable position on this issue. How is an 'education' related to the state's need for a certain kind of public servant; is 'training an orator' really 'giving a man the best general education', or merely 'filling the necessary job-spaces in government'? How is a programme of reading, or a technical training in

---

[15] On culture, and the relation between Literature (the canon), culture and society, see R. Williams, *Culture and Society, 1780-1950* (London, 1958), especially the concluding chapter; *The Long Revolution* (London, 1961); *Marxism and Literature* (Oxford, 1977), Part I, 11-71.

[16] See the writings of Pierre Bourdieu, most recently (and accessibly) P. Bourdieu and J.C. Passeron, *The Inheritors* [= *Les héritiers*] (Chicago, 1979); P. Bourdieu, *Distinction: A Social Critique of the Judgement of Taste* [= *La Distinction: Critique sociale du Jugement*], tr. R. Nice (Cambridge, Mass., 1984), Part I ('A social critique of the judgment of taste'), 9-96.

grammar, rhetoric and dialectic, related to personality formation and character training? Should an education produce the broadly cultured or the proficiently specialist?

These are the kinds of question which Cicero raises, and to which he appears tentatively to offer the following answers. It is part of the function of an educational system that it should produce the key figures the society needs (in the case of Rome, 'perfect orators'). Because culture and curriculum are intimately related (both derive from an 'ideal' Greek model), a mastery of the literary canon and a thorough drilling in the technical linguistic disciplines will together contribute to the moral formation of the individual (the student will be made both clever and virtuous). And, by and large, a general education is superior for this purpose to a narrowly specialised one. On what is ostensibly the central issue of the dialogue – the question of the relative effectiveness of teaching by gradual accumulation and teaching by drilling in an all-purpose method – Cicero deliberately suspends judgment. He avoids a decision by indicating that the success of any such programme must in the end depend on the natural gifts of the aspiring orator.

We have seen that all these are also assumptions made by humanist educators throughout the period with which this book has been concerned. From fifteenth-century Italy to late-sixteenth-century England, wherever humanist educators set about providing further education for a minority of the population, the goals of that education were set as Cicero had defined them: the production of a small, politically active minority who were heirs to a mature foreign culture, and who were thereby (it is claimed) hallmarked as of the requisite moral and intellectual calibre to make substantial contributions to their own developing communities.[17] Behind Renaissance western culture and the societies it enhanced and supported stands ever-present the legacy and the example of an idealised Rome, and Cicero, perfect orator.

---

[17] On the profound and lasting long-term consequences of commitment to such a liberal arts education on the part of European governments and dominant power groups, see M.J. Wiener, *English Culture and the Decline of the Industrial Spirit, 1850-1980* (Cambridge, 1981); E.N. Suleiman, *Politics, Power and Bureaucracy in France: The Administrative Elite* (Princeton, New Jersey, 1974).

Index